Robert Ezra Park

RACE

AND

CULTURE

THE FREE PRESS OF GLENCOE

COLLIER-MACMILLAN LIMITED, *London*

FIRST FREE PRESS PAPERBACK EDITION 1964

For information, address:
The Free Press of Glencoe
A Division of The Macmillan Company
The Crowell-Collier Publishing Company
60 Fifth Avenue, New York, N.Y., 10011

Collier-Macmillan Canada, Ltd., Toronto, Ontario

DESIGNED BY SIDNEY SOLOMON

This book was originally published in its clothbound edition as Volume I of *The Collected Papers of Robert Ezra Park,* edited by Everett Cherrington Hughes, Charles S. Johnson, Jitsuichi Masuoka, Robert Redfield, and Louis Wirth.

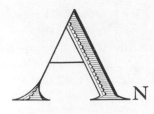N AUTOBIOGRAPHICAL
NOTE
(Dictated by Dr. Park to his secretary at Fisk University and found among his papers after his death)

I CAN trace my interest in sociology to the reading of Goethe's *Faust*. You remember that Faust was tired of books and wanted to see the world—the world of men. At any rate, after leaving college I gave up a position as teacher in a high school at Red Wing, Minnesota, and went to Minneapolis on the chance of getting a job as a reporter. I got the job, and I saw a lot of the world—the kind of a world that a reporter does see. I finished with Minneapolis in about three years and started out for New York. New York was the mecca of every ambitious newspaperman. I did not get to New York at that time but stopped six months in Detroit; went from there to Denver, finally got to New York. But once there I was shortly disenchanted with the prospect. The life of the average newspaperman seemed, at that time to be about eight years. After that if he remained in the profession his value steadily declined.

Meanwhile I had gained an insight into the functioning of the newspaper. The newspaper and news became my problem. About that time I was introduced by John Dewey, who was then at Ann Arbor, to a very interesting man named Franklin Ford. Ford had been a newspaper reporter. He had reported Wall Street and gained a conception of the function of the press by observing the way in which the market responded to news. The market price was, from his point of view, a kind of public opinion, and, being a man of philosophic temperament, he drew from this analogy far-reaching inferences. I cannot go into that. Suffice it to say he came to believe, and I did too, that with more accurate and adequate reporting of current events the historical process would be appreciably stepped up, and progress would go forward steadily, without the interruption and disorder of depression or violence, and at a rapid pace.

It was interest in the newspaper that sent me back to the university. I had graduated at Ann Arbor. I decided to go to Harvard. I studied philosophy because I hoped to gain insight into the nature and function of the kind of knowledge we call news. Besides I wanted to gain a fundamental point of view from which I could describe the behavior of society, under the influence of news, in the precise and universal language of science.

I spent a year at Harvard and then went abroad. I intended to stay abroad for a year, but I remained for four years. There, listening to the lectures of Georg Simmel, at Berlin, I received my only formal instruction in sociology.

While I was in Berlin I ran across a little treatise on the logic of the social sciences by a Russian, Kistiakowski. It was the first thing I had found anywhere that dealt with the problem with which I was concerned in the terms in which I had come to think of it. Kistiakowski had been a student of Wilhelm Windelband, so I went to Strassburg and later to Heidelberg, when Windelband succeeded Kuno Fischer in the chair of philosophy in that university. I wrote a thesis under Windelband. I called it *Masse und Publikum* ("Crowd and Public"). I returned in 1903 to Harvard, giving my thesis the final touches there. It was during that period that I was assistant, not assistant professor, in philosophy.

By this time, however, I was sick and tired of the academic world, and I wanted to get back into the world of men. I had never given up the ambition I gained from reading Faust—the ambition to know human nature, know it widely and intimately.

While I was at Harvard, William James read to us one day his essay on "A Certain Blindness in Human Beings." I was greatly impressed at the time, and, as I have reflected upon it since, the ideas suggested there have assumed a steadily increasing significance.

The "blindness" of which James spoke is the blindness each of us is likely to have for the meaning of other people's lives. At any rate what sociologists most need to know is what goes on behind the faces of men, what it is that makes life for each of us either dull or thrilling. For "if you lose the joy you lose all." But the thing that gives zest to life or makes life dull is, however, as James says, "a personal secret" which has, in every single case, to be discovered. Otherwise we do not know the world in which we actually live.

Well, this is merely to suggest how, after I had grown tired of books, and while I was looking about for something more thrilling than a logical formula, I discovered a new interest in the study of the Negro and the race problem.

This new interest grew out of meeting Booker Washington. The result of that meeting was that I spent seven winters, partly at Tuskegee but partly roaming about the South, getting acquainted with the life, the customs, and the condition of the Negro people.

It happened in this way: While I was living outside of Boston, having just completed the writing of a Doctor's thesis and having lost for the moment any ambition to teach, as I had once intended to do, I was invited to become secretary of the Congo Reform Association. There were at the time reports of great scandals in the Congo, and the secretary of the Baptist Foreign Missions, Dr. Barbour, wanted someone to help him advertise the atrocities in order to prepare for some sort of political action which would insure reform. I was not, at that time, strong for missions, but I undertook the job. Eventually, however, I became genuinely interested. I discovered what I might have known in advance—that conditions in the Congo were about what one might expect, what they have since become, though not by any means so bad, in Kenya. They were, in short, what they were certain to be whenever a sophisticated people invades the territories of a more primitive people in order to exploit their lands and, incidentally, to uplift and civilize them. I knew enough about civilization even at that time to know that progress, as James once remarked, is a terrible thing. It is so destructive and wasteful.

I was so interested by this time that I was about to go to Africa to study the situation at first hand. It was at this moment that Booker Washington invited me to visit Tuskegee and start my studies of Africa in the southern states. I think I probably learned more about human nature and society, in the South under Booker Washington, than I had learned elsewhere in all my previous studies. I believe in firsthand knowledge not as a substitute but as a basis for more formal and systematic investigation. But the reason I profited as much as I did from this experience was due, I am sure, to the fact that I had a long preparation. As a result I was not, as I found later, interested in the Negro problem as that problem is ordinarily conceived. I was interested in the Negro in the South and in the curious and intricate system which had grown up to define his relations with white folk. I was interested, most of all, in studying the details of the process by which the Negro was making and has made his slow but steady advance. I became convinced, finally, that I was observing the historical process by which civilization, not merely here but elsewhere, has evolved, drawing into the circle of its influence an ever widening circle of races and peoples.

Since then I have been around a good part of the world. I was a year in Honolulu as research professor, at the University of Hawaii. I was in Peiping a few months, where I learned a great deal about China from the members of my class at Yenching University. I attended the Fourth Pacific Science Congress in Java in 1929. Two years later I visited India, South Africa, and South America. In July, 1937, I went again to Brazil, to visit the city of Bahia, which is a kind of center of African culture, so much as remains of it, in Brazil.

I have told you how I came to be interested in the newspaper, in the crowd and the public, in collective psychology, generally. I have indicated how I came to get interested in the races and racial attitudes and the incidental problems of cultural conflict and cultural change. There remains the studies of the city, of urban and rural communities, what R. D. McKenzie and I call, quite properly I believe, "human ecology."

While I was a newspaper reporter I used to do a good deal of writing for the Sunday papers. In those days the daily papers wrote their own Sunday papers and did not depend to the extent they do now upon syndicated articles.

I found that the Sunday paper was willing to publish anything so long as it concerned the local community and was interesting. I wrote about all sorts of things and became in this way intimately acquainted with many different aspects of city life. I expect that I have actually covered more ground, tramping about in cities in different parts of the world, than any other living man. Out of all this I gained, among other things, a conception of the city, the community, and the region, not as a geographical phenomenon merely but as a kind of social organism.

My interest in the newspaper had grown out of the discovery that a reporter who had the facts was a more effective reformer than an editorial writer who merely thundered from his pulpit, no matter how eloquently.

According to my earliest conception of a sociologist he was to be a kind of super-reporter, like the men who write for *Fortune*. He was to report a little more accurately, and in a manner a little more detached than the average, what my friend Ford called the "Big News." The "Big News" was the long-time trends which recorded what is actually going on rather than what, on the surface of things, merely seems to be going on.

PREFACE

INTO this first volume of the collected writings of Robert E. Park are gathered his twenty-nine articles, lectures and introductions to books concerning the contacts of peoples different from each other in culture or race or both. The earliest of them was published in 1913, when, a man of nearly fifty years, he was entering upon the only part of his academic career which can be called regular, the years in which he was professor of sociology at the University of Chicago.

It was in the early Chicago years that he started that collaboration with his much younger colleague, Ernest W. Burgess, which produced the *Introduction to the Science of Sociology* (Chicago: University of Chicago Press, 1921). This book, which the authors looked upon as prolegomenon to further research and theory, is especially known for its development of a scheme of four basic processes of social interaction: competition, conflict, accommodation and assimilation. These concepts have been widely applied in the study of the contacts of peoples: perhaps more so by others than by Park himself. Park by no means regarded them as instruments to be used only for study of what happens when people migrate to a strange land, or when people of one race are enslaved by another. It will also be evident to any reader that Park used the term "social contacts" not for the contacts of peoples or cultures only, but to refer to "the simplest aspect of interaction."

After the first Great War, Park published two books on immigrant problems: *The Immigrant Press and Its Control* (New York: Harper and Brothers, 1921) and, with Herbert A. Miller, *Old World*

Traits Transplanted (New York: Harper and Brothers, 1921). Both were products of the special interest in the loyalty of immigrant populations during and after the war; in neither is an answer given to the question of loyalty, but in both the reader is led to consider the processes of adjustment to a strange land and culture in a more general way. There is external and internal evidence that William I. Thomas had a hand in the *Old World Traits*. Thomas had been influential in bringing Park to Chicago. The two remained friends so long as both lived. Thomas' pioneer work on *The Polish Peasant in Europe and America* gave much of the method and much of the conceptual scheme for the *Old World Traits*. The study of European immigrants in North America was the second leg, after his years with the American Negro problem, of Park's exploration of cultural and racial contacts.

The third was an expansion of his interests to include contact of Orient and Occident. In the middle twenties he conducted a survey of communities of Oriental people in our Pacific states and in British Columbia. The "Autobiographical Note" sketches his travels on the rim of the Pacific.

About half the items were written in the period when, having been "retired" from his duties at the university, he travelled about the world to witness the effects of the more dramatic contacts of the races and finally settled down to teaching at Fisk University. These pursuits of "retirement" were shared by his wife, Clara Cahill Park, who put into charming pastels many of the "marginal" men and women of whom he wrote. The last of the papers was published, without his final editing, after his death in 1944.

In an earlier phase of his career, he had written about the same problems in another mood and in another role. It was Park, the muck-raking journalist and press agent who, in 1906, exposed King Leopold of Belgium's exploitation of the natives of the Congo in *Everybody's Magazine*.[1]

The "Autobiographical Note" contains hints of a restless search for a career he could continue to find zest in; that is, one that he could continue to believe in. Thus the change from the Park of "The

---

[1] "A King in Business: Leopold II of Belgium, Autocrat of the Congo and International Broker," *Everybody's Magazine*, Vol. XV (1906), 624-633; "The Terrible Story of the Congo," *Everybody's Magazine*, Vol. XV (1906), 763-772; "The Blood-Money of the Congo," *Everybody's Magazine*, Vol. XVI (1907), 60-70.

Blood-Money of the Congo," to the Park who wrote, "In the relations of races there is a cycle of events which tends everywhere to repeat itself," was not a mere evolution. It was one of several turns from academic speculation to action and back again. Only after his several years of association with Booker T. Washington, including the latter's trip to other parts of the world in search of "The Man Farthest Down," did Park turn finally to an academic career in which he found an enduring, if often uneasy, synthesis of action and thought. But he did not find it; he made it. For there existed no ready-made pattern for his ways of teaching. Indeed, he often seemed much more concerned to learn from the student than to teach him. And it was essentially this desire to learn—even from students—that made him a a great teacher. He made his students curious about themselves, and about the social worlds in which they lived; then he gave them a perspective in which to see themselves and thus satisfy the curiosity. The perspective was a system of concepts abstract enough to comprehend all forms of interaction of men with one another, anytime and anywhere, yet vivid and suggestive. Many a student saw himself and others in a new light because of Park's invention of the phrase, "Marginal Man." But because the phrase referred not merely to one's self, but to an order of things, the student also forgot himself, in some measure, and became more curious about others. This dialectic of focus upon the individual case and upon the genus runs through all that Park did.

It is, in a sense, the dialectic of his own life: reform and action as against detached observation; writing the news of the unique event as against the discovery of the eternal themes and processes of history; sympathy for the individual man as against concern for the human race. From this dialectic proceeds the paradox of his work on race relations, and, for that matter, on other aspects of human life. For, as the reader will see, this book contains little or no news of the racial and cultural fronts of the world. It refers to racial news, such as the first major modern defeat of a "white" nation by a "colored" one, and to Hitler's persecution of the Jews. (Park was always an avid follower of the news.) The references are but the occasion for the development of general ideas concerning race relations.

The paradox goes further. Park probably contributed more ideas for analysis of racial relations and cultural contacts than any other modern social scientist. Yet he was not a specialist in race relations. To be sure, he was endlessly curious about peoples of all races and

Preface

cultures. He maintained the unspoiled reporter's interest in human behavior. The characters of the play could be of the alley or of the avenue; his middle-class American neighbors, the freaks in a circus, or the people of ancient times or of some exotic country. His interest was more catholic than even the wide field of racial and cultural contacts. It was human. His essays on race relations are, in fact, essays on social processes and social interaction in general. And that is why we who have undertaken to put them into a more accessible form, have done so.

You have before you part of the record of a passionate, but speculative man's thinking about a great theme of human life and history.

EVERETT CHERRINGTON HUGHES

The University of Chicago

BIBLIOGRAPHY

"The Problem of Cultural Differences," Preliminary paper prepared for the Institute of Pacific Relations, Hangchow, China, 1931. New York: American Council Institute of Pacific Relations, 1931

"Culture and Civilization." Unpublished paper

"Culture and Cultural Trends," *Publications of the American Sociological Society*, XIX (1925), 24-36

"Reflections on Communication and Culture," *American Journal of Sociology*, XLIV (September, 1938), 187-205

"A Memorandum on Rote Learning," *American Journal of Sociology*, XLIII (July, 1937), 23-36

"The Negro and His Plantation Heritage," being "Introduction" to C. S. Johnson, *Shadow of the Plantation* (Chicago: University of Chicago Press, 1934), pp. xi-xxiv

"The Nature of Race Relations," in Edgar T. Thompson (ed.), *Race Relations and the Race Problem* (Durham, North Carolina: Duke University Press, 1939), pp. 3-45

"Race Relations and Certain Frontiers," in E. B. Reuter (ed.), *Race and Culture Contacts* (New York: McGraw-Hill Book Co., 1934), pp. 57-85

"Our Racial Frontier on the Pacific," *Survey Graphic*, LVI (May, 1926), 192-196

"Experience and Race Relations," *Journal of Applied Sociology*, IX (1924), 18-24

"A Race Relations Survey," *Journal of Applied Sociology*, VIII (1923), 195-205

« xv »

"Politics and 'The Man Farthest Down'," being "Introduction" to Harold F. Gosnell, *Negro Politicians* (Chicago: University of Chicago Press, 1935), pp. xiii-xxv

"The Etiquette of Race Relations in the South," being "Introduction" to Bertram W. Doyle, *The Etiquette of Race Relations in the South* (Chicago: University of Chicago Press, 1937), pp. xi-xxiv

"The Race Relations Cycle in Hawaii," being "Introduction" to Romanzo Adams, *Interracial Marriage in Hawaii* (New York: The Macmillan Company, 1937), pp. vii-xiv

"The Career of the Africans in Brazil," being "Introduction" to Donald Pierson, *Negroes in Brazil* (Chicago: University of Chicago Press, 1942), pp. xi-xxi

"Racial Assimilation in Secondary Groups with Particular Reference to the Negro," *Publication of the American Sociological Society*, VIII (1913), 66-83

"Race Prejudice and Japanese-American Relations," being "Introduction" to J. F. Steiner, *The Japanese Invasion* (Chicago: A. C. McClung and Co., 1917), pp. vii-xvii

"The Bases of Race Prejudice," *The Annals*, CXXXX (November, 1928), 11-20

"Behind Our Masks," *Survey Graphic*, LVI (May, 1926), 135-139

"The Concept of Social Distance," *Journal of Applied Sociology*, VIII (1924), 339-344

"Education in Its Relation to the Conflict and Fusion of Cultures: With Special Reference to the Problems of the Immigrant, the Negro, and Missions," *Publication of the American Sociological Society*, XIII (1918), 38-63

"Negro Race Consciousness as Reflected in Race Literature," *American Review*, I (September, October, 1923), 505-516

"Racial Ideologies," in William F. Ogburn (ed.), *American Society in Wartime* (Chicago: The University of Chicago Press, 1943), pp. 165-183

"Education and the Cultural Crisis," *American Journal of Sociology*, XLVIII (May, 1943), 728-736

"Missions and the Modern World," *American Journal of Sociology*, L (November, 1944), 177-183

"Human Migration and the Marginal Man," *American Journal of Sociology*, XXXIII (May, 1928), 881-893

"Personality and Cultural Conflict," *Publication of the American Sociological Society*, XXV:2 (May, 1931), 95-110

"Cultural Conflict and the Marginal Man," being "Introduction" to
E. V. Stonequist, *The Marginal Man* (New York: Charles Scribner's Sons, 1937), pp. xiii-xviii

"Mentality of Racial Hybrids," *American Journal of Sociology*,
XXXVI (January, 1931), 534-551

ACKNOWLEDGMENTS

THE FIRST steps toward collecting the Park papers and bibliography were made in the Department of Social Sciences at Fisk University, under the leadership of Charles S. Johnson with the collaboration of Professor Park himself. The other editors of the present volume are grateful to Dr. Johnson, to the several members of the faculty and to the many students of Fisk University who had a hand in the work.

In each case where a chapter has previously appeared in print, an exact citation is made as to place of publication and publisher. We would like to express our gratitude to the following publishers, journals, and individuals for the use of copyrighted material:

Mrs. Nellie C. Adams, American Institute of Pacific Relations, *The American Journal of Sociology*, The American Sociological Society, *The Annals of the American Academy of Political and Social Science*, Mr. Alfred O. Brown, Duke University Press, Department of Social Sciences at Fisk University, *Sociology and Social Research*, McGraw-Hill Book Company, Inc., Charles Scribner's Sons, Professor Jesse F. Steiner, *Survey Graphic* and The University of Chicago Press.

The photograph for the frontispiece was provided by Mrs. Park.

CONTENTS

Contents

PART ONE: *Culture and Civilization*

CHAPTER I

THE PROBLEM OF CULTURAL DIFFERENCES

CULTURE, which is a character we ordinarily attribute to communities and peoples, is a term not unlike personality, which is a character we attribute to individuals. Personality has sometimes been described as the individual and subjective aspect of culture. In that sense we may say that culture consists of those habits in individuals that have become customary, conventionalized, and accepted in the community.

Culture includes, therefore, not merely all that Sumner has described as the folkways but it includes, also, art, science, philosophy and formal law, all the technical and rational devices, in fact, by which men have at all times sought to control not only their environment but themselves. It is because what is customary in the community becomes habit in succeeding generations that the fund of tradition which we call culture persists and accumulates. Once habits formed by individuals have become conventionalized, sanctioned, and transmitted they become a communal possession.

It is the community that conserves and transmits them. It is characteristic of culture that it is at once diffused and transmitted, and by the diffusion and transmission of its folkways society at once extends and gives permanence and consistency to the influences that it exerts upon the individuals who compose it.

"Society exists," as Dewey expresses it, "through a process of

---

Robert E. Park, Preliminary paper prepared for the Institute of Pacific Relations, Hangchow, China, 1931. (N.Y.: Am. Council Inst. of Pac. Relations, 1931.)

transmission, quite as much as biological life. This transmission occurs by means of communication of habits of doing, thinking, feeling from the older to the younger. Without this communication of ideals, hopes, expectations, standards, opinions from those members of society who are passing out of the group life to those who are coming into it, social life could not survive." [1]

Every individual is the inheritor of a double inheritance, physical and moral, racial and cultural. It is, however, by association, by education and, fundamentally, by communication, that these individuals come into possession and become the bearers of their cultural heritage.

All this indicates what culture is. It is not an artifact merely, nor something that can be bought, sold, and "distributed." It is not even something that can be collected, classified, and exhibited in anthropological museums or in art galleries. The exchange of economic goods and the distribution of foreign commodities unquestionably does modify and eventually transform indigenous cultures. But cultural traits cannot be exported or transported. They can be transmitted and diffused. A cultural trait is transmitted from one generation to another, or diffused from one culture to another, when it has been incorporated into the traditional culture complex and thus become an integral part of the customary and accepted practice of the community in which it has been "diffused."

Transmission and diffusion inevitably involve, as Malinowski has insisted, some modification in the character of the traits diffused and some accommodation and adaptation of the culture into which diffusion takes place. "Just because no idea and no object can exist in isolation from its cultural context, it is impossible to sever mechanically an item from one culture and place it in another. The process is always one of adaptation in which the receiving culture has to re-evolve the idea, custom or institution which it adopts. . . . Diffusion, invention, are always mixed, always inseparable." [2]

It is because the transmission and diffusion of cultures involve some re-discovery and re-evolution of the ideas, customs, or institutions transmitted that one may say that culture exists in and through transmission and diffusion, in the same sense that society may be said to exist in and through communication.

A society may be described as a group of individuals who are

---

1 John Dewey, *Education and Democracy*, New York, 1916, pp. 1-11.
2 Elliott G. Smith, B. Malinowski, Herbert J. Spindon, A. Goldenweiser, *Culture, The Diffusion Controversy*. New York, 1927, p. 106.

capable of some sort of concert and collective action. This usually implies the possession of institutions by means of which collective action can be maintained and controlled. The diffusion of culture makes it possible to act collectively over a wider area and to maintain some sort of concert among, and control over, a larger number of individuals. The transmission of a cultural tradition, on the other hand, tends to make that action more consistent and more intelligent.

Culture, as the anthropologists conceive it, is a constellation of individual elements and of complexes of elements or traits. A cultural trait is, theoretically at least, a unit of cultural description and analysis. In practice it is any increment or item of any existing culture that is capable of independent diffusion or modification.

"A trait," said Wissler, "grows out of an idea or an invention, as the case may be, but does not rise to the level of a cultural trait until a standardized procedure is established in the group. A single individual may have started it, may have practiced it for a long time, but until a number of his fellows adopt it and pass it on to the rising generation, it is not a trait for culture." [3]

As a matter of fact, under the influence of cultural contact, migration and conquest, cultural complexes break up into smaller units and are transmitted and diffused independently of the cultural context in which they had, presumably, their origin. One of the first and most perplexing problems of cultural anthropology and sociology is to, discover the conditions and the processes by which cultural traits have been diffused and modified. In regard to the exact nature of this process of diffusion there is a growing diversity of opinion, but there is, at the same time, an increasing appreciation of its complexity and its importance.

Cultural diffusion inevitably involves, as I have suggested, a breaking up of cultures and cultural complexes. Cultural traits are not taken over wholesale from one culture to another. What ordinarily happens when people of widely divergent cultures come into contact and conflict is that certain elements of the invading or borrowed cultures are assimilated first, while others are incorporated in the complex of the invaded culture only after a considerable period of time, if at all.

Diffusion of cultures takes place, in some instances, in a manner analogous to that in which, in a plant community, an existing "formation" is broken up by the invasion of alien species. In this case

---

[3] Clark Wissler, *An Introduction to Social Anthropology*, New York, 1929, p. 358.

the plant formation corresponds to the cultural complex. This plant formation, like the cultural complex, "is a highly complex structure in which the interruption of one function tends to throw the whole into confusion."

Diffusion does not always take place by a process that can be described as invasion nor by the imposition of one culture upon another. It sometimes takes place by what Wissler describes as "spontaneous borrowing." Individuals and peoples borrow from the cultures of their neighbors, particularly from the peoples with whom they are in competition and conflict, and more particularly from the people by which they have been subjugated and reduced to a status of conscious inferiority.

Anthropologists have generally sought to preserve, as far as possible, the native cultures of the peoples with whom they have become acquainted, and in order to do this they have sought to protect these peoples from the corroding and destructive effects of contact with traders and missionaries. They have not always reckoned, however, with the human nature of the natives themselves. Wissler quotes from the experience of a correspondent, writing from Africa, who has discovered "that if you tell a native to do a thing in as native a manner as possible, he will do it in his best possible imitation of a Euorpean way. If you try to persuade him to wear suitable indigenous clothing rather than follow the most unsuitable castoffs of Europeans, or if you try to persuade him to develop his own educational system, he at once becomes suspicious and angry; to him all that is European represents civilization and if you want him to follow his own customs then you must try to keep civilization from him and to keep him a serf race! The greatest enemy of the whole experiment is the native himself." [4]

It is evident, however, that in what seems like similar circumstances not all natives behave in precisely the same way. Maurice Evans, observing the native rickshaw men in Natal, South Africa, is impressed by their "barbaric splendor and mighty physique," but he is amazed that living, as they do, in the midst of the strange intriguing sights of a European civilization, with its imposing structures, complicated machinery, and its stimulating bustle and movement, the native, the *Abantu,* is quite unimpressed and seemingly untouched by the wonders of the white man's world. He neither understands nor cares to understand what it is all about, and presently, when the desire comes upon him to see his home again, no wage offered him, no sense

---

4 Clark Wissler, *op. cit.,* p. 360.

of gratitude or of loyalty, nothing will keep him away longer "from the kraal by the rushing Umbagi, from the girls and the cattle." [5]

What one cultural group borrows from another is determined first and last by the use it can make of what is borrowed. Cultures diffuse in much the same way that news travels, but not so rapidly. What is interesting and disturbing travels most rapidly and most widely, and other things being equal, it reaches the people most concerned first. One of the marvels of the modern world is the rapidity with which knowledge of world events reaches peoples in the most remote corners of the earth. On the other hand, it is shocking to discover how ignorant people in different parts of the world are likely to be of events which do not immediately concern them, or of events the import of which they do not fully understand. In the modern world, which the telegraph and the radio have converted, as has so often been said, into one vast whispering gallery, the only obstacle to the circulation of intelligence seems to be the inability of the purveyors of news to make the reports of events not merely accurate but interesting and intelligible.

To recognize that culture is transmitted and diffused rather than transported and distributed, is to recognize that cultural traits have their roots and their sources in the instincts and habits of human beings. It is this that gives them that dynamic character by which they interact and modify one another. They are not merely diffused, but in the process of diffusion they are transformed, recreated.

This is no doubt what Teggart had in mind when he wrote: "It should be observed that the word 'culture' is frequently used to designate the sum-total of the acquisitions of any human group, in language, in rites, customs, practices, material objects, in ideas. Strictly speaking, however, 'culture' signifies the work of cultivation; it means the *activity* through which the products which we assemble in ethnological museums, and which we describe in books, have been brought into existence." [6]

It is in this sense that we must conceive the folkways as Sumner describes them. They are cultural traits from the point of view of action. They are ways of doing things, action patterns, habits arising in the individual, conventionalized and transmitted by society as part of the cultural heritage.

---

[5] Maurice Evans, *Black and White in Southeast Africa*, London and New York, 1911, p. 3.

[6] Frederick J. Teggart, *Theory of History*, New Haven, 1925, pp. 189-190.

"Arts and crafts, language, science, political organization and institutions are merely the extension of structures and of functions of which the habits of the individuals and the customs of the group are the most elementary expression." [7]

Cultural traits seem to spring up spontaneously and, in certain historic periods, burst forth in great diffusion, manifesting themselves in changing fashions and innovations and inventions of all sorts. Among these there is, naturally, a struggle for existence; and of the multitude of novel ideas and devices that appear, relatively few survive and are permanently incorporated in existing cultures. There is, furthermore, as Sumner has noted, "a strain toward consistency" in the folkways and among the different traits which constitute any particular culture. Traits which were at first antagonistic, by modification and selection, achieve a stable equilibrium in which competition and conflict disappear and the different traits seem to cooperate and mutually support one another against the invasion of any foreign elements. The effect of this cooperation is to still further stabilize the existing equilibrium and prevent cultural change. This is what we have had, apparently, in China, and what we may expect in any civilization that has achieved any degree of antiquity.

It is this congruence and integration of the elements that constitute a particular culture, also, that gives it that harmonious and individual character which makes it possible to compare the civilization of one period and the culture of one people with that of others.

"The two great cultural divisions of the human race," says Sumner, "are the oriental and the occidental. Each is consistent throughout; each has its own philosophy and spirit; they are separated from top to bottom by different mores, different standpoints, different ways, and different notions of what societal arrangements are advantageous. In their contrast they keep before our minds the possible range of divergence in the solution of the great problems of human life, and in the views of earthly existence by which life policy may be controlled. If two planets were joined in one, their inhabitants could not differ more widely as to what things are best worth seeking, or what ways are most expedient for well living." [8]

Wissler thinks that the dominant characteristics of American culture—those traits, namely, that one would meet, if one should look

---

[7] Stuart A. Rice, *Methods in Social Science, A Case Book.* Chicago, 1931, pp. 150-156.

[8] William Graham Sumner, *Folkways.* New York, 1906, p. 6.

for them in every American village, may be reduced to three general categories: mechanical invention, mass education, and universal suffrage.

These are indeed universal characteristics of American life. A little reflection will suggest that there is a more intimate connection between them than is likely to appear at first glance. In fact, these connections are so close and so real that it is difficult to conceive any one of them existing in the absence of the others. These three characteristics, mechanical invention, mass education, and universal suffrage, include not merely a multitude of individual traits but they represent, as Mr. Wissler puts it, "a core of ideas and beliefs actuating the [American] people and in large measure, controlling their career." They give to American life, in short, that consistency and unity which impresses the stranger but which is not always manifest to Americans themselves.

An analysis of culture will almost certainly reveal the fact that every single trait presupposes the existence of most others. This is more particularly the case in those societies in which the constituent traits have achieved a relatively permanent and stable equilibrium, as is notably the case with China and the Orient as compared with America and the Occident.

One of the notorious differences between the Orient and the Occident concerns the attitudes prevalent in these two grand divisions of culture in the world in respect to change. The soul of the East, we have been told, is repose. By the same token, the genius of the West is action. The unchanging East is the antipodes of the mobile West.

As a matter of fact, most of the ideas, beliefs, and practices peculiarly characteristic of the Occident are associated with the fact of change. The Western outlook on life is prospective rather than retrospective. Its mood is one of anticipation rather than of reflection. The Western attitude towards change is embodied in the concept of progress. Progress, says J. B. Bury, is "the animating and controlling idea of Western civilization."

The control that this conception exercises, however, is not that of an ideal, like the notion of democracy. It is that of an article of faith, like the belief in Providence or in Fate. In fact, Progress has superseded Providence as a dogma of popular religion in the modern world, just as Providence has replaced Fate or Destiny in the ancient.[9]

---

[9] J. B. Bury, *The Idea of Progress*. London, 1921, p. 1.

There are, however, dissenters who do not accept the dogmas of the popular religion. Among the most eminent of these is Dean Inge, who speaks of progress as a modern superstition which has only established itself as a popular belief during the last one hundred and fifty years. Among its prophets is Herbert Spencer, who asserts the perfectability of man, as Dean Inge says, "with an assurance which makes us gasp." [10]

Not only do the East and West differ in their traditional attitudes toward the fact of change, but they have differed in the past, and probably differ still, in the extent of change which is actually taking place in their different worlds.

Recently Rudolph Heberle published a survey of American contemporary life in which he sought to estimate, on the basis of statistical studies, the extent of the population movement of the United States, and to indicate its consequences as reflected in the structure of American society and in the personal characteristics of the American people.

To a European observer, the outstanding characteristic of American life, as compared with that of Europe, is the extraordinary mobility and restlessness of the American population.[11] This mobility, so strikingly exhibited in America, is characteristic of the modern world. It is peculiarly characteristic, however, of the Occident as compared with the Orient.

Migration and movement are not always, perhaps, original causes of social change, but they are at least incidental to it. When the existing economic and social order is disturbed, migration and population movements take place in an effort to achieve a new equilibrium.

It is, no doubt, the machine and the progressive application of machine methods—i.e., routinization, standardization, coordination and, in general, what is called rationalization—to the collective activities of an ever-expanding world economy that is responsible for the speed and tempo of modern life. But this has been accomplished and accompanied by an increasing mobility of the population involved. Thus, one of the indices, if not the causes, of cultural change is the increased use in recent years of new means of locomotion and of communication.

---

[10] William Ralph Inge, *Outspoken Essays* (Second Series). London, 1923, p. 163.
[11] Rudolph Heberle, *Mobilität der Bevölkerung in den Vereinigten Staaten.* Jena, 1929.

So far as mobility is a measure of social change, present indications are that—in spite of all that has taken place in the Orient in recent years,—the pace and tempo of the Occident, and particularly of the United States, is now, as it has been in the past, more rapid than that of the rest of the world. In a recent issue of the *American Journal of Sociology*, statistics showing the increased use in the United States, during the year 1930, of the automobile, the aeroplane, the radio, the telephone; the increased attendance of motion pictures and circulation of newspapers have been summarized. The authors of this report, Malcolm M. Willey and Stuart A. Rice, in summing up the results of their inquiry, say that while it is impossible to follow "the ramification of the most obvious changes in American life" summarized in the data presented, they are nevertheless led to "marvel at the way in which American life and the habits of the individual citizens are being transformed." [12]

One may, perhaps, discount the conclusions which are likely to be drawn from the statistics of mobility in the United States, since Americans, who have long been habituated to social changes of every sort, have become, like the Gypsies, more or less immune to their consequences.

Cities have always been the centers of social change because they have been the points at which people came together to exchange their products and to get the news. Modern life is characteristically urban, but modern cities are notoriously the products of the steamship, the locomotive, the automobile. Modern life is, by the same token, the product of the telegraph, the telephone, and the newspaper, particularly since communication has, in the long run, the same social consequences as locomotion. Both tend to break up what Bagehot calls the "cake of custom," to release the individual from the routine of tradition, and to stimulate him to undertake new enterprises.

Differences in customs, manners, philosophy, and in general, the style of life, between a society that is mobile and one that is relatively immobile are likely to be, in the long run, very great. In an immobile society, habits are inevitably fixed. All the activities of life tend to be controlled by custom and to conform to the normal expectation of the community. In an immobile society, personal and social relations tend to assume a formal and ceremonial character. Social status is fixed by tradition; social distances are maintained by social ritual and

---

[12] Malcolm M. Willey, and Stuart A. Rice, "Communication," *American Journal of Sociology*, Vol. 36, No. 6, May, 1931.

etiquette. The individual is born into an established tradition, his place and function are defined by ancestral custom. Subordinated in most of his activities to the traditional interests of the group, he tends to lose his individual initiative and spontaneity of action. It is, with a society as with an individual: as they grow older, security seems more desirable than adventure.

On the other hand, in a mobile society, such as exists in America, particularly on the frontier and in the cities, where changes of fortune are likely to be sudden and dramatic, where every individual is more or less on his own, the influence of tradition is inevitably minimized. Personal relations are easily established but quickly dissolved. Social forms are flexible and in no sense fixed. Fashion and public opinion take the place of custom as a means and method of social control. The individual is emancipated, and society is atomized.

Under these circumstances the character of law and legislation changes. Statutory regulations take the place of general consensus, and of that form of common sense known as the common law. Law, no longer supported by a body of mores common to a whole community, assumes the character of a traffic regulation. There is nothing sacred about social regulations whose authority rests upon a changing public opinion rather than upon a venerable tradition.

What I have described as the atomization of society eventually affects the individual's sense of inner security, upon which the control and direction of his personal life finally rests. This sense of insecurity is reflected in art, in literature, and in a general lack of religious conviction. As Walter Lippmann has put it, "surveying the flux of events and the giddiness of his own soul, he comes to feel that Aristophanes must have been thinking of him when he declared that 'Whirl is King, having driven out Zeus'." [13]

These divergencies in the character of civilization, which rest, the one upon a mobile, and the other upon an immobile population, have by no means escaped the observation of students of society and civilization. Ferdinand J. Tönnies, in his volume, *Gemeinschaft und Gesellschaft*, has made a classic statement of the characteristic traits of what one may, perhaps, describe as the sacred and secular societies. [14]

What characterizes a sacred society is not so much antiquity as

---

[13] Walter Lippmann, *A Preface to Morals,* New York, 1920, p. 4. See also the *Melody of Chaos,* by Houston Peterson, New York, 1931.

[14] Ferdinand J. Tönnies, *Gemeinschaft und Gesellschaft.* Leipzig, 1897. See also Durkheim, Emile, *La Division du Travail Social.* Paris, 1902.

immobility. The sacred society is typically a small, isolated community and more particularly the primary group—i.e., the family, the clan, or the religious sect,—a society, in short, where everything is known and every one is bound to every one else by obligations that are at once personal and sacred.

The thing that characterizes secular society, on the other hand, is its mobility. It is composed of people who come together because they are useful to one another; because they have interests, permanent or temporary, that make association profitable; or merely because they are curious one about another, and about the world in which these others live. The inevitable focus of such a society is the market place, where people come together, not because they are alike, but because they are different, not for collective action, but for trade; for exchange of goods, of services and of ideas. The ideal type of such a secular society is the bourse, the money market, or the gaming table, where nothing is sacred, and where men are moved to action neither by piety nor by duty but by an intense and undivided interest in the gains and losses that their decisions are likely to entail.

In a sacred society the typical virtue is that of piety, filial piety, and respect for tradition. Under the influence of the sentiment of piety, one does what is right, proper, and expected. In a secular society, on the contrary, the typical virtue is efficiency, and the thing one seeks to achieve is not conformity, but success.

It is evident that these two types of association, *Gemeinschaft und Gesellschaft*, societies sacred and secular, can, and do, exist in the same community. The history of the Jews proves that it is possible to maintain a vigorous family life and, indeed, a form of tribal culture, with an extraordinary degree of mobility and a lively interest in, and aptitude for, trade.

On the other hand, one cannot escape the conclusion that mobility tends, not merely to undermine the existing social order, but to progressively complicate social relations, and by so doing, release and emancipate the social units of which society is composed.[15]

What has been said suggests the significance of the statement that Chinese and Oriental civilization generally are based on the family. There they have had their origin, and from that source they have

---

[15] See Frederick J. Teggart, *Theory of History*, Chapter XV, "The Methods of Hume and Turgot," where he reviews the theories of those writers, including Waitz and Bagehot, who have sought to explain progress as an incident of the migration and movement of peoples.

derived those controlling ideas that constitute their philosophy of life—the ideas that maintain the unity of their diversified but closely integrated cultures.

On the other hand, Occidental, and particularly modern and American, culture may be said to have had their origin and to have found their controlling ideas in the market place, where men come together to barter and trade, and by the exchange of commodities and services in order to improve—each for himself, and according to his own individual conception of values—his condition in life.

One of the characteristic traits of Occidental, as contrasted with Oriental, civilization is that marriage is the proper termination of courtship and romance. Romantic love as a phenomenon is not unknown in other parts of the world, but it is only in Western Europe, and particularly in America, that it has come to be regarded as a sufficient ground for marriage or for divorce.

Men and women have always been disposed to fall in love, but not until very recent times have they assumed that a romance was a safe or proper basis upon which to establish a family. There is probably no institution, outside of the Protestant Church, where the individualism of the West, as compared with the communism of the East, has found a more decisive or more characteristic expression.

Romantic love, like progress, is a conception which has exercised a controlling influence upon the life and institutions of Western peoples. Only recently has this notion invaded the Orient. It has come in with the American cinema and with the "social dance." With the acceptance of the dogma which asserts that a man is entitled to choose his own wife, and the woman is entitled to choose her own husband, the ancient and inherited type of family, one of the foundation pillars on which Oriental society is based, has begun to crumble. But then, everything in our modern world, under the pressure of changing conditions, has begun to crumble. This is even true, as one gathers from Oswald Spengler's *The Decline of the West*, of the Western world's conviction of its own superiority; the one indomitable idea on which its faith in its future is finally based, has also begun to crack.

CHAPTER 2

CULTURE AND CIVILIZATION

THE terms society and community as ordinarily used are not co-extensive. A family may be a society but we do not ordinarily think of it as a community. There may, of course, be in a family that mystic element of communion. In our own country, as contrasted with China, we have *community* with very little *society* or consensus. When we think of community we have in mind people settled on the land each carrying on some economic activity for himself. There is little society here; there is little collective action. A community does not as such maintain a religion. The members may have little in common in the way of etiquette and social form. Our society represents a police state. Our notion is that the least government is the best government and in such a society we find freedom of belief, of movement and of values.

In contrast with such a society as ours let us look at the small ethnocentric we-groups that Sumner describes as the proto-types of all societies. In these we-groups there is order and discipline and the institutions become fixed and hardened. The solidarity in the we-group depends upon the animosity with the out-group. The we-group has a cult, a religion and a moral order of its own. Commercial relations, where they exist at all, exist between such groups that are more or less in conflict with one another. The territorial relations are the basis of the market and of the trade. Within the we-group we have a moral order. Between the groups which are struggling against

---

Unpublished paper.

one another there arises an economic and political order. A minimum of formal understanding is necessary to carry on trade. A territorial community may have an ecological order and an economic and political order, but it does not have a moral order, which is found only inside of a we-group and not between such groups.

Culture is the sort of order existing in a society which has a cult or a religion. It preserves morale and enables the group to act collectively. Most of our institutions enable us in our society to act with unanimity in times of danger. They enable us to face the physical "evil forces." They serve to maintain the integrity of a system. If we could use the word *culture* to refer to a society that has a moral order and *civilization* to refer to the order that applies to a territorial group, we could bring out the important distinction more clearly. What we call civilization is always a territorial affair. It comes about by trade and commerce. We cannot be satisfied with a mere recognition that there are culture areas, as the anthropologists have used that term. Civilization is built up by the absorption of foreign ethnic groups, by undermining them, and by secularizing their cult and sacred order.

In an *imperium*, people of different cultures are allowed to reside side by side. In the end, one culture becomes dominant and extends its influence over the others. In Soviet Russia we see today the attempt to bring together in one political system peoples of different races and cultures. There Russian authorities have sought to maintain the individuality of these cultures, but they cannot continue very long. A process of homogenization will inevitably take place. The integration of people over a wider territory rests upon extending the economic and political and moral order to these other peoples.

This is the main problem which civilization faces. What actually happens is that the smaller ethnic groups become secularized and break down. Civilization is fundamentally a territorial affair. It undermines the smaller cultures and by secularizing them furnishes release to the individual from the controls to which he is accustomed. We see this process in various stages in the second and third generation of immigrants, who tend to become detached from the moral order of their ancestors. In many such communities there is nothing aside from the police controlling individual behavior. The only order arising in such a community is that produced by the conflict between groups. The relations between Nazis and Jews represent a case in point.

The caste society is a term which applies to a society that is unwilling to incorporate strange tribes on an equal basis. Trade relations tend to break down such a society. In China, we find that the invaders have absorbed the various aboriginal groups. There are sharp differences between China and Mongolia. But as China expands, the Mongolians see the advantage of Chinese order and begin to want it for themselves. They feel inferior alongside of the Chinese and want to be accepted into Chinese society. Such a process has been going on for centuries. Likewise in European life through the conquest of different states, cultural absorption has been going on. In the beginning, there was much race mixture. Later, this race mixture stopped. The advantage of race mixture for culture is that wherever you have races mixing, acculturation goes on more rapidly than it otherwise would. Wherever superior and inferior peoples meet those who speak the language of the superiors have better opportunities. Those who live in cities get an education; those in the country continue to speak the mother tongue, get no education, and are put at a disadvantage.

The sect represents a new cult. It adopts new conceptions of life which differentiate its members from others. The sect, therefore, is to be seen as on a level with society, culture, and ethnic groups, over against which we place community, civilization and the state. The sect like the caste adopts a distinguishing mark of dress and manners, if it has no original mark. The function of the sect is to protect people against disintegration and against a sense of inferiority. The sect preserves its own solidarity and its own moral order. In the case of the community, of civilization and the state, we are dealing with essentially different principles of organization. A theory of the origin of the state is that it is established through conquest. In the state we get social and racial classes instead of age and sex groups. In the state, furthermore, we can see the hierarchization of law and authority.

How do outside cultures gain prestige? As long as the internal culture is maintained intact, the external culture has no appeal. There can be no culture except where there is some consensus. Consensus is a matter of understanding. It is transmitted through communication, through example and through participation in a common life. It is not merely habit. The term consensus, for the time being, had best remain loosely and tentatively defined.

Every group, with the possible exception of the trading group, that carries on a common life has something equivalent to a cult. When we speak of civilization we are thinking of the consequences of the coming together of different ethnic groups, which were formerly spread over a wide area and which are usually brought together by trade. When we speak of culture, on the other hand, we think of a small, familiar, ethnocentric group. The larger groups are based upon contractual relations. They are political in character.

This indicates the significance of the contrast pointed out by Sir Henry Maine between status and contract. Culture and civilization are words often used to cover the same things but with different emphasis. Culture is unique; not so with the objects that constitute civilization, which can be bought and sold and which embrace something wider than culture. We do not find anything corresponding to the mores in civilization. The things that make it up are not sacred. They constitute our technique of which science is typical. It is typical because it belongs to everybody and is a thing of utility.

The philosopher of history usually deals with civilization, not with culture. Anthropologists have supposedly dealt with culture. Sociology, however, grew out of the philosophy of history. Spengler thinks that every culture tends to develop into a civilization and grows through various phases which resemble a process of succession. He points out that the city destroys culture and develops civilization. The more cosmopolitanism there is, the more certain the destruction of culture. In the course of the growth of cities, people leave their homes in the country and come to a heterogeneous environment which the city offers. In the course of this, they become emancipated. If people go to war they may thereby strengthen their culture, but if they come to the city they become secularized, individuated in their cultural life and personal relations.

The city offers freedom, including freedom of speech, for in the city nothing is sacred. This is largely because the city is based on trade, and trade is the most impersonal of all human relationships. There is always the conflict between the sacred order which we try to preserve and that order based on trade which brings about the co-mingling of strange peoples and through which people become detached from their cultural moorings. Civilization breaks down solidarity and results from the loss of culture. The growth of cities, the use of money and the rationalization of life activities are characteristic of the displacement of culture by civilization.

Professor Teggart has another way of conceiving of civilization, which might be contrasted with that of Spengler. The processes that go on in one civilization are comparable to those going on in others. Cities have been centers of empires. They have had their sophisticated, intellectual people. Teggart believes that all important advances in civilization come through migration and, though he does not actually say so, through conquest. This idea is very old and was widely current in the 18th century. If the mixture of blood destroyed civilization, it must also have made civilization. If the peoples who are now mixed were to get pure again, they would be lost. Europe, despite all of its diversities, is a culture unit.

The history of the expansion of Europe offers abundant material for the study of the growth of civilization. Europe resembles a unit much as China does. The growth of European cities is coincident with the expansion of Europe. It may be that Europe has now actually reached the physical limits of its expansion, for there are no unknown territories left to bring under its dominion and those that have already been brought under its dominance have begun to live an independent career. The growth of cities and the expansion of empires are always coincident. People go to cities to produce articles of commerce, which are distributed through trade; hence the interconnection between the growth of cities and of empires.

In such a case we get propaganda and counter-propaganda. If any group, such as a clan or an in-group, has to fight opposition, it tends to build up solidarity and moral discipline. Unless there is significant rivalry between groups, we do not build up this morale within. If in America, for instance, we can keep up the rivalries between groups instead of Americanizing and demoralizing our immigrants, we can hope for morale. This is a problem to which Mr. Elton Mayo in his *Human Problems in an Industrial Civilization* has called attention.

The historical process by which culture develops is not different from the expansion of a single civilization such as the expansion of European civilization. Living cultures tend to expand, but with expansion changes come in. New ideas arise. We moderns scarcely realize how complete a society a family was. The family transmitted its own traditions. It did not fight with its neighbors, to be sure, but it entered into marriage relations in a formal way. It called upon the minister for funerals, marriages and christenings, and celebrated birthdays and anniversaries. In short, the family was a cult and an ethnic unit. Marriage relations with other groups were formal, but within the in-group the individual acquired status and was subjected to discipline.

Religious sects still retain the same quality. In a religious sect a humble man may be lifted up to be one with God, and experience an expansion of personality. Even in the smallest groups, such as in playground groups, there is some order that is non-logical as Mayo calls it, but in general the world in which we live shows a trend from persons to things. People who happen to use the same kind of automobile do not usually have much of a cult.

When we talk about a civilization, we think of an aggregate of people who use the same artifacts and who have no solidarity at all. Culture, on the other hand, is the function of groups that can act collectively. Culture grows up in situations calling for collective action. A study of the more or less universal phases of the evolution of civilizations is to be found in Herman Shneider's *History of World Civilization*. The author points out that the history of each civilization starts with a background of racial composition and evolution.

The distinction to which we should call attention is not so much that of Sumner's distinction between we-groups and others-groups but rather that between intimate, familial, ethnic groups and territorial or civilizational groups. This point is illustrated by Goethe's distinction between the little world of intimacy and naivete and the larger world of cosmopolitanism. It is interesting to compare the sophistication expressed in the first and second parts of *Faust* respectively.

Economic organization is almost impossible in the intimate groups and is most easily carried on and is, in fact, almost inevitable in territorial groups. Ethnic solidarity may indeed be maintained in a group for a long time before it is thoroughly corrupted. A small ethnic group represents a moral order, but the intellectual and economic life is carried on in larger groups of different ethnic origin. The familial group has primarily age and sex groupings within, while the territorial, cosmopolitan group is characterized by classes and castes. Castes grow up where inter-marriage is not permitted. The bonds in the small, intimate group that hold the individuals together are the sentiments, the obligations and loyalties. In the larger group the bond is territorial and commercial. In the latter there is a type of organization not to be found in the family.

The individual represents the human being outside of society. The person represents the individual in society. All that is characteristic of human beings as human beings is developed in society. In Chinese society we have a sentiment which is very thoroughgoing in the form of filial piety. It means that a person in such a society has duties but has no rights against society. Outsiders who come for business demand fair play or justice. We go to the outsider for justice and rights, but inside the group we have only duties and loyalties.

A familial society irrespective of the soil it occupies is based upon ethnocentrism. Patriotism is the substitute for ethnocentrism in a territorial society. It is loyalty to a society that occupies the soil and is really different from ethnocentrism, which is identification with the group. In familial society we get solidarity; in a territorial society there is developed a sentimental attitude toward freedom. Freedom may be regarded as a development of the frontier. In familial society we get an attitude that things are sacred. In our society we are guided less by sentiment and more by interest. It is difficult to argue oneself into a sentiment. Our order is more of a rational order in which utility is the decisive element. In a familial society we get consensus. Formal law hardly exists. In a territorial society we get cooperation, which usually turns out to be competitive cooperation based upon individual interests. In familial society there is a moral order which means a customary and expected order. We know what we are expected to do. In the other kind of society there is a political order based not on custom but on public opinion which is in constant change and under which laws are hard to enforce. To stop automobile thefts, for instance, in the city of Chicago, we virtually have to organize a crusade. To enforce the multitudinous rules of our own society we need constant agitation. We live more or less in both of these orders and in these we get the character we call human. There may indeed be feelings and loyalties in animal societies, but at least there is no conversation, no religion, or no politics. It takes a long time for creatures to develop that peculiar egocentrism which we call self-consciousness and which makes them into persons.

The family, the clan, the gang, the sect, the secret society are cases of familial groups. From the beginning we have communication in these groups, but we do not have merely communication. We have, in addition, the inter-penetration of minds. Human beings are immensely sensitive and suggestible. In our emphasis on the rational behavior of men, we greatly neglect this social weather in which we live. We feel an expansion and exaltation if we find our communication confirmed by others and we feel depression and despair if it is not so confirmed and if it is disapproved.

Habit is not merely individual custom and custom is not merely collective habit. There is an attitude of expectancy in what is customary. We cannot even think of breaking absolutely with our conventions. Some people would rather face Gatling guns than face the consequences of a violation of custom. Society really begins with communication. We meet people and they make a psychic assault upon us and get a claim on us. There is a feeling of expectancy which is largely absent from economic and other external relations.

There is a realm of physics which represents a closed system. Similarly there is a biological world, a web of life as Thompson and Darwin call it, which again represents a level of existence and of explanation. In social science we are dealing with the realm of the social, which consists of social and personal relations. It is not psychological but social. If a pebble should drop on our head from the roof we would look up and if there were no one there that we could discover who had dropped it, we would not be inclined to hold anyone responsible; or if someone had dropped it inadvertently, we would not feel particularly resentful; but if we suspected someone of doing it out of mischief, we would feel quite differently. What we would resent is not so much his act as his motive. It is the same with praise that drops on us. It is not the words but the fact that someone said them that matters.

In the little worlds where people come close together, human nature develops. The family, the tribe, the local community are instances. To the extent that we have intimate relations, we get responsiveness to one another. The definite personalities that we know grow up in intimate groups. In the larger society we get etiquette, urbanity, sophistication, finish. Urbanity is a charming quality but it is not a virtue. We don't ever really get to know the urbane person and hence never know when to trust him. It is more or less fundamental traits of personality which arise in the intimate group which enable us to act with definiteness and assurance towards others. Manners are of secondary importance.

It is not music, not drama, but news that is the most important thing in society. Thus as a result of news, some action or change of attitude in us is called forth. Of course not everything in the newspaper is news to everyone, but what calls for a change in attitude or action in those communications that come to us through the newspaper is news. News in the long run becomes the basis for control in modern society. In familial society this same function is exercised by custom or by the rules of the chief. If a ruler, even in an African society, wishes to do something unexpected, he must prepare for it by getting his notion into circulation. News circulates rapidly. It is like the diffusion of other elements of culture. News becomes interesting if we can interpret it, and it spreads only where people are ready to receive it.

In an individualistic society, every rule assumes the form of what Tönnies calls *Kürwille*—of arbitrary will, of traffic rules, as over against *Wesenswille*, which is more like natural law. Natural law is something anybody would obey, but there is little of it left in our society. Almost all of our law is positive law. In such a society news is important. The stock exchange is hence a typical institution in our society, for it reflects news from every part of the world. Everyone watches the tape because the tape makes the price. This is the mark of a civilized, secular society.

We may ask why, despite all shifts and changes, the London Stock Market still dominates the world. It is because London has investments all over the world and has men in every part of the world to keep it aware of what is going on in the world. Everything affects the money market—the weather, war and peace. There are people in London who know how to interpret the news and know where to get it. The fact that they know how to interpret the news means they are enabled to act on it promptly and intelligently. People with money to invest will usually seek the best possible news sources and the sources of news are close to the sources of power. It is not unlike the Roman Catholic Church. The Roman Catholic Church is stronger today than it ever was.

In a society like ours the élite rules because it has a wider horizon and is capable of responding over a larger area. The middle class fails to see the world fully and gets its news second-hand. On the bottom of the social pyramid is a class which is lost in the woods. Here sects and revolutionary movements germinate. But these movements had their doctrines and their leadership supplied when members of the élite attached themselves to the revolution. The middle class, not knowing how to interpret the news, is disturbed by reading it. The popularity of the *Christian Science Monitor* in that group is an evidence of this. The disturbing news in such a publication is left out. In a real sense we live in the world only when we keep up with the news of the world. If a person lives in a foreign country for any length of time with the expectation of returning to God's country, meaning his own, he is subject to disillusionment.

CHAPTER 3

CULTURE AND CULTURAL TRENDS

I. CULTURE AS FORM AND AS CONTENT

IN A PAPER published in 1911 in *Nature*, W. H. Rivers sought to distinguish between those elements of culture which are embodied in external, visible, and tangible objects, and those other less obvious, less formal aspects of culture which he called "social structure."

I shall not attempt to define social structure as Rivers uses the term. The conception is, at best, a dubious one. Interesting and important, however, is the distinction he has tried to make between elements or aspects of a culture which may be transmitted, as he says, by mere contact, and those other cultural complexes which remain in the background of the folk mind, invisible but active, coloring and modifying the overt behavior of the people of whom they are, perhaps, a forgotten heritage.

We find in Oceania . . . . people wearing European clothes and European ornaments, using European utensils, and even European weapons when they fight; we find them holding the beliefs and practicing the ritual of a European religion; we find them speaking a European language, often even among themselves, and yet investigation shows that much of their social structure remains thoroughly native and uninfluenced, not only in its general form, but often even in its minute details. The external influence has swept away the whole material culture, so that objects of native origin are manufactured only to sell to tourists; it has substituted

Publications of the American Sociological Society, XIX (December 1925), pp. 24-36.

a wholly new religion and destroyed every material, if not every moral, vestige of the old; it has caused great modification and degeneration of the old language; and yet it may have left the social structure in the main untouched. And the reasons for this are clear. Most of the essential social structure of a people lies so below the surface it is so literally the foundation of the whole life of the people, that it is not seen; it is not obvious, but can only be reached by patient and laborious exploration.[1]

It is always easier to transmit our language than our ideas. It is less difficult to inculcate the forms of a religious cult than it is to translate the religious experiences in which these religious practices originated. It is easier to sell a sewing machine in China than to establish a parliamentary form of government. It is easier, in short, to introduce among any people tools or technical devices the usefulness of which is obvious than to transplant an alien institution which has had a history and embodies in its motives and its structure the accumulated experience of successive generations.

The most striking illustration of the sudden and successful adoption of an alien culture is Japan. And yet those observers who have had an opportunity to know Japan intimately assure us that as yet European culture has merely changed the exterior of Japanese life. Japan has taken over the science, the technique, and many of the external forms of European culture, but is, perhaps, less disposed today than it was sixty years ago to adopt the mores of the occidental world.

The adoption of Western civilization was not nearly such an easy matter as unthinking persons imagined. And it is quite evident that the mental readjustments, effected at a cost which remains to be told, have given good results only along directions in which the race has always shown capacities of special kinds. Thus, the appliances of Western industrial invention have worked admirably in Japanese hands, have produced excellent results in those crafts at which the nation had been skilful, in other and quainter ways, for ages. There has been no transformation—nothing more than the turning of old abilities into new and larger channels.[2]

In one limited sense, Western art has influenced Japanese literature and drama; but the character of the influence proves the racial differences to which I refer. European plays have been reshaped for the Japanese stage, and European novels rewritten for Japanese readers. But a literal version is rarely attempted, for the original incidents, thoughts, and emotions would be unintelligible to the average reader or playgoer. Plots are

---

[1] W. H. R. Rivers, "The Ethnological Analysis of Culture," in *Nature*, LXXXVII (1911), 358-60.

[2] Lafcadio Hearn, *Kokoro* (Boston: Houghton Mifflin Co., 1896), pp. 9-10.

adapted, sentiments and incidents are totally transformed. 'The New Magdalen" becomes a Japanese girl who married an Eta. Victor Hugo's *Les Misérables* becomes a tale of the Japanese civil war, and Enjolras a Japanese student. There have been a few rare exceptions, including the marked success of a literal translation of the *Sorrows of Werther*.[3]

This does not mean that changes in Japanese life are not profound. It does mean that the Japanese *ethos*, rooted in temperament and reinforced by tradition, will, like any other living organism, persist, using the changed conditions to further and fortify its continued existence in a changed environment. The external adventitious elements of its culture will change first and change more rapidly. What Rivers calls the structure of Japanese national life will change also, but more slowly.

The contrast which Rivers draws between the changing, superficial aspect of culture and its relatively unchanging core, seems to reduce itself finally to the contrast between form and content. Those traits which are external and visible are form; those which are deep and inaccessible are content. We know what the external aspects of a culture are: they are its arts, its ceremonial, and its tools. But what of the content; in what, precisely, does this thing we call content consist? It consists, apparently, in memories, that is to say, in tradition; in a relatively unorganized social experience; something which is, at any rate, less structure than will.[4]

Rivers' discussion of blended cultures is concerned with the processes by which cultural traits are transmitted horizontally from one cultural group to another. But cultures are transmitted vertically from one generation to another in the same cultural group. The process is probably much the same, but the results are different. Children seem to take over intuitively and without resistance just those elements of a foreign culture which an adult alien finds most difficult to understand and assimilate. Children do not inherit the cultural complexes of their parents, and when children of immigrants grow up in the country of their adoption they inevitably take over all the accents, the inflections, the local cultural idioms of the native population. This is true of the Chinese in America, even though they are reared—as most of them are—in a ghetto. Most of the native sons among the

---

[3] Lafcadio Hearn, *Kokoro* (Boston: Houghton Mifflin Co., 1896), pp. 10-11.
[4] This will is probably related to the *libido* of the psychoanalyst and to the *élan vitale* of Bergson. It is anything you please, so long as the term is used to describe a fact, and is more than the name of a mystical and metaphysical entity.

Chinese in California are outrageously American in their manners and in their sentiments. It is only in later life, if at all, that they revert to the ancestral tradition and acquire a secondary racial loyalty.

If it turns out—as it frequently does—that the culture of the second generation seems a little thin and superficial as compared with that of the first, it is due, no doubt, to the fact that this second generation, having lost or abandoned the older cultural heritages, is not quite in possession of the new. In the long run this undoubtedly affects American life as a whole. It manifests itself, I suspect, in the proverbial restlessness of the American; in the extraordinary extent of family disorganization, i.e., divorce, desertion, as well as in the amount of juvenile delinquency and crime.

For this and other reasons, the distinction between the form and the content of cultures, which Rivers found useful in his studies of his primitive folk, is even more important in the study of conflicts and fusions of racial and national cultures in our cosmopolitan and contemporary life.

The significant thing about the whole matter is that, with the fusion and blending of culture, form and content tend to fall apart, and gain each a more or less independent existence. The significance of this will appear later, when we come to define the changes we have called trends.

II. TECHNIQUE AND THE MORES

The distinction between form and content, as applied to the analysis of cultures, has a parallel and an analogy in the contrast between technique and the mores.

Among primitive peoples, what Sumner calls "folkways" seem to have been identical, or nearly so, with what he later describes as mores. Folkways are not merely ways of doing all the common things of life as they have become defined in custom and transmitted through tradition, but they are the "right" ways.

There is a right way to catch game, to win a wife, to make one's self appear, to cure disease, to honor ghosts, to treat comrades or strangers, to behave when a child is born, on the warpath, in council, and so on in all cases which can arise. The ways are defined on the negative side, that is, by taboos. The "right" way is the way which the ancestors used, and which has been handed down. The tradition is its own warrant. It is not held subject to verification by experience. The notion of right is in the folkways. It is not outside of them, of independent origin, and brought to them to test them. In the folkways, whatever is, is right.[5]

Folkways, however, become in the course of time the object of reflection. Crude and vague notions of societal welfare grow up in regard to them and serve to explain and justify them. Then, according to Sumner, folkways assume the character of mores. The mores are not themselves a philosophy of life, but they hold a philosophy of life in solution. But folkways are not merely customary ways of doing things. They are, at the same time, devices and contrivances for getting things done and for doing them effectively. The folkways are practices which embody the elements of technique. Practice leads inevitably to experiment and then to reflection on these experiments. Out of these reflections we get eventually science, i.e., natural science. When science has explained the arts, ceremonies, and practical devices by which we do things and get them done, these arts, ceremonies, and other devices assume the character of technique.

The effect of this experimentation upon the folkways is to secularize them; to take them out from under the mores—that is to say, out from under the control of custom and the group—and put them at the service of the individual man. In this way, they cease to be a form of social ritual and become a kind of tool, a means to an end, rather than an end in themselves.

This process of secularization begins with simple and elementary practices like sowing and reaping, the making of gins and traps, the manufacture of tools. It extends itself eventually to all the activities of life.

Furthermore, when customary practices are made intelligible in the manner described, they are more easily transmitted from one cultural group to another. They can be bartered and sold in the marketplace, they lose their institutional character, and become part of that general culture of mankind which we ordinarily call civilization.

The history of modern civilization, viewed from one point of view, is the history of the continued secularization and rationalization of human activities, in the course of which ritual has become technique.

The natural sciences, at least in the occidental world, have long since entirely lost their local and national character. Philosophy and

---

[5] W. G. Sumner, *Folkways* (Ginn and Company, 1906), p. 28.

art, on the other hand, still reflect temperament and the historical experience of nations and of peoples of whose cultures they are a peculiarly intimate expression.

The effect of these international labors has been to destroy the clearly marked differences of national thought. At least in the domain of science, the peculiarities of the French, the German, and the English schools are rapidly disappearing. The characteristics of national thought still exist; but in order to find them in the present age we should have to study the deeper philosophical reasonings, the general literature, and the artistic efforts of the three nations. . . . . The establishment of an observatory or a laboratory in our age lays under contribution almost every civilized country in the world, and the most international of sciences—that of electricity—fixes its units by the names of discoverers of many countries.[6]

Those cultural traits which have so completely lost their local, tribal, and national character that they have ceased to be expressive, have, at the same time, lost their character as culture. They may be regarded as a part of nature. Civilization, on the other hand, is a more abstract conception than culture. Civilization includes both technique and the mores.

Civilization, as we ordinarily use the term, is not a local phenomenon in the same sense in which that is true of culture. It is not a term which describes what is individual and unique in the life of races or peoples. Civilization is the term we apply to those aspects of culture which have been generalized, rationalized, and are generally intelligible. So far as there is any distinction in the use of the terms, civilization emphasizes technique as culture emphasizes mores.

It has been a frequent observation of students of society that social groups, although consisting of individuals each with his own private opinions and purposes, frequently acts as if each group had a mind of its own, a group mind. We may, as James Harvey Robinson says we must, have to "reconcile ourselves to novel and revolutionary conceptions of the mind, for it is clear that the older philosophers, whose works still determine our current views, had a very superficial notion of the subject with which they dealt." [7]

Without venturing to discuss the question as to whether the group mind is "real" entity in any such sense as the mind of the individual

---

6 John Theodore Merz, *European Thought in the Nineteenth Century* (London: William Blackwood and Sons, 1907), I, 305.

7 James Harvey Robinson, *The Mind in the Making* (New York: Harper & Bros., 1921), p. 36.

is supposed to be, we may at least use the analogy to describe the way in which social groups do actually behave.

We are already familiar with such expressions as the "rural mind," "the urban mind," "the medieval mind," "mind in the making," etc. What we look for in the materials which the study of cultures offers us is something which enables us not merely to estimate their mentality, but to know their minds, using the term "mind" as Henry Osborne Taylor does when he speaks of the "medieval mind," or as Bliss Perry does when he speaks of the American mind.

That is what is meant by saying that cultural materials must be expressive. We can only know the minds of peoples, as we know a work of art, in so far as we are able to re-create, in our own minds, the experiences which have made them what they are.

Lafcadio Hearn, who was an adept in the art of "feeling himself," as the Germans say, into the lives of strange people, speaks with authority on this topic:

> Sympathy is limited by comprehension. We may sympathize to the same degree that we understand. One may imagine that he sympathizes with a Japanese or a Chinese, but the sympathy can never be real to more than a small extent outside of the simplest phases of common emotional life, those phases in which child and man are at one. The more complex feelings of the Oriental have been composed by the combinations of experiences, ancestral and individual, which have had no really precise correspondence in Western Life, and which we can therefore not fully know. For converse reasons, the Japanese cannot, even though they would, give Europeans their best sympathy.[8]

Whether the distinction between technique and the mores, with which I started out, or the distinction between culture and civilization, with which I ended, are wholly tenable or not does not greatly matter for the purposes of this paper. It is at least true that civilization is the broader term, and that within the wide embrace of a civilization, local, tribal, and even national, cultures may be found to exist. It is perhaps only when we consider civilization and culture in this relation to each other that the significance of the distinction between them becomes impressive. Using the terms with this definition, we might say of America today that it has, to be sure, a civilization, but not a culture. This is, in fact, pretty nearly what Horace Kallen does say in defense of his program of cultural pluralism.

---

[8] Lafcadio Hearn, *Kokoro* (Boston: Houghton Mifflin Co., 1896), pp. 11-12.

Decidedly, the older America, whose voice and whose spirit were New England, has, by virtue of business, of communications, of the immigrant, gone beyond recall. Americans of British stock still are prevailing the artists and thinkers of the land, but they work each for himself, without common vision or ideals. They have no *ethos* any more. The older tradition has passed from a life into a memory, and the newer one, so far as it had an Anglo-Saxon base, is holding its own beside more and more formidable competitors, the expression in appropriate form of the national inheritances of the various populations concentrated in various states of the Union, populations of whom their national self-consciousness is perhaps the chief spiritual asset, as their labor-power is their chief economic asset.[9]

I am not defending the view here expressed. I do not accept it; I merely quote it. But the fact that this view has been uttered and defended by a mind of unusual perspicuity and intelligence is itself significant.

III. CULTURAL TRENDS

The unifying element in every cultural complex is, in the language of Clark Wissler, "a core of ideas and beliefs, actuating a people and in a large measure controlling their career." The core of ideas and beliefs and the material objects in which these ideas and beliefs are embodied mutually interact upon one another to produce a harmonious whole. We are constantly remaking the world in accordance with our desires, but that world, once created, inevitably reacts back upon our desires to reshape them and define them in conformity with itself.

"Our experience with the world," says Wissler, "indicates that whenever we find sharp contrasts in such homely affairs as housing and feeding, we are certain to find equal, if not even sharper, contrasts in beliefs, social ways, ideals, and ethics, and in fact all mental attitudes toward things of whatever sort."

This admirable harmony between the ideal and material, between the subjective and objective aspects of culture, is probably a good deal more characteristic of the Eskimo, which is the illustration Wissler uses, than it is—to take an extreme case—of the hobo, or in fact of any other representative of our modern, cosmopolitan, urban life. Between the material objects of the hobo's cultural world and his beliefs and wishes the contrast is so great as to amount to conflict.

---

[9] Horace Kallen, *Culture and Democracy in the United States* (Boni and Liveright), p. 105.

The same is true, however, of almost every other class in modern society.

It is not merely true that the hobo as an individual is not always able to make ends meet, but the hobo's ideals of life are out of harmony with the general scheme of things. His life lacks form, and he is restless, migratory, and unsettled in his mind.

But this is characteristic of every class in modern society. Even our most solid citizens have a sense of insecurity which probably rests finally upon a sense of incongruity between our material culture and our aims and ideals of life.

The reason seems to be that the changes in our material culture are moving at a tempo with which our ideas and ideals have not been able to keep pace. This lack of congruity manifests itself not merely in our art and in our religion, but in our politics. Our institutions— we hear it repeated on all sides—are out of touch with life. Our art and architecture, like the hobo's career, is free, but lacks form. As Von Ogden Vogt has put it, our art is nondescript.

The arts constitute the description of the world as an age or a people apprehends it. The spiritual life of a time is depicted with unescapable exactness in its artistry. A spiritual movement that does not find expression in the arts cannot attain self-consciousness or dominance or survival. An age or a people that does not reach any self-realization or any unity of thought or feeling that breaks forth into artistic expression is nondescript.[10]

And then he adds:

Rebels, prophets, protestants, are in every time and place, but if they are in the majority, the community is nondescript, and the voices of the arts are mute, for they have no great thing to say. . . . .[11]

This is a nondescript age in which we live. The old isolations within which the older cultures grew up have broken down. "No race can again form so separate a culture and artistry as that of Siam or Japan. The world is one as never before. And it is nondescript as never before."[12]

On the other hand, religion, as it has found institutional expression in the church, is likewise out of touch with modern life and thought.

---

[10] Von Ogden Vogt, *Art and Religion* (New Haven: Yale University Press, 1921), p. 9.
[11] *Ibid.*, p. 11.
[12] Charles A. Ellwood, *The Reconstruction of Religion* (New York: The Macmillan Company, 1922), p. 2.

Science and practical life have moved on and left the church with its creeds behind.

The crisis in the religious world has been brought about by the failure of existing religion to adapt itself to the two outstanding facts in our civilization—science and democracy..... Of these two, science is the more outstanding and dominant. It is the foundation of our views of life and of the universe, as well as of our material progress, and so it has largely created the conditions which have favored the rise of modern democracy. Yet the maladjustment of religion with science remains pronounced.[13]

Roscoe Pound has made similar observations in regard to our political and judicial institutions:

To understand the administration of criminal justice in American cities today we must first perceive the problems of administration of justice in a homogeneous, pioneer, primarily agricultural community of the first half of the nineteenth century, and the difficulties involved in meeting those problems with the legal institutions and legal doctrines inherited or received from seventeenth-century England. We must then perceive the problems of administration of justice in a modern, heterogeneous, urban, industrial community, and the difficulties involved in meeting those problems with the legal and judicial machinery inherited or received from England and adapted and given new and fixed shape for pioneer rural America.[14]

Disease has been described as an evidence and an effect of a lack of adjustment between the organism and its environment. Social disorganization may, with probably equal justice to the facts, be described as an evidence of conflict or incongruity between the subjective and objective aspects of culture, between the group mind and the instrumentalities through which that mind acts.

It is the thesis of this paper that what we ordinarily call cultural trends are changes that take place in the mores, in law, in public opinion, and in philosophy in the struggle to bring these into some sort of consistent and harmonious relations with social conditions and, as we so often say, actual life.

There is a fashion in public opinion, in law, in the mores, and in culture generally, as there is in all things that express the life and the will of the social group. The general direction which fashion takes is what I should like to describe as a cultural trend.

---

13 *Ibid.*, p. 16.
14 Roscoe Pound, *Criminal Justice in Cleveland* (Cleveland: The Cleveland Foundation, 1922), p. 590.

The classic illustration of such a trend is Dicey's account of the changes in public opinion in England in the period beginning with the end of the eighteenth century and ending with the twentieth.[15] Dicey speaks of law and public opinion, but the public opinion that he describes includes what Sumner calls the mores. It is the change in the mores, as they were reflected in law, with which he is mainly concerned.

What he says, in effect, is that from the end of the eighteenth century to the end of the nineteenth, changes in English law, with, to be sure, many divagations and shiftings, took one general direction. On the whole, these changes represented a shift from a more individualistic to a more communistic conception of government and human relations. The direction which this change took was a trend.

Similar changes have been taking place in our own society. Without intending to do so, without clearly realizing that they are doing so, our legislatures, in seeking to regulate the railways and other public or quasi-public corporations, have been steadily undermining the conception of private property inherited from England. The labor organizations, in their struggles with the employers of labor, have worked, consciously and unconsciously, in the same direction. The latest and most radical expression of the labor movement is embodied in the phrase "citizenship in industry." Citizenship in industry is an assertion of labor's right, in conjunction with its employers, to fix wages and define the conditions under which industry should be carried on.

The expression, "boring from within," is simply a description and a rationalization of the process by which labor has actually undermined the institution of property upon which the employer's right to control the industry rests.

If now we consider causes, the systematic character of these changes and the apparent failure of both parties to understand their fundamentally subversive character seem to preclude the notion that they were the result of design, or consciously intended by the persons who brought them about. The causes were deeper and more impersonal.

When we review what actually has taken place in the nineteenth century, we observe that with the growth of cities the multiplication of the means of transportation and communication, and the consequent division of labor, the interdependence of individuals and of

---

[15] A. V. Dicey, *Law and Public Opinion in England.*

peoples has been vastly extended. And this extension of the division of labor, with the consequent economic interdependence which it involves, has undermined not only the independence of the working-man, but of every one of us. Under conditions of modern life the workingman bears, or did at one time, most of the economic costs of the fluctuations of industrial production. Every new industrial machine puts the hard-won skill of a group of workers on the scrap-heap. Every fluctuation in trade threw large numbers of men out of work. With this increasing extension of economic interdependence of all individuals and classes, it was inevitable that eventually laws should be passed that recognized this interdependence and sought to control it.

In general, one may say that changes in what Rivers calls the less material culture always and inevitably reflect changes in the more material culture. In other words, technique and the mores are so related that any change in the former inevitably brings corresponding changes in the latter. The relation is, however, probably not reversible. This is, perhaps, one explanation of the fact as well as the illusion of progress, progress being a cultural trend in which we see social conditions constantly in process of amelioration in one direction while they are just as steadily deteriorating in others.

Nothing inspiring or uplifting seems to follow from the cleavage I have attempted to point out between the core of the cultural complex and its expression in physical objects; there is no immediate practical significance, either, to the fact that what we call cultural trends seem to arise out of the struggle for coherence among elements, subjective and objective, within the cultural complex.

It is significant, however, that these distinctions have in every case arisen, not merely in an attempt to analyze primitive cultures, but in the effort to deal practically with the problems of racial and cultural conflicts as they manifest themselves, among people with whom we are brought in everyday contact, within the limits of what Henry James calles the "American scene."

What does strike one as hopeful, is that further investigation on the lines here indicated, will throw a new and a more searching light upon the whole cultural process, so that in the future we may hope to study it empirically, rather than discuss it philosophically, as this paper has been compelled to do.

CHAPTER 4

REFLECTIONS ON COMMUNICATION AND CULTURE

I. COMMUNICATION IN THE CULTURAL PROCESS

COMMUNICATION is so obvious and pervasive a factor in social life that I have often wondered why so little had been said or written about it. Now that I have attempted to write something on the subject, I no longer wonder, I know.

One reason that there has been so little written on this subject is because there has been so much to write, and because much that has been written has been concerned with communication as it functions in some special way in some specific region of social life.

In any case, this paper has turned out to be little more than a record of my explorations and mental prospecting, seeking to define the limits of a subject of which I believed before I started that I already had some general knowledge.

There is, to be sure, an extensive literature on the subject of speech and language, including technical devices as different as the ideographs of the Stone Age and the newspaper and radio of the modern world, by which man has sought to perfect his means of communication and expand the effective limits of his world. The radio and newspaper, however, have been mere instrumental extensions of speech. Less has been written about the manifold types of symbolism, including the so-called fine arts, by which sentiments and attitudes as well as ideas are communicated.

American Journal of Sociology, XLIV (September 1938), pp. 187-205.

There is also an extensive psychological and sociological literature which approaches the subject of communication obliquely and from the point of view of some ulterior interest. In the writings of the Scottish moral philosophers, from Bishop Butler to Hume and Adam Smith, one notes an insistent reference to the facts of sympathy and of imitation as offering at once an evidence and an explanation of that understanding and solidarity which is the basis of the moral order. A little later, in 1872, Walter Bagehot, in a volume, *Physics and Politics*, which has become a sociological classic, emphasizes the importance of imitation and indicates its role in the cultural process and in social life. Eighteen years later when Gabriel Tarde published his *Laws of Imitation*, he identified imitation, which he described as "action of one mind upon another at a distance," with the fundamental social and cultural process. The forms in which communication takes place are obviously protean. They include not merely sympathy and imitation, which are generally recognized as such in the literature of the subject, but discussion, dialectic, and suggestion.

The nature and function of communication appears in a new light in the studies of personality and self-consciousness and in the writings of men as widely divergent in their several points of view as J. Mark Baldwin, Charles H. Cooley, and George H. Mead. Communication and the nature of the process by which one mind knows another turns up again as a cardinal problem of the so-called "understanding sociology" (*verstehende Soziologie*) of Max Weber and in the writings of Wilhelm Dilthey, who preceded and influenced him.

Finally there are the Semanticists, of whom C. K. Ogden and I. A. Richards, authors of *The Meaning of Meaning*, seem to be the most eminent representatives. They are interested not primarily in communication but in intelligibility, which as far as I am concerned, they have not always achieved. And finally as I write these words, I note the appearance of a new volume by Stuart Chase, *The Tyranny of Words*, in which he undertakes to tell us in simple language what Ogden and Richards meant when they wrote *The Meaning of Meaning*.

Implicit in all this discussion—and that, it seems to me is the important thing—is the notion that communication is a form of interaction or a process that takes place between persons—that is to say, individuals with an ego, individuals with a point of view, conscious of themselves and more or less oriented in a moral world. Communication is, therefore, not a form of interstimulation merely. The term would not properly apply to two individuals who by occupying the same bed kept one another warm. Communication when completed involves an interpretation by A of the stimulus coming from B, and a reference of that interpretation back to the person of whose sentiment or attitude it assumes to be an expression.

Let me illustrate. If innocently, as is my wont, I am walking along the street and a brick falls on my head or close enough at least to interrupt my meditations, that in itself is a mere physical fact. If, however, looking up I see a face grinning down on me maliciously from the wall from which the brick came, the fall of that brick ceases to be a mere physical phenomenon and becomes a social fact. It changes its character as soon as I interpret it as an expression of attitude or intent rather than an act of God—that being the secular language in which we describe a happening that is wholly without intention of any sort, and one, therefore, for which no one can be made responsible.

Communication is then a form of interaction that takes place, typically at least, between individuals with an ego. I am leaving out of the reckoning, for the present, the kind and quality of the communication which obviously takes place among less articulate creatures than ourselves.

You have no doubt observed the ceremonious way in which two strange dogs approach each other. This is not mere interstimulation; it is communication. These dogs understand one another, even when they do not speak. So it is with the hen clucking to her chicks. This is not conversation, but it is communication. What the natural history of the process is I shall not undertake to discuss. The origin of language is one of the classic problems of the students of linguistics. The case of hen and chicks was one of the favorite themes of George Mead's lectures on social psychology.

The most interesting thing I have been able to find in the books on the subject of communication is Edward Sapir's article on "Language" in the *Encyclopedia of the Social Sciences;* that, and two briefer articles by the same author, one on "Communication" and the other on "Symbolism." Sapir, following in this Ogden and Richards, distinguishes between language that is symbolic and impersonal—like a mathematical formula or the number system—and language that is expressive and personal, like a gesture or an expletive, or even a voice crying in the wilderness. In the first case the function of language is purely "referential," as in scientific discourse. It points out its object, identifies, classifies, and describes it.

In the second case, language, modulated by accent, intonation, and inflection, tends to be expressive merely. In that case the function of words seems to be to reveal the mood and the sentiments of the person who utters them, rather than to define and express an idea.

The same distinction applies, in varying degrees, to forms of communication as different as the sign language used by deaf-mutes and what I may call the "expressive arts," particularly music and dancing. In every form which the process of communication assumes and in all the variations involved due to the different means employed, the distinction between the referential or didactic function —where ideas are communicated—and the expressive function—where sentiments and attitudes are manifested—persists. In the one case ideas, and in the other sentiments, attitudes, and emotions are communicated, partly through the medium of conventional symbols and partly through gesture and expressive behavior, by which I mean behavior that can be interpreted intuitively. Music and dancing are expressions of this sort. They seem to be expressions of what Schopenhauer calls pure will. In the same sense mathematics and logic may be described as expressions of pure form or idea.

To pursue these divergent lines of inquiry farther, however, would lead into a discussion of the manner in which logic and science on the one hand, and the expressive arts on the other, have developed out of the impulse and the efforts of human beings to communicate their ideas and express their sentiments. My purpose is rather to emphasize the fact that communication as I understand it is, if not identical with, at least indispensable to, the cultural process. Culture may assume among different peoples at different times and places many and varied forms, material, and nonmaterial—language, marriage customs, and artifacts, like the hoe and the plow, all alike are cultural traits. It is, however, the fact that they are understood by a particular people, by a cultural group, that gives them the character we describe as cultural. Culture includes then all that is communicable, and its fundamental components, whatever the forms and symbols in which they may be anywhere embodied, are, in the sense in which Schopenhauer seems to have used those terms, Will and Idea. Attitudes and sentiments, folkways and mores, are the warp and woof of that web of understanding we call "culture." I follow Sapir in the assumption that the essence of culture is understanding.

II. COMMUNICATION AND COMPETITION

What does communication do and how does it function in the cultural process? It seems to do several different things. Communication creates, or makes possible at least, that concensus and understanding among the individual components of a social group which eventually gives it and them the character not merely of society but of a cultural unit. It spins a web of custom and mutual expectation which binds together social entities as diverse as the family group, a labor organization, or the haggling participants in a village market. Communication maintains the concert necessary to enable them to function, each in its several ways.

Family group or labor organization, every form of society except the most transient has a life-history and a tradition. It is by communication that this tradition is transmitted. It is in this way that the continuity of common enterprises and social institutions is maintained, not merely from day to day, but from generation to generation. Thus the function of communication seems to be to maintain the unity and integrity of the social group in its two dimensions—space and time. It is in recognition of this fact that John Dewey has said: "Society not only continues to exist by transmission, by communication, but may fairly be said to exist in transmission, in communication."

Implicit in Dewy's statement, however, is a conception of society that is not generally nor everywhere accepted, since it seems to identify the social with the moral order. By so doing it limits the term "social" to those relations of individuals that are personal, customary, and moral.

When individuals use one another to get results, without reference to their emotional or intellectual disposition and consent, says Dewey, they are involved in relations that are not social. To make the matter clear, he adds, "So far as the relations of parent and child, teacher and pupil remain upon this level, they form no true social group, no matter how closely their respective activities touch one another."

It is obvious, however, that communication, if it is the typical social process, is not the only form of interaction that goes on among the individual units of a social group. "We are compelled to recognize," he admits, "that even within the most social group there are many relations which are not yet social"—not social, at any rate in the sense in which he uses the term. Competition, for example, performs a social function of a somewhat different sort, but one that is at least comparable to that of communication. The economic order in society seems to be very largely a by-product of competition. In any case, competition is, as Cooley observes, "the very heart of the economic process." What we ordinarily designate as economic competition, however, is not competition in the Malthusian sense of that term in which it is identical with the struggle for existence. Economic competition is always competition that is controlled and regulated to some extent by convention, understanding, and law.

The investigations of plant and animal ecologists have discovered that even where competition is free and unrestricted, as it is in the so-called plant and animal communities, there exists among creatures living in the same habitat a kind of natural economy. What characterizes this economy is a division of labor and an unconscious co-operation of competing organisms. Wherever in nature competition or the struggle for existence brings about a stable organization among competing individuals, it is because they have achieved in some form or another a division of labor and some form of conscious or unconscious co-operation. In such case the competing species or individual, each occupying the particular niche in which it fits, will have created an environment in which all can live together under conditions where each could not live separately. This natural economy of plant and animals is called symbiosis.

Man's relation to other men is, to a very much larger extent than has hitherto been recognized, symbiotic rather than social, in the sense in which Dewey uses that term. Competition among plants and animals tends to bring about an orderly distribution as well as a mutual adaptation of the species living together in a common habitat. Competition among human beings has brought about, or at any rate helped to bring about, not merely a territorial, but an occupational distribution of races and peoples. Incidentally, it has brought about that inevitable division of labor which is fundamental to every permanent form of society from the family to the nation.

If the struggle for existence, as Darwin conceived it, was a determining factor in producing that diversity of living types described in the *Origin of the Species*, then economic competition, the struggle for a livelihood, seems to have been a decisive factor in bringing about among human beings a comparable occupational diversity.

But this division of labor wherever it exists in human society is limited by custom; and custom is a product of communication.

As a matter of fact, competition and communication operate everywhere within the same local habitat and within the same community, but in relative independence of each other. The area of competition and of the symbiotic relationship is, however, invariably wider and more inclusive than the area of those intimate, personal, and moral relations initiated by communication. Commerce invariably expands more widely and rapidly than linguistic or cultural understanding. It is, it seems, this cultural lag that makes most of our political and cultural problems. But the main point is that communication, where it exists, invariably modifies and qualifies competition, and the cultural order imposes limitations on the symbiotic.

Most of you will perhaps recall Sumner's description of primitive society, a territory occupied by little scattered ethnocentric groups, each the focus and center of a little world in which all members are bound together in ties of mutual understanding and loyalty.

Outside of these little tribal and familial units, on the other hand, men live in relation with one another not unlike those in which they live with the plants and animals, that is to say, in a kind of symbiosis, very little modified by mutual understanding or agreements of any sort. Under these circumstances the fundamental social and economic order is enforced and maintained by competition, but competition modified and controlled to an ever increasing degree by custom, convention, and law.

As a matter of fact, society everywhere exhibits two fundamental forms of organization—the familial and the communal. Familial society seems to have had its source in the interest and in the urge of individuals, not merely to live as individuals but to perpetuate the race. Thus the family seems to rest, finally, on an instinctive basis. Communal society, on the other hand, has arisen out of the need of the individuals to survive as individuals. Under these conditions men have come together, not in response to some gregarious impulse comparable with the sexual instinct, but for the more pragmatic and intelligible reason that they are useful to one another.

In spite of the changes which time and civilization have wrought in the existing social order, man lives as he always has, in two worlds —the little world of the family and the great world of commerce and politics. In the little world the order which predominates is intimate, personal, and moral. In the larger world man is free to pursue his individual interests in his own individual way, relatively uninhibited by the expectations and claims which, in a more intimate social order, the interests of others might impose upon him. In the family it is communication and the personal influences which communication mediates that are the source and principle of order. In the world of commerce, and to a less degree in politics, it is competition, and competition in the more sublimated form of conflict and rivalry, which imposes such order as exists.

What all this suggests, though not perhaps so obviously as I should like, is that competition and communication, although they perform divergent and unco-ordinated social functions, nevertheless in the actual life of society supplement and complete each other.

Competition seems to be the principle of individuation in the life of the person and of society. Under the influence of this principle the individual adapts and accommodates himself, not merely to the human habitat but to the occupational organization of the society of which he is a member. He follows the vocation and does the thing he can, rather than the thing he might like to do. Communication, on the other hand, operates primarily as an integrating and socializing principle.

It is true, of course, that when new forms of communication have brought about more intimate associations among individuals or peoples who have been culturally isolated, the first consequence may be to intensify competition. Furthermore, under the influence of communication, competition tends to assume a new character. It becomes conflict. In that case the struggle for existence is likely to be intensified by fears, animosities, and jealousies, which the presence of the competitor and the knowledge of his purposes arouse. Under such circumstances a competitor becomes an enemy.

On the other hand, it is always possible to come to terms with an enemy whom one knows and with whom one can communicate, and, in the long run, greater intimacy inevitably brings with it a more profound understanding, the result of which is to humanize social relations and to substitute a moral order for one that is fundamentally symbiotic rather than social, always in the restricted sense of that term.

III. DIFFUSION

Communication, whether it takes place through the medium of gesture, articulate speech, or conventional symbols of any sort whatever, always involves, it seems to me, an interpretation of the attitude or intent of the person whose word or gesture supplied the stimulus. What anything means to anyone at any time is substantially what it means, has meant, or will mean, to someone else. Communication is a process or form of interaction that is inter-personal, i.e., social in the narrower sense. The process is complete only when it results in some sort of understanding. In other words, communication is never merely a case of stimulus and response in the sense in which those terms are used in individual psychology. It is rather expression, interpretation, and response.

In some cases, in most cases perhaps, and particularly where the persons involved are *en rapport*, the response of individual A to an expressive action of individual B is likely to be immediate and well-nigh automatic. This is obviously so in the case of hypnotic suggestion, and particularly so under the condition of what is called "isolated rapport," where the subject responds to the suggestions of the hypnotizer and to those of no one else.

We must conceive individuals in society as living constantly enveloped in an atmosphere of subconscious suggestion. In this atmosphere they are constantly responsive, not merely to the overt acts but to the moods and the presence of other persons, in somewhat the same way that they are to the weather. What we call the fluctuations of public opinion, public sentiment, and fashion, are, in fact, a kind of social weather. These changes in the social weather evoke changes in internal tensions of persons who are *en rapport*: changes so subtle that they amount to a kind of clairvoyance. It is only in moments of abstraction that this condition of clairvoyance is interrupted and then only partially. A suggestion is, of course, not a mere stimulus, but a stimulus that is interpreted as an expression of a wish or an attitude. The literature of hypnotism indicates how subtle suggestions may be and how responsive under certain conditions individuals may be to them.

Sometimes, to be sure, the sense and meaning of the behavior and language of those about us are obscure; this sets us thinking, and leaves us sometimes with a sense of frustration and confusion. At other times it arouses us, not to definite action, but to vague emotional protest or inarticulate opposition. This emotional expression of unrest, multiplied and intensified by the reflex influence of mind on mind, may take the form finally of a social brain storm like the dancing mania of the Middle Ages or the commercial panic of 1929. Under more normal conditions unrest may express itself in social agitation or in the less violent form of discussion and debate.

These are some of the manifold ways in which communication operating within the limits of an existing culture group changes, directly and indirectly, the pattern of cultural life. If I merely refer to these manifestations here in passing it is because a fuller discussion of them would involve problems of collective behavior which are so diverse and manifold that they have become the subject of a special discipline of the social sciences.

The cultural process ordinarily presents itself in two dimensions or aspects which are intimately bound up with and determined by the condition under which communication inevitably takes place. They are: diffusion and acculturation.

As communication takes place between persons, it is necessarily involved in all the complexities incident to the transmission of a stimulus from the source *a quo* to a terminus *ad quem*—i.e., from a person of whose mind it is an expression to the person in whose mind it finds a response. The obvious conditions which facilitate or obstruct these processes are mainly physical and in modern times they have been progressively overcome by means of technical devices like the alphabet, printing-press, radio, etc.

The less obvious obstacles to effective communication are the difficulties that grow out of differences of language, tradition, experience, and interest. By interest in this instance I mean what Thomas refers to as the "run of attention." Everywhere and always, certain interests, persons, or events are in the focus of attention; certain things are in fashion. Whatever has importance and prestige at the moment has power to direct for a time the currents of public opinion, even if it does not change, in the long run, the trend of events. All these things are factors in communication and either facilitate or make difficult the transmission of news from one country to another. The manner in which news circulates is typical of one way in which cultural diffusion takes place.

Discussions of the deficiencies of the press often proceed on the implicit assumption that the communication of news from one cultural area to another—from the Orient to the Occident, for example, or from Berlin to New York—is an operation as simple as the transportation of a commodity like bricks. One can, of course, transport words across cultural marches, but the interpretations which they receive on two sides of a political or cultural boundary will depend upon the context which their different interpreters bring to them. That context, in turn, will depend rather more upon the past experience and present temper of the people to whom the words are addressed than upon either the art or the good will of the persons who report them.

Foreign correspondents know, as no one who has not had the experience, how difficult it is under ordinary circumstances to make the public read foreign news. They know, also, how much more difficult it is to make events happening beyond his horizon intelligible to the average man in the street. In general, news circulates widely in every direction in proportion as it is interesting and intelligible. In that respect it is not unlike any other cultural item, the oil cans of the Standard Oil Company or the Singer sewing-machine for example, which are now possibly the most widely dispersed of all our modern cultural artifacts.

Each and every artifact or item of news inevitably tends to reach finally the places where it will be appreciated and understood. Cultural traits are assimilated only as they are understood, and they are understood only as they are assimilated. This does not mean that a cultural artifact or an item of news will have everywhere the same meaning; quite the contrary. But the different meanings they do have in different places will tend to converge, as diffusion is succeeded by acculturation.

It is extraordinary to what extent and with what rapidity news tends to reach the minds of those to whom its message, if intelligible, is important. On the other hand, just as important, if less remarkable, is the difficulty of communicating a message that is neither important nor intelligible to the persons to whom it is addressed. This latter is a problem of the schools, particularly the problem of rote learning.

Thirty-three years ago the conclusion of the Russian-Japanese War made news that I suspect circulated farther and more rapidly than any other report of events had ever traveled before. One heard echoes of it in regions as far apart as the mountain fastnesses of Tibet and the forests of Central Africa. It was the news that a nation of colored people had defeated and conquered a nation of white people. The same item of news might travel farther and with greater speed today, but it would not have the same importance. The question of how and why and under what circumstances news circulates is an important one and deserves more attention than has yet been given to it.

It is a familiar observation of students of the cultural process that artifacts, the traits of a material culture, are more easily diffused and more rapidly assimilated than similar items of a nonmaterial culture—political institutions and religious practices, for example. That is no more than to say that trade expands, on the whole, more rapidly than religion. But that, too, depends upon circumstances. Consider, for example, the sudden rapid diffusion in the modern world of communism.

One reason the terms of a material culture are so widely diffused and easily assimilated is because their uses are obvious and their values, whatever they be, are rational and secular. One needs no rite or ceremony to initiate him into mysteries involved in the use of a wheelbarrow or rifle. When the first plow was introduced into South Africa, an old chief who was invited to be present and see the demonstration recognized its value at once. He said, "This is a great thing the white man has brought us." Then after some reflection he added: "It is worth as much as ten wives."

What we call civilization, as distinguished from culture, is largely composed of such artifacts and technical devices as can be diffused without undermining the existing social institutions and without impairing the ability of a people to act collectively, that is to say, consistently and in concert. Institutions seem to exist primarily to facilitate collective action, and anything that involves a society rather than the individuals of which that society is composed is hard to export. Diffusion takes place more easily when the social unity is relaxed.

It is no secret, I suppose, that there is inevitably an intimate and indissoluble relation between commerce and the news. The centers of trade are invariably the centers of news; the centers to which the news inevitably comes and from whence it is diffused, first to the local community and then, according to its interests and importance, to the ends of the earth.

During this diffusion a process of selection necessarily takes place. Some news items travel farther and more rapidly than others. This is true even when all or most of the physical obstacles to communication have been overcome. The reason of course is simple enough. It is bound up with the inevitably egocentric character of human beings and the ethnocentric character of human relations generally. An event is important only as we believe we can do something about it. It loses importance in proportion as the possibility of doing that something seems more remote. An earthquake in China assumes, in view of our incorrigible provincialism, less importance than a funeral in our village. This is an example of what is meant by social distance, which sociologists seek to conceptualize and, in some sense, measure personal relations and personal intimacies. Importance is ultimately a personal matter; a matter of social distance.

The principle involved in the circulation of news is not different from that involved in the cultural process of diffusion, wherever it takes place. Individuals and societies assimilate most readily, as I have said, what is at once interesting and intelligible.

IV. ACCULTURATION

If the market place is the center from which news is disseminated and cultural influences are diffused, it is, likewise, the center in which old ideas go into the crucible and new ideas emerge. The market place, where men gather to dicker and chaffer, is in the very nature of things a kind of forum where men of diverse interests and different minds are engaged in peaceful controversy, trying to come to terms about values and prices; trying, also, by a process that is fundamentally dialectical, to explore the different meanings things have for men of different interests; seeking to reach understandings based rather more on reason and rather less on tradition and the prejudices which custom has sanctioned, if not sanctified. It is for this reason that the great metropolitan cities—Rome, London, and Paris—cities to which peoples come and go from the four ends of the earth, are in a perpetual ferment of enlightenment; are continually involved—to use a German expression, in an *Aufklärung*. Under such conditions the historical process is quickened, and acculturation, the mutual interpenetration of minds and cultures, goes forward at a rapid pace.

When peoples of different races and divergent cultures seek to live together within the limits of the same local economy, they are likely to live for a time in relations which I have described as symbiotic rather than social, using that term in this connection as Dewey and others have used it, namely, as identical with cultural. They live, in short, in physical contiguity, but in more or less complete moral

isolation, a situation which corresponds in effect if not in fact, to
Sumner's description of primitive society.

This has been and still is the situation of some of those little religious sects like the Mennonites, which have from time to time sought
refuge in the United States and elsewhere, settling on the frontiers of
European civilization, where they might hope to live in something
like tribal isolation—untrammeled and uncorrupted by intercourse
with a Gentile world.

It was to preserve this isolation that some of Pennsylvania's "plain
people," the Amish, protested a few months ago against a gift of
$112,000 of P.W.A. funds which the government was pressing upon
them for new schoolhouses. New schools, in this case, involved the
use of busses, to which the "plain people" were opposed. They believed, also, and no doubt quite correctly, that intimate association of
Amish children with the mixed population of a consolidated school
to whom Amish folkways would certainly seem quaint would undermine the discipline and the sacred solidarity of Amish society.

This situation, in which peoples occupying the same territory live
in a moral isolation more or less complete, was historically, so long
as they lived in the seclusion of their religious community, the situation of a more sophisticated people than the Amish, namely, the Jews.
It has been, to a less extent, the situation of every immigrant people
which has for any reason sought to find a place in the economic order
of an established society and at the same time maintain a cultural tradition that was alien to it.

Inevitably, however, in the natural course, under modern conditions of life, both the immigrant and the sectarian seek to escape from
this isolation in order that they may participate more actively in the
social life of the people about them. It is then, if not earlier, that they
become aware of the social distance that sets them apart from the
members of the dominant cultural group. Under these circumstances
acculturation becomes involved in and part of the struggle of immigrants and sectarians alike for status. Everything that marks them
as strangers—manners, accent, habits of speech and thought—makes
this struggle difficult. The cultural conflict which then ensues—
whether openly manifested or merely sensed—tends, as conflict invariably does, to heighten self-consciousness in members of both cultural
groups, in those who are classed as aliens and in those who count themselves native.

However, anything that intensifies self-consciousness and stimulates introspection inevitably brings to the surface and into clear consciousness sentiments and attitudes that otherwise would escape rational criticism and interpretation. Otherwise they would probably, as the psychoanalysts tell us, continue active in the dark backgrounds of consciousness. They would still function as part of that "vital secret" to which William James refers in his essay *A Certain Blindness in Human Beings*—a secret of which each of us is profoundly conscious because it is the substance of one's own self-consciousness and of one's individual point of view—but for which we look in vain to others for sympathy and understanding. But conflict, and particularly cultural conflict, in so far as it brings into the light of understanding impulses and attitudes of which we would otherwise remain unconscious, inevitably increases our knowledge not merely of ourselves but of our fellows, since the attitudes and sentiments which we find in ourselves we are able to appreciate and understand, no matter how indirectly expressed, when we find them in the minds of others.

Acculturation if we conceive it in radical fashion, may be said to begin with the intimate associations and understandings that grow up in the family between mother and child and somewhat later with other members of the family. But while mothers are necessarily, and under all ordinary circumstances, profoundly interested and responsive to their children, it is notorious that they do not always understand them.

The situation differs, but not greatly, with other members of the family—notably with the relations between husband and wife. Men are naturally and instinctively interested in and attracted by women, particularly strange women, but they often find them difficult to understand. In fact men have felt in the past and still feel in some obscure way, I suspect, that women, no matter how interesting, are not quite human in the sense and to the degree that this is true of themselves.

If this is not true to the same extent today that it once was, it is because men and women, in the family and outside of it, live in more intimate association with one another than they formerly did. They still have their separate worlds, but they get together as they formerly did not. They speak the same language. But this is true also of parents and children. Both understand each other better than they once did.

Men and women have learned a great deal about one another from experience, but they have learned more—in the sense of understanding one another and in the ability to communicate—from literature and the arts. In fact it is just the function of literature and the arts and of what are described in academic circles as the humanities to give us this intimate personal and inside knowledge of each other which makes social life more amiable and collective action possible.

I am, perhaps, wrong in describing the intimate associations which family life permits and enforces as if they were part and parcel of the cultural process. That may seem to be employing a term in a context which is so foreign to it as to destroy its original meaning. I am not sure, however, that this is quite true. At any rate, in the family in which husband and wife are of different racial stocks, with different cultural heritages, the process of acculturation—and acculturation in the sense in which it is familiar to students—takes place more obviously and more effectively than it does elsewhere. It is this fact and not its biological consequences which gives recent studies of race mixture and interracial marriage, like the studies of Romanzo Adams in Hawaii, a significance they would not otherwise have. It is in the life-histories of mixed bloods whose origin ordinarily imposes upon them the task of assimilating the heritages of two divergent cultures, that the process and consequences of acculturation are most obvious and open to investigation. The reason is that the man of mixed blood is a "marginal man," so called, that is, the man who lives in two worlds but is not quite at home in either.

In discussing cultural diffusion I have taken news and its circulation as an illustration of the process of diffusion. In doing so I have had in mind the wide distribution of news that has taken place with the extension of the means of communication through the medium of the printing-press, telegraphy, and the radio. I should add, perhaps, that not everything printed in the newspaper is news. Much that is printed as news is read, at least, as if it were literature; read, that is to say, because it is thrilling and stirs the imagination and not because its message is urgent and demands action. Such, for example, are the "human interest" stories, so called, which have been so influential in expanding and maintaining newspaper circulation. But human-interest stories are not news. They are literature. Time and place are the essence of news, but time and place impose no limitations on the circulation of literature and art. It is art and literature, and particularly the art of the moving picture rather than the newspaper which exercise, I suspect, the most profound and subversive cultural influences in the world today.

If the newspaper and the circulation of news seem to be the most obvious illustration of diffusion, the cinema and the motion picture seem to be the most obvious example of acculturation. The cinema deals with themes that are closer to the interests and the understanding of the ordinary man than are those of the newspaper. Besides news is very largely concerned with business and politics, and the ordinary man, as Mr. Mencken and other newspaper men have discovered, is not profoundly interested in either. Furthermore, the moving picture touches and enlivens men on a lower level of culture than it is possible to do through the medium of the printed page.

I have observed Negro audiences in some of the remote islands of the West Indies, where the level of literacy is very low, convulsed with laughter and mad with delight in watching the antics of Fatty Arbuckle; and I have seen the startled, cynical laughter of native audiences in the Pedang Highlands in Sumatra witnessing for the first time some of the, to them, incredibly intimate scenes of a Holly-wood wooing. Anyone who has had an opportunity to observe the influence of the moving picture in any of the outlying regions of the world and upon peoples to whom its vivid transcripts of contemporary American life have come as a sudden and astonishing revelation, can have no doubt about the profound and revolutionary changes they have already wrought in the attitudes and cultures of peoples, even in the most remote parts of the world.

It is not possible, on the basis of my limited observation, to determine whether the influence of the newspaper, the cinema, or the radio has been more effective in the cultural process or more decisive in bringing about cultural changes. The influence of each has at least been different.

In conclusion, I shall revert to the distinction with which I started —the distinction between language and forms of communication which are referential, as in scientific description, and language and forms of communication which are symbolic and expressive, as in literature and the fine arts. It seems clear that the function of news is definitely referential. If it does not have the status in science of a classified fact, it is at least indispensable to governmnet and to business. On the other hand, the function of art and of the cinema is, on the whole, in spite of the use that has been made of it for educational purposes, definitely symbolic, and as such it profoundly influences sentiment and attitudes even when it does not make any real contribution to knowledge.

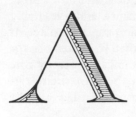 MEMORANDUM ON

ROTE LEARNING

IN CHICAGO recently I met George Axtell, of the department of pedagogy at Northwestern University. I had known him several years before when he was head of the "experimental school," as it was called, in Honolulu. I knew that he must have had some experience with rote learning while teaching Orientals in Hawaii and suspected that he would be keen on the subject. He was. He told me that the whole education policy of the department of education at Northwestern revolved around the problem of rote learning, and he was much interested in my observation on Negro education in the South. I gathered from what he said that there had been few if any attempts to study rote learning in what I may call its cultural context; no attempt, at any rate, to study its natural history, i.e., to discover the conditions under which it arises or the conditions under which it is superseded by more sophisticated and fundamental educational processes. This assumes that, somewhere and under certain circumstances, rote learning is the natural and normal response to the situation.

The fact seems to be that no studies have thus far been made that are designed to reveal the specific nature and function of learning by rote in the total educational process.

Rote learning seems to be learning without, or with a minimum of, insight. But we do not know the conditions under which experience is transformed into insight, and we do not know the processes by which individual insights are transformed into communicable ideas.

American Journal of Sociology, XLIII (July, 1937), pp. 23-36.

We do not understand the role, in the process of communication, of question and answer, argument and counterargument, and of the whole dialectical proceeding by which ideas are defined as they arise; achieve logical precision in language and concepts; and eventually evolve a logical structure within which discussion can take place. It is mainly by classroom discussion, however, that it is possible for either the pupil or the teacher to find out what things learned by rote do actually mean. Without discussion words may perform their original function of expressing sentiments, but they will not become the symbols of intelligible ideas.

I have found it difficult, in some of my classes, to induce students to ask questions. I found it difficult, in fact, to get them to admit they did not understand what they had read in the textbook or had heard in the classroom. On the other hand, they were often eager to get the correct, authoritative answers to questions they were likely to meet on examination, and they were adepts in formulating vague, suggestive verbal, and often meaningless, replies to such formal and general questions as I asked.

This is not, under the conditions which the ordinary classroom imposes, conduct that is either unusual or unexpected. I encountered the same sort of thing at Harvard years ago, when, as assistant in philosophy, I had to read papers in the introductory courses. But it seemed to me that what I encountered in my classes at Fisk last fall was an inveterate disposition—a tradition, in fact, not by any means local in origin—that had its sources in the historic condition under which Negro education has grown up in the South. It had its origin partly, no doubt, in the fact that Negro children have been handicapped by the lack of books and of a tradition of education in the home. The majority of Negroes have started life at a lower cultural level than the majority of the white people, and in their haste to catch up they, and their teachers, have relied too much on the authority of textbooks and too little on personal experience, observation, and common sense. Negroes have not had the opportunities for education that white people have had, and the task of raising the cultural level of a population of 122,000,000 even under the most favorable circumstances, is stupendous and, at any rate, takes time. The facts are well known, but their significance is not, I am convinced, fully comprehended.

Children can and do pick up an extraordinary amount of knowledge at home, especially where they are exposed to an association with books and of parents who encourage them to ask questions and to pursue further the inquiries and experiments that their naïve interests and curiosity suggest. It seems as if there is hardly anything that cannot be learned in this informal and natural way if the child's spontaneous interests are wisely directed and controlled. But this is not the way of formal education, however, and this is not the method of the schools. On the other hand, formal education invariably presupposes the informal education of the home and of the playground. That suggests the importance of the studies which Jones and Junker have been making of Negro rural communities and the cultural backgrounds of the rural school.[1]

In so far as formal instruction seeks to supplement or replace the informal education of the home or the local community, success will probably depend on the ability of the teacher to integrate the knowledge which the school seeks to inculcate with the experiences of pupils and with the tradition of the local community. Often the disparity between the language and tradition of the textbook and of the schools and that of the pupils and the local community is very great. I recall Booker T. Washington's story: Going into a rural school in Mason County he found the pupils, some of them almost grown men and women, learning to read from a textbook entitled *Little Steps for Little Feet*. The trouble was, as he remarked, that "there were no little feet there."

When the knowledge which the school is seeking to impart is remote from the experience of the pupil, the task of translating it into language that the pupil understands is a difficult one. There are, I suspect, few teachers in the South as capable as Miss Argrett in translating the formal, and more or less abstruse, language of the textbooks into the idiom and vernacular of the average rural Negro community.[2] Teachers are not prepared, in the ordinary normal school, for such formidable tasks. But it is just where this divorce between the school, on the one hand, and the local community, on the other, is most obvious that the tendency to relapse into rote learning is, I suspect, most likely to prevail. Just to the extent that the language in which ideas are expressed is unintelligible, words tend to assume the character of something mystical and sacred. Under these circumstances education

---

[1] Lewis Jones and Buford Junker are just completing a compendium, shortly to be published, of local studies of Negro rural schools, the purpose of which is to reveal the local condition and cultural background of the Negro rural schools.

[2] Virginia Argrett, graduate student at Fisk in 1936 and 1937.

inevitably assumes the rigid and formal character of ritual. In such case its function is more or less identical with the puberty rites by means of which the children of preliterate peoples make the transition from the status of a child to that of an adult. Under these circumstances the ritual has the more prestige, the more severe the ordeal to which the candidate is subjected.

It is much the same in the schools. Education is too often conceived by the student, if not by the instructor, as a series of preparations for a series of ordeals by which one makes the transition from a status socially inferior to one socially superior. This is, perhaps, as it should be, except for the fact that there is always danger that in the process all intellectual curiosity and all the natural incentives to seek and pursue knowledge will be systematically rooted out.

Few people pursue knowledge anymore, it seems; and, if they do, there is nothing very exciting about the pursuit. This seems, however, more or less inevitable where rote learning prevails. Fisk University probably stands at the peak of the Negro educational structure, but it is a structure erected on a system of rote learning. The trouble with Fisk as well as all other Negro colleges begins, I suspect, in the "common school."

I am not now raising the inquiry of how far rote learning prevails elsewhere. The fact that Dr. Axtell seems to regard it as the fundamental problem of education everywhere leads me to believe that rote learning is not confined to Negro schools. On the other hand, so far as the historic conditions under which Negro education came into existence have made rote learning in Negro schools more or less inevitable, it would seem that it is in these schools that rote learning might most effectively be studied. Here, as elsewhere, the things we may learn from a study of the black and the brown should help a lot with the white.

In reflecting upon the subject of rote learning, my attention has been directed to folk schools like the Jewish Chedar, or the Moslem schools, where education consists almost wholly in learning verses— in the one case from the Talmud and in the other from the Koran— much as when I was a boy we used to learn to recite verses from the Bible. Sometimes, when there was a contest, and, particularly when prizes were offered, these contests assumed the character of a sporting event. We acquired in this some valuable phrases but very few ideas that were helpful in later life. It seems that wherever formal education has replaced natural and informal education it has first of all adopted the methods of rote learning. In the folk schools pupils have been taught to chant the texts they learn. That is the way I learned the alphabet, and it is a very good way to learn an alphabet or anything else where verbal memory is the important factor. One can, as a matter of fact, learn most anything—rules of grammar, historical facts, the names of the presidents or Roman emperors, verses from the Bible or the Koran—by rote. One can even learn the rules and formulas for solving mathematical problems and the manipulations of fractions and the demonstrations of geometry in this same mechanical way, without reflection and without insight. But this sort of knowledge is relatively of little value in a changing, dynamic world, where encyclopedias and reference books supplement and supersede memory, and the important thing is the ability to think and apply general principles to particular cases. In the routine of simpler and more stable societies this necessity did not exist, certainly not to the extent that it does in the modern world.

I remember, thirty years ago, visiting a school at High Point, North Carolina, where I had occasion to listen to a recitation in geometry. Neither pupils nor instructor had any notion whatever as to what it was all about. Certainly, neither pupil nor teacher had the slightest idea of the proposition they were demonstrating, or that it had any application in the art of the land surveyor, in the navigation of a ship, or even in the erection of a house. The whole exercise was so utterly unintelligible, and so obviously a matter of educational ritual and ceremony, that I did not venture to ask a question lest I embarrass the teacher in the presence of his pupils.

As long as education is conceived by the teacher and the student as a preparation for a recitation or an examination, and recitations and examinations are regarded as ordeals by which one acquires merit and distinction merely, such methods are likely to persist. In that case the notion that education—a liberal education at least—is an attempt to satisfy the natural desire of the normal human being to explore and to understand the world about him completely disappears.

One thing that makes the conditions in the classroom seem artificial, as compared with conditions outside it, is the fact that in the classroom it is the teacher, while outside it is the pupil, who asks the questions.

But, even at that, the questions of the teacher are not those of one who is seeking to understand the pupil. A question, in such case, is not an attempt to get the pupil's peculiar slant or notion about the matter in hand. Few grown-ups know how to engage children, or other inferiors, in conversation on such a friendly and man-to-man basis as this implies. In any case the atmosphere of the classroom is not one which encourages understanding. In the classroom, as too often happens, teacher and student are pitted against each other. Where that is not the case, pupils are likely to be in competition with one another for the recognition and commendation of the teacher. The organization of the classroom, furthermore, is designed to maintain tension and discipline. The teacher is in command. The student's function is to obey. It is the circumstance that gives to those occasions when the teacher indulges in a personal anecdote, or replies to some irrelevant question, the character of a blessed interlude during which teacher and pupils associate, for a brief space, on terms that are quite informal and wholly human.

One must distinguish between (1) learning by experience and the acquisition of habit and routine by a process of "conditioning"; (2) learning by rote, i.e., formal education; and (3) the assimilation of a tradition, using that term in the sense in which it is ordinarily used by anthropologists.

One cannot say that any cultural trait is assimilated until it is fully comprehended and understood. It is not assimilated, in short, until it has become so thoroughly part and parcel of the communal tradition as to be second nature in the individuals who compose the community. Education conceived in this way includes the whole cultural process. It is not, therefore, complete until things "learned" are sufficiently incorporated in habit and common sense as to form the basis for thought and action in the ordinary affairs of life. Things learned or studied are integral parts of the individual's mind. The mind of a man is, in short, all the instincts, attitudes, experiences, and memories that co-operate to enable him to think and act.

The individual cannot, at once, understand the significance and meaning of all that he "learns." He discovers what present experience means by incorporating it with earlier experiences. This invariably involves a lot of experimentation, reflection, and rumination in the course of which he is likely to have, now and then, moments of illumination—moments in the light of which familiar and known things appear suddenly in a new and different light.

When, on the other hand, learning involves neither rumination, reflection, nor experimentation, there will be no moments of illumination and insight. When there is no attempt to integrate the things learned in the schoolroom with the experience and problems of actual life, learning tends to become mere pedantry—pedantry which exhibits itself in a lack of sound judgment and in a lack of that kind of practical understanding we call common sense. Sometimes this pedantry takes the form of a shallow verbosity or a general disposition, characteristic of a college intelligentsia, to play with ideas in a wholly irresponsible way as if they were mere mental toys. This is a defect proverbially attributed to academic training wherever it exists.

Rote learning is likely to occur in schools where the standards are "high" or where the tradition, language, and learning of the school is so different in form and content from the ordinary experience of the ordinary student that he is unable to interpret what he learns in school in terms of the language and tradition of the community in which he lives.

This inevitably happens where the only source of knowledge for both teacher and pupil is a textbook. Manifestly, the teacher who has had few opportunities for general reading is wholly dependent upon a textbook for his or her knowledge of the subject taught and is, therefore, going to find it difficult to translate the text into a language that is wholly intelligible to the pupil. On the other hand, it is only as the pupil is able to ask questions and the teacher to answer them—questions, I mean, that traverse an experience familiar to both pupil and teacher but not covered in the text—that the student is likely to assimilate what he learns.

Negro rural schools, like city schools in the case of the immigrant, are handicapped by the fact that parents and children live in different worlds. To most immigrant parents the atmosphere that surrounds the life of their children in the schools is an impenetrable mystery. The consequence is that a child who has the privilege of growing up in a home where parents participate in the education of their children has a very real advantage. But the children of immigrants who live in cities pick up, in the vivid life of the city streets, an immense amount of knowledge. Much of this is permanently valuable; but much more, as far as it contributes to the making of a career, is positively detrimental.

One of the consequences of the effort of the child to live in two, and perhaps three, wholly dissociated worlds—(1) the world of the family circle; (2) the world of the playground and the associates he makes there; and (3) the world of the schoolroom and formal knowledge—is that, in the absence of a cultural background, he tends to become disillusioned and cynical. The result of pupils' efforts to meet the artificial requirements of the school and to get through and out in the easiest and quickest way is frequently to make even those who have good natural abilities appear stupid in the classroom. Frequently, the natural abilities of students who seemed dull in the classroom assert themselves later, outside the school, in real life. On the other hand, under similar conditions, the fate of the industrious and "good" student is often worse, since his natural destiny is to become a teacher or "professor"—condemned for life to inflict upon future generations of pupils, as well as the general public, the pedantries he acquired at such great cost in school. It used to be the case that almost the only reason one studied Latin was in order that one might teach other persons to study Latin. This is part of the rote-learning complex.

I have been thus far discussing rote learning mainly from the point of view of my observations in the South. These observations have led me to believe that the conditions I found in the high schools and colleges were mainly due to the character of Negro education in the common schools. It is, as I have said, a system, and one that has grown up under conditions that were inherent in the racial and economic situation in the South—conditions that cannot very easily or very quickly be altered.

The problems of Negro education probably begin in the rural schools; in the education of a people whose condition corresponds, in general, less to that of an Iowa farmer than to that of a European peasant.

In this connection I am reminded of a remark made to me by Dean Redfield. He said that Embree [3] had just returned from Japan and that he had turned up during his studies in a peasant village at least one very interesting fact. At the present time, it seems, many, perhaps most all, Japanese peasants have become literate. But this literacy had apparently made no appreciable difference in the general routine of life in the peasant community. Literacy in their case seems to be a pure luxury. The government might just as well, perhaps, have presented each head of each peasant household with a diamond ring. He would have been proud of it. It would have been a distinction, but it would not make any great difference in his life.

---

[3] John F. Embree, of the department of anthropology, at the University of Chicago, has been for two years in Japan studying Japanese life in a peasant village.

I am reminded of what Dr. George Hall once said about Negro education. "Why," he said, "at that time we thought of education as a purely personal distinction. It was something you were expected to wear like a decoration. We had no notion that education had any practical value. That was a later discovery."

This seems to be the case of the Japanese peasant, but with this difference! Dr. Hall found later what he could do with an education. In the case of the Japanese peasant, on the other hand, unless the traditional scheme of his economic and cultural life should change, he may continue to find little if any use for the education he now possesses.

The man who goes to the city and aspires to live in the modern world must have an education. He must, at least, know how to read. Life in a city is well-nigh inconceivable without a daily newspaper. But in the village a newspaper is not a necessity.

In studying the foreign-language press some years ago, I was impressed with the fact that very few of the peasants who read a paper in the United States had been accustomed to read a paper at home. They were literate, but they did not read. Literacy does not seem to be an essential part of a peasant culture. This raises the question whether, under the conditions which prevail today on the plantation in the South, literacy will not continue to be in the future, as it has in the past, a luxury.

It undoubtedly marks an epoch in the history of any people when it begins to lose interest in fairy and folk tales and learns instead to read the news. That seems to be a change that is going on in China today, at least in port cities like Shanghai. But there are very considerable areas in different parts of the United States where this change has not yet taken place.

Interest in the news is the mark of an urban civilization. In the modern world, and particularly in America, everyone seems to be either in the city or on his way to it. Everyone seeks at least to live in an urban atmosphere. In most European countries, on the other hand, with the notable exception of Denmark, peasant peoples are apparently little troubled by the influence of the press, of the machine age, or, indeed, of the modern world. Perhaps we shall have to wait for the introduction of the cotton picker to change the system of rural education in the South. Perhaps the growth of the tenant-farmer class will finally create there and elsewhere in America a permanent class with the traditions and outlook of a European peasantry. America, as compared with the rest of the world, seems to be settling down. Immigration has ceased, and the population is approaching a condition that may be regarded as stable.

We have, however, the automobile, the cinema, and the radio to reckon with. They may do what the rural school has thus far failed to do, namely, destroy the moral and intellectual isolation in which the Negro on the plantation, the "Cajans" in the swamps of Louisiana, and the Appalachian mountaineers have continued, until very recently, to live.

In view of all these considerations and some others, I suggest one might try, at Mount Bayou in the Yazou Delta, for example, or on the territory of the Tennessee Valley Authority—where it might be welcomed—a somewhat novel experiment. We might discover a public school in which it would be possible to set up a form of education in which the emphasis was upon a method and procedure just the opposite of those now prevailing in rural Negro schools or elsewhere for that matter. We might establish a school in which the community rather than the pupils would have first consideration of the teacher. In this school pupils and teacher might conceive themselves engaged in a joint enterprise the purpose of which was to interest the adult members of the community in a communal program—public health, for example. In such a school, teacher and pupils would be engaged in acquainting themselves first of all with the local needs and, second, with sources of disease and the methods of public health in combatting them. The local health board and civil authorities would presumably wish to assist such a project.

Part of the task of the school might be to prepare a primer dealing with the subject of public health in which the nature of the prevailing and preventable diseases and the necessary measures of prevention would be described—and described in the language of the local community. In preparation for such a primer it would be desirable that the teacher or an assistant make a study of local medical practices and, particularly, of traditional folk beliefs and usages. The pupils would assist the teacher and her assistant in collecting this information. This should serve to advertise the project in the community and to enlist the interest and aid of its more alert and influential members.

In the writing and in the preparation of such a primer, the technical training of pupils in the essentials—reading, writing, and arithmetic—would be regarded as incidental to the main task of the school, namely, public health education, or any other public service which the school might properly undertake.

In connection with this program it would be advisable to publish from time to time, once a week perhaps, a news bulletin, written in the simplest possible language and reporting progress. In this chronicle the names—names are always news—of all the personalities involved; their contributions to the program; the difficulties and adventures connected with the enterprise, particularly in getting and recording information and in achieving a working relation between the school and the community; difficulties in the matter of getting and publishing the local news and in the use of the news bulletin as a kind of supplementary reader in the schools in the community should be fully and carefully reported.

I have some notion of what can be done with such a local newspaper in a rural school because I know what happened some thirty years ago when Tuskegee published such a paper for the Negro farmers of Macon County. The results were surprising and, on the whole, quite happy. I have often wished the paper might have been continued. It was merely part of Booker Washington's program to secure the financial support of the Negro farmers in extending the terms and improving the buildings of the Negro rural schools. After the schools had been built, however, and the school terms extended, the paper went out of existence. The importance of the experiment— as indicating how and to what extent local news can be employed to stimulate the interest of pupils and parents in the work of the school —was never fully understood or appreciated.

In a school that is intended to educate the community first and the pupils and teacher second, it would be possible, and perhaps necessary, to base instruction largely on news—"local" and "foreign" —but not exactly in the sense of the daily paper.

By "news" I mean almost anything which is not yet history. To be more precise, I mean by news (1) an event which has, or seems to have, some importance for the community concerned and (2) an event the significance of which is still under discussion. As soon as news is interpreted and generally understood, it ceases to be news— it becomes history. And, if news does not make some difference worth discussing in the lives of the people concerned, it is not news. There is no such thing as news in the abstract. News is always local, at least in the sense that it visibly touches the interests of individual men. It is neither knowledge, history, nor literature, in the ordinary sense of this term. So far as the curriculum of our school is based on news, it will be necessary, at the very outset, to find out what news is and, particularly what is news in the community in which the school is planning to operate.

One purpose of such a school as here proposed would be to widen the intellectual horizon, or what I may describe more precisely as "the area of orientation" of the community. That means the area over which events are news. This area of orientation, as here conceived, would be for that community identical with the area over which the import and importance of such news as was published was sufficiently understood to be a subject of general conversation. News, as Dana, of the *Sun*, once remarked, is anything that makes people talk.

The physical boundaries of the world in which a peasant population lives is, as we know, very narrow. Polish peasants (see Thomas and Znaniecki *The Polish Peasant*) have a specific name for this world. They call it "the region round about." The school should seek to widen the dimensions of the "region round about" not merely for the pupils in the school but for the community as a whole. This might be done in part by the use of the radio, by week-end excursions by auto, truck, or train, and by weekly meetings for discussion of events of the larger world outside.

It should be the purpose of the school not only to widen, for the local community, the area over which events are news but also to attempt to make news. A health campaign such as I have suggested might make news for some considerable time and might be followed by a program dealing with some other aspect of community life in which everyone, pupils and parents, should as far as possible participate.

One possible way of making news is by means of the cinema. A few years ago a representative of the Y.M.C.A. made a great stir in China by presenting to popular audiences illustrations of some of the marvels of Western science. This was news for the masses of the Chinese people who cannot read, although most of the scientific tricks performed at these lectures were probably familiar to Chinese students who had had the advantage of a Western education.

There are now available educational films—one of which I saw a few years ago—which are of a character to be news to almost any audience. The film I refer to was a picture of the death struggle between two, or rather two species of, microbes—one a phagocyte, guardian of the blood stream, and the other that of an invading disease germ. The whole drama took place within the limits of a blood corpuscle—a clear crystalline pool as it appeared—of an infected rat. The picture was not interesting merely—it was terrifying and instructive! Pictures like these are news.

With regard to the Y.M.C.A. lectures, intended to awaken China's interest in Western culture, I ought to add that, while the Chinese were interested in these scientific marvels, they interpreted them as magic, pure and simple, and the lecturer who presented them gained the reputation of a great magician, like Houdini. This was, of course, not just what the lectures were intended to do. The fact, however, illustrates that news, and particularly anything foreign to the common experience and understanding of the community in which it circulates, must be assimilated to the prevailing cultural tradition in order to be understood.

News, unlike history as taught in the classroom, must be interpreted rather than remembered and repeated merely. Otherwise it is not news.

One of the interesting and important by-products of an experiment such as I am proposing would be the light it would throw upon the process of acculturation, if I may use that term in this context. It would be interesting to find out, at any rate, how the community —children and adults alike—do interpret the news, and particularly the news presented to them through the camera.

If what the community got from the film interested them, it would be because they were able to interpret it in terms of their own experience. Their interpretations, as gradually elaborated in the course of discussion, would undoubtedly turn out, in some cases, something quaint and interesting—a contribution of science and folklore. That is, in fact, what popular knowledge, in spite of all the effects of the schools, inevitably tends to be. It would, however, reveal what the experiences were on which these interpretations of the news were based. It should reveal, better than anything else can, what the cultural background of the community actually is—what is, in short, the character of that body of tradition with which members of the community do their thinking.

It should throw light upon rote learning, too, because it is just those things we "learn" but cannot assimilate that constitute the knowledge we call "pedantry." Pedantry—knowledge "learned" but not assimilated—is responsible for many, if not most, of the present difficulties in Negro schools and formal education everywhere.

CHAPTER 6

THE NEGRO AND HIS PLANTATION HERITAGE

SOME time during the winter of 1898 and the spring of 1899 William James read to his students in philosophy a notable paper he had then just finished writing, to which he later gave the quaint and intriguing title, "A Certain Blindness in Human Beings."

The "blindness" to which James here refers is a kind of blindness to which we are all subject, by the very limitation of our human nature and of our individual experience, our blindness, namely, "to the feelings of creatures and peoples other than ourselves."

"We are," as James says, "practical beings each with limitations and duties to perform. Each is bound to feel intensely the importance of duties and the significance of the situations that call these forth. But this feeling in each of us is a vital secret for sympathy with which we vainly look to others. The others are too much absorbed in their own vital secrets to take an interest in ours." [1]

It is not possible to suggest in a word the significance which this fact of the isolation and loneliness of the individual—each in his own little world, hugging his own personal secret—assumes in James's interpretation of it. Suffice to say that the fact connects up directly with a definite philosophy to which James subscribed and to a theory of knowledge to which—if he did not first formulate it—he lent a powerful support.

Being "Introduction" to C. S. Johnson, *Shadow of the Plantation* (Chicago: University of Chicago Press, 1934), pp. xi-xxiv.

[1] William James, *Talks to Teachers on Psychology; and to Students on Some of Life's Ideals.*

I

My reason for referring to this essay here and to the conception of human relations and of knowledge, which it so persuasively sets forth, is that it seems to shed light, from an unexpected source, upon the problem and method of this present study [*Shadow of the Plantation*] and of social studies generally, particularly when they are concerned with the customs and institutions of isolated and provincial peoples; peoples who, though they live close to, and dependent upon us, as we upon them, are still outside the orbit of our ordinary life and understanding.

Shadow of the Plantation is concerned with the Negro peasants of the southern plantations, but the Negroes of the "black belts" are not the only peoples in America who live on the outer margins of our understanding and to whose vital secrets we must confess a certain blindness. There are other peoples, white peoples, like the Acadians of southwestern Louisiana; the Mennonites and so-called Pennsylvania Dutch of Lancaster County, Pennsylvania, and vicinity. There are also the mountain whites of the Appalachians and the peoples of mixed racial ancestry like the Mexicans of New Mexico and the little isolated communities of Indian, Negro, and white mixtures, scattered about in remote parts of Virginia, North Carolina, Alabama, and Louisiana. All of these are peoples who live, to be sure, within the political boundaries of the United States but live nevertheless on the margins of our culture. In this sense, and for the further reason that they occupy a place somewhere between the more primitive and tribally organized and the urban populations of our modern cities, they may be called "marginal peoples." The distinction between them and the peoples by whom they are surrounded is that they are not merely people, but folk people, and their culture, in so far as it differs from that of the majority of us in the United States, is a folk culture.

What is a folk culture and what is the folk? A very simple way to state the matter is to say that the "folk" is a people whose current history is recorded, if at all, by the ethnologist rather than by the historian or the newspaper. Not that folk peoples do not have history, but it exists for the most part in the form of unrecorded ballads and legends which, with its folk lore, constitutes a tradition that is handed down from generation to generation by word of mouth rather than through the medium of the printed page.

It is characteristic of the folk that it has a habitat and that its culture is local. Gypsies are folk, too, but they are the exception. Though they wander, they manage somehow to preserve a cultural isolation and a tribal solidarity as complete as that of any other preliterate people. In all our various attempts to study human nature we invariably encounter these exceptions. They constitute, in fact, the most valuable data that an investigation ordinarily turns up: first, because they are the starting-points for fresh observation and further reflection; and, second, because in the long run the exceptions always prove the rule.

Redfield in his volume *Tepoztlán*, which is a study of one of the marginal peoples of Mexico, similar in some respects to those in the United States, is at some pains to define what he conceives the folk to be. He says:

Such peoples enjoy a common stock of tradition; they are the carriers of a culture. This culture preserves its continuity from generation to generation without depending upon the printed page. Moreover, such a culture is local; the folk has a habitat. And finally, the folk peoples are country peoples. If folk lore is encountered in the cities it is never in a robust condition, but always diminishing, always a vestige.[2]

And then he adds:

The southern Negro is our one principal folk. He has a local tradition orally transmitted; he makes folk songs. Except for him we have to search for folk peoples in the United States. In the mountains of the South and Southeast we have a sort of vestigial folk. And here and there, in such occupations as involve long periods of isolation and a relative independence of the printed page—as, for example, among lumbermen or cowboys—a sort of quasi-folk develop, who write anonymous folk songs and sometimes build up, around campfires, folk sagas of the Paul Bunyan variety.

On the other hand, the folk are not to be confused and identified with the peasant who has left the soil to live and work in the city. Such peoples constitute what might be described as the "populus" or, better still, the "proletariat."

So the Negro of the plantation—though the two are closely related and the history of the one goes far to explain the existence of the other—is not to be identified with the mobile and migratory Negro laborers who crowd the slums of southern cities, or, like the hero of Howard Odum's *Rainbow round My Shoulder*, go wandering about

2 Robert Redfield, *Tepoztlán, A Mexican Village* (University of Chicago Press, 1930), pp. 1-6.

the country celebrating their freedom and their loneliness by singing "blues."

These blues, which, by the way, first gained recognition as a form of popular ballad in night clubs of Beale Street, Memphis, are the natural idiom of the Negro proletarian, just as the "spirituals" have been, and to a very considerable extent still are, the natural expression of the mind and the mood of the plantation Negro. The distinction between the folk of the villages and the open country and the proletarians or populus of the city is expressed and symbolized in the difference between the folk song and the popular ballad, the spirituals and the blues.

II

Marginal peoples, peoples in transit between simpler and primitive and more sophisticated and complex cultures, such as characterize our modern industrial and urban civilization, constitute, as I have suggested, a special problem in method, but one which is after all fundamental to studies of society and human nature everywhere.

There are no special difficulties in describing the external forms and the obvious expressions of a local culture. The difficulty consists in making that culture intelligible; in discovering the meaning and the function of usages, customs, and institutions.

Anthropologists, in their studies of primitive peoples, have distinguished between (1) material and (2) non-material elements of a culture. Material culture is represented by the tools, artifacts, and in general the technical devices employed by a people in their dealings with the external world. Non-material culture, on the other hand, includes all those institutions, ceremonial customs, ritual dances, and what not by which a people maintains its morale and is enabled to act collectively.

Institutions are, generally speaking, devices which come into existence in the effort to act collectively and exist in order to make collective action more effective.

But customs persist and preserve their external forms after they have lost their original meaning and functions. Institutions are borrowed or imposed upon peoples to whose traditions, instincts, and actual needs they are quite foreign, or have not yet been fully assimilated. Fashions change, and with the change institutions, though they still persist, are looked upon with profoundly changed attitudes.

Considerations of this sort have led anthropologists in studying culture to distinguish between form and function, and to emphasize the subjective and less obvious aspects of the cultural complex. The study of a society or of a people turns out under these circumstances to be the study not merely of its institutions but of its mentality.

What is meant by mentality in this sense is stated impressively by Redfield in the concluding chapter of his volume *Tepoztlán*. "If by mentality is understood," he says, "a complex of habits employed in meeting unfamiliar problems," then mentality, too, is an aspect of culture. "If the individual undergoes experiences of a very different sort from those undergone before, he develops a correspondingly new organ, a new mind."

But there is a less obvious aspect of social institutions in which they appear in even more intimate and vital association with the people whose life they serve. It has been observed that as long as their social institutions are functioning normally, primitive peoples ordinarily exhibit an extraordinary zest in the life they lead, even when that life, like that of the Eskimo in the frozen North or the pigmies in the steaming forest of Central Africa, seems to be one of constant privation and hardship.

On the other hand, when some catastrophe occurs which undermines the traditional structure of their society, they sometimes lose their natural lust for life, and that euphoria which enabled them to support the hardships of their primitive existence frequently deserts them. That catastrophe may be, and frequently is, the sudden advent of a more highly civilized people intent upon their improvement and uplift by incorporating them in a more highly organized industrial society.

Under such circumstances, a people may be so completely obsessed by a sense of their own inferiority that they no longer desire to live as a people; and if they live as individuals, they will prefer to identify themselves, as far as they are permitted to do so, with the invading or dominant people.

It is in some such way as this, i.e., by the incorporation of defeated or merely disheartened people into some larger and more complex social unit, that castes are formed.

It is evident, in spite of all that has been written of human nature and of human behavior, that the sources of joy and sorrow are still obscure. It is evident also that, as Stevenson says, in a passage in *Lantern Bearers* quoted by James, "to miss the joy is to miss all." That is to say, if you miss the joy you miss the one aspect of a people's life which more than anything else gives vitality to cultural forms and ensures their persistence, possibly in some new and modified form, under changed conditions. For this reason, the most subjective and least obvious aspect of the life of peoples and cultures is nevertheless one that cannot be neglected, particularly in the case of peoples who, as I have said, are in process of transit and subject to all the vicissitudes of profound cultural change.

This zest for life is just that personal and vital secret which, for each one of us, gives meaning and significance not merely to the life of the individual but of the society, of whatever sort it be, of which he is a member and a part.

III

Although it describes itself as a study of "social and cultural change," the materials on which *Shadow of the Plantation* is based are not those with which anthropologists are familiar or are likely to approve. As a matter of fact, the study starts with a different tradition—the tradition, namely, of the rural sociologist, who conceives his community rather as a statistical aggregate than as a cultural complex. One reason for this is the convenience and the necessity of making use of the available statistics, which have been collected and classified on the basis of existing administrative units rather than of the region or of any other sort of natural area.

Thus the investigation assumed at the outset the character of a survey and study of a population rather than of a people, and the plan, as originally conceived, was, by a process of sampling, to describe and characterize statistically a population area.

The area chosen for this survey was a slice of one of the familiar "black belts," historically the region of cotton culture in the South. Macon County, of which Tuskegee is the county seat, is the seat also of Booker Washington's famous industrial school for Negroes and the county which, during his lifetime, was, so to speak, the rural laboratory in which he carried on his experiments in rural education—experiments which graduates of his school and others, with the assistance of the Rosenwald Fund, have extended to most other parts of the South.

It was assumed, no doubt, that Macon County offered a fair sample of Negro rural population, and that a study of its population would indicate what Negro education—unaccompanied, to be sure, by any special or systematic effort to reorganize on any considerable scale the plantation system—had been able to do to keep the Negro on the soil and, by raising the general level of his intelligence and encouraging him to take the initiative in improving his own condition, to improve the condition of the country as a whole.

There were other reasons why a study of Negro culture should assume the technical form of a survey beside the desirability of starting with the available information in regard to the region. One was the character of the Negro community itself, and of the very tenuous lines of connections which hold the rural population into any sort of solidarity that could be described as communal. Another was the fact that the Negro community is so completely interpenetrated and dependent upon the dominant white community that it is difficult to conceive it as having any independent existence.

Outside of the plantation the only centers of Negro life are the rural churches and rural schools. The social situation is reflected in the human geography of the county.

A bird's-eye view of Macon County discloses a country of softly rolling uplands and interspersed with fragrant, wooded swamps.

Plantation, hamlet, and town, still rather widely dispersed, are connected by a network of rural roads which, except for a few stretches of recently constructed thoroughfare, wind their way leisurely along rolling ridges in order to escape as far as possible the perils of the sometimes heavy spring rains. Closer observation of this same countryside discloses the existence of another, narrower, and less obvious network of footpaths which—unplanned, unplotted, and without official recognition—intersect, connect, and supplement but never compete with the public highways.

These two systems of transportation—the public highways connecting the towns and the plantations and the footpaths connecting the humbler habitations of the Negro tenant farmers—suggest and symbolize the complicated interrelations and divisions between the races in Macon County and in the South generally, suggest also some of the complexities and some of the difficulties of studying one section of a population without taking some account at the same time of the other.

IV

If the study of culture is to reveal what makes life for individuals or peoples either significant and exciting or merely dull, what are the kinds of facts most likely to disclose this vital secret?

Undoubtedly the most revealing portions of the present study are the candid comments of the peoples studied on their own lives. As recorded here, in the language and accents in which they were uttered, most of these statements have the character of a human document.

The value of a human document as a datum is that it brings the object that is under investigation closer to the observer. Like a magnifying glass, it brings into view aspects of the object that were before that time not visible or only partially so. It sometimes happens that a casual remark, like a ray of light through a keyhole, will illuminate a whole interior, the character of which could only be guessed at as long as one's observations were confined to the exterior of the structure.

A good many of the remarks recorded in this study are so concrete, so pregnant with human interest, that they might have been written by Julia Peterkin or Du Bose Heyward, whose stories of Negro life exhibit an insight and "acquaintance with" the life they are describing that is unusual even in writers of realistic fiction.

As a rule, the individuals whose conversation and comments are here recorded are not in any sense a selected group of outstanding personalities in the community; rather they are just the ordinary mine-run of the population. A good many of them are old women, grandmothers, who with the freedom traditionally accorded to "old mammies" on the plantation are accustomed to express themselves more vigorously and more volubly than other members of the family. Besides, grandmothers, partly because they are less mobile than other members of the families and therefore more likely to be at home, are in a position to speak with authority in regard to marriages, births, deaths, and all the other facts that the investigators' schedules called for.

The statements recorded, while they do not represent a selected group of individuals, do exhibit an interesting diversity of types such as one would expect the intimate associations of an isolated community would inevitably produce. It is true that every kind of cultural association produces a certain degree of cultural homogeneity, but it invariably produces at the same time characteristic personality types. Among these an occasional individual is sufficiently outstanding to achieve a recognition in this record that is not accorded to the others. This was the case of Zach Ivey, who was clear and convinced that he had had a better time when he was a slave than he had ever had since; and by way of contrast to Zach Ivey there was Riny Biggers, who had early been impressed with the high value of literacy and differed profoundly from the views on slavery which Zach Ivey professed.

It is interesting to know that the relative merits of slavery and freedom are still a matter in regard to which there are differences of opinion among the Negroes on the plantations in the South. It is indicative of the immense weight of the tradition which still supports the plantation system. It makes significant and intelligible a remark made to me years ago by an old Negro farmer in Macon County who, though he could neither read nor write, owned and conducted successfully a plantation of eleven hundred acres. He said, with the peculiar quizzical expression of a man who would like more light on an obscure problem: "You know we'se jus' so ign'rint down heah we don' see much dif'rence 'tween freedom an' slavery, 'cep' den we wuz workin' fer ole marster an' now we'se workin' fer oursel's."

V

One can hardly escape the impression in viewing the facts of this survey that it is the inheritance of a tradition, embodied in the present plantation system, which more than anything else inhibits the progress, not merely of the black tenant but the white landlord, and that with the persistence of that tradition the small and independent farmer cannot make headway.

Under these conditions the Negro rural school, instead of creating a settled class of Negro peasant proprietors, seems, particularly since the World War, to have conspired with other tendencies to hasten the movement from the rural South to the northen cities. On the whole, the plantation, as at present organized, seems to be a sick and dying institution. It still remains, however, what it was before the Civil War, the focus and center of the Negro life in the rural community; but it is no longer able to maintain either the discipline or the morale of an efficiently functioning institution; and plantation life has apparently lost whatever zest it may ever have had for the generations of white folk and black that it once nourished.

The plight of the cotton plantation is probably due not entirely to its inability to shake off its ancient heritage, which involves among other things the tradition of Negro racial inferiority. The prosperity of the cotton plantation in the southern states is dependent, finally, upon its ability to compete with other cotton-raising areas in the world-market.

Most that is still problematic in the condition of the Negro peasant seems to focus about two quite different institutions: (1) the plantation and (2) the Negro peasant family. What is the future of either or both, since the fate of the one seems to be bound up in that of the other?

The Negro peasant family, as it exists today, is certainly a rather amorphous social organism. In slavery, parents had little or no personal responsibility for the provision and care of their children, since that office was early taken over by the planter or his overseer, who assigned some older and experienced woman to the task. The consequence was that natural maternal affection, rather than any common economic interest, constituted the tie that held the family together. The male member of the family did not count for much in this arrangement. The family was, and still is, matriarchal in character.

It was not until freedom imposed upon the Negro tenant the necessity of making his farm pay that the Negro farmer began to reckon his children as a personal asset. The effect of this was that parents began to discourage the early marriage of their children, the consequence of which would be to deprive them of their children's services.

When a Negro farmer reached the position where he owned property of his own, he had a new incentive and found a new means for maintaining the permanence of the family, since he was eager to transmit this property to his children, who in turn looked forward to inheriting it. The permanence of the property interest became the basis for a continuing family tradition, and for a more consistent life-program for both the family as a whole and its individual members.

As long, however, as the freedman continued to live under the shadow of the plantation, these changes made but slow progess. With the advent of emancipation the status of the Negro on the plantation had been suddenly transformed from that of a field hand to tenant farmer. But the actual change was not as great as might have been expected. The freedman was not able at once to enter into the spirit and tradition of a free competition and industrial society. He had no conception, for example, of the secret terror that haunts the free laborer; the fear, namely, of losing his job and of being out of work. On the contrary, his first conception of freedom was that of a condition in which he would be permanently out of work. So far, therefore, from being possessed by that mania for owning things which is the characteristic, as the communists tell us, of a capitalistic society, his first impulse and aim were to get as deeply in debt as possible. If, therefore, the agents of the "Third International" find that such Negroes are as yet not ripe for communism, it is undoubtedly because they have not had as yet the opportunity to realize the evils of a free and competitive society.

What the findings of this survey suggest, then, is: (1) the necessity of a wider—in fact, a world-wide—and comparative study of the cotton plantation not merely as an economic and industrial but as a cultural unit; and (2) a comparative study of the actual conditions of the world in which the people on the plantation live.

VI

One thing that complicates any attempt to study Negro peasant institutions and culture is the fact that, though the white man and the Negro have lived and worked together in the United States for three hundred years and more, the two races are still in a certain sense strangers to one another. One way in which this fact finds expression is in the statement that the Negro has not yet been, and perhaps never can be, assimilated. Another and more drastic expression of the same conviction is the familiar statement, repeated in most every part of the world in which Europeans have settled: "This is a white man's country."

It is very curious that anyone in America should still think of the Negro, even the Negro peasant of the "black belts," as in any sense an alien or stranger, since he has lived here longer than most of us, has interbred to a greater extent than the white man with the native Indian, and is more completely a product than anyone of European origin is likely to be of the local conditions under which he was born and bred.

There is, nevertheless, a sense in which the Negro, even though culturally he be a purely native product, is not assimilated, though in just what sense this is true it is difficult to say.

One is reminded of the old lady who, visiting the Indian Village at the World's Fair, was moved to speak a friendly word to one of these aborigines. What she said was: "How do you like our country?"

It was her view that, this being a white man's country, an Indian would naturally feel a little strange in it. It did not occur to her that an Indian might not share this common-sense assumption.

It is just these naïve assumptions, which are matters of common sense in one class, caste, sect, or ethnic group but not in others, that seem to constitute the final obstacle to the assimilation of peoples. They reveal social distances between individuals and peoples otherwise unsuspected.

William Graham Sumner has invented a word to describe the state of mind that these innocent and generally unconscious prejudices betray. He calls it "ethnocentrism." In savage people ethnocentrism betrays itself in the disposition to call themselves "men" or "human beings." Others are something else not defined. They are, perhaps, like the flora and fauna, part of the landscape but not human.

This trait is not confined to nature people. We are all disposed to assume that other peoples, with other customs, are not quite human in the sense that we feel this is true of ourselves. This is part of that blindness to which James refers.

The incurable ethnocentrism of peoples makes it difficult to communicate freely and candidly with strangers, particularly when the purpose of the inquirer is to go behind exteriors and discover what is behind their faces, namely, their attitudes.

The great value and the great vogue of psychoanalysis is due to the fact that it has developed a technique for getting behind visible forms and the external expressions of the people to discover the subjective aspect of personal behavior and culture, the thing which at once intrigues and baffles the student of personality and of culture.

If this ethnocentrism makes it difficult, on the one hand, to discover the subjective aspect of a people's culture, it makes it difficult, on the other hand, to describe realistically their customs and usages when one knows that such descriptions are likely to be misinterpreted. One is often tempted under such circumstances to state things in a manner to meet and correct in advance the expected misinterpretation. But that, too, is impracticable and no solution of the difficulty. Realistic descriptions of manners and customs are always likely to be a little shocking. In the final analysis, however, it is undoubtedly true that if anything, at least anything customary and accepted in any human society, seems shocking or merely quaint, it is because that custom or usage is not quite intelligible.

There is an old French adage to the effect that "to comprehend all is to forgive all," and not merely forgive but accept as something not alien but indubitably human, like ourselves.

Only so far as this is anywhere achieved can such studies of human nature as this be said to have wholly achieved their purpose.

PART TWO: *Race Relations*

CHAPTER 7

THE NATURE OF RACE RELATIONS

I

RACE relations, as that term is defined in use and wont in the United States, are the relations existing between peoples distinguished by marks of racial descent, particularly when these racial differences enter into the consciousness of the individuals and groups so distinguished, and by so doing determine in each case the individual's conception of himself as well as his status in the community. Thus anything that intensifies race consciousness; anything, particularly if it is a permanent physical trait, that increases an individual's visibility and by so doing makes more obvious his identity with a particular ethnic unit or genetic group, tends to create and maintain the conditions under which race relations, as here defined, may be said to exist. Race consciousness, therefore, is to be regarded as a phenomenon, like class or caste consciousness, that enforces social distances. Race relations, in this sense, are not so much the relations that exist between individuals of different races as between individuals conscious of these differences.

Thus one may say, without doing injustice to the sense in which the term is ordinarily used, that there are, to be sure, races in Brazil—there are, for example, Europeans and Africans—but not race relations because there is in that country no race consciousness, or almost none.

In Edgar T. Thompson (ed.), *Race Relations and The Race Problem* (Durham, North Carolina: Duke University Press, 1939), pp. 3-45.

One speaks of race relations when there is a race problem, and there is no race problem in Brazil, or if there is, it is very little if at all concerned with the peoples of African and European origin.[1]

On the other hand, when one speaks of race relations and the race problem in South Africa one does not think of the African and the European. The African does, to be sure, constitute a problem, but in South Africa, it is described as the "native problem." South Africa has, also, the problem of the Cape Coloured, a hybrid people of mixed Hottentot and European origin. The native, as the term is there used, is a Bantu, and of a quite different racial origin than the "native." South Africa has, likewise, the problem of the East Indian. Hindus were first imported into Natal about 1860 in the interest of the sugar industry in that province. However, when one speaks or writes in common parlance of the race problem in South Africa, it is to the relations existing between the English and the native Dutch or Africanders that this expression refers.

In this context and in this sense the expression race relations seems to describe merely the sentiments and attitudes which racial contacts invariably provoke and for which there is, apparently, no more substantial basis than an existing state of the public mind. For the purpose of this chapter, however, the term has been employed in a somewhat wider universe of discourse, in which it includes all the relations that ordinarily exist between members of different ethnic and genetic groups which are capable of provoking race conflict and race consciousness or of determining the relative status of the racial groups of which a community is composed.

Race relations, in this more inclusive sense, might comprise, therefore, all those situations in which some relatively stable equilibrium between competing races has been achieved and in which the resulting social order has become fixed in custom and tradition.

Under such circumstances the intensity of the race consciousness which a struggle for status inevitably arouses, where it did not altogether disappear, would be greatly diminished. The biracial organizations of certain social institutions that have come into existence in Southern states since emancipation exhibit the form which such racial accommodations sometimes take. Some of these, as in the case of the churches and the labor organizations, seem to have grown up quite spontaneously and have been accepted by both races as offering a satisfactory *modus vivendi*. In other instances, as in the case of the

---

[1] See unpublished MS by Donald Pierson, *The Black Man in Brazil*.

public school, the segregation which such dual or biracial organizations necessitate, in spite of certain advantages they offer, has been bitterly opposed even when they have later been reluctantly accepted by the colored people. They were opposed (1) because of the discrimination they inevitably involve and (2) because the separation of the races in the schools as elsewhere has seemed to imply the acceptance of an inferior civic and social status.

All this suggests that the term *race relations,* as here conceived, includes relations which are not now conscious or personal, though they have been; relations which are fixed in and enforced by the custom, convention, and the routine of an expected social order of which there may be at the moment no very lively consciousness.

Historically, the races of mankind at different times and places have lived together in a wide variety of ways. They have lived over long periods of time in a relationship not unlike that existing between the plant and animal species occupying the same territory, that is to say, a relationship of biotic interdependence, without interbreeding. Under these conditions the different races, like the different species, have been able to maintain their integrity as distinct races while living in a form of association that might be described as symbiotic rather than social. Examples of this sort of symbiosis among human creatures are the gypsies of Western Europe or the Wild Tribes of India, particularly the so-called "Criminal Tribes."

On the other hand, other racial stocks, notably those that have fused to create the existing peoples of Europe, have lived together in an intimacy so complete that the original racial differences that once distinguished them have almost wholly disappeared, or at best can now only be clearly determined by the formal investigations of anthropologists. This is the case, for example, of the Germanic and Slavic tribes which, politically united by the conquests of the Markgraf of Brandenburg and the Teutonic Knights, in the thirteenth century, eventually fused to produce the Prussian people.[2]

---

[2] "In 1226 the Polish Duke Conrad of Masovia invited the Teutonic Knights into his territory to combat the heathen Prussians. After a difficult struggle, the Order conquered the territory of the heathen Prussians, exterminated most of the native population, and invited German peasants and townspeople into the country as settlers. In the fourteenth century the State ruled by the Knights was a power in northeastern Germany. It acquired Pommerellia and for a time the Neumark also, and through its connection with the Order of the Sword, of Livonia, extended its influence as far as Estonia. A string of flourishing cities sprang up along its coast" (*Encyclopaedia Britannica,* 14th ed., XVIII, 654).

Evidence of this modern instance of racial amalgamation are the occasional "racial islands," particularly in East Prussia, where, because the process of fusion has not been completed, some remnants of the Slavic peoples and their cultures still persist. Perhaps the most notable example of this incomplete amalgamation and assimilation is the existence, a short distance from Berlin, of an ancient Wendish folk, which still preserves its language and culture, and still cherishes a kind of tribal identity. They are called the *Spree-wälder*, i.e., the people of the Spree Forest, where they exist in the midst of a German population, as a kind of racial and cultural enclave.

There are, however, numerous examples of such isolated racial islands nearer home. There are, for example, the interesting little communities of Negro, Indian, and white mixed bloods, of which there are a great number scattered about in out-of-the-way corners of the Southern and Eastern states. Perhaps the most notable of these is the community of white and Negro half-castes, living near Natchitoches, Louisiana, described by Lyle Saxon in his recently published novel, *Children of Strangers*.[3]

All these various and divergent types of isolated, and more or less outcast racial and cultural groups, have recently been classed, for the purposes of comparison and study, as minority groups, although the term as originally used acquired its meaning in a European rather than American context. Among these such sectarian and religious groups as the Amish of Eastern Pennsylvania, or the Mormons of Utah, have sometimes been included.

The classic examples of such racial minorities, however, are the Jewish communities in Europe and the Near East, where Jews have maintained, in spite of their very intimate association with other peoples, their racial identity and their ancient tribal religion.

All these relations of cultural or racial minorities with a dominant people may be described, for our purposes, as types of race relationship, even though no evidences exist either of active race conflict, on the one hand, or of obvious racial diversity on the other.

II

The races of mankind seem to have had their origin at a time when man, like all other living creatures, lived in immediate dependence upon the natural resources of his habitat. Under pressure of the food

---

[3] Boston, 1937.

quest, man, like the other animals, was constantly urged to roam farther afield in search of (1) a more abundant food supply and (2) of some niche or coign of vantage where life was relatively secure. This was the period of what one may describe as "the great dispersion."

The first movements of mankind seem, therefore, to have been like the migrations of plants and animals, centrifugal. It was as if they were engaged in a general recognizance and exploration in order to spy out the land and discover the places where the different species might safely settle. It was, presumably, in the security of these widely dispersed niches that man developed, by natural selection and inbreeding, those special physical and cultural traits that characterize the different racial stocks.

The process of dispersion still continues, and no permanent biotic equilibrium is yet in sight. As a matter of fact, the dispersion of living organisms, including human beings, is taking place today as a result of the multiplication of new means of transportation, more rapidly than ever before. However, the consequences, so far as they concern human beings at least, are profoundly different now from what they were at earlier stages in the historical process. As populations have increased and man—having learned to subjugate and domesticate not merely other animals but other men—has become the dominant species, his dependence upon cultural, as distinguished from natural, resources has vastly increased. One consequence of this is that human migrations have taken a different direction. The movements of peoples that had been centrifugal, away from the centers of population, have long since begun to take the opposite direction, and have become, particularly in recent times, centripetal, i.e., toward the cities. Settled villages have taken the place of nomadic tribes, and villages have become more and more dependent upon, or superseded by, urban and metropolitan communities. The result of this is that man is no longer so immediately dependent, as he once was, upon the natural resources of his habitat but has become increasingly dependent upon society. For the same reason the condition of isolation in which the different races slowly accumulated and funded, so to speak, their different racial and cultural traits, no longer exists, certainly not to the extent that it once did. Evidence of this is the increasing hybridization of peoples which seems everywhere to be the inevitable consequence of racial contact.

"The degree of ethnical purity of a human race," says Pittard, "is first and foremost a function of its geographical isolation. An unmixed stock is assured to a human group by the very difficulty it experiences in leaving its natural environment or, and this comes to the same thing, the difficulty any other group experiences in approaching it." [4]

On the other hand, he continues, "primitive races became mixed from the time that the wanderings of humanity over the continents became intensive." In fact, the mingling of races has increased progressively from that time to the present day so that it is impossible, as far as Europe is concerned, to speak of pure races. "In Europe the Lapps and the Samoyeds," says Pittard, "are better protected by their geographical position from admixture, than others. However, the Lapps have very largely mixed with the Scandinavians and the Samoyeds with Russians." [5]

If it is true that the different races, like the different species, came into existence under conditions imposed by their dispersion, it is likewise true that civilization, if not society, is a product of the city. In the city peoples of diverse races and cultures come together not to participate in and perpetuate a common life as is the case of a family, kinship group, or a religious sect, but as individuals who have discovered that they are useful to one another. Society and the moral order indubitably have had their origin in the family, but civilization has grown up around the market place and has expanded with the expansion of the market.

Sumner suggests that we should conceive primitive society as

---

[4] Eugène Pittard, *Race and History: An Ethnological Introduction to History* (New York: Alfred A. Knopf, 1926), p. 17.

[5] The conditions under which racial purity is maintained have been briefly summarized in a paragraph by Pittard: "The isolation of high valleys, great poverty (bad economic conditions have never attracted strangers from without), religious fanaticism and extreme conservatism in the matter of ancestral customs, all conduce to a fierce hostility to anything new; still other reasons may explain the comparative lack of mixed blood in certain districts. In such conditions of ethnical preservation we have the chance of finding a considerable percentage of individuals of the same type. Many European countries can still show smaller or larger groups of this kind today, relatively well preserved. We can count on a similar percentage in still another set of circumstances, as when the primitive 'human kingdom' finds itself situated far from the beaten tract—Scandinavia, for example—and when, in addition, the conditions of existence offered by this 'kingdom' are very poor. Consequently its more favored neighbours did not seek to fall upon it. If a high birthrate increased its population unduly, portions of it would swarm from the hive and settle elsewhere; the groups that remained behind, being almost undisturbed by foreign elements, were able, like an untroubled spring, to maintain their primitive purity. The anthropological map of Scandinavia is of almost uniform tint. Furthermore, all the other reasons for preservation already indicated—or some of them—can add their quota to this geographical cause for homogeneity." Pittard, *op. cit.*, p. 18.

composed of little ethnic and ethnocentric groups scattered over a territory—a territory with no very clearly defined limits. Within this territory every ethnic or tribal unit lives with every other in a state of potential, if not actual, warfare. Under these conditions one may expect to find peace, order, and security within the family or tribe, or as Sumner describes it, the "in-group." On the other hand, the permanence of this peace, security, and solidarity within is more or less determined by the degree or imminence of conflict without. The "in-group" and the "out-group" are to be conceived, therefore, as in a relation like that of compensating or countervailing forces. The sentiments with which these different groups regard one another reflect the moral isolation in which they live, and they define, in so far as races rather than mere tribal units are involved, the racial situation.

Ethnocentrism, as Sumner explains, "is the technical name for this view of things in which one's own group is the center of everything, and all others are scaled and rated with reference to it." [6] Under such circumstances the members of every little society or ethnic group tend to regard the members of every other as somewhat less human than themselves. People living in tribal isolation think of themselves as "men" or "human beings." All others they are likely to regard, as they do the trees in the forest, or the animals who inhabit it, as part of the flora and fauna. As such they may appear interesting or quaint, but such interest is always qualified by the fact that one cannot tell what those "foreign devils," to use a term with which the Chinese have made us familiar, will do next.

This does not mean, of course, that in primitive society the stranger and the alien may not be welcomed if they come endowed with a certain amount of prestige. When Captain Cook made his first visit to the Hawaiian Islands he was received by the natives with divine honors. But that did not prevent his being killed and, it is suspected, ceremonially eaten, when the natives discovered later that he was not wholly immune to attack by the weapons of ordinary mortals.

All this indicates that primitive peoples have lived, and to an extent which it is difficult for most of us to comprehend, still do live in an isolation which I have described as "moral." By moral in this sense I mean a relation which exists only when, and in so far as, one individual recognizes another as human like himself. Physical distances which separate races and peoples are important socially only as they serve

6 William Graham Sumner, *Folkways* (Boston: Ginn and Co., 1906), p. 13.

to maintain social distances. Social distance is measured by the degree of intimacy and understanding which individuals or social groups have anywhere achieved.

Primitive society, so far as it is organized on the basis of the kinship group, survives only to the extent to which it is able to maintain and transmit a tradition of solidarity and interdependence which has grown up in the intimate association of primary groups and is maintained by custom and tradition. In a civic society, in which kinship has been replaced by citizenship, relations are more formal and not so binding.[7]

III

Preliterate peoples do not, however, live in complete isolation, and the routine of their tribal life has not infrequently—until Europe imposed its peace upon them—been interrupted by the alarms of tribal wars as well as the milder excitements of intertribal trade. With the increase of commerce and communication, however, a form of association eventually came into existence of a sort very different from anything primitive man had hitherto known. The new and more inclusive social unit which emerged included all the peoples within a territory of which the market place was the center. For this reason and for others it tended to assume, with the growth of permanent setlement, the character of a territorial, as distinguished from the familial, organization, such as is characteristic of primitive and particularly nomadic peoples. Such a society, held together in unstable equilibrium by a process of competitive co-operation, is obviously of a very different sort from the little genetic and ethno-

---

[7] So-called primitive societies resemble the most perfect animal societies in the rigidity of their organization. Quoting a recent writer, an author adds, "The individual from the moment of his birth is the prisoner of the group to which he belongs, which imposes upon him its customs, its beliefs, its manner of life, which obliges him to take a wife from a specific circle. The solidarity of members of this group extends to every domain." It involves, he continues, the responsibility of all for the faults of one of their number, the responsibility of descendants for the faults of their ancestors. Property has a social character. The rites, in which all collaborate, aim at ensuring the prosperity of the group. The social bond is indurated, and life, as it were, mechanized within the narrow sheath of institutions. Not only the activity of individuals, but their very thought is subject to social constraint—no less than to the burden of heredity. Henri Berr in the Foreword to *From Tribe to Empire: Social Organization among Primitives and in the Ancient East,* by A. Moret and G. Davy (New York: Alfred A. Knopf, 1926), pp. xiii-xiv.

centric societies of which it is composed. It is a type of association that is fundamentally economic in the sense in which plant and animal ecologists use that term.[8]

The thing that most definitely characterizes it is, perhaps, the absence of that mystic sense of solidarity which, at certain times and seasons, unites the members of a family, a clan, or religious sect into a consensus so intimate that it can be felt but hardly analyzed. I mention the religious sect in this connection because of all forms of a society, not genetic in origin, it seems to be one that more nearly conforms to the organization of the clan and tribe. It is an interesting fact in this connection that, in the breakup of primitive societies under the impact of European civilization, a mission station of some religious society, with its little community of converts—or if not the mission then some newly organized sect—has frequently performed functions that had formerly been performed by the class or tribe. In a religious community, it seems, the detribalized native feels himself at home once more—perhaps more than ever before—in a world in which he had been otherwise quite lost.[9]

The conditions under which men buy and sell, have undoubtedly had a profound influence on human relations and upon human nature. Not all that is characteristically human is the product, as Cooley seems to say, of man's relations in the primary group.[10] Men go to market and women too, not as they go to church, namely, to revive a sense of their social solidarity and of their participation in common destiny. One meets at the market place, not friends merely, but strangers, possibly enemies. They have all, each motivated by interests presumably personal to himself, come together because they need one another and because, by an exchange of goods and services, they hope

---

[8] "In every habitat we find that there is a sort of community or society of organisms not only preying upon but depending upon each other, and that certain balance, though often a violently swaying balance, is maintained between the various species so that the community *keeps on.* . . . The particular name given to this subject of vital balances and interchanges is called Ecology. Ecology is a term coined by Haeckel, the celebrated German biologist, in 1878; its root is the Greek οικος, a house, which is also the root of the kindred older word economics. Economics is used only for human affairs; ecology is really an extension of economics to the whole world of life" (H. G. Wells, Julian S. Huxley, and G. P. Wells, *The Science of Life*, New York, 1931, III, 961).

[9] The government of South Africa a few years ago registered the names of no less than 206 native separatist churches. All of them were organized by detribalized natives. See J. Merle Davis, *Modern Industry and the African* (London, 1933), Appendix E.

[10] Charles H. Cooley, *Human Nature and the Social Order* (New York, 1902).

not only to satisfy their own needs but also profit by the needs of others. Besides, the market place, aside from the mere social excitement of being a member of the crowd, offers the prospect of hearing the latest news, and that is always an interest that is as intriguing to primitive as to more sophisticated peoples. There is, also, the consideration that in the market one may have, among strangers, a better chance to drive a bargain since it is always difficult to bargain with friends and relatives. On the other hand, it is notoriously easy and interesting to trade with strangers. It is even possible, under certain circumstances, to carry on a rather brisk trade with the enemy.

The familiar rule of the market place, *caveat emptor*, "Let the purchaser beware," is an indication of what was, and still is, the normal relation between buyer and seller. The situation in which men bargain and chaffer is psychologically complex and tricky, and for that reason, perhaps the capacity to trade is one of the last of the fundamental human traits that mankind has acquired. Among the many definitions of man that seek to identify him with, but at the same time distinguish him from, the other animals is that which describes him as a trading animal. Man is the only animal that has learned to dicker and trade.[11] But trade is necessarily a complex affair since it requires that one know, at the same instant, both his own mind and that of the other party. Each must understand the need of the other in order that each may make for himself the best bargain. This is inevitably the case because in this unique form of co-operation one man's necessity is another man's opportunity. But at the same time one does not wish to know the other party and his necessity too well either. One must, if possible, remain objective. It is for this reason, among others, that trade has so frequently gotten into the hands of foreigners.[12] It is easier to be objective if one maintain the normal distances. Detachment is the secret of the academic attitude.

It was around the market place that cities originally grew up. When city states first came into existence in Egypt and Asia Minor, later in Greece, they seem to have been at first and in many instances little more than market places with walls around them. The market, with the industries that grew up about it, may have been there first

---

[11] See Edward Westermarck, *History of Human Marriage* (3d ed., London, 1901), p. 400.

[12] See Gustave Glotz, *Ancient Greece at Work* (New York: Alfred A. Knopf, 1926), pp. 170-177.

and the place later fortified, or a market may have grown up under the protection of a citadel.[13]

City states came into existence, not always perhaps, but often, when some nomadic chieftain with his tribal followers invaded and conquered a settled and sedentary population. In that case he made the market place the seat of a totalitarian government. Every city as it became a center of political power acquired its local deity, just as among more primitive peoples every clan had its totem. It was at once the emblem of its authority and the symbol of its solidarity.

"The war-like character of the nomads," says Friedrich Ratzel, "is a great factor in the creation of states. It finds expression in the immense nations of Asia controlled by nomad dynasties and nomad armies, such as Persia, ruled by the Turks; China, conquered and governed by the Mongols and Manchus; and in the Mongol and Radjaputa states of India, as well as in the states on the border of the Soudan. . . . Their importance lies in the capacity of the nomads to hold together the sedentary races who otherwise would easily fall apart. This, however, does not exclude their learning much from their subjects. . . . Yet all these industrious and clever folk did not have and could not have the will and the power to rule, the military spirit, and the sense for the order and subordination that befits a state. For this reason, the desert-born lords of the Soudan rule over their Negro folk just as the Manchus rule their Chinese subjects."[14]

The rise of the city state gave a new direction to the historical process which profoundly affected and presently transformed tribal and racial relations. The first consequence was to change a relationship between ethnic groups, which had been territorial—modified and mitigated to be sure by commerce and politics, that is to say, intertribal war and peace—into a relationship of dominance and subjection, a relationship which eventually assumed the hierarchical form of caste and class organization. The second consequence was to hasten the process of ethnic amalgamation which, up to that point, had taken place mainly, but not wholly, by the incorporation of the women and

---

[13] "The agora, the town market, was originally a neutral, sacred ground where the members of different *gene* met for peaceful transactions such as exchange and arbitration. When the sovereignty of the city was extended over a larger territory there were 'border agoras,' protected against violence by religious laws" (*ibid.*, p. 113).

[14] Friedrich Ratzel, *Völkerkunde* (2d ed., Leipzig and Wien, 1894-95), p. 370. Quoted by Franz Oppenheimer, *The State*, trans. John M. Gitterman (Indianapolis, 1914), pp. 54-55.

children of the conquered tribes into the tribal organizations of the conquerors.

It was inevitable, perhaps, that a state based on conquest should seek to extend its boundaries so as to include more territory and more peoples. But there were always limits to territorial expansion, and as the city state approached these limits, the possibility and the necessity for amalgamation disappeared with the necessity for conquest. With peace, society tended to crystallize, and the form which it invariably took, particularly in a society based on conquest rather than trade, was that of a caste and class system. As a matter of course, there was, particularly at first, a certain amount of miscegenation between the different castes, but caste distinctions were still based on ethnic differences. In short, the contrast and conflict of ethnic groups were still the basis of the new social and political, as they were earlier of the tribal, society. But race consciousness and race conflict were in process of supersession by class consciousness and class conflict.

The existence of a permanent caste system in India seems to have had its origin in the obvious diversity of racial types in the Indian population. It is a well-recognized fact that visibility is an important factor in maintaining social distances and incidentally making class distinction hereditary. It is notable in this connection that while domestic slavery has always, apparently, existed in China where racial differences in the population are slight, there has never been anything that could be described as caste among Chinese people, although the relation between the Hakka and Punti peoples in South China tends to assume that character. In China, also, where feudalism disappeared relatively early, social classes were not closed and social status was not based on inheritance. In Japan, on the other hand, where society is notoriously more regimented than elsewhere in the Orient, there still exists, in spite of efforts to ameliorate their condition, an outcaste group called the Eta, which in origin seems to have been foreign although it has been recruited from all classes, even from the Samurai at times when these knightly warriors sought oblivion, because for some reason, perhaps as a consequence of defeat in battle, they had lost caste.

IV

In Greece the outstanding examples of the city state were Athens and Sparta, and, in spite of the fact that we know a great deal more about the life of the people of these two cities and of the territories that they dominated than we do of any others in the ancient world, the knowledge that we have of the rise and evolution of their political and social institutions shows that these conform rather consistently to the pattern suggested by Oppenheimer in his natural history of the state.[15]

The Spartans like the Athenians owe their existence to the invasion of Greece by Nordic nomads who imposed themselves as overlords upon the native peasantry. In Attica the invaders seem to have fused with the native population more completely than they did in Laconia, where a military aristocracy, having reduced the native peasantry to the position of serfs or helots, seems to have devoted itself rather consistently to war and knightly pursuits, as described in Homer's *Iliad*.

The Athenians, for reasons that are not wholly obvious—perhaps because their position was less secure than that of Sparta—were the more responsive to changing conditions in the world about them. The consequence was that Athens passed through a series of political transfigurations which resulted finally in a democratic society, qualified by slavery.

Sparta, meanwhile, sitting in proud isolation on her impregnable hills, retained her original form of government, relying upon her superiority in arms to maintain her supremacy at home and on the land. Athens, on the other hand, sought her fortunes on the seas, and succeeded eventually by conquest, colonization, and by successful competition with the Phoenician traders, in building up a political and commercial empire which extended at one time from the Black Sea to Etruria in northern Italy.

Trade was everywhere despised in Greece and nowhere more than in Sparta. In Athens, likewise, even after that city had become the commercial center of the Greek world, and largely dependent for such wealth as it possessed upon its foreign commerce, not merely petty trade, but even banking, strange as it seems to one reared in a capitalistic society, was in ill repute.

Nevertheless, Athens was able to achieve commercial supremacy first in the Aegean and later in the Mediterranean, but mainly through the enterprise of its Metic, that is to say its resident alien population. These foreigners became eventually so numerous as to constitute a distinct middle class or caste in Athenian society.

Gustave Glotz, in his volume, *Ancient Greece at Work*, devotes

---

[15] Oppenheimer, *op. cit.*, pp. 51-81.

one of his chapters to the Metics in Athens. I have attempted to outline briefly, and mainly in his own words, what that author says with regard to the place and role of these foreigners in Athenian life that seems important, because it seems typical of race relations everywhere.

Athens refused citizenship to the foreigners domiciled on her territory. At first she was not very particular; an Athenian formed a line of Athenians, whatever the country of his wife. But when the development of trade drew masses of foreigners to Attica mixed marriages became frequent. In 451 B.C. a law proposed by Pericles himself provided that to be a citizen a man must be born of a citizen father and a citizen mother. The Athenian who presented a son to his phratry must swear that his wife was an Athenian; if not, the child was impure, a bastard, a *nothos*. Athens consented to confer citizenship on a foreigner only as a national reward for distinguished services.

The Athenians, as I have said, had a very poor opinion of trade. Although they did, when poverty forced them to do so, permit themselves to engage in it in competition with Metics, they do not seem to have been eminently successful.

"Go through the speeches of Demosthenes," says Glotz, "not one of the ship-owners or bankers who have retained the great advocate is a citizen by birth, and at the most one of them has become a citizen because he did big business as a Metic. Not one of the great firms known to us belongs to a citizen." The Athenians were still more reluctant to carry on a petty retail business. They must be driven by poverty. In such business they are quite lost, especially the women; mingling with Metics and freedmen, they exposed themselves to being confused with them. The enemies of Euripides reproach him with having had a greengrocer for a mother; they hope that they will thus deprive him of his citizenship.

The condition of the foreigner, which was hard at the beginning, had greatly improved in the fifth century. The Athenians were proud of the good reception which they gave to the foreigner, and especially to the resident alien or Metic.

He was inhibited from owning land to be sure. In respect to justice he was less protected than the citizen in his person, but not in his goods. In return for her kindness Athens obtained valuable services from her Metics.

With their genius for business and their foreign connections, the Metics were in a perfect position for appropriating the higher branches of business, and especially import trade. But the merchants whose transactions most affected the prosperity and the very existence of the Athenian people were those whose business extended from Sicily, Egypt, and the Euxine to the Peiraeius, and from the Peiraeius to every port in Greece—the corn merchants. Whether importers or brokers, they were almost always Metics.

Traffic in money was almost entirely in the hands of the class which tapped movable wealth almost at all its sources. The great banks were often managed by former slaves who had become Metics. Thus in all branches of industry and trade the most important firms, the record of which has been preserved, had Metics at their head. Their strength lay in their wealth. They held the capital. The citizens had the land, the houses, and the public offices. For the Metics, movable property was everything, and they owned a great part of it.

The liberal careers also attracted the Metics. From the humblest stations to the highest, they made themselves a place there which was very respectable. The intellectual professions offered to many Metics the opportunity of making a great reputation and to some of leaving a glorious name.

Most of the philosophers who taught in Athens before Socrates and after Plato came from abroad. They exercised a powerful influence on the moral and social evolution of the Athenian people. They brought with them all the ideas which were being worked out in the Hellenic world, but especially those which best suited men who were emancipated from local prejudices and eager for practical novelties.

Lastly, it was a merchant from Cition, Zeno, who based human dignity and personal liberty on Stoicism, and the audience which he collected in the Porch was amazingly cosmopolitan.

With the expansion of Athenian trade there was a corresponding growth in Athenian industry and an increasing demand for laborers, that is to say, for slaves. To the Greeks slavery was a natural and necessary incident of a civilized life. Plato, to be sure, condemned the practice of holding Greeks as slaves. However, in the *Laws*, where he attempted to formulate not an ideal but a practical scheme of society and government, he accepts the institution as necessary and advises for the safety of masters, that natives from different countries should be mixed and well treated.

Most slaves were, it seems, of other than Greek origin, and it was no doubt quite as true in the ancient as in the modern world that a slave was more valuable the farther he was from home. But any Greek ran the risk of enslavement from hostile forays or from piracy. Children were frequently kidnapped and raised as slaves, and there was a systematic slave trade with the peoples in Asia Minor and the Balkan Peninsula. Of the foreigners, the Asiatics were regarded as most valuable because of their skill in the arts and their familiarity with the refinements of the more civilized East. Slaves from the rude countries of the North were used in the mines, the workshops, and in transport. As slaves "born in the house" were never very numerous most of the slaves in Greece were purchased abroad. Although the more enlightened Athenians deplored the necessity of slavery, Athens, as it assumed the character of a metropolitan and imperial city, became at the same time a center of the slave traffic.

Slavery as practiced in Athens, with all its inevitable abuses and hardships, tended to assume forms less severe than elsewhere in the ancient world. The slaves employed in the mines, where they were treated, as Aristotle described them, as "living tools," were indeed condemned to a bitter existence. But slaves employed in the domestic service were frequently treated as members of the family. Slaves employed in industry were frequently permitted to work on their own account, or even in command of a shop. Furthermore, the city owned slaves and employed them as clerks in the government service where they constituted a kind of bureaucratic organization that was permanent, in contrast with the constant shift in officials which a democratic form of government, as the Greeks conceived it, necessarily entailed. "It was," says Glotz, "this body of unassuming, trustworthy servants which caused the hidden machinery of the State to work and, in a commonwealth which was ever moving, ensured the continuity of the government." [16]

As there were many degrees of slavery, so there was always for the slave the prospect of an improvement in his actual status as well as the hope of eventual emancipation. Once the slave secured his freedom he was not relegated to a separate class, as was the case in other Greek cities and in Rome, but was ranked with Metics, beside but below the citizen.[17]

The thing that makes the career of the Metics in Athens significant for present purposes is that it so aptly illustrates another and later phase in the natural history of race relations.

The expansion of commerce in bringing about a wider division of labor incidentally effected the emancipation of the individual man.

---

[16] Glotz, *op. cit.*, p. 213.
[17] *Ibid.*, p. 215.

Freed from the claims of custom and tradition, the alien or Metic, like the freedman, found himself faced with the opportunity and the necessity of exercising whatever individual talents he possessed. At the same time a lively sense of the inferiority of his status, in comparison with that of an Athenian citizen, inspired him with an invincible determination to rise. This struggle of the foreigner and the freedman to find a place for himself in the freer and more spacious existence of the expanding metropolis changed, in a relatively short time, not only the character of race relations but of society, within the limits of the Greek world.[18]

The barbarian, who was condemned to servitude, as the Greeks believed, as a consequence of a natural and invincible inferiority, might still hope for freedom. Evidence of this fact is not so much the numbers of the freedmen in Athens as the extent to which they aroused the prejudice of Athenian citizens. The freedman was described as "greedy and coarse." It was said of him that "he thinks only of material needs. All trades are good to him, and all means of succeeding in them. He obtains wealth by fraud and position by adulation. He marries his master's daughter. He dazzles the town with his ridiculous ostentation. There is no harder despot to his slaves than the upstart from slavery." [19]

All of these, the foot-loose foreigner, the freedman, and the man of mixed blood, all of them typical city dwellers, are examples of a personality type that has been aptly characterized by Franz Oppenheimer in his account of the genesis of the "maritime state," founded as he says by "sea nomads," as the territorial state was by land nomads. He says:

The psychology of the townsman, and especially of the dweller in the maritime commercial city, is radically different from that of the country-

---

[18] "The point that has come to impress itself, in recent years, on the minds of students is that, as a result of the breakdown of customary modes of action and of thought, the individual experiences a 'release' from the restraints and constraints to which he has been subject, and gives evidence of this 'release' in aggressive self-assertion. The overexpression of individuality is one of the marked features of all epochs of change. On the other hand, the study of the psychological effects of collision and contact between different groups reveals the fact that the most important aspect of 'release' lies, not in freeing the soldier, warrior, or berserker from the restraint of conventional modes of action, but in freeing the individual judgment from the inhibitions of conventional modes of thought" (Frederick J. Teggart, *Theory of History*, New Haven: Yale University Press, 1925, p. 196).

[19] Glotz, *op. cit.*, p. 218.

man. His point of view is freer and more inclusive, even though it be more superficial; he is livelier, because more impressions strike him in a day than a peasant in a year. He becomes used to constant changes and news, and thus is always *novarum rerum cupidus.* He is more remote from nature and less dependent on it than is the peasant, and therefore he has less fear of "ghosts." One consequence of this is that an underling in a city State is less apt to regard the "taboo" regulations imposed on him by the first and second estates of rulers. And as he is compelled to live in compact masses with his fellow subjects, he early finds his strength in numbers, so that he becomes more unruly and seditious than the serf who lives in such isolation that he never becomes conscious of the mass to which he belongs and ever remains under the impression that his overlord with his followers would have the upper hand in every fight.

This in itself brings about an ever progressive dissolution of the rigid system of subordinated groups first created by the feudal state.[20]

The city dweller, as a personality type, is a product of conditions which his persistent struggle to rise created. The person and his world constitute, it seems, a vicious circle, each being an effect of the other. Furthermore, this struggle for status, as here described, is the very source and origin of the race problem as we know it.

The man of lower caste, who is usually a man of a different racial stock, is invariably "all right in his place." It is when he seeks to rise that his presence, his occupation, and his position in society—if it is one in which his superiors are not accustomed to seeing him—is resented. This resentment is naturally intensified when the intruder exhibits, as he is almost certain to do, the ignorance, arrogance, and bad manners of an upstart. To the extent that individuals of a particular caste or class are identified with a particular racial stock, the conflict of races and nationalities tends to become involved with the conflict of classes. Finland is a modern instance. The Finnish nationalists and the Finnish socialists are likely to be organizations of the same persons, just as the politically dominant Swedish minority, with which Finnish nationalists are in conflict, is likely to be identical with the dominant capitalist class.

In a democratic society, where every individual is free, or relatively so, to rise and to improve his social status on the basis of his individual achievement, or whatever represents success in the society in which he lives, caste distinctions tend to dissolve and disappear. In that case race distinctions also are obliterated, or forgotten and neglected. To be sure, race distinctions which inhibit intermarriage

---

[20] Oppenheimer, *op. cit.,* pp. 167-168. (By permission of The Viking Press, Inc. Copyright 1914 and 1922.)

may be maintained even after caste distinctions have wholly or largely disappeared. This is the case of the Negro in the United States, and of the Jew in Europe and elsewhere. Under these conditions the nationality, race, or what not—because inbreeding still preserves certain distinctive physical traits—is regarded as a race, and tends to assume the character of a racial and cultural minority.

The struggle of the classes to rise and find a more secure place in the social order of the Athenian world was repeated or continued in Alexandria, when that city had become the center of the Hellenic world. It was continued or repeated in Rome when that city had become the capital of an empire that included the whole civilized world. To these cities foreigners of every description thronged. Adventurers, fortune hunters, sophists, soothsayers, every one who found himself oppressed and was enterprising enough to seek his fortune abroad—all that was human and foot-loose—sought to find in the metropolis, if not a happier, at least a more intriguing world.

The philosopher Seneca, reflecting on the significance of this cosmopolitan life, has left us a very vivid picture of the crowds that thronged the streets of Rome. "Look, I pray you," he says, "on these vast crowds, for whom all the countless roofs of Rome can scarcely find shelter: the greater part of those crowds have lost their native land: they have flocked hither from their country towns and colonies, and in fine from all parts of the world. Some have been brought by ambition, some by the exigencies of public office, some by being entrusted with embassies, some by luxury which seeks a convenient spot, rich in vices, for its exercise, some by their wish for a liberal education, others by a wish to see the public shows. Some have been led hither by friendship, some by industry, which finds here a wide field for the display of its powers. Some have brought their beauty for sale, some their eloquence; people of every kind assemble themselves together in Rome, which sets a high price both upon virtues and vices." [21]

In the freedom and ferment of this cosmopolitan world not merely tribal distinctions and tribal animosities vanished, but national and territorial units lost all or most of their significance, particularly when citizenship was finally in 212 A.D. granted to every freeman within the Empire.

[21] Seneca, in Minor Dialogues, XI, vi, quoted in *Social Thought from Lore to Science*, by H. E. Barnes and Howard Becker (Boston: D. C. Heath and Co., 1938), I, 175.

The outstanding exception was Palestine. Jews persisted in their determination to preserve their national autonomy and their national religion. The result was that after repeated revolts Jerusalem was finally destroyed in 135 A.D., and the Jewish people were dispersed throughout the Empire.

In this Roman world, in which all, or almost all, racial and national distinctions were abolished, there occurred about this time two events of world-wide significance. One was the rise of the Stoic philosophy at Rome, and the other, the appearance of the Christian religion in Palestine.

The Stoic philosophy seems to have been, in some sense, a response to the cosmopolitan character which the world had now definitely assumed. Conceiving himself a citizen of the world, the stoic philosopher found very little to interest him in the actual life about him. For him, as for so many others, the world in which he once lived had almost ceased to exist. The euphoria which had given a zest to life while the Empire was expanding was succeeded at this time by a sense of ennui which, like an insidious disease, attacked the noblest Romans, manifesting itself in a disposition to suicide or to permanent withdrawal from the world.

Christianity, on the other hand, which had come into existence as an obscure Jewish sect, rose rapidly to the position of a world religion. Inspired by the consciousness of a great mission, seeking to bring together in the bonds of a common fellowship all men, without distinction of race or class, its rise was like the annunciation of the end of the old era and the beginning of the new. From this time the bonds that held the empire together were gradually relaxed. The processes of acculturation continued, but the world that remained was neither wholly Greek nor Roman. It was barbarian, mainly, but Christian.

V

In the modern world, and particularly outside of Europe, wherever race relations—or what, in view of the steadily increasing race mixture, we have called race relations—have assumed a character that could be described as problematic, such problems have invariably arisen in response to the expansion of European peoples and European civilization.

In the period of four hundred years and more since Vasco da

Gama rounded the Cape of Good Hope and Columbus landed at San Salvador, European discoveries and European enterprise have penetrated to the most remote regions of the earth. There is nowhere now, it seems—either in the jungles of the Malayan peninsula or the remote islands of New Guinea—a primitive people that has not, directly or indirectly, come under the influence of European peoples and European culture.[22]

The growth of European population is, among other evidences of European expansion, the one that is perhaps least obvious. However, the growth and decline of populations are basic to every other form of social or cultural change.

Between 1800 and 1930 the population of Europe increased from 180,000,000 to 480,000,000, and the number of individuals of European origin overseas amounts at the present to 160,000,000. During this period, and indirectly as a result of this emigration of European peoples, a corresponding movement of African and Asiatic peoples has been in progress. The number of people of African origin in the New World, that is, in North America, the West Indies, and South America, is at the present time, as near as can be estimated 37,000,000. Of this number, something over 12,000,000 are in the United States and Canada; 8,148,000 are in Bermuda, Central America, and the West Indies; 14,200,000, including, according to the best estimates, 8,800,000 mulattoes, are in Brazil. The remainder, 2,400,000, are in South America.

Meanwhile oriental peoples, mainly Chinese and East Indians, in response to the demands for crude labor to do the rough work on Europe's advancing frontier, have been imported into almost every part of the world outside of Europe. There are settlements of both Hindus and Chinese in the West Indies, in Australia, South and East Africa, and the islands of the Pacific, particularly the Dutch East

---

[22] The situation seems to have brought about something approaching an anthropological crisis. Since there are now, or soon will be, no living examples of primitive peoples to investigate, anthropologists seem to have arrived at a crossroads with the following result: One school of thought is directing its attention more exclusively to antiquarian and prehistorical investigation, seeking to extend the limits of our knowledge of historical facts; another school is more particularly interested in the historical processes they observe going on about them in contemporary life—the processes of history in the making. But the processes of history, so far as they reveal the manner in which new societies and new civilizations have arisen on the ruins of their predecessors, are the processes by which new and more sophisticated types of personality have succeeded earlier and simpler types. Anthropology thus merges into sociology.

Indies, the Philippines, and the Hawaiian Islands. They are employed mainly, but not wholly, in plantation agriculture. They are imported to work in the gold mines. There are Chinese in Cuba, in Jamaica, and British Guiana. They were imported in the first instance to replace Negroes on the sugar plantations after emancipation. There are Japanese in Brazil as in the United States. They were brought to Brazil to work in the coffee plantations in São Paulo and to the United States to work in the fruit and vegetable gardens of the Pacific coast.

The number of Chinese, Indians, and Japanese who have gone abroad and are now living outside of their native states has been estimated at 16,084,371. There is in South Africa a Chinese community in the Transvaal and an Indian community in Natal. The Chinese were imported as laborers to work in the Rand gold mines; the Indians, to work on sugar plantations in Natal. In the West Indies, Indians and Chinese took the places, after emancipation in 1834, of Negroes on the plantations. Japanese, who are more recent emigrants, have gone mainly to Hawaii and Brazil.

There are, at the present time, between 16,000,000 and 17,000,000 people of Asiatic origin living in the diaspora, if I may use that term to designate not merely the condition but the place of dispersion of peoples.[23]

Of the Orientals in this diaspora, 10,000,000, it is estimated, are Chinese, 2,125,000 are Indians, and 1,973,960 are Japanese. There are 1,900,000 Chinese in Siam; 1,800,000 in Malaya; 1,240,000 in the Dutch East Indies; 700,000 in Indo-China; 150,000 in Burma; 74,954 in the United States; 45,000 in Canada; and 4,090,046 in other parts of the world.

Of the 4,125,000 Indians abroad, 1,300,000 are in Burma; 628,000 in Malaya; 1,133,000 in Ceylon; 281,000 in the island of Mauritius;

---

[23] Diaspora is a Greek term for a nation or part of a nation separated from its own state or territory and dispersed among other nations but preserving its national culture. In a sense Magna Graecia constituted a Greek diaspora in the ancient Roman Empire, and a typical case of diaspora is presented by the Armenians, many of whom have voluntarily lived outside their small national territory for centuries. Generally, however, the term is used with reference to those parts of the Jewish people residing outside Palestine. It was used at first to describe the sections of Jewry scattered in the ancient Greco-Roman world and later to designate Jewish dispersion throughout the world in the twenty-five hundred years since the Babylonian captivity. Diaspora has its equivalents in the Hebrew words *galuth* (exile) and *golah* (the exiled), which, since the Babylonian captivity, have been used to describe the dispersion of Jewry. *Encyclopaedia of the Social Sciences*, V, 126-127.

278,000 are in South and East Africa; 133,277 are in the British island of Trinidad; 181,600 in British and Dutch Guiana; 76,000 are in the Fiji Islands; 6,101 in the United States and Canada; and 100,225 in other countries.

Of the 1,969,371 Japanese living outside Insular Japan, 1,351,383 are in Korea, the Island of Sakhalin, Manchuria, Formosa, or other parts of the world including China, which have become, or are in a process of incorporation in, the Japanese Empire. Of the remaining 617,988 Japanese abroad, 162,537 are in Brazil, and 297,651 are in the United States and Canada. Of the number of Japanese in the United States, 139,634 are in Hawaii.[24]

The Hawaiian Islands are occupied by what, from the point of race and cultural differences, is probably the most thoroughly scrambled community in the world. The census for the Hawaiian Islands, where, different from continental America, the population is classified by racial origin, recognizes twelve different racial categories, two of them hyphenated. They are: Hawaiian, Caucasian-Hawaiian, Asiatic-Hawaiian, Other Caucasian, Portuguese, Chinese, Japanese, Korean, Porto Rican, and Filipino. Among the laborers that have at various times been imported to perform the work on the plantations a considerable number were from Europe, among them Scandinavians, Germans, Galicians, Russians, Poles, Portuguese, and Spaniards.

Of the total population of 347,799 in Hawaii in 1930, 236,673 were Orientals, 562 were Negroes, and 46,311 were hybrids. Of this 46,311, or 47,560 according to another and different calculation, 5,040 were persons who counted their ancestry in more than two races.[25] Commenting on the situation, one of these products of miscegenation, a very charming young lady, incidentally, remarked: "Mixed? Yes; I am a kind of league of nations in myself."

I have conceived the emigration of European peoples and the emigration of extra-European peoples—since most, if not all, of these movements have taken place in direct and indirect response to conditions in Europe—as integral parts of a single mass migration. So considered, this is, undoubtedly, the most extensive and momentous movement of populations in history. Its consequences, likewise,

---

[24] Radhakamal Mukerjee, *Migrant Asia* (Rome, 1936), Appendix A. The figures for the Japanese in the United States and Brazil have been corrected in accordance with more recent figures.

[25] Romanzo Adams, *Interracial Marriage in Hawaii* (New York, 1937), pp. 12-20. See also Appendix C, pp, 334-345, for data relating to interracial marriages.

have been in proportion to its numbers. Everywhere that European peoples—including their commerce and culture—have penetrated they have invariably disturbed the existing population balance; undermined the local economic organization; imposed upon native societies, sometimes a direct form of control, more often political and judicial processes which were strange to them, but processes which have, at any rate, more or less completely superseded those of the native and local authorities. The invaders have frequently, but not always, inoculated the native peoples with new and devastating diseases. They have invariably infected them with the contagious ferment of new and subversive ideas.

All this disorganization and demoralization seems to have come about, however, in the modern world as it did in the ancient, as an incident of ineluctable historical and cultural processes; the processes by which the integration of peoples and cultures have always and everywhere taken place, though not always and everywhere at a pace so rapid or on so grand a scale.

It is obvious that race relations and all that they imply are generally, and on the whole, the products of migration and conquest. This was true of the ancient world and it is equally true of the modern. The interracial adjustments that follow such migration and conquest are more complex than is ordinarily understood. They involve racial competition, conflict, accommodation, and eventually assimilation, but all of these diverse processes are to be regarded as merely the efforts of a new social and cultural organism to achieve a new biotic and social equilibrium.

The fact that these adjustments involve different processes, each operating in relative independence of one another, suggests that one may conceive race relations as existing and assuming different forms at different levels of association. Thus the invasion by one race or one people of the territories occupied and settled by another involves first of all a struggle for mere existence, that is to say, a struggle to maintain a place on the land and in the habitat which has been invaded. This has often resulted in a catastrophic decline in the numbers and sometimes, as in the case of the Tasmanians, in the extinction of the native population, who seem to have been hunted like wild animals by the European immigrant as were, at one time, the Indians in the United States.[26] But disease is often more deadly to primitive

---

[26] During the Indian wars in the United States bounties were frequently offered for Indian scalps to encourage settlers and frontier men to kill Indians

people than war. The native population of Hawaii declined in the period from 1778 to 1875 from 300,000 or more to 55,347. Since that time the total population of the islands has increased, largely by the importation of Orientals to work on the plantations, until in 1930 it was 368,336, inclusive of military personnel.[27]

In other parts of the Pacific the native population has multiplied under European domination. The population of Java has increased in the centenary 1830 to 1930 from about 5,000,000 to 36,745,537.

The effects of infections and contagious diseases introduced by foreigners are the more devastating in the first years of the intercourse. Eventually some sort of biotic equilibrium is achieved, but racial competition on the biotic or ecological level continues, although its consequences are not so obvious. "Throughout human history," says S. J. Holmes, "stocks have continually been replaced, peacefully or otherwise, by their successful rivals. Even relatively stable populations represent but a temporary retardation in the general course of racial change. What is of greater importance than military prowess in the biological fortunes of peoples is the more obscure factors which affect the balance of births and deaths." [28] But any change in the conditions of life which affects the biotic or population balance is inevitably reflected at every other level on which race relations may be said to exist. This is particularly well illustrated in a recent analysis by S. J. Holmes of the vital statistics of the Negro in the United States. He has described his investigation as "A Study in Human Ecology." However, his estimate of the Negro's chances of survival in the American environment is, as he himself admits, necessarily inconclusive. It is inconclusive because there are factors to be reckoned with for which we have as yet no adequate statistical data.

---

as they would be encouraged to kill wolves and other pests. In a note in the volume, *Alien Americans* (New York: The Viking Press, Inc., 1936), p. 5, B. Schrieke states: "This method was introduced in 1641 by Wilhelmus Kieft, Dutch director-general of New Netherlands—presumably imitating a similar practice in the East Indies—and later on was adopted by the Puritans. It was, in a way, a money-saving expedient. If the frontier farmers could be encouraged to make offensive war against the Indians on a commission basis, fewer regular soldiers—paid and maintained by the government during long periods of inactivity—would be needed. The last American scalp bounty was offered by the Territory of Indiana in 1814 as an 'encouragement to the enterprise and bravery of our fellow citizens.'" (By permission of the publisher. Copyright, 1936.)

[27] Adams, *op. cit.*, pp. 1-12. Also George H. Pitt-Rivers, *The Clash of Cultures and the Contact of Races in the Pacific* (London, 1927).

[28] S. J. Holmes, *The Negro's Struggle for Survival: A Study in Human Ecology* (Berkeley: University of California Press, 1937), p. 2.

"There are," he says, "four ways in which the racial struggle may conceivably work out:

1. We may all become black;
2. We may all become white;
3. Whites and blacks may fuse into a hybrid stock; or
4. We may become permanently biracial, either mingled together, or occupying different local areas.[29]

But this list does not include all the factors that one needs to take account of in making such a forecast as is here proposed. The Negro population, for example—and this is characteristic of almost every other population element in America—is sometimes slowly, sometimes rapidly, but continuously in motion, moving out of its original location and settlement into some other part of the country. There has been a very considerable concentration of Negro population in recent years in Northern cities. Nevertheless, the population is with every decade more widely dispersed. Associated with this dispersal is a tendency for Negroes, as for all other races, living in communities where they are a small or negligible minority, to intermarry and interbreed and so lose their racial identity. On the other hand, in the Black Belt where the Negro is, or has constituted, 50 per cent or more of the population, the Negro's complexion has not noticeably changed.

The migration and dispersion of Negroes involves new social contacts and new race relations. Negroes in every part of the country, even on the plantations in the Southern states, are now, as they were not formerly, in a competition with whites for jobs and places of relative security in the occupational organization of the community in which they live.

In one of its aspects this competition is not merely a struggle of the individual to find a place in the local economy, it is at the same time a struggle of a racial unit to discover a niche in which Negroes will enjoy relative security from competition with white competitors. This is the way in which the caste interest and caste organization, where it exists, cuts across class interest and class organization. When, and to the extent that the Negro finds the niche into which he fits, or into which he has succeeded in accommodating himself, then the degree of this economic security will be registered in the balance of births and deaths.

Moving North, the Negro has become a factor in politics to an

---

[29] *Ibid.*, p. 2.

extent that was not permitted him in the South. The Northern migration and dispersion have given him opportunities for education which he did not have in the South. But the effect of education, and conspicuously the education of Negro women, has had a devastating effect upon the Negro birth rate. There is apparently no way in which a people can so effectively commit race suicide as by educating its women. At the present time colored women have more opportunities for education, and for higher education, than colored men.

The effect of education, especially higher education, in so far as it has increased the number of occupations, particularly in the professions to which Negroes have access, has brought into existence a Negro middle class, which fact has also had effects that will eventually be registered in the balance of Negro births and deaths. In proportion to the numbers of Negroes in the population, I might add, the number in the professions is much smaller than is normal for the population as a whole.[30]

The effects of education and dispersion in so far as they tend to increase the number of Negro occupations tend likewise to undermine the caste system. The consequence of this is, on the one hand, to diminish the distances between the races at the different class levels and, on the other, to transform the status of the Negro in the United States from that of a caste to that of a racial minority.[31]

It seems, then, that one may think of race relations as existing not only on different levels, that is (1) ecological, (2) economic, (3) political, (4) personal and cultural, but one may think of these different levels as constituting a hierarchy of relations of such a nature that change upon any one level will invariably have repercussions, not immediately, but finally, upon every other.

VI

There are, it seems, two distinct and opposite points of view from which it is possible to survey an historical movement, such as that referred to by historians as "The Expansion of Europe." From one point of view this movement appears as a progressive extension of European culture and domination in the world, accompanied by an increasing integration of, and intimacy with, the races and peoples

---

[30] Charles S. Johnson, *The Negro College Graduate* (Chapel Hill, 1938).

[31] Bertram W. Doyle, *The Etiquette of Race Relations in the South* (Chicago, 1937), Introduction, p. xxii.

within this imperium. The movement may, however, be viewed in a temporal perspective in which it presents itself as a succession of changes which have come about in connection with, and incidental to, the expansion and integration of a vast and new social organism, if it is permissible to apply that term to any or all of the typical forms of interdependence—ecological, economic, political, and cultural— which the European social and cultural complex has assumed in the course of its expansion. At any rate, the changes which have come about with the expansion of European dominance seem to have come about everywhere, though not everywhere at the same pace.

The earliest cultural and racial contacts seem to have arisen out of the necessities of trade and barter. At the outset this trade was likely to proceed very cautiously as in the case of the so-called "silent trade." [32]

There is always, it appears, something uncanny about people who are complete strangers, particularly when they arrive in great ships, or, as has recently happened in the New Guinea archipelago, in flying boats. However, as trade relations progress, everything foreign tends to acquire a certain prestige, partly because it is unfamiliar and exotic. Presently barter is superseded by something like commercial exploitation. Articles of foreign manufacture replace the native products because, being machine made, they are cheaper.

Trade relations are invariably succeeded, eventually if not immediately, by some form of political domination. This is made necessary in order to protect not merely trade but the trader. Political domination may, in the natural course, take forms as different as that represented, on the one hand, by a crown colony, to use an English expression, or on the other, by "spheres of influence." At this point in the race relations cycle the foreign missionary is likely to make his appearance.

We ordinarily think of missionary societies, so far as their secular activities are concerned, as agencies for salving the wounds and

---

[32] This area (the Congo forest) "is famous for the development of 'silent trading' between the pygmies and the Negroes. Many pygmy groups are tacitly attached to a Negro village and have an understanding for the barter of game for agricultural crops. After a successful hunt the negritoes enter the banana groves of the villagers, gather fruit, and hang suitable meat in its place; the villagers when needing game will also lay out agricultural produce in an accustomed place for the hunters, who will in due course bring to that place a portion of their bag." C. Daryll Forde, *Habitat, Economy and Society* (2d ed., New York: Harcourt, Brace and Co., 1937), p. 23. See also Sir P. J. H. Grierson, *The Silent Trade* (Edinburgh, 1903).

mitigating the grievances which an unregulated commerce inevitably provokes. This conception is justified when one considers to what extent colonial or "missionary peoples," if I may use that term in a general and generic sense, have benefited by the schools, hospitals, and other welfare agencies which European missionary societies have established in every part of the world in which Europeans are now or have been dominant. But missions, in planting the seeds of a new and competing culture, in countries like India and China—that is, in countries which are now, or will be presently, involved in a struggle to emancipate themselves from European domination and tutelage— have sometimes intensified the confusion and raised new points of conflict. But that, too, is an inescapable incident of the historical process. As a matter of fact, the formal education begun in the missionary schools is carried on and completed by the informal education which native peoples inevitably receive on the plantations, in the factories, and the commercial establishments where they work within the limits of a European economic and social system, and under the direct supervision of European agents.

Thus every plantation in Java, the Philippines, or Hawaii, every factory, commercial organization, or bank in Hong Kong, Calcutta, or Bombay, is a means of completing the education begun by the missionary schools, and incidentally of hastening the time when the native peoples will be able to dispense with the luxury of foreign tutors and foreign tutelage.

The final stage in European expansion is reached when Europe begins to export not goods but capital, capital first of all to finance mining operations, the tin mines of Billiton, in the Dutch East Indies, for example, or the rubber plantations in Sumatra and the Malay peninsula, and finally, to build factories to employ native laborers in the manufacture of commodities which are then sold not only in the colonies, but, as in the case of Japan, in Europe and in competition with European products.

This imposes upon European expansion the limit to which it has been steadily trending. The cycle is now complete. Communication, to be sure, is still expanding and acculturation continues, but the great migration is, apparently, ended. In a recent volume, entitled *An Island Community*, Andrew Lind describes this movement as it is reflected in the history of economic and race relations in the Hawaiian Islands.

Here we may see, as in a microcosm, within the compass of a territory smaller than Massachusetts and within a period of 160 years, the operation of processes which Oswald Spengler has described in cosmic proportions and in the grand style of a philosopher of history, in his *Decline of the West (Untergang des Abendlandes)*.[33]

From a somewhat similar point of view Hermann Schneider has written a *History of World Civilization*. In this unique history—unique because it attempts to make history systematic—the civilizations of Egypt, Babylon, Crete, Persia, Greece, and Rome, and the Jews are treated as individual organic units, each repeating with individual variations the same life cycle. It is Schneider's thesis that every civilization begins with migration, invasion, and conquest. There follows a period of miscegenation, in the course of which a new race is formed by the fusion of the invaders with the natives. After a period of internal conflict a class organization finally crystallizes, and then, in due course, a new culture arises which finds expression in a characteristic literature, philosophy, and technology. This process is repeated with the rise of each succeeding civilization, except that, in so far as each later civilization is able to appropriate and assimilate the inheritance transmitted to it from its predecessors, the latter represents an advance over the earlier. In this way progress is achieved. The transmission of a cultural heritage from an earlier to a later civilization is always problematic, never complete, and its advance, when achieved at all, is not as continuous and consistent as the popular conception of progress assumes.

One of the consequences of the European expansion that is not ordinarily taken into the reckoning is the appearance, in the wake of every European invasion, of a mixed blood population due in part to the intermarriage and interbreeding of Europeans with the native populations and in part to the mixture of races outside of Europe im-

---

[33] From Spengler's point of view there is no such thing as civilization; there are only civilizations, each an organism unique and individual, limited in its possibilities, and expressing itself in a characteristic rhythm, form, and duration. "I see," he says, "in place of that empty figment of *one* linear history which can only be kept up by shutting one's eyes to the overwhelming multitude of the facts, the drama of *a number* of mighty Cultures, each springing with primitive strength from the soil of a mother-region to which it remains firmly bound throughout its whole life-cycle; each stamping its material, its mankind, in *its own* image; each having *its own* idea, *its own* passions, *its own* life, will and feeling, *its own* death." Oswald Spengler, *The Decline of the West* (New York: Alfred A. Knopf, 1926), I, 21.

ported into the colonies to do the rough work on the plantations for which natives are not fitted.[34]

Hybrid peoples, particularly if they are the product of the interbreeding of stocks so physically divergent that the resulting hybrid can be readily distinguished from both parents, will ordinarly occupy a status somewhat below that of the colonizing European but above that of the native or pure blood. In this situation the half-caste tends to conform to the personality of the so-called "marginal man," that is to say, a man who is predestined to live in two cultures and two worlds. It is characteristic of marginal types that they are able to look with a certain degree of critical detachment upon the diverse worlds of their parents. At the same time they are likely to feel themselves not quite at home in either.[35] This is especially the case when, as has happened in Hawaii, the parents speak habitually each a different language, Chinese and Hawaiian for example. In that case the offspring will probably speak English. They will have, in short, no mother tongue.

Living, so to speak, on the margin of two races, the half-caste ordinarily functions either as a mediator or a buffer between the European and the Asiatic or African. In some cases, as for example in the West Indies, the man of mixed blood may, indirectly and quite

---

[34] No attempt has been made to estimate the number of persons in the world who are today reckoned as "mixed bloods." As a matter of fact, unless the races which interbreed are sufficiently different in respect to those traits by which we ordinarily distinguish races, no mixed or half-caste arises. Thus if a Jew marries a Christian, their offspring become either Jews or Gentiles. The individual may, to be sure, be reckoned as a part-Jew and part-Gentile, but there is no part-Jew-part-Gentile class or caste. The opposite is the case with an African or an Asiatic who is born of mixed parentage.

However the number of persons who are of recognized racial origin, but are not sufficiently amalgamated to constitute them as distinct racial varieties, is considerable.

There were in the United States 1,660,554 persons reckoned as mulattoes in 1920. The Cape Coloured, mainly mixed Hottentots and Dutch, numbered 545,548 in 1930. The Eurasians of India, or Anglo-Indians, as they prefer to call themselves, numbered in 1921, 113,090. In Brazil "persons of color," that is, persons recognized as of mixed Negro-white origin, numbered 8,800,000. Forty-three per cent of the population is of mixed Indian and Europian origin. In Java the Indo-Europeans, or Eurasians, numbered 290,408.

If we add to the numbers of those who are recognized as of mixed racial origin those who have been or could properly be classed as "racial and cultural minorities," that is, those who, because of racial or language differences, have not been wholly assimilated or regard themselves in any sense as alien in the country in which they live, we should know how extensive the diaspora—that is to say, the region in which peoples live more or less as strangers, the region in which race relations may be said to exist—actually is.

[35] Everett V. Stonequist, *The Marginal Man* (New York, 1937).

unintentionally, assist in keeping the African of pure blood in subordination and by so doing make the position of the dominant European more secure. This happens when the man of mixed blood, representing a rising middle class, interposes himself between the European at the top and the man of pure blood at the bottom in such fashion that no man of pure blood can rise except in so far as he is accepted by the mulatto middle class or caste. This is, in a general way, the situation in India though the racial situation is complicated by the existence of a caste system—and a caste system maintained by religious as well as social sanctions. The caste system of the Hindu necessarily affects the status of every other ethnic or religious unit in India. The Anglo-Indians, being Christians, actually occupy a position in the Indian Empire comparable with that of the Parsis in Bombay. They are described in the report on which the new Indian constitution is based as a "community," although as employees of the state they are dispersed throughout the Empire.

In Brazil, where *métis*, or mixed bloods, are neither a class nor a caste but merely the advance guard of a population of African origin in process of assimilation, the mulatto seems to have no special social function. The situation in the United States, on the other hand, is profoundly different. Here, where every man with a tincture of the African in him is classed as Negro, and racial distinctions within the race have been pretty thoroughly abolished, the Negroes of mixed blood have made themselves protagonists of the American Negro minority. They have been likewise the most aggressive leaders of the race.[36]

VII

One of the incidental consequences of European expansion that inevitably impresses the world traveler is the sudden rise along great ocean thoroughfares through which the currents of world commerce flow, of a succession of great metropolitan cities. Most of them are new cities and if they are not wholly European in character they all sport a European façade. The most outstanding of these cities, which circle the world like a girdle, are: San Francisco, Yokohama, Shanghai, Hong Kong, Colombo, Bombay, Marseilles, London, and New York. And then there is Johannesburg, one of the world's most interesting

---

[36] Alfred Holt Stone, *Studies in the American Race Problem* (New York, 1908), chap. ix, "The Mulatto Factor in the Race Problem," pp. 425-439. See also Robert E. Park, "Mentality of Racial Hybrids," *American Journal of Sociology*, XXXVI, 534-551 (Jan., 1931).

metropolitan cities, which has apparently strayed inland, but which, as the primary market for most of the world's gold, performs a distinctly metropolitan function. Aside, also, from the fact that Johannesburg is much like San Francisco in the early years of the Gold Rush, it is interesting from the point of view of race relations because in its gold mines some two hundred thousand tribal natives are getting their first lessons in European civilization.

The function of the great port cities in the new world economy is to facilitate the movement of raw materials and commodities from their sources in the interior through continental gateways, into the world market. Almost all the great and growing cities of the world are now located on this main street of the world.

Spengler has described these cities as the centers "in which the whole life of broad regions is collecting while the rest dries up." These are the places where "the type-true people, born of and grown on the soil," are being superseded by "a new sort of nomad, cohering unstably in fluid masses, the parasitical city dweller, traditionless, utterly matter-of-fact, religionless, clever, unfruitful, deeply contemptuous of the countryman and especially that highest form of countryman, the country gentleman." [37]

If it is true that in the cosmopolitan life all that was characteristic of earlier and more provincial cultures is obviously losing its local characteristics and disappearing in a welter and mishmash of local cultures and that we are now living, most of us, in a world which, in comparison with the life-forms of a more mature and stable social order, is almost without form and wholly without distinction, it is nevertheless equally true that in these cities a new civilization, new peoples, the modern world, with new local varieties of culture, is visibly coming into existence.

One of the evidences of this is the sudden and widespread interest in nationalism and in local nationalities. The struggle of minor racial and language groups for some sort of independent and individual expression of their traditional and national lives, which began in Europe in the early part of the last century, has now spread, as if it were contagious, to every part of the world; every part of the world, at any rate, which has felt or still feels itself oppressed in its local, provincial autonomous life, or for any other reason, inferior in its international status.

It is interesting that this ambition of minority nationalities, if I may

[37] Spengler, *op. cit.*, I, 32.

so describe them, to control and direct their own destinies, in accordance with their own tradition and sense of values, has not in the least diminished their interest in, or determination to possess and use, in their own interest, all the technical knowledge and all the technical devices upon which the dominance of Europe in the modern world seems to have been based.[38]

The present nationalist movement, associated as it is by the practical cessation of migration and the so-called "devolution" of missions, is evidence that we are at the end of one epoch in human and racial relations and at the beginning of another.

What then, finally, is the precise nature of race relations that distinguish them, in all the variety of conditions in which they arise, from other fundamental forms of human relations? It is the essence of race relations that they are the relations of strangers; of peoples who are associated primarily for secular and practical purposes; for the exchange of goods and services. They are otherwise the relations of people of diverse races and cultures who have been thrown together by the fortunes of war, and who, for any reason, have not been sufficiently knit together by intermarriage and interbreeding to constitute a single ethnic community, with all that it implies.

Obviously that does not imply as much in the modern world as it did in the ancient; it does not imply as much in the Occident as it does in the Orient, where society is still organized on the familial pattern. It possibly implies less in America, or parts of America where divorce is easy and people are not generally interested in genealogies, as it does in Europe.

Although people in America and the modern world are no longer bound and united as people once were by familial and tribal ties, we are, nevertheless, profoundly affected by sentiments of nationality, particularly where they have an ethnic and a cultural basis. Furthermore, national and cultural differences are often re-enforced by divergence of physical and racial traits. But racial differences would not maintain social distances to the extent they actually do if they were not symptoms of differences in custom, tradition, and religion, and of sentiments appropriate to them. Differences of race and custom

---

[38] The only instance of an outstanding personality in the modern world who has opposed this tendency to appropriate European technology is Mr. Gandhi, of India, who in other respects seems to be the most modern of moderns. He advised the Indian people to go back to the spinning wheel rather than forward to the factory. See René Fülop-Miller, *Lenin and Gandhi* (London, 1927), p. 289.

mutually re-enforce one another, particularly when they are not broken up by intermarriage.[39]

Traditions and customs are ordinarily transmitted through the family and can be most effectively maintained by intermarrying, i.e., endogamous groups. Evidence of this is the fact that every religious society tends to assume the character of a caste or endogamous group in so far at least as it prohibits or discourages marriage outside of the church or the sect. The Catholic clergy are profoundly opposed to marriage outside of the church, and the Jews who are, perhaps, the most mixed of peoples, have only been able to preserve their tribal religion for three thousand years and more because by endogamy they converted a religious society into a racial minority.

It has become commonplace among students of anthropology that most of the traits which we attribute to the different historic races are, like language and a high-school education, acquired by each succeeding generation for itself, sometimes by painful experience and always by a more or less extended formal education. Nevertheless, it is likewise becoming more obvious to students of human nature and society that the things that one learns in the intimate association of the family are likely to be the more permanent and more profound in their effects upon one's character in determining the individual's conception of himself, his outlook on life, his relations to other people.

It is obvious that society, so far as it is founded on a familial or genetic basis is concerned—as a secular society based on commercial and political interest is not—with maintaining not merely a definite life program, but a manner, moral order, and style of life consistent with that conception.

All this implies that the family and religion, the home and the church, in spite of public schools and social welfare institutions of every sort, still have the major responsibility for directing the career of youth and transmitting that intimate personal and moral order in accordance with which individuals freely govern themselves. Where custom breaks down, order may still be maintained, not by custom but by the police.

The consequence of this is that where there are racial and cultural minorities, whether Jews, Negroes, Catholics or religious sects that do not intermarry, the conflicts ordinarily described as racial but which are mainly cultural, do everywhere tend to arise. They arise even in an equalitarian society, like our own where "all men are,"

---

[39] See Romanzo Adams, *op. cit.*

in principle if not in fact, "born equal," and they arise perhaps more readily here than they do in a society based on caste, because in theory they should not arise.

The obvious source and origin of most, if not all of the cultural and racial conflicts which constitute our race problems, are, therefore, conflicts of the "we groups" and the "other groups," as Sumner calls them, groups which are, however, integral parts of a great cosmopolitan and a free society. They are the ineluctable conflicts between the "little world" of the family in its struggle to preserve its sacred heritage against the disintegrating consequences of contact with an impersonal "great world" of business and politics.

They are, in fact, individual instances of an irrepressible conflict between a society founded on kinship and a society founded on the market place; the conflict between the folk culture of the provinces and the civilization of the metropolis.

Looking at race relations in the long historical perspective, this modern world which seems destined to bring presently all the diverse and distant peoples of the earth together within the limits of a common culture and a common social order, strikes one as something not merely unique but milennial! Nevertheless, this new civilization is the product of essentially the same historical processes as those that preceded it. The same forces which brought about the diversity of races will inevitably bring about, in the long run, a diversity in the peoples in the modern world corresponding to that which we have seen in the old. It is likely, however, that these diversities will be based in the future less on inheritance and race and rather more on culture and occupation. That means that race conflicts in the modern world, which is already or presently will be a single great society, will be more and more in the future confused with, and eventually superseded by, the conflicts of classes.

CHAPTER 8

RACE RELATIONS AND CERTAIN FRONTIERS

HUMAN geographers have been accustomed to divide the world into regions which are (*a*) politically active and (*b*) politically passive. In somewhat the same sense one may speak of culture areas that are (*a*) active and (*b*) passive.[1]

Active areas are those in which there is a great deal going on. New ideas are burgeoning, new technological advances are in progress, and both are changing the conditions, the structure, and the content of social life.

Passive areas, on the contrary, are those in which life continues, on the whole, to revolve in the same unbroken and traditional routine. In such regions, where population, natural resources, and the standards of living have achieved some sort of equilibrium and where custom and tradition provide for most of the exigencies of life, changes still take place, to be sure, but take place silently, continuously, and at an almost imperceptible pace.

It is characteristic of active, as contrasted with passive, areas that they are at the same time centers of increasing population, of expand-

In E. B. Reuter, (ed.). *Race and Culture Contacts* (New York: McGraw-Hill Book Co., 1934), pp. 57-85.

[1] Jean Bruhnes and Camille Vallaux, in a volume published in 1921 describing the existing distribution of the world's population, referred to zones of concentration, some of which are active and some of which are passive. Later on in the same volume the authors, in recording their observations on present-day political geography, characterized certain regions as those that are politically active "where there are numerous and powerful states in a condition of fermentation," and regions that are politically passive, that is, those "upon which societies

ing commerce, of political and cultural dominance, and that the outer margin of any such area constitutes an ever-widening frontier.

As one ordinarily understands the term in the United States a frontier is an incidental product of migration and designates an area, with somewhat indefinite boundaries, which gets its special character from the alarms, excursions, and rapid changes incident to the invasion and settlement of a new population in a relatively vacant or sparsely settled territory. In this sense of the word, a frontier is not so much a mark or boundary as a zone on the margin of an advancing population. The thing that gives the frontier, so conceived, its peculiar character and significance is the fact that the invading people in their efforts to accommodate themselves to the conditions of life in a new country invariably discard or lose their inherited and traditional ways of life and as a result new peoples and new cultures arise. It follows that a frontier is not merely a mark where peoples meet but a zone of transition where they intermingle.

For four hundred years and more Europe, and particularly Western Europe, has been preeminently the seat and center of greatest intellectual and political activity. During this period European commerce and European culture have penetrated to the most remote corners of the habitable world. As a result of this expansion, most of the world outside Europe has been reduced to a position of political and cultural subordination and dependency—a condition that is rather suggested than described by the term colonial. Thus the sphere of Europe's dominance includes not merely its colonies, in the narrow sense of that word, but those more nebulous forms of sovereignty which we call protectorates, spheres of influence, mandated and mission territories. It includes also those former European colonies in America and elsewhere which, with the completion of the colonial process, have now achieved the status of independent states, although some of them, as the British Dominions, are still included within the confederation of the British Commonwealth.

European colonies are, however, of two types: colonies of settlement and colonies of exploitation. The latter are located, for the most part, in the tropics and in territory believed to be unsuited to European settlement, or in territory already densely populated where the

---

politically active are projecting their shadows, and into which they are extending their ramifications."—Jean Bruhnes and Camille Vallaux, *La géographie de la historie; géographie de la paix et la guerre, sur terre et sur mer*, pp. 131-190, 269-319.

native populations cannot be displaced. Thus Europe, in drawing within the steadily widening orbit of its political and cultural influence an ever-increasing portion of the habitable world and an ever larger quota of the world's population, has actually advanced on two frontiers: a frontier of settlement and a frontier of commercial and industrial exploitation. In either case the frontier has invariably advanced by stages; stages distinguished less by the increasing numbers of the invading population than by the character of the artifacts and technological devices which each successive advance of population had invariably introduced. Thus the introduction of an artifact, idea, or institution, provided it is sufficiently innovating and disturbing to the existing social order, may mark the rise of a new frontier, not in every instance a frontier of settlement but in any case a cultural frontier.

Thus one might, conceivably, considering their world-wide distribution, speak of the oil-can frontier, that is, the frontier where kerosene has been substituted for tapers and torches.

One might, in the same sense, speak of the Singer sewing-machine frontier, or the automobile, cinema, and radio frontiers, and it is quite possible that, were we able to plot the distribution of these contributions of the so-called active to the so-called passive areas of the world, it would appear that they have all followed each other in some sort of regular succession, such a succession as one finds on the advancing American frontier, where "the vanguard of the advance was led by 'long hunters,' exploring scouts, outlaws, prospective gold rushers, Indian traders, and *coureurs de bois*"; followed a little later by "the main stream of hunters, ranchers, frontier farmers, traders, and miners," and still later by more settled and less romantic types of migrant, bringing with them the institutions and technological devices of a permanently settled community including, among other things, churces, the printing press, and eventually bathtubs and modern plumbing.[2]

The latest and most significant index of European cultural expansion is, however, Europe's capital export, machinery, and factories. These are significant because they mark the end of Europe's monopoly of the products of machine industry and because they indicate a rising competition between Oriental and Occidental industry. They probably mark also the limits of Europe's last cultural frontier. There is, in fact, evidence that Europe's influence in the world has already reached its zenith—has, in fact, already begun to decline. At any rate

[2] Frederick L. Paxon, "Frontier," *Encyclopaedia of the Social Sciences.*

there are everywhere in Asia the evidences of a recession of European political power.

CULTURAL EXPANSION AND RACE MIXTURE

The expansion of Europe has been the expansion not merely of a civilization but of a race. It is estimated, on the basis of such statistics as exist, that the European population has increased from 180,000,000 in 1800 to 640,000,000 in 1930. Of this total, 160,000,000 represents those Europeans, and their descendants, who migrated overseas. As near as can be estimated, this indicates a rate of increase in the European population during this period three times as great as the increase in the population of the world as a whole. Most of this outward movement of population was directed to the colonies of settlement, but the number of Europeans and Americans, including commercial agents, colonial officials, soldiers, and missionaries resident abroad, most of them located in the foreign trade settlements, is considerable and up to the beginning of the World War was undoubtedly increasing.

One evidence and consequence of this racial expansion is the existence, in both the colonies of settlement and the colonies of exploitation, wherever Europeans have gone to live in fact, a population of half-castes and mixed bloods, usually relatively small in numbers but of sufficient importance to be assigned a separate classification in the statistics of population. The mixed-blood populations are, as a matter of fact, one of the inevitable and invariable products of every racial frontier. It is with these half-castes and mixed bloods, as products and indices of Europe's social frontier, that this paper is concerned.

In actual numbers, if not in percentages of their total populations, the United States and Brazil have the largest contingents of mixed-blood peoples—as that term is ordinarily construed—of any countries of the world. The total mulatto population of the United States, a mixture of European, Indian, and Negro, was as recorded by the census of 1920—the last census in which an attempt was made to record the mulatto population separately—1,660,554, which is 15.9 per cent of the total Negro population and a little more than one-tenth of one per cent of the total population, Negro and white, in the United States. Incidentally these figures indicate a decrease of 390,132 from those of the 1910 census, when the mulatto population was stated to be 2,050,686. These figures, if accepted as accurate, would indicate a reversal, during the decennial period, of the secular trend of mulatto population growth which up to that point had shown a steadily increasing number of mixed-blood, as compared with pure-blood, Negroes in the population of the United States. However, in view of the fact that in the United States a person, for census purposes at least, is a Negro only when he is known to be or passes for a Negro in the community in which he lives, this decline in number of mixed bloods in the population from 1910 to 1920 may be merely another indication of what is known from other sources to be a fact, namely, that many mulattoes who migrated during the decennial period are not known as Negroes in the communities in which they now live.

In contrast to any inferences which might be drawn from the census statistics in regard to the amount of European, African, and Indian race mixture in the United States, Herskovits, basing his estimates on anthropometric measurements made in Washington, D. C., New York City, West Virginia, and some other places, has come to the conclusion that 78 per cent of the American Negro population shows traces of mixed European or Indian descent.[3]

The last census in Brazil, which attempted to distinguish the European, African, Indian, and mixed-blood contingents in the population, was made in 1890. It indicated that 44 per cent of the total population was of European origin. Of the remaining 56 per cent, 9 per cent was Indian, 14.6 per cent was Negro, and 32.4 per cent was "persons of color," that is, people of recognized mixed racial origin. In estimating the value of these statistics it is important to take into account the fact that, if in America one drop of Negro blood makes a white man black, the reverse is likely to be the case in Brazil. At any rate the definition of what constituted a *branco*, a white man, is more liberal and less pedantic than it is in some parts of the United States.[4]

More recent investigations based on anthropometric measurements of Brazilian Army recruits indicate that the tendency to what Brazilian savants describe as progressive Arianization, namely, the tendency for the white population to absorb the *mestizos*, and the *mestizos* to absorb the Negro and Indian, continues. Meanwhile the Arianization of Brazil's colored population has been greatly expedited

---

[3] Melville J. Herskovits, *The American Negro: A Study in Racial Crossing.*
[4] Monroe N. Work, *Negro Year Book: An Annual Encyclopedia of the Negro*, 1931-1932, pp. 79-80.

by the influx in recent years of European immigrants from Italy, Spain, and Portugal.[5] A few years ago Italy contributed the largest quota to the total Brazilian immigration. At the present time Portuguese immigrants outnumber the Italian. German immigration, so important seventy years ago, has shrunk to insignificant proportions.

One does not know whether to attribute the high percentage of mixed bloods in the Brazilian population to the fact that race relations are more amiable there than elsewhere or, adopting the contrary hypothesis, to explain the apparent lack of race consciousness in Brazil's European population by the amount of race mixture that has already taken place. It is probably a little difficult to maintain any high degree of race prejudice in a country where, owing to the indiscretions of distant ancestors, every family is likely to have had an Indian or Negro grandmother.

However, Portuguese have always mixed freely with the native populations of the countries in which they established colonies. In the very early days of European colonization, it was the policy of the Portuguese government, as it was of the Catholic Church, to encourage intermarriage between the colonists and the natives. Comparatively few of the Portuguese soldiers sent out to the colonies in that early period ever returned to Portugal. A good many of them died but those who survived invariably took up with native women and presently acquired a brood of half-caste children. The priests hastened to sanction and regularize the unions thus made and in that way brought parents and children within the control and discipline of the church. It was in this way that the Goanese in western India and the Macanese in Southern China, who are descendants of these early Portuguese mixtures, came into existence. Goa was the first territorial possession of the Portuguese in Asia and was for a long time the administrative center of the Portuguese colonial empire.

Macao, which is thirty miles west from Hong Kong at the entrance to the Canton River, is the oldest outpost of European trade with China. It was originally settled by one thousand Portuguese families, whose descendants have intermarried with the Chinese to such an extent that they are now predominantly Chinese in blood, if not in culture. Macao is a beautiful and gaudy city, particularly at night when the streets in the Chinese quarter, where the gambling hells are

---

[5] Pinto Roquette, *Ensaios de Anthropologia Brasileira*. See also Oliveira Vianna, *Evolucao do Povo Brasileiro*, 2d ed., pp. 172-185.

located, are ablaze with light and banners. Macao is in fact the Monte Carlo of Southern China.

Though the Goanese and Macanese have been more completely assimilated, culturally and biologically, with the native peoples among whom they live than any of the other European half-castes, they are, nevertheless, like most Portuguese, devout Christians in a pagan world, and this fact has doubtless assisted in preserving their racial identity.

Like other Eurasians the Macanese and Goanese are city folk. They are found all up and down the coast of Asia and as far south as Mombassa, Africa, where they function as clerks, stenographers, and general intermediaries between the Oriental and Occidental worlds. In Mombassa and Zanzibar, the points at which India and the Orient come in contact with Africa, Goanese clerks and Parsi merchants from Bombay compete with the Arabs for the trade of Africa.

After Brazil and the United States, South Africa probably has the largest mixed-blood population of which the numbers and racial composition are known with something approaching accuracy. Mexico, the Philippines, and the West Indies have, to be sure, large mixed-blood populations. In the Philippines, Europeans and Chinese have intermarried and interbred with the native Malay stocks. The population of Mexico is very largely Spanish and Indian with a tincture of Negro, which is one reason, no doubt, why the 698,090 Mexicans in the United States were classed as "colored" in the census of 1930, whereas previous to that time they had been reckoned as white.[6] In the West Indies, particularly in the French and Spanish islands, there are considerable numbers of European and African hybrids, but little or no attempt has been made to segregate the *mestizos* from the parent stocks. In Santo Domingo, which is the part of the Island of Haiti which the close of the revolution left in the possession of mulattoes rather than blacks, amalgamation has gone so far that the Santo Dominicans, like the Macanese and Goanese, may almost be said to constitute a new race.[7]

---

[6] Monroe N. Work, *Negro Year Book*, p. 339. According to the 1940 census three major race classifications are distinguished namely white, Negro, and "other races." Persons of Mexican birth or ancestry who were not definitely Indian or of other nonwhite race were returned as white.—Ed.

[7] During the colonial period in Mexico there were three classes of people: Indians were called *mexicanos*, creoles or *mestizos* were called *americanos*, and men of pure white blood were *espaniols*. *Espaniols* were also called *gachupin*, "he who wears shoes." From such statistics as exist, it appears that mixed blood

Race and Culture

In South Africa, on the contrary, the distinctions between races—Europeans, Bantu, Indians, and Cape colored—have been rigidly maintained, although there is, as the very moderate decennial increase in the colored or mixed-blood population indicates, a certain amount of crossing on racial frontiers. This happens especially when colored people from the Cape migrate, as they do in spite of the loss of status involved, from the communities in which they were born to other parts of the union.[8]

The Cape colored population, estimated for 1930, amounted to 545,548 out of the total population in South Africa of 6,928,580. However, this total includes 4,697,813 natives (Bantu) and 165,731 Asiatics, mostly descendants of Hindu laborers imported to work in sugar plantations of Natal. Of the total Cape colored population 80 per cent is now living in Cape Colony. The increase in the Cape colored population from 1921 to 1931 was 3.73 per cent, while that of the Bantu population during the same period was 16.89 per cent, and that of the Asiatics 8.89 per cent.

The colored population of South Africa has its origin, as was the case of mixed-blood people elsewhere, in the early days of the Dutch settlement of the Cape. One way in which immigrant peoples have frequently got themselves rooted and established in new countries has been by adopting the customs of the country and by interbreeding with the indigenous peoples. The other alternative, the one which was eventually adopted in the Cape, has been the introduction of slavery. Transplanting a people, like transplanting any other organism, is a ticklish business, and interbreeding is one way of successfully accomplishing the transition. This explains, in part at least, the tolerance with which the Dutch population, in the early days of the settlement, regarded racial intermarriage and racial interbreeding. In fact, this tolerance is so characteristic of the early period of settlement in any new country that it may properly be regarded as a stage in the colonial process.

Once the Cape Colony was fairly established and the Dutch

in Mexico was 22 per cent in 1810, 40 per cent in 1900, and 43 per cent in 1921. The population of Jamaica was 916,620: white population 2 per cent, "colored" 18 per cent, black 77 per cent, East Indian and unknown 3 per cent.

The population of Cuba in 1927 was 3,568,552. Of this number 62.8 per cent was native white; 27.7 per cent was Negro and mixed; 9.5 per cent, including 10,300 Chinese, was classed as foreign white.

[8] The Cape colored and the educated Bantu have the right to vote in Cape Colony, and a very limited right, which is expressly denied them in the constitution of the other South African states, in Natal.

housewives had measurably succeeded in banishing the native concubines, the attitude of the community changed. At the present time there is probably nowhere a more grim determination to preserve the integrity of their racial stock than there is among the descendants of those first Dutch settlers and of the French Huguenot and German immigrants who followed and fused with them to form the Boer people.

On the frontier, however, and particularly on the northwestern frontier where the colonists encountered and eventually subjugated the Hottentots, miscegenation continued. Evidence of this is the number of mixed racial communities that once flourished there, some of which still persist. The most notable of these were the *Griquas* of Cape Colony and the so-called *Rehobother Bastaards* of German Southwest Africa.

The Griquas of Griqualand have greatly declined in recent years and are apparently fated to be absorbed and assimilated, as other of these so-called *bastaard* communities have been, into that melting pot of races in South Africa, the Cape colored.

The Rehobother Bastaards, an isolated community of mixed Boer and South African natives, of which there exists a very interesting and innovating study by Eugen Fisher, still maintains its independence, its isolation, and its integrity as a people if not as an ethnic unit.[9]

The Cape colored, in contrast to the Bastaards, are a composite not of two but of several races, Bushmen, Hottentots, and the slaves imported into South Africa from the very much mixed populations of Madagascar, Mozambique, and Java. Malays from Java were, and have remained, orthodox Mohammedans; all the other racial elements which have contributed to the composition of the Cape colored are Christian. The Mohammedans regard themselves as a little superior to the Christians but are otherwise on good terms with them.

The amount of Bushman blood in the colored population is slight. The Bushmen proved to be intractable and difficult to domesticate. But the Hottentot nomads were finally settled on the land, sometimes under the protection of missionaries, sometimes as serfs on the widely dispersed farms. It was under these circumstances that they were assimilated, physically and culturally, and incorporated in the South

---

[9] In the vernacular of South Africa *bastaard* means simply mixed blood. In the past it has been a title of which the men who bore it were proud. It set them apart from the aborigines with whom they refused to identify themselves, regarding them—the aborigines—as inferior.

African racial complex. The Kafirs on the northeastern frontier, who came in touch with the Europeans later, have to a considerable extent maintained their tribal organization and, like the other Bantu peoples, have contributed little or nothing to the racial composition of South Africa's mixed peoples.[10]

The South African peoples, white, black, and colored, are still more or less in the making. The time has perhaps not yet arrived when it is possible to determine with any sense of finality the form which, under the influence of the peculiar racial situation, South African institutions are likely to take. There is, however, abundance of material, in view of the diversity of races and of social divisions and cleavages in the South African population, for an investigation of the origins of peoples, and for the observations of some of the elementary processes of civilization which these racial and social cleavages have laid bare.

The Boers themselves are rather more an indigenous than an immigrant people and almost as much a product of the soil as the Kafirs who invaded South Africa only a little earlier than they did.

The original Dutch population in South Africa was small. After 1707 no new European immigrants arrived. During the first fifty years of the history of the colony, the European population increased to about 2,500 of whom about half were Dutch. However, there were more Dutch women than there were German or French in the colonies and for that reason Dutch dialect became the language of the people.

The Boer population has reached its present numbers almost wholly by the natural increase of these first immigrants. The Africans' language, originally a low Dutch dialect, assumed its present form about 1760. One factor in the formation of the Boer people has been the long struggle of Boer nationalism with British imperialism. When one speaks in South Africa of the race problem, it is the struggle between Briton and Boer that is meant. The silent conflict in progress between the Boer and the Bantu—silent because the Bantu people are, as yet, not quite articulate—constitutes another and a different problem, namely, the problem of the native.

The Griquas and the Rehobother Bastaards are not by any means the only instances of hybrid peoples who came into existence on the South African frontier and have been, or are now, in process of absorption and assimilation into the South African melting pot. They

---

[10] Kafir is a name given by the Mohammedans to the infidels and all who are not Mohammedans are infidels, unless they are Christians.

occupy a place in the history of race relations in South Africa not unlike that of those communities of mixed Negro, Indian, and white which still exist on the outer margins of white settlement in the southern states. Like their American analogues they deserve more study than has yet been given them by those who are interested in ethnogeny and the origin of races.

Among the anecdotal and legendary material awaiting the historian of South African race relations, there are many remembered or recorded episodes which throw an interesting light upon not only racial but social origins. One of these to which one finds frequent references is the story of the Boer outlaw Coenraad du Buis. Buis was one of those wild Dutchmen from whom the Boer *Vortrekkers* were later recruited; one of those men who, spurning the restraints of the more civilized Cape, abandoned the settlements and eventually took up and lived with the natives. He was a man of gigantic stature and of a sort to make his way among simple and savage peoples. Everywhere he went he intermarried and interbred with the native women and eventually accumulated a considerable following, consisting almost wholly of his wives, children, and children's children. His descendants, whom he ruled during his lifetime in patriarchal fashion, now live in the Zoustpansburg Mountains of the North Transvaal. They have refused to intermarry with the natives by whom they are surrounded and have interbred to such an extent that they now constitute a relatively distinct and homogeneous ethnic group which occupies an intermediary position between the native and the white man. While they discourage intermarriage with the natives, they do not oppose interbreeding with such white men as come their way. In fact, they encourage such intermarriages in order, as the Negro women on the plantations used to put it, "to raise the color of their children."

Another anecdote which one occasionally meets refers to the career of the missionary Dr. Jacobus Theodorus Vanderkemp, who was probably the first representative of the London Missionary Society in South Africa, an institution which has played a memorable rôle in South African affairs.[11]

Vanderkemp was a Dutchman who resigned a high position in Europe in order to devote his life to mission work. He is a quaint, quixotic, but genuinely heroic figure in the history of race relations in South Africa. What is best remembered in regard to him is the fact

[11] William M. Macmillan, *The Cape Colour Question, a Historical Survey.*

that he married a *native* woman in order to identify himself wholly with the native people among whom he lived and worked.

The Vanderkemp saga seems to have suggested the theme, if it did not furnish the materials, for Gertrude Millin's story of South African life, *God's Stepchildren*. God's stepchildren were the colored descendants of a missionary who, like Vanderkemp, married a native wife. The story is an account of the long, pathetic struggle of the descendants of this ill-assorted pair who, by thinning their blood through three generations and by raising the cultural level of each succeeding generation, sought to achieve in South Africa the status of white folk, and of poor white folk at that.

Probably nothing thus far written on the racial situation in South Africa has so nearly succeeded in touching the nerve of the problem, since in the last analysis the problem of the South African races, whether they are Boers, Britons, Indians, Cape colored, or poor whites, revolves around a struggle for status. It is the struggle for status, however, among races and peoples that are at the same time involved in a very elementary struggle for existence.

ANGLO-INDIANS AND INDO-EUROPEANS

The half-caste communities of Asia are more numerous, more scattered, and not so formidable, in comparison with the native populations, as those of South Africa, the United States, and Brazil. Europe's invasion of the Orient has not anywhere resulted in large or permanent settlements outside the cities, and such European communities as were established have grown up for the most part about the trading outposts located on the seaboard. Some of these trading outposts have, to be sure, grown to the size of great metropolitan cities—Shanghai, Hong Kong, Singapore, Calcutta, and Bombay. Bound together by the invisible ties of their multitudinous commercial connections, with the other metropolitan and seaboard cities of the world, they dominate and constitute the structure of a new and rising world economy.

It is in these great cities that the Eurasian populations are mainly located. The largest half-caste community of India is in Calcutta. It is located midway, interestingly enough, between the European and the native quarters of the city. There are other such communities in Rangoon, Bombay, Madras, and Colombo, but none of them is so large and important.

The Anglo-Indian population of India, according to the census of 1921, was 113,090, which represents an increase of nearly 13 per cent for the decennial period. There is, however, some question about the accuracy of these figures, in view of the fact that the line which divides the Anglo-Indian of mixed blood and the Anglo-Indian who is now classed as a resident European is not very clearly drawn. Formerly all European residents were called Anglo-Indians, and the desire of the Eurasian population to be identified with their European rather than their Indian ancestors explains why they rejected the title of Eurasian and adopted that of Anglo-Indian.

The Ango-Indians are mainly of British origin and are not to be confused with the Portuguese and Indian mixtures of Goa which represent an earlier colonial settlement and earlier racial intermixture.

In Java, where there is a similar Eurasian population of Dutch and Javanese origin, the half-castes call themselves Indo-Europeans and are classed as Europeans in the population statistics of the Netherlands Indies. In the city of Batavia, out of a total population of 290,408, 28,753 are classed as "Europeans and Eurasians." The Asiatic population of Batavia, mostly Chinese and Chinese half-castes, is 45,408.[12]

The Portuguese came to Java early in the sixteenth century. They established factories and stayed for some time. They held slaves and around the factories there grew up a mixed people. They frequently brought slave women with them. The children remained in the *kampongs*. The fathers first began to take care of their children by native women as far back as 1600, about the time the Dutch arrived. These children were registered as Dutch.

Some of the half-breed children were sent to Holland. Some stayed. It is those who stayed who constitute the Indo-Europeans. A great majority of the half-castes became natives so that one can never be quite sure whether a person in Java is a full-blood native or half-caste. There are *kampongs* that are known to be full of mixed bloods.

Indo-Europeans who do not get a European education constitute a separate class. They are likely to be inferior government officials. They frequently enter the minor offices. They sometimes speak the

---

[12] L. S. von Romer, who was himself of mixed Dutch, German, Singhalese, Indo-Chinese, and Javanese origin, in an article on race mixture published in the proceedings of the first congress for the study of language, land, and ethnology in Java, after reviewing the history of several distinguished Eurasians and of others of mixed racial origin in Java, says that of 1,361 marriages in the year of 1917 in the Netherlands Indies, 179 represented mixtures of Europeans or persons of mixed European blood with native Javanese.

Indisch-Pidgin-Dutch. A Sinjo is a half-breed with half education. They usually become small officials, but they are good civil servants.

In 1890 the ethnic policy was changed. This meant that natives would have schools. The conception of race dominance was dropped.[13]

During the first period of English colonization in India, which lasted from the founding of the English factories in Madras until 1775, the "intermarriage between British residents and native women was encouraged and the offspring of such marriages were treated in all respect as English." [14]

An abstract from a dispatch addressed by the Court of Directors to the President of Madras and dated April 8, 1687, states:

> The marriage of our soldiers to the native women of Fort St. George, formerly recommended by you, is a matter of such consequence to posterity, that we shall be content to encourage it with some expense, and have been thinking for the future to appoint a pagoda to be paid to the mother of any child that shall hereafter be born of any such future marriage, on the day the child is christened, if you think this small encouragement will increase the number of such marriages.[15]

The future of the Anglo-Indian community in India, as of the Indo-Europeans in Java, is at present precarious. In both the Netherlands Indies and in British India the superiority of the Eurasians to the natives seems to have rested mainly upon their special opportunities for acquiring a European, that is, English or Dutch, education. As soon as European schools were opened to natives and native peoples were permitted to prepare themselves for government service, the half-caste lost the privileged position he had up to that time enjoyed. With the rising tide of nationalism in the Orient, and particularly in India, the Eurasian population is finding it increasingly difficult to maintain its European standard of living. The Salvation Army in Calcutta dealing with the "down and outs" has found itself mainly occupied with the Anglo-Indians who are out of work because they cannot find "suitable" jobs.[16]

---

[13] The Dutch in Java seemed to have been quite as liberal in their views of intermarriage as they were in the Cape Colony in the early history of that settlement. One man, a Hollander, who was very free with the native women on his plantation and who kept track of his children had over fourteen hundred descendants in thirty years.

[14] Elmer Hedin, "The Anglo-Indian Community" (unpublished paper).

[15] India Office Records, Letter Book 8, 290 and 493, quoted by Hedin, *op. cit.*

[16] In the spring of 1933, the Salvation Army established a shelter for homeless men in Calcutta. Most of the men who found shelter there were young men with

There are, of course, Eurasian communities outside British India and the Netherlands Indies. Every important port city along the Asiatic coast from Yokohama to Port Said has as a part of its cosmopolitan population a community, small or large, relatively, of half-castes. In Rangoon, Pedang, and Singapore these communities are organized. In Hong Kong Eurasians have no permanent organization but are held together by a sense of common interest and a conviction that their fortunes are involved in a common destiny. In the foreign settlements at Shanghai the Eurasian community is in the process of being absorbed into the very mixed population of that cosmopolitan city. The Hanbury School in Shanghai, established originally for Eurasians, has been recently consolidated with the municipal schools for Europeans. There is now or was a few years ago a Eurasian Mission and Sunday School, the members of which called themselves The Endeavorers.

Most mixed-blood communities, in Africa and Asia, have already achieved a stage of relative stabilization and race mixture has declined. This, however, is not everywhere true. In islands like Reunion, off the east coast of East Africa, in the South Sea Islands, in Samoa, for example, or the Hawaiian Islands of the mid-Pacific, miscegenation is still taking place. This is due in part to the fact that the importation of laborers from China, Japan, the Philippines, and elsewhere has continued until very recently. Now that such importations have ceased, it seems probable that race mixture will measurably decline. At the present time Romanzo Adams estimates that of every hundred births in the Hawaiian Islands thirty are individuals of mixed racial origin.

Not all the racial frontiers are seaport cities. Johannesburg, the capital of the gold region of South Africa, Elizabethville, the center of the Katanga copper mining region in the Belgian Congo, and Nairobi, capital of Kenya, in Central Africa, to which European immigration has turned since the World War, are younger and less important but, in other respects, characteristic frontier cities, in which the typical cycle of race relations has just begun.

Harbin, on the Russian-Chinese border of Manchuria, is notorious as a racial melting pot. Official statistics are not available but a recent

---

a European education whose ordinary vocation would have been a clerical job in a business or government office. Failing this, they were in a way to become outcasts, abandoned by the Europeans and despised by the Indians. A good many of the men who found shelter here were said to be the ne'er-do-well sons of European tea planters in the Darjeeling district.

estimate fixes the number of children of mixed Chinese and Russian parentage, living in the railway zone of Manchuria, at something more than 60,000.[17]

Hybrid peoples are interesting and significant for several reasons: (*a*) because they offer the most obvious and tangible evidence of the extent and character of European cultural contact; (*b*) because their numbers and the particular rôle assigned in the communities in which they live are indices of the character of existing race relations and of the extent to which racial and cultural assimilation between the parent races has taken place. This fact has suggested the possibility, and the desirability, of a miscegenation map of the world which, by locating the places where race mixture has gone on in the past or is now in process, would make it possible to study comparatively the conditions under which the miscegenation and assimilation take place as well as the social and political consequences which accompany them.

There are, of course, consequences in any case when different ethnic groups seek to carry on a common life, whether there is a cultural and racial fusion or not. The history of the Jews, who have preserved their ancient tribal culture during the whole period of their dispersion, testifies to that fact. The Jews have maintained their ethnic unity but always at the cost of living more or less as aliens and strangers in the countries of their adoption. In any case the consequence of a policy or course of action that leads to ultimate assimilation and one designed to preserve the ethnic integrity of a people are profoundly different.[18]

PROCESSES AND TRENDS

A somewhat cursory survey of the conditions under which peoples of obviously mixed blood exist today does not reveal any principle

---

[17] A United press report dated Harbin, Sept. 12, 1929, and published in the *Japan Advertiser*, Sept. 29, makes the following interesting statement in regard to the miscegenation of white and yellow races in northern Manchuria:

"In North Manchuria more than anywhere else in the world, intermarriages are occurring between fair-skinned Russian and deeper hued Chinese. Economic necessity appears to be playing a leading part in bringing the races together."

More than 150,000 White Russians live in the Chinese-Eastern-Railway zone, and nine-tenths of them have been compelled to live for the twelve years since the Russian revolution on the living standard of the Chinese lower classes. The result has been a fusion of races such as seldom has occurred anywhere else.

[18] It is, of course, true that the Jews like every other people are racially mixed. However, they are an endogamous group and have preserved to a remarkable extent their ancient tribal traditions and culture.

which permits a wholly satisfactory explanation of their present status or of the tendencies which control their destinies.

On the basis, however, of what is known one may venture to formulate a few general hypotheses.

1. Miscegenation takes place most readily and rapidly upon the frontiers. It takes place among primitive people when their tribal organizations have been undermined by slavery or by sudden incorporation, in some other way, into the industrial systems of more highly civilized peoples. It occurs in the early period of any invasion of an alien population before stable conditions and a normal distribution of the sexes has been achieved.

2. The progeny of these early intermixtures, unless they are promptly absorbed into one or the other of the parent stocks, tend by inbreeding to amalgamate and to create thus a relatively homogeneous racial stock which with time tends to assume the character of a new race and a new people, with traditions and institutions peculiarly its own. Actually it becomes a "racial minority" which in its relations with the racial majority tends to assume the character of: (*a*) a caste or (*b*) a nationality.

3. One principle which seems to have been everywhere operative in determining the amount of miscegenation that anywhere exists, as well as the various permutations and patterns of race relations dependent on it, has been the principle of hypergamy, as it is called in India. This is a rule which in Hindu law prescribes that a woman may only marry into a caste that is equal to, or higher than, the one in which she was born.

It is the ambition of every Hindu family that its daughters should, where humanly possible, marry up. From the point of view of the caste system, it is inconceivable that any woman, if she marries out of the caste or subcaste in which she was born, should ever marry down. As the possibilities of marrying under the caste system are limited in any case, and as the possibilities of marrying up are still more restricted, it often happens that the head of an Indian household will go to extravagant lengths and indulge in ruinous expenditure to secure for the daughter of the family a dowry which will insure her not only a suitable but a desirable marriage.[19]

The principle which is thus recognized in Hindu custom and law seems to be a principle in human nature—one of those principles which operates spontaneously and needs no formal legislation to insure its

[19] H. H. Risley, *The People of India.*

enforcement. It is the principle which is represented in the familiar phrase: "How would you like to have your daughter marry a Negro?"—a phrase which possibly has its counterpart elsewhere. In orthodox Jewish circles, it would probably take the form: "Do you want your daughter to marry a *Goy?*" In any case, whatever form it assumes in any given society, this is a question that is invariably the touchstone and final criterion in determining what restrictions it is necessary to impose on race relations where they involve any sort of intimate contact. It suggests, and fairly demonstrates, the inconceivability of a parent's permitting the marriage of a daughter to a man of a class or caste beneath him.

The same question when applied to a son is not so convincing. It is curious that this should be so, in view of the fact that almost everywhere, outside the United States or other countries where frontier traditions obtain, sons are regarded as a more important family possession than daughters.

If the principle of hypergamy prevails even where it is not expressly formulated in law or custom, it is not because women are less venturesome than men in matrimonial choices but because they are more controlled and protected.

Romantic interest invariably attaches to the strange, the distant, and unfamiliar, and the disposition of men to go abroad for wives and of women to welcome these roving strangers is probably part of original nature. Human beings are naturally exogamous. Endogamy, on the contrary, has grown up in the interest of the family, the clan, and the community.[20]

One consequence of this principle of hypergamy is that in a society where a caste system, or something approaching it, prevails there is always a tendency on the part of the women of the lower

---

[20] The ultimate source of the rule of hypergamy seems to be the possessive attitude of the male toward the female. It is partly chivalry. He wants to protect her and he is not willing to delegate this office to any other male. If he finally does consent to do so, it will be under conditions that he himself imposes or accepts. Fielding's novel *Tom Jones* offers some testimony, by a keen analyst of human nature, on this subject. The manner in which Squire Western finally hands over his daughter Sophia to Fielding's hero Tom Jones is a naïve but typical expression of the male attitude. The Squire had resisted Tom's courtship of his daughter through many chapters of a racy narrative. At the end, however, he is compelled to capitulate. Once the thing was finally settled, however, the Squire is as impatient as any lover to have the marriage consummated, and he announces his purpose with the hearty and somewhat naïve comment: "d'n me, if he [Tom] shan't have the tousling her."

caste to become the concubines of the men in the higher caste. These were the conditions under which, during the period of slavery in the United States, a system of concubinage grew up which was connected with the famous Quadroon Balls of New Orleans. The situation is succinctly stated in an introductory essay to an anthology of Afro-French poetry in Louisiana by Edward Larocque Tinker:

> The position of these women in the society of their day was anomalous. They formed a separate class halfway between the Whites and the Negroes. They could not marry white men, for caste prejudice was all-powerful and was reinforced by drastic laws against miscegenation, so the women, as their mothers had before them, took the only course open and became the mistresses of white men. They had their own social existence and amusements, the most famous of which were the Quadroon Balls given in the old *Salle d'Orleans,* which is now, oddly enough, a convent housing colored nuns.[21]

No such institution exists among the Cape colored people in South Africa, but it is notorious that colored women are disposed to live as concubines of white men, and sometimes of Indians, when law or custom does not permit them to marry.

If the principle of hypergamy operates to intensify the tendency to miscegenation in a settled community where the normal balance of the sexes prevails, one can understand how it has operated under frontier conditions, where the number of males in the invading population invariably outnumbers the females.

On the other hand, as frontier conditions pass and the normal balance of the sexes is restored, the interests of traditional and established society reassert themselves, and the interests of individuals are subordinated to the vested interests of the family and the community.

4. Generally speaking, half-caste peoples are city folk. This is true in the Orient where the Eurasians are the by-products of the foreign settlements. It is true, likewise, in the United States, where the statistics of migration show that the mulattoes have invariably been the first to move from the plantations to the towns and from the towns to the northern cities.

Generally speaking, also, the mixed blood is the more mobile man. He is at the same time likely to be intellectually the more alert and emotionally the more responsive. This may be a matter of tempera-

---

[21] Edward Larocque Tinker, "Les Cenelles, Afro-French Poetry in Louisiana," *The Colophon,* September, 1930. See also Frederick L. Olmsted, *Seaboard Slave States,* pp. 243-248.

ment. It is at any rate a fact that mixed bloods do gravitate to the cities, and particularly to the great cities, which have always been the final refuge of the detribalized, denationalized, and emancipated, and of that particular type of man elsewhere referred to by the author as the "marginal man," that is to say, the individual whose fate is to be born into, and to live on, the margins of two cultures.[22]

The marginal man migrates to the city because he finds there an opportunity to play the rôle for which, if he is a mixed blood, his racial origin has predestined him, namely, the rôle of an intermediary and interpreter between the two races and the two cultures, represented so often in his own person.

He finds there, also, an opportunity to gain an European education which is for him a prime necessity if he is to continue to enjoy the position between the European and the native which he has so long occupied and to which he clings so tenaciously—the anomalous position of a man born in a country of which he is never quite a native nor yet a citizen.[23]

Anthropologists have noted the fact that the points at which different culture areas intersect are often, if not always, the points at which new centers and new cultures arise. As far as this is anywhere true it is probably due to the fact that points of contact beween peoples of divergent cultures are inevitably the loci of the greatest cultural ferment and fusion. In the modern world the points of contact between the civilizations of the Orient and the Occident— between the old world and the new—are the great metropolitan cities, where peoples from the antipodes meet to compete and co-operate in the vast collective enterprise of international commerce. It is here that a new civilization world wide and without local boundaries seems to be coming into existence.[24]

---

[22] Robert E. Park, "Human Migration and the Marginal Man," *The American Journal of Sociology*, 33 (1928), 882-883.

[23] The legal status of the Anglo-Indian was defined by the Under Secretary of State at India in 1925 as follows:

"For purposes of employment under the Government, and inclusion in schemes of Indianization, members of the Anglo-Indian and Domiciled European Community are statutory natives of India. For purposes of education and internal security, their status in so far as it admits of definition approximates that of European British subjects."—*Report of the Indian Statutory Commission*, 17, 527.

[24] "The great fact of the twentieth century is the definite emergence of a new type of civilization different from anything that the world has known hitherto. All through the nineteenth century the new forces which were to transform human life were already at work, but their real tendency was to a great extent

It is significant, therefore, that the mixed bloods, like all other racial and cultural minorities, looking across national boundaries for moral support and protection against the aggressions of a sometimes fanatical nationalism, invariably trend to these centers of a new and cosmopolitan civilization.

The Jews, who have been described in Germany as a "permanent minority," are the historical and classical example.[25]

A more thorough investigation of the facts would probably show that minorities, racial cultural, and national, have always sought the freedom and protection of the more inclusive imperium. The political power of the British Empire in its Dominions and in India—a candidate for Dominion status—rests very largely upon the racial, national, and cultural minorities in those territories. The little states of Europe are the most vigorous supports of the League of Nations. The continued existence of the British Empire is probably dependent upon its ability to transform itself into a league of independent states. On the other hand, divergences of race may make that impossible.

---

veiled by current modes of thought and preconceived ideas which had their origin in political and philosophical doctrines. The mind of the nineteenth century was dominated by the ideals of Nationalism and Liberalism, and the actual process of social and economic change was interpreted in terms of these doctrines. In reality, however, the forces that were at work were only partially amenable to such theories; in many respects they were moving in a contrary direction.

"Thus, while the peoples of Europe were consciously accentuating their national idiosyncrasies and their political independence, they were at the same time becoming more and more alike in their customs, their ideas, and their whole apparatus of material culture. At the same time, they were losing their economic self-sufficiency and being drawn into the meshes of a supernational industrial and commercial system, which transcends political frontiers and renders each people dependent on the rest for the very necessities of material existence."—Christopher Dawson, *Enquiries into Religion and Culture*, p. 3.

[25] Max Hindebert Boehn, "National Minorities," *Encyclopaedia of the Social Sciences*, X, 518-524.

CHAPTER 9

OUR RACIAL FRONTIER ON THE PACIFIC

"The race relations cycle—contact, competition, accommodation and eventual assimilation—is apparently progressive and irreversible"

WHAT is taking place around the Pacific is what took place some centuries ago around the Mediterranean; what took place a little later around the Atlantic. A new civilization, or, as Ramsay Traquair puts it, a new Commonwealth of the Pacific is coming into existence. For civilization is not, as some writers seem to believe, a biological, but a social, product. It is an effect of the coming together for trade and for intercourse of divergent races of divergent cultures.

We may observe the effect of this impact of divergent peoples and cultures around the whole rim of the Pacific, as well as in the scattered islands that lie within its wide circumference. The present ferment in Asia and the racial conflict on the Pacific Coast of America are but different manifestations of what is, broadly speaking, a single process; a process which we may expect to continue until some sort of permanent equilibrium has been established between the races and peoples on both sides of the oceans.

In the course of the long struggle which began with the Sand Lot riots in 1876, and ended with the Exclusion Law of 1924, the Pacific Coast has formulated a policy with reference to the peoples of the Pacific, the effect of which is to set the people of Asia apart from the people of Europe and the rest of the world. This policy, now formally written into the federal statutes and supported by a long series of legislative enactments and court decisions, has come to have something of the character, in so far as it represents the deliberate

Survey Graphic IX (May, 1926), pp. 192-196.

intention of the American people, of a constitutional enactment. These laws have created on our Western Coast a barrier to immigration that is distinctly racial. Its purpose is not merely to limit but to stop immigration from Asia. It is as if we had said: Europe, of which after all America is a mere western projection, ends here. The Pacific Coast is our racial frontier.

All the problems of the Pacific tend to focus about this racial barrier. Will it be maintained? What will be its reflex influence upon Asia? Will it tend in the long run to give Japan the hegemony of Asia? What effect will the inhibition of Asiatic immigration have upon international commerce? Will it hasten the industrialization of Asia, now well under way? Will it give Asiatic states a common cause sufficient to guarantee united political action? Incidentally, it may be said that if America, the front door of Europe, is closed to Asiatic immigration, Russia, the back door, is wide open.

What follows is not to be regarded as an attempt to answer the questions raised. Most of them are, for the moment, probably quite unanswerable. It is intended rather to serve the purpose of what in natural science is called a *frame of reference;* it is intended to define the problem; to indicate the limits within which it is possible to think and estimate the consequences of specific acts and specific tendencies.

What are races and what are racial relations which racial barriers seek to regulate?

I. GEOGRAPHY AND RACE RELATIONS

Race relations are, or were, primarily geographic rather than human and social. The races grew up in isolation and acquired distinct racial characteristcs slowly by adaptation and by inbreeding. Man, like every other animal, has been and is a creature of his environment, even when that environment has consisted largely of other men. Biological and inheritable differences represent man's responses to the kind of world in which he has learned to live. They are, so to speak, his biological capital; the accumulations of successive generations of men in their struggle to live.

The tendency of man to achieve some sort of equilibrium between himself and his environment is constant. But this is merely one instance of that more general tendency which has brought all living things, plant and animal alike, into relations of vital interdependence. This interdependence of all living organisms is what J. Arthur Thomson has described as "the web of life."

So close and complex are the relations of man and his living environment that the introduction of a new insect or the extermination of an existing micro-organism may change the course of history. It was not until the American Yellow Fever Commission of 1900 discovered the "yellow fever" mosquito, the *aedes calopus*, that the completion of the Panama Canal, which had cost the French government nearly two million francs and an unestimated number of human lives, was rendered practicable.

If it is impossible to predict the ultimate consequences of the migrations of organisms so minute and seemingly insignificant, it is certain that we cannot estimate the remote effects upon human life and human relations of the vaster and more subversive migrations of man. And this is true for one reason if for no other—because man is himself a carrier of disease.

Steamships and railways have effectually altered the geography of the world, and the barriers which formerly protected the races from one another have been swept away. With the multiplication of modern means of transportation, and with the increasing movement and migration of peoples, no part of the world is so remote from one another as to be secure from the invasion of the diseases of which man is the principal carrier.

Under these conditions race relations take the very elementary form of biological competition, which means the struggle to determine, within any geographical area, which race and which races are to survive. Some races have already disappeared, others are dying. The Moravians, the oldest and the most zealous of missionary denominations, maintain a mission devoted to the dying races. Most of these dying races are located on the inlands of the Pacific—Polynesia and Melanesia—or in the countries bordering it.

Back of every other objection and prejudice of the people of the Pacific Coast to oriental immigration is the desire to survive. They see the older New England stocks being replaced by French-Canadians and Slavs; they do not want to see the Native Sons of the Pacific replaced by Asiatics.

The fact is that for almost the first time in history the world has become "race conscious." We have in the past sought immortality in various ways, in our family and our clan, in our tribe and in our nation. Now we are seeking it in that somewhat mythical entity that we call race.

II. RACE RELATIONS AND WORLD ECONOMY

If racial differences are the effects of geography and isolation, civilization, on the other hand, seems to be a product of contact and communication. Every civilization, in extending the area of human intercourse, has invariably brought about new concentrations of population and a new intermingling of races.

This means that in the long run it is difficult if not impossible to maintain, in America or elsewhere, racial frontiers. All the deeper currents of modern life run counter to a policy of racial or national isolation.

One thing that has invariably tended to widen the circle of human relationship has been the very natural desire of individuals and peoples to effect an exchange of goods and services. Just because they are different physically and culturally, the races are useful to one another. The best evidence of this is the enormous expansions in very recent times of international commerce.

The effect of the steady expansion of international commerce has been to create over the whole earth a vast unconscious cooperation of races and peoples, such that a wheat corner in Chicago a few years ago caused a bread riot in Liverpool, and the price of rubber on the London market has been at times a matter of life and death to the native of Central Africa.

This world-wide division of labor, which every new device of transportation and communication has progressively made possible, and every new application of science to industry has made increasingly desirable, has not been effected without some costs and some disorganization of industrial and social life.

The effect upon European agriculture of the growth of railway transportation in America is an illustration in point:

In 1870 the cost of transporting a bushel of grain was so great as to prohibit its sale beyond a radius of two hundred miles from a primary market. By 1883, the importation of grains from the virgin soil of the western prairies in the United States had brought about an agricultural crisis in every country in Western Europe.

The effect of the agricultural crisis in Europe was immediately reflected in the rising tide of immigration to America. If this immigration since 1880 has continued to come in in an increasing degree from southern and southeastern Europe it is because these regions have not developed in the meantime the machine industries and the great cities which have absorbed the population in the northern European States.

What has already taken place in the region around the Atlantic is apparently taking place around the Pacific.

The expansion of trade has been followed by a vast movement of populations. The same motives and the same devices of transportation and communication have mobilized both goods and persons. It is natural enough that the same interests which have led merchants to sell in the highest markets and buy in the lowest, should—once the ties that bind man to the soil are loosened—lead the populations in overcrowded regions, with limited resources, to seek their fortunes, either permanently or temporarily, in the new countries of undeveloped resources.

The motives which have inspired Asiatic migrations are, on the whole, not different from those that have led to similar movements in Europe. Asia is, to be sure, not Europe, and the United States is no longer a country of open resources. Yet the population pressures in Asia, in the long run, provoke the same tendencies and the same migration as population pressures in Europe.

What, under all the circumstances, may we expect of the racial barrier on the Pacific Coast? We do not know as yet how far it will be possible to enforce exclusion regulations. As long as there is work that the immigrant, European or Asiatic, can perform better and more economically than the native population can or will, exclusion laws will make migration more of an adventure but will not wholly inhibit it.

For some years past there has been no adventure that has so inflamed the imagination of the European, and even more of the Asiatic peasant, as the great adventure of migration, and especially migration to America. The files in the offices of the United States inspectors of immigration contain the records of some of the most romantic episodes in the history of smuggling in any country. The earlier records are mainly those of the unsuccessful attempts of Chinese laborers to cross the American border, or they are the records of some enterprising tongman seeking to conduct a Chinese slave girl through the perils of the American customs office. But since the passage of exclusion laws, other races are, in increasing numbers, surreptitiously crossing our borders. A new underground railway has come into existence.

Since the period of the fugitive slaves, there has been no chapter in American history just like it, unless it is that earlier and even more romantic episode of the slave pirates who smuggled African slaves into the United States.

The thing that is significant in this connection is that the competition of goods, which is an effect of foreign trade, tends inevitably to bring about a competition of persons, which is an effect of immigration. Finally, both the movements of goods and of populations seem to be merely aspects of a general tendency to redress the economic balance and to restore the equilibrium between population and food supply, labor and capital, in a world economy.

III. RACE RELATIONS AND WORLD POLITICS

It was inevitable that a world which had become, through the medium of international commerce, an economic unit, should eventually seek to establish a political organization capable of protecting international trade. In order that the continually expanding industrial processes might not be interrupted, it was necessary for the European states to find markets for their manufacturers and secure the sources of raw materials for their industries and for the rapidly increasing populations for which the industrial revolution had made a place.

The result of the colonial wars in Asia and Africa, and of the political maneuvers in Europe, has been to create over and above the economic organization of the world not a super-state, to be sure, but a political organization loose and ill-defined but world-wide. This political organization came into existence first of all as a result of exploration, conquest, and settlement. The two Americas are actually nothing but extensions of Europe, so largely have Europeans displaced with their populations and cultures the native peoples. In other regions— West and Central Africa, for example—political control has taken the form, first, of spheres of influence, and, since the world war, of political mandates. Where Europe has not extended its control by conquest and immigration, or by conquest without immigration, it has established a political control through the medium of international understandings and treaties. Whether we accept the existence of such an international government as the League of Nations, or not, there is no doubt about the actual existence over the whole world of a political organization so complete that any future struggle between the peoples of the world is bound to assume more and more the character of an internecine war.

Within the organism thus established, it was inevitable that there should arise, irrespective of all other interests, a struggle of the subject peoples to be free and of the peoples occupying an inferior position to improve their status. Among the independent peoples, status goes by the name of prestige. For a nation or a people to be without prestige, is to be without status. Among the subject peoples status is defined in terms of independence or self-determination.

In a recent volume dealing with international and interracial relations, Herbert A. Miller has sought to describe what he calls the "oppression psychosis." The oppression pyschosis occurs when the wish or urge for independent action of one group, i.e., race or nationality, is frustrated and inhibited by another. This wish, urge, or will, as he expresses it, is "created to struggle." That is its function. "Opposition stimulates it to struggle harder." At bottom the struggle to maintain national prestige and the struggle for national self-determination are one and the same. They are struggles to gain, to increase and maintain international recognition and status.

One of the evidences of the existence of an international society and an international political order is just this fact of national and racial consciousness. Where nations and races are not at all concerned about their position in the "family of nations," political relations may be said not to exist.

But the demands that one nation, race or people makes upon another for consideration of its interests or recognition of its status are the very stuff of which politics is made. The fact that such demands made by one people are entertained by another implies the existence of an understanding, a law, a code, or rule of some sort, to which either party may appeal. The struggles of peoples and races for independence and self-determination have been, after all, but the struggles for recognition and status in an international or political order that is maintained by the common consent of the peoples involved.

That is the meaning of the nationalist movements which have made so much of the history in Europe during the past seventy-five years. That is the meaning, also, of the rising nationalism in Egypt, in Korea, in India, and in China. India, Korea and the Philippines want independence, or something as near that as it is safe to hope for in an armed world.

China, like Turkey, wants to be mistress in her own house. Japan wants, in the councils of the dominant powers, the status of a political equal.

It is for this reason that Japan insists that Japanese in America should have the same rights and privileges as European immigrants; the right to enter, to settle, and eventually to make her contribution, racial and cultural, to our present "racial and cultural pluralism," to use a phrase which has already gained certain popularity in the United States.

The Japanese government has been very explicit in regard to this matter. In a note of June 4, 1913, the Japanese ambassador declared that in the opinion of the Japanese government:

The provisions of law, under which it is held that Japanese people are not eligible to American citizenship, are mortifying to the government and people of Japan, since the racial distinction inferable from these provisions is hurtful to their just national susceptibility . . . when that distinction is made use of, as in the present case, for the purpose of depriving Japanese subjects of rights and privileges of a civil nature, which are freely granted in the United States to other aliens, it becomes the duty of the Imperial Government, in the interest of the relations of cordial friendship and good understanding between the two countries, to express frankly their conviction that the racial distinction, which at best is inaccurate and misleading, does not afford a valid basis for the discrimination on the subject of land tenure.

The Handbook of International Organizations, published at Geneva in 1923, lists not less than 350 international organizations of various sorts. Of these, at least twenty are either organizations seeking to exercise some sort of political control, or they are organizations which seek to educate and form public opinion in respect to some matter of international importance.

The result of every conference and of every investigation in the field of international relations is to prepare the way for new agreements and new treaties, these being at present the only forms in which international legislation takes place.

With this continuous expansion of international communication and international politics, race relations have ceased to be a domestic problem.

The rigid enforcement of racial distinctions at home leads "oppressed" races to seek alliances abroad. The First Universal Races

Congress, in London, in 1911, is an instance. The Pan-African Congress, which followed, is another. Race has in recent years come to be what religion has always been since the dawn of Christianity, an interest which divides and unites peoples irrespective of national boundaries.

As far as concerns race relations, at any rate, the distinctions which we seek to enforce at home are complicated with the relations which we seek to maintain abroad.

The fact is that races and peoples are coming out of their isolation, whether it be geographical, economic or political. In a world in which every act, every significant gesture, reverberates around the globe, the concept of national independence, in the sense in which that word was once used, becomes a mere legal fiction.

IV. RACE RELATIONS AND THE MELTING POT

The distances which in the past have separated peoples and races have been not only physical, but moral and social. The races have looked at one another invariably with curiosity, but they have not always understood what was behind the faces into which they looked. The sense of distance has made them wary, and often a little lonely, in one another's company.

Social distances maintain themselves longest, but eventually they, too, give way. One of the means by which this change has been effected in recent times has been by the rapid increase in literacy among the masses of the people in all parts of the world. "In the great centers of Islamic life," it is said, "the shrill call of the newsboy is as much a part of daily life as the sonorous cry from the minaret," and in the gulf ports of Iran the most popular literature is likely to be a translation of a penny dreadful published in London. The introduction of universal education in Japan, the reform and simplification of the written language in China, and the multiplication of newspapers and journals in both countries, have opened for great masses of people new windows upon a world no longer bounded by the horizon of their earlier villages. The expansion of commerce and the rise of great cities have likewise accelerated the movement. The growth of literacy seems to run parallel to the growth of cities. In the cities, literacy ceases to be a mere luxury for a special class of intellectuals, and becomes a necessity for the common man. The common man cannot keep pace with the changes in modern life; he can not know how to use the new mechanical devices which are constantly multiplying, unless he knows how to read. The amount of knowledge the ordinary man must have in the modern world in order to live, requires that he be able to get it through the printed page rather than by mere rule of thumb or oral tradition, as he used to do.

An incidental consequence of the extension of international trade and travel has been to extend vastly the use of these European languages which have become the medium of international communication in business, in politics, and in science; namely, English, French and German.

Just as there is a struggle, silent and often unnoticed, to determine what races shall survive, and what places, occupations and states they shall have in the new world society, so there is competition among the great world-languages to determine what form of speech shall survive and become the accepted medium of communication in what Graham Wallas calls The Great Society.

Life is more than food and shelter. Human beings, when they live at all, live in their memories and in their imaginations; in their hopes and their dreams. The ability to read, to gain visual impressions through photographs of other lands and other peoples; to learn through literature something of motives and human passions behind their strange exteriors, has enormously intensified the curiosity of every part of the world in regard to every other. These vicarious experiences have aroused new hopes, new ambitions, and stimulated the desire to travel and seek new adventures, in new and strange worlds.

This is today the most romantic period in the history of the whole world; not even the period of the discovery of America has influenced man's imagination more. And, still more significant, this flair for adventure in the modern world has not merely taken possession of the upper classes, the literati and the intellectuals, but has penetrated to the great masses of the people who in previous generations, and until very recent years, have been living in the peaceful seclusion of their peasant communities.

Migration has had the effect of an emancipation, upon most of the immigrant peoples. But books and literature have greatly enhanced the effects of these migrations. And now the printing-press has been supplemented by the cinema and the radio. The American films, with their realistic and thrilling pictures of American life, have transmitted to the Orient some of the restlessness and romanticism of the Occident. Particularly in the outlying regions and among the common people, where America is more a legendary place than it is elsewhere, the effect of the American movies has been more devastating than elsewhere.

A few years ago the average man in China and in Japan got his most lively conceptions of America from two sources: the returned immigrant and the missionary. From the former, America acquired the title "the mountain of gold." From the latter, the oriental students sometimes gained the impression that America was a nation of missionaries. These sources of information have since been superseded by a press founded more or less upon western models; a press, at any rate, that is directed more or less to an understanding of the common man. But, as Walter B. Pitkin has pointed out, in discussing Japanese-American relations, the news despatches are no longer the most important sources of knowledge and understanding of the Occident by the Orient. "They are," he says, "little more than confirmatory of hypotheses which they [the Japanese] derive from another source so much more widely known in the islands, so vivid, and so copious that every other channel of knowledge has become petty in comparison. This source is the American motion-picture."

The films exported to Asia, to the West Indies, and to South America are largely of two classes: those which have failed in America because they were inferior, and, as Pitkin puts it, are "dumped on the helpless heathen, who can pay only the lowest rentals, and hence ought not to expect much," or they are films that have never been exhibited in America because they were forbidden by the board of censors. "The mildest description of these films," he says, "is unfit to print. Yet missionaries and business men both testify that they are being shown regularly in all the larger cities of Asia, and a high official of the government of India personally told me that the effect of these loathsome displays on the natives of that country was so evil that plans for a severe censorship were being considered, especially against what Asia knows as the American film." In Japan a censorship has already been established, and a similar censorship would be established in China, I am told, if China were master of her own house.

The cinema may be regarded as the symbol of a new dimension of our international and racial relations which is neither economic nor political, but cultural. But culture is merely the objective and collective aspect of the inner and personal life of individuals and peoples, and it is in men's minds and in their intimate personal experiences that the most profound and significant changes in the world are taking place today. It is in the obscure, dream-haunted recesses of our inner lives that the future of the world is taking form and shape.

As long as races and peoples remained imprisoned within the limits of their differing languages; as long as we knew them only through records of their overt acts, communication was difficult and understanding not always possible. But the silent drama is now bringing the great masses of peoples, who have known each other only indirectly and at second hand, face to face. In the movies we see strange peoples in action, and these actions reveal to us behind their alien manners and foreign faces, passions that we can both understand and share; motives that we admire or fear or hate.

It is impossible to estimate at the present time the consequences which the realism of the motion pictures is likely to bring about in the relations of races and peoples. It has at least brought the ends of the earth into an intimacy unimaginable a few years ago. In this intimacy all that was individual, strange and peculiar in the customs and manners of different races and peoples has been brought into solution and is in process of change. If America was once in any exclusive sense the melting pot of races, it is so no longer. The melting pot is the world.

The really new factors in international and race relations are the devices like the cinema and the radio; these, with the rapidly increasing literacy, are steadily bringing all the peoples of the earth measurably within the limits of a common culture and a common historical life.

V. THE RACE RELATIONS CYCLE

The impression that emerges from this review of international and race relations is that the forces which have brought about the existing interpenetration of peoples are so vast and irresistible that the resulting changes assume the character of a cosmic process. New means of communication enforce new contacts and result in new forms of competition and of conflict. But out of this confusion and ferment, new and more intimate forms of association arise.

The changes which are taking place on the Pacific Coast—"the last asylum," in the language of Professor Ross, "of the native-born"—are part of the changes that are going on in every other part of the world. Everywhere there is competion and conflict; but everywhere the intimacies which participation in a common life enforces have created new accommodation, and relations which were merely formal or utilitarian have become personal and human.

In the relations of races there is a cycle of events which tends everywhere to repeat itself. Exploration invariably opens new regions for commercial exploitation; the missionary, as has frequently been said, becomes the advance agent of the trader. The exchange of commodities involves in the long run the competition of goods and of persons. The result is a new distribution of population and a new and wider division of labor.

The new economic organization, however, inevitably becomes the basis for a new political order. The relations of races and people are never for very long merely economic and utilitarian, and no efforts to conceive them in this way have ever been permanently successful. We have imported labor as if it were mere commodity, and sometimes we have been disappointed to find, as we invariably do, that the laborers were human like ourselves. In this way it comes about that race relations which were economic become later political and cultural. The struggle for existence terminates in a struggle for status, for recognition, for position and prestige, within an existing political and moral order. Where such a political and moral order does not exist, war, which is the most elementary expression of political forces, creates one. For the ultimate effect of war has been, on the whole, to establish and extend law and order in regions where it did not previously exist.

The race relations cycle which takes the form, to state it abstractly, of contacts, competition, accommodation and eventual assimilation, is apparently progressive and irreversible. Customs regulations, immigration restrictions and racial barriers may slacken the tempo of the movement; may perhaps halt it altogether for a time; but cannot change its direction; cannot at any rate, reverse it.

In our estimates of race relations we have not reckoned with the effects of personal intercourse and the friendships that inevitably grow up out of them. These friendships, particularly in a democratic society like our own, cut across and eventually undermine all the barriers of racial segregation and caste by which races seek to maintain their integrity.

It was the intimate and personal relations which grew up between the Negro slave and his white master that undermined and weakened the system of slavery from within, long before it was attacked from without. Evidence of this was the steady increase, in spite of public opinion and legislation to the contrary, of the number of free Negroes and emancipated slaves in the South. Men who believed the black man fore-ordained to be the servant of the white were unwilling to leave the servants they knew to the mercy of the system when they were no longer able to protect them.

In spite of the bitter antagonism that once existed toward the Chinese, the attitude of the Pacific coast is now generally amiable, even indulgent; and this in spite of the nuisance of their tong wars and other racial eccentricities. The Chinese population is slowly declining in the United States, but San Francisco, at any rate, will miss its Chinese quarter when it goes.

There has never been the antagonism toward the Japanese in this country that there once was toward the Chinese. Even such antagonism as existed has always been qualified by a genuine admiration for the Japanese people as a whole. Now that the exclusion law seems finally to have put an end to Japanese immigration, there is already a disposition to relax the laws which made the permanent settlement of Orientals on the Pacific coast untenable.

It does not follow that because the tendencies to the assimilation and eventual amalgamation of races exist, they should not be resisted and, if possible, altogether inhibited. On the other hand, it is vain to underestimate the character and force of the tendencies that are drawing the races and peoples about the Pacific into the ever narrowing circle of a common life. Rising tides of color and oriental exclusion laws are merely incidental evidences of these diminishing distances.

In the Hawaiian Islands, where all the races of the Pacific meet and mingle on more liberal terms than they do elsewhere, the native races are disappearing and new peoples are coming into existence. Races and cultures die—it has always been so—but civilization lives on.

CHAPTER 10

EXPERIENCE AND RACE RELATIONS

Opinion Attitudes, and Experience as Types of Human Behavior

EXPERIENCE DEFINED

IN THE STUDY of race relations, we are concerned with more than the formal facts. We are concerned with experiences and with the personal reactions of individuals and races.

It is not sufficient to know what happened; we want to know how the transaction looked through the eyes of individuals seeing it from opposing points of view. If there were not racial points of view there would be no race problems.

What is experience? How shall we distinguish experience from other forms of knowledge? The same experiences may be data for both the historian and the sociologist, but these different sciences deal with these data differently. How differently and why?

Experience, in the limited sense in which we ordinarily use that term, as distinguished from other forms of knowledge, is concrete, personal, and unique. To say that it is personal is merely to say that it is the result of action rather than reflection. We may describe experience, from this point of view, as James Harvey Robinson has described history, as "the reaction of man's instincts and traditions to new conditions." [1]

To say on the other hand that experience is unique is merely to

---

[1] See *Saturday Review of Literature*, August 9, 1924, "These Eventful Years," James Harvey Robinson.

say that experiences do not repeat themselves. We sometimes say that we had today the same experience that we did yesterday or a week before. This, however, is never quite accurate. We never have the same experience twice. An experience is like an historical fact; it always has a date and a location and it happens only once. Ideas on the other hand, as Plato first of all observed, are timeless and not located.

Experience is not fact, not even historical fact. It is merely A's or B's personal reaction to, and interpretation of, an event. Until A's experience has been checked up with B's and with C's experiences of the same event we would not call it an historical fact.

WHERE HISTORY AND SOCIOLOGY PART

This is, however, just the point of view at which the historian and the sociologist part company. The historian is quite as interested in the experiences of individuals, and groups of individuals, as is the sociologist, but for a somewhat different reason. The historian wants to know what actually happened. His material is, to be sure, the *naïve* narratives of the persons participating in the transaction. Out of this mass of circumstance he seeks to disentangle and interpret the actual transaction.

The sociologist is not primarily concerned with the event itself. He rather takes that for granted. What he is more particularly concerned about are the attitudes of the persons involved, as they are reflected in their very differing accounts of the same historical event. He is interested in anything, in fact, that will throw light upon these attitudes and make them intelligible. It is just this difference in the points of view of the different groups,—racial and political,—that he seeks to discover and record. It is not the event but the attitude—the individual or the group mind—that the sociologist, as distinguished from the historian, is seeking to describe and explain.

For that reason, any expression of those different points of view, whether it pretends to be fact or not, just so long as it fairly reflects the sentiments and attitudes, is interesting and important.

MYTH AND LEGEND AS SOCIOLOGICAL DATA

Much that the historian might characterize as myth and legend; much that is pure poetry, even gossip, so far as it reflects the dominant attitude of the races and parties involved, may furnish material for the student of race relations—may, in fact, furnish material for the student of society. What is society, finally, but just this whole vast complex of human relations in which parties, races, and nations are involved?

The value of "experiences" to the sociologist is then that they are the sources, not the only, but perhaps the best, from which the student can gain a knowledge and an understanding of the attitudes of strange and unassimilated peoples.

Attitudes, however, are not opinions. An individual's own account of his attitude is his opinion; but opinions are after all largely what the psycho-analysists call a "rationalization." They are his explanations and justifications of his attitudes, rather than his actual "tendencies to act."

It is certain, at least, that every man's opinion becomes more intelligible if we know the particular circumstances under which it was conceived; particularly if we know also, the circumstances that have reaffirmed and intensified it. It is for this reason that, in studying opinions, we seek to go back to the point of genesis, seek to define the concrete circumstances under which opinions took form, and the motives which inspired them. Knowing these things we may say we not only *know* an opinion but we *understand* it. An opinion becomes intelligible in one sense at least, not when we approve of it, but when, knowing the *circumstances*, we are able to appreciate the motives that inspired it.

WHAT IS MEANT BY MAKING OPINIONS

To make an opinion intelligible in the sense here indicated is to discover and describe the concrete experiences in which it is imbedded. There is always some sort of complex behind every motor tendency, every motor tendency that is not a mere reflex.

To make an attitude intelligible it is necessary to study its natural history; to reproduce the circumstances under which it arose so completely that the observer can enter imaginatively into the situation and the experience of which the attitude is a part. This, at any rate, is the first step.

Reproducing an experience in such a way that it can be made an object of observation involves what Ellwood calls "sympathetic introspection." Let us see how this reproduction, and the subsequent *interpretation* and *explanation*, actually take place. The experience *contains*, so to speak, both the event and the attitude. As students of race-relations we are not concerned primarily with the event. The event is what actually happened.

What actually happened is a matter for historical investigation. What the student of race-relations wants to know is: (1) the social situation, (2) the individual's reaction in that situation, as reflected in his experience.

What is a social situation? Well, it is always something more general than an historical situation. I may begin a narrative by saying: "I once had the experience of an earthquake in Java." The social situation here is defined by "earthquake," not by the fact that it was in Java, although the fact that it took place in Java may be found later to introduce some important modification in the situation that it is necessary to take account of. However, in general this is an "earthquake situation" and I go on to tell how I felt and acted in that situation.

Some one else relates a similar experience. The two experiences are different but they have points of comparison. The student of human nature is interested in this comparison, in the similarities and in the differences. He gathers from a comparison of these experiences something about the way people in general behave in earthquakes.

Here again the sociologist parts company with the historian. The historian is interested in these generalizations about human nature in so far as they enable him to determine just what actually happened in a given place and at a given date. The historian *interprets* the experience. The sociologist is interested in the particular experience only so far as it enables him to say something about human nature in general, irrespective of any particular time or place. The sociologist classifies the experience and so *explains* it. Let us return for a moment to our earthquake in Java.

If the experiences in the earthquake are peculiar and quite foreign to ordinary experiences, the student may want to gather a number of cases to see how true to type the individual cases are. Having found the type, he is interested mainly in the variations from it. The question he asks is: Taking account of the variations in the situation, how far can they be reduced to certain general types?

The procedure here is just the same as in any of the natural and explanatory sciences. We explain things by putting them under some general category, classifying them, in short, and then discovering where we can, the reason for the deviation from type.

Of course, the situation cannot always be defined so simply and so explicitly as we have sought to do here. It might be described, for example, as "earthquake plus fire, general terror, and crowd excitement." The crowd excitement might have so intensified the reaction as to almost totally change it.

Most of the experiences of the alien and oriental population will fall under certain general and familiar categories, there will be certain modifications that need to be explained by further observation and analysis. The presumption is that they will be explained by differences in the situation. These differences may be (1) the physical appearance of the Oriental, (2) his traditions, (3) minor changes in the situation defined by time, place, and circumstance.

TYPICAL EXPERIENCES

The general assumption is that experiences are likely to be more intelligible than opinions, which are the inferences we draw from them. If we are able to reproduce the experience we will be able to appreciate the motives and share the feelings that entered into them. Ordinarily the behavior of another individual becomes intelligible as soon as we are able to reproduce all the circumstances, including perhaps the previous history of the individual involved.

Ordinarily explanation of an experience does not mean more than such an imaginative reproduction of it. If the thing is still strange, if it is still unintelligible, we need more details and we ask further questions. If, however, we can bring ourselves to feel how, under the circumstances, we might have behaved the same way: as soon, in short, as we can reduce this new and strange experience to some pattern that we are familiar with, it becomes intelligible.

The fact is, however, that as soon as we are able imaginatively to reproduce an experience, we have already classified it. Our general class or category, under which the particular experience is subserved, may be explicitly stated, may in fact be quite below the level of clear consciousness—still it is there and functions as a category.

When the class or general pattern under which the particular experience is subserved is explicitly stated, we have an explanation of the experience in the more formal sense of that word.

We may re-state the matter this way: We explain opinions when we refer them to the attitudes of which they are a rationalization. We make attitudes intelligible when we are able to reproduce the experiences, in which they are imbedded. We explain experiences as we are able to reduce them to general types—types of human behavior —where behavior includes not merely the external act but the feelings ordinarily associated with it.

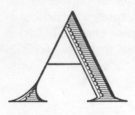 RACE RELATIONS

SURVEY

*Suggestions for a Study of the Oriental Population
of the Pacific Coast*

I

THE PROBLEM DEFINED

THERE have been two, perhaps three, previous studies that clearly fall within the field of "race relations" as the term is here used. The first was made by Ray Stannard Baker for the *American Magazine*, and was subsequently published in the volume, *Following the Color Line*. The occasion of this investigation was the Atlanta riot of September, 1906.

In this study Mr. Baker sought first of all to go behind the newspaper reports and investigate the events that led up to the catastrophe. But he did more; he sought to discover what were the conditions which made such an outbreak of elemental passions possible. His researches took him a long way and his report is not merely the first authentic account of a race riot, but the first disinterested study of the peculiar character of the racial relations under which these social eruptions arise.

Thirteen years later a second and somewhat similar investigation was undertaken under the auspices of the Chicago Commission on Race Relations, appointed by Governor Lowden to investigate and

Journal of Applied Sociology, VIII (1923), pp. 195-205. EDITORIAL NOTE: This paper was written in answer to the question: "What is a Survey of Race Relations?" It is a tentative outline, intended to indicate and emphasize what is, perhaps, novel and unusual in studies of this kind, rather than an attempt to offer a complete outline for such studies.

report on the causes of the Chicago race riot of July 27, 1919. This is probably the most complete and thoroughgoing study of any racial group that has yet been made in the United States.

Race conflicts have their biological and economic aspects but it is the attitudes that they express and provoke which are of first importance.

The Chicago report is unique in one respect: more than any previous study it has succeeded (a) in uncovering the sources of racial friction, and (b) in showing the effects of these sometimes obscure irritations upon public opinion.

Modern medicine has made us familiar with the fact that the aches and pains from which we suffer are frequently due to infection from unsuspected sources. A pain in the back may lead a physician to examine the patient's teeth and tonsils. It is possibly true that many of the ills and pains of which the community complains have a more obvious origin, but human nature is quite as complicated as physical nature, and quite as much in need of study and observation. For this reason, a Race Relations Survey, whatever else it may be, will inevitably turn out to be a study of public opinion.

Other investigations which fall in this field are studies in Americanization, like those made a few years ago under the direction of Allen T. Burns. These studies attempt to throw light upon the processes by which the foreign-born and their descendants are incorporated into the economic life and the social traditions of American communities. The problems of the European and the Asiatic, though different in certain respects, are enough alike to be comparable.

What is then the specific problem with which a survey of race relations is concerned? Briefly stated, it is the problem which arises from the difficulty, if not the impossibility, of peoples of a markedly different racial type, as well as standards of living, entering freely, and without conflict, into the competitive cooperation of an individualistic and democratic society; that is to say, a society in which there are no generally recognized castes or class distinctions by which free competition is restricted. Competition is used here broadly to include not mere economic competition but competition in the indirect sense of that word—the struggle for existence of races and peoples.

The Oriental, partly because of his language, but more particularly because of his color, and other physical characteristics, is a marked man. Like the Negro, he wears a racial uniform which he cannot lay aside. The effect of this is to intensify racial consciousness, both in himself and in the community of which he seeks to be a part. Race consciousness, in turn, produces racial segregation. It tends to set the yellow, as it has the black, man socially and economically apart from the other peoples among whom he seeks to live. The result is that the Oriental, like the Negro, rarely attains to a position where he is accepted simply on his merits, as an individual. On the contrary, he is invariably regarded as a representative of his race. Under these circumstances, outside of his own racial group, he almost ceases to be a person: he is likely to be regarded as another example of the species merely. And this, in turn, accounts for the fact that competition between Orientals and Occidentals ceases to be individual and personal and becomes impersonal and racial.

Racial competition leads easily, and more or less inevitably to racial conflict. The only situation in which the Oriental is able to live without prejudice is in some occupation in which he does not come into too direct competition with other members of the community. This exclusion, although not always formally and legally recognized, is enforced by the prejudices and public opinion that racial conflict engenders.

These seem, in general, to be the inevitable tendencies of the racial situation, and the problem for investigation is to discover how far, in spite of them, the different immigrant races, because of their differences in culture or organization, have been able successfully to accommodate themselves in the local communities in which they live.

The problem thus defined in terms of economic competition has its reverberations in political and in social life. All these are necessarily part of an investigation which seeks, not merely to describe but to explain, in terms of fundamental human nature, the existing race relations.

II

MATERIALS WANTED

Materials for the study of any immigrant group may be classified under four general headings:

1. Geographical distribution of racial groups i.e., Orientals, Mexicans, etc., (a) on the land, (b) in cities.

It is important to note (1) the changes in distribution of the different racial groups within the limits of the period within which each group has been a factor in the industrial life of the community, (2) present tendencies, (3) movement to or from the cities, or from one rural area to another.

Maps should eventually be made of the agricultural areas in which the races to be studied are settled. These maps should distinguish the type of organization of the agriculture in each area.

    (a) Kind of agricultural product, i.e., citrous fruits, vegetables, etc.

    (b) Irrigated and non-irrigated lands

    (c) Large estates, resident owners

    (d) Large estates, tenant farmers

    (e) Small farms

A series of maps will make it possible to visualize these facts for different periods, exhibiting at the same time, (a) changes that have taken place in the organization of the industry and, (b) present tendencies.

Maps for cities should indicate to what extent the various racial groups are segregated and isolated, delineating, where possible, residential and business areas.

2. Division of Labor, i.e., occupations of the different Oriental and competing immigrant groups.

    (a) First occupations

    (b) Changes in occupations

    (c) Occupations now dominant

    (d) Present tendencies

    (e) Extent to which business of Orientals is limited to members of their own race.

3. Competition, Conflict and Accommodation.

    (a) With what native American groups are the immigrant races in competition: that is, as laborers, tenant farmers, land owners, business men, etc.?

    (b) When and where have conflicts arisen: that is, where has complaint been made, and what, in general, has been the character of the complaints?

    (c) In what region and in what relations have complaints been more bitter: that is, in relation of servant and master, employee and employer, in business, in schools, in the relation of neighbor, etc.?

    (d) In what situations and under what conditions, if at all, have the several racial groups succeeded in reaching an accommodation with the native born American, so that they have been able to live and work on friendly terms?

4. Public Opinion.

    (a) What has been the nature and how intimate have been the racial contacts in different geographical regions and in different occupations?

    (b) What are the *sources* of irritation in the relation of the immigrant races with the native born population?

    (c) What are the *actual experiences* in any of the relations that have been most exasperating and least tolerable?

    (d) How far do the racial contacts and sources of irritation differ for the different racial groups, i.e., the Chinese, Japanese, Mexicans, etc.?

(e) How far do these racial differences in attitude seem to depend upon the extent and character of the racial contacts, and, in general, upon the personal experiences of the individual, class, occupational or social group of which each is a member?

(f) To what extent do native born Americans differ among themselves in their attitude toward immigrant groups?

III

THE COLLECTING AND RECORDING OF MATERIALS

1. In general the materials for a Race Relations Survey will take the form of single documents, i.e., letters, narratives of personal experiences, newspaper clippings, detailed descriptions of individual cases, i.e., case-histories, autobiographical materials and life histories.

In addition to these it will be necessary to collect official reports, monograph studies, statistics, etc. In general, the latter are not difficult to obtain. It is the documents based on personal observation in which the experiences of individual groups, classes and communities are deposited and recorded that are important.

In general a study of this nature requires the materials that an historian might want, fifty or a hundred years hence, if he were to give a lively, intimate and authentic picture of the relations of the immigrant races and the native population of the present day. Such a picture would tell us not merely what took place, but how the people felt about the matter, and why.

2. The sources of such materials will naturally be:

(a) The memories of "old settlers," the first inhabitants, those who have lived long in the country and who have had experiences with the Indians, Mexicans, Chinese, Japanese and others.

(b) Employers of labor, business men, and those who have known the races to be studied in any or all of the ordinary relations of life.

(c) Farmers, laborers, and others who have come into personal competition with these races or have known them as neighbors or in business.

(d) Scientific observers, travelers, missionaries, etc., all those who have known the immigrant races in their own countries, and particularly those who have succeeded in establishing intimate and friendly relations with them, and can therefore assist in securing materials that would explain their so-called "racial traits."

3. A census of persons who have known the races studied in any one of the ways indicated is one of the first things to be undertaken. The names of these persons should be written on small 3x5 sheets, including notes on occupation, extent and character of their contacts and associations with the races studied, thus:

> Jones, Ralph, M.D., 1215 L St., Los Angeles. Owner estate 350 acres, San Diego County. Has employed Chinese, Japanese, and Mexican labor. Knows Chinese best. Remembers the Sand Lot agitation and is familiar with the whole history of the effort to exclude Orientals from the United States.

4. Case studies may be made of (a) City neighborhoods, (b) Urban and rural communities, (c) Small farms and farmers, (d) Estates.

Case studies should be first of all, "case histories," indicating how and to what extent the regions and persons studied have been affected by (a) the growth of immigrant populations, (b) the co-incidental expansion and reorganization of industry, (c) the arrival of successive racial groups, i.e., Chinese, Japanese, etc.

The case history should include, of course, any incidents that seem likely to throw light upon past or present race relations, or upon local opinion in regard to the several racial groups.

Particular care is necessary in writing out a case history to describe accurately locations, physical boundaries, etc., and to suggest the general social and historical setting. Names, dates, and addresses are important. Local personages who are sources of information should be characterized; differences of opinion, where there are two or more recognized opinions in a given community should be carefully noted.

A case-study should eventually be typewritten in three copies and each be given eventually the form of a single document. Names and addresses recorded in the case-study are confidential and should not be used in the final report of the survey except where permission is given.

5. Life Histories are in the long run the most important materials for the purpose of a race relations survey. A life history, for the purposes of this study, is the account which one individual is able to give of his own first-hand encounter, in a problematic situation, with members of another race. In such an encounter of the alien with the native-born and of the native-born with the alien the following items are important: (a) first contacts and impressions, (b) early impressions,

particularly those formed before the age of reflective thought and formal opinion, (c) later opinions and attitudes, particularly those based on experiences, (d) conclusions and reflections which these experiences have enforced.

A life history may be autobiographic, that is, one in which the writer tells his own story; it may be elicited and recorded by a third person through the medium of an interview. In the latter case the interviewer should set down freely his or her own impressions of the subject of the interview. In any case a life history should be anecdotal, a record of first-hand experience, and like the Padre's description of a confession, it should be "sudden, bitter, and complete." These are the sort of materials which throw most light upon race relations and the fundamental traits of human nature which, in the long run, not only determine the character of race relations but, at the same time, explain them.

6. Interviews should be recorded as far as possible in the language and reflect the accents and emphasis of the person interviewed. Answers to leading questions are usually misleading unless both question and answer are recorded in the precise form in which they were uttered. Formal language is an imperfect instrument of expression of attitudes, which are only adequately revealed in actual behavior. What one does is always the best commentary on what one says. For this reason a record of personal experience, in which action and sentiments are recorded as integral parts of the whole transaction, are the best indices as to what the attitudes actually are.

7. An attitude is a tendency to act. Individuals are frequently surprised and chagrined by their own behavior and this serves to emphasize the fact that individuals are not always the best judges of their own minds.

It is important, in recording an interview, to distinguish between attitudes, opinions, convictions, and theory, all of which are ordinarily recorded as opinion. Attitudes are formed quite unconsciously, on the basis of experience. Opinions, on the other hand, arise usually in discussion, in the effort of the individual to define and to justify an attitude already defined. Opinions are usually expressed in conventional phrases, and if formulated under attack, are inevitably framed to meet that attack. Opinions, therefore, are usually public opinion; they reflect the fighting attitude of the group or party to which the persons who hold them belong. Such opinions pass over into doctrines or theories, more or less philosophical in character. As such they represent the efforts of the intelligentsia to rationalize the attitudes and wishes of the group to which they belong.

As Dean Inge has remarked, "Philosophy is always an attempt to find out, not what is, but what we want." A scientific theory, on the contrary, is an attempt to describe what we may expect to happen, irrespective of what we want.[1]

Opinions are of course right or wrong in so far as they are justified by all the facts, but we are very little concerned, in a study of public opinion, with the question of justification. Most opinions, as far as they are individual opinions, are justified by the experience of the people who hold them, and so far as they are not the opinions of a single individual only, but of a group, they will be justified by the tradition of the group.

Tradition is simply vicarious experience, which individuals inherit from other individuals. That is the reason why, in the study of public opinion, it is important to get the actual experiences upon which opinions rest.

In collecting opinions, or rather, materials spoken or written in which attitudes are directly or indirectly reflected, it is important not merely to state the opinion, but to indicate also the intensity with which it is held. As Lowell pointed out long ago, it is not merely the number of persons who subscribe to an opinion that counts, but the conviction with which they hold it, that determines in the long run whether one view or another shall prevail. It is the convinced minorities that make legislation.

The conviction with which men hold their opinions is largely determined by the character of the experiences in which these opinions are rooted. What one wants, therefore, in studying opinion is not merely the formal statements and theories which men advance to rationalize and justify their views, but something that reveals the sources and intensity of their convictions.

It frequently turns out, in disputes, that arguments fail to convince because words do not mean the same to the parties at dispute. One of the purposes of studying public opinion upon a particular issue is to bring the parties into the same "Universe of Discourse" and make them in this way intelligible to one another. Perhaps that is the most that such an investigation can hope to do.

---

[1] What Dean Inge actually said was: "The object of studying philosophy is to know one's own mind, not other people's. Philosophy means thinking things out for oneself." William Ralph Inge, Dean of Saint Paul's, *Outspoken Essays,* (Second series) Confessei Tidei, p. 1, London, 1923.

CHAPTER 12

Politics and "The Man Farthest Down"

I

SOME twenty-five years ago, in the summer of 1910 to be exact, Booker T. Washington conceived the notion that he would like, for once, to get quite away from the United States and see what this America, in which he had been so long and so actively immersed, looked like from the outside. Accordingly, he took seven weeks out of a very busy life to visit and see Europe.

What made this journey unique was the fact that, though he visited most of its capitals, he did not, in the sense of the ordinary traveler, see Europe at all. So far from visiting the historical shrines and seeing the customary sights he sedulously avoided them, limiting his observations to the life and labor of what he described as "the man farthest down." His purpose was, so far as possible in the time at his command, to meet and make the acquaintance of the classes in Europe which, in respect to their opportunities, their handicaps, and their conditions of life generally, were comparable, not, to be sure, with the élite, but with the masses of the Negro people in the United States.

What Washington wanted to see abroad, and from the distance and point of view of Europe, was America, and not America merely but the American Negro. He therefore visited in preference the slums of London instead of the art galleries; hunted out the abandoned

Being "Introduction" to Harold F. Gosnell, *Negro Politicians* (Chicago: University of Chicago Press, 1935), pp. xiii-xxv.

ghettos of Prague and Cracow; explored the sulphur mines of Sicily and discovered in remote villages returned Polish or Italian immigrants. Eventually he published his observations in a volume to which he gave the title, suggested by his own description of the object of his journey, *The Man Farthest Down*.

Booker Washington's conception of "the man farthest down," it perhaps needs to be said, was not racial. He did not, at any rate, think of him either as a man foredoomed to be a hewer of wood and drawer of water, nor as one whom the oppression of a more favored class had reduced to a position of hopeless inferiority. On the contrary, with an optimism characteristic of other self-made Americans, Washington was disposed to believe that all men were predestined to rise and that those who found themselves behind were, in all probability, merely those who, like the Negro, had started late and were now, or would soon be, on their way.

In any case, the backwardness of peoples seems to be, on the whole, a historical and not a biological phenomenon. So conceived it loses some of the tragic interest ordinarily attributed to it. The Negro's case was not at that time and is not now as exceptional as it has sometimes seemed. There are, for example, in the Appalachian Mountains, on the high plains of New Mexico, and in the swamps of southern Louisiana, other peoples who have not yet emerged, or are just beginning to emerge, from their ancient isolation. They are, like the "Habitants" of Quebec, the "Pennsylvania Dutch" of Pennsylvania, and the so-called "Cajuns" of southern Louisiana, what Benton MacKaye calls "the indigenous and colonial" as contrasted with "metropolitan" peoples. They are, in short, the provincial peoples who have not yet left home to try their fortune in cities and centers of civilization.[1]

America and, perhaps, the rest of the world, can be divided between two classes: those who reached the city and those who have not yet arrived.

Now it happens that since Booker Washington went to Europe twenty-five years ago in quest of the man farthest down, there has been a great migration of the Negroes from the plantation and small towns of the South to the manufacturing cities and metropolitan centers of the North. This migration has brought about, for good and for all, a great change in the condition and in the outlook of the

---

[1] Benton MacKaye, *The New Exploration: A Philosophy of Regional Planning* (New York, 1928).

Negro people in America—a change that Washington, who assumed that Negroes were destined to remain for an indefinite period in the rural South—could not have foreseen.

In the cities rural Negroes have become involved in a competition —biological and economic—more intense and pervasive than they had ever known. On the other hand, in this stimulating environment the Negro has developed an intellectual life and produced a literature for which otherwise and elsewhere there would have been neither the occasion nor the opportunity. Finally, in the city the masses of the Negro have gone into politics.

When in January, 1901, George H. White, the last Negro member of Congress from the southern states, delivered his valedictory speech, the incident, although it attracted little attention at the time, marked the end of an epoch. Since that time the public—the public at any rate that gets its politics from the press—has become accustomed to the notion that the Negro was, humanly speaking, out of politics, if not for good and all, at least for an indefinite period.

The public was therefore surprised and a little disconcerted when in 1928 Republicans of the First Congressional District of Illinois elected a Negro to Congress. Still more surprising, six years later, a Negro was elected from the same district on the Democratic ticket to succeed a Republican. This shatered all traditions.

What makes this the more interesting and significant is that both Republican and Democratic congressmen were presumably elected by the votes of Negro migrants from the South, voters who at home had been effectively dispossessed of the franchise. The First Congressional District includes Chicago's First and Second wards, where Negroes constitute 58 per cent of the population, most of them comparatively recent arrivals.

It is still true of the Negro in America, as it once was of the serfs in Europe, that city air makes men free, and this is true in more ways than are ordinarily conceived of. The great cities are now what the frontier and the wilderness once was, the refuge of the footloose, the disinherited, and all those possessed by that undefined *malaise* we call social unrest.

This volume [*Negro Politicians*], if I might characterize in a word, is at once a chapter in the local history of Chicago and at the same time an account of the way in which the rural Negro, "the man farthest down," came to the city and got into politics.

II

The motives which, since 1914, have turned the faces of the Negro people cityward have been primarily economic rather than political. However, the prospect of regaining in the North some measure of the political power they had lost in the South undoubtedly did speed up the exodus. There are, besides, historical reasons why the ballot should have for Negroes a sentimental and symbolic significance, quite out of proportion to any positive value it may have had in the past or is likely to have in the future.

The Negro's first experience in politics was gained during the anti-slavery agitation which—so far as Negroes participated in it—may be said to have begun with the publication in 1829 of *Walker's Appeal,* an anti-slavery pamphlet which General Giles of Virginia referred to at the time as "a seditious pamphlet sent from Boston." Coming as it did as few years after the Denmark Vesey conspiracy in Charleston in 1822 and just before the Nat Turner insurrection in Virginia in 1830, its influence upon public opinion, North and South, was profound.

In the course of the anti-slavery struggle, which began at this time and in this way, Frederick Douglass, who had been a fugitive slave before he became an anti-slavery orator and journalist, played a leading rôle. It is probably the prestige he gained at that time, rather than the prominence he achieved afterward during the period of reconstruction, that has made him the one outstanding figure in Negro politics.

It was unfortunate in some respects, but not in others, that Negroes got their introduction to politics in connection with a radical and more or less revolutionary movement. It was inevitable that the abolition crusade should have created expectations that could not, at the conclusion of the Civil War, be suddenly and miraculously fulfilled. The failure of reconstruction to realize the millennial hopes it had inspired was the first and most tragic disillusionment which emancipation brought to the Negro.

It has been customary to refer to Negro politicians of the reconstruction period as if they deserved the contempt that a partisan public opinion has bestowed upon them. The fact seems to be that very few of them were the downright rascals they are sometimes described to be. Politicians are rarely either as noble or as despicable as their contemporaries conceive them to be, and Senator Tom Reed's saying, "a statesman is a politician who is dead" is quite as likely to be true of black men as of white.

Not all Negro office-holders under the reconstruction government were either as ignorant or as incompetent as they have been represented to be. Among them were, for example, men like John Mercer Langston, who graduated in 1844 from Oberlin College, and Robert Brown Elliott, born in Boston and educated in England, who seems to have been, of all the twenty-two Negro members of Congress, the one man who could be described as brilliant.

Of the two colored United States senators elected at different times from Mississippi, Blanch K. Bruce had been a school teacher in Missouri, and Hiram Revels, after graduating from Knox College, Galesburg, Illinois, had been a preacher and lecturer before he got into politics.

Men such as these, who had succeeded either at the cost of a long and desperate struggle, or by the grace of some unusual good fortune, in getting any kind of superior education, were disposed to take themselves seriously and to be, if anything, a little too conscious of their responsibilities. In fact, if I might base an opinion upon men of that period whom I have known I should say it was characteristic of them that they put too high an estimate upon their respectability, and were rather more ambitious than would be true of the Negro intelligentsia of today to behave correctly and in what James W. Garner describes as "an Anglo-Saxon manner."

It was said of John R. Lynch, who was a member of the legislature of Mississippi in 1872, that he presided over the deliberations of the House with a dignity and impartiality to which, upon his retirement, even his political opponents bore testimony.[2]

Another reconstruction legislator, Hannibal Thomas, a Negro carpet-bagger from Ohio, was so shocked by what he heard and saw after he went South, of the life of the Freedman, that he was impelled to write a book describing "the insensate follies of a race blind to every passing opportunity."

The book is mainly interesting now as an evidence of the idealism of the politicians of the reconstruction era. It is characteristic of idealists that they expect too much of human nature and are hence

---

[2] James W. Garner, *Reconstruction in Mississippi* (New York, 1901).

likely to become embittered and pessimistic when they discover how far ordinary human beings fall short of what they expected of them.[3]

There were at the time, and there have been since, among Negro leaders those who shared the misgivings with regard to the future of the Negro in America which Hannibal Thomas has so candidly expressed, but they have not, as one might expect, been effective leaders of the masses. They have not been successful politicians.

Not all of the Negro politicians of the reconstruction shared the illusions of the anti-slavery crusaders. There were men like Isaiah Montgomery, the founder of the Negro town at Mound Bayou, who was born, reared, and educated on the plantation which he, his father, and his brother later purchased and conducted.[4] Isaiah Montgomery was the only colored man to participate in the constitutional convention of 1890, which adopted a constitution which effectively disfranchised the Negroes in that state.

In that convention he made a notable speech in defense of his race, which was so moderate, wise, and realistic in tone that it attracted wide comment at the time and was regarded of sufficient importance to be printed in full in the New York World.

The Negro politicians described in this volume are perhaps not as moderate and as considerate of white folks as they should be. They have very few illusions, however, in regard to the people they seek to represent. On the other hand, they are making no apologies for them either.

III

Reconstruction in the South seems to have passed through most of the characteristic phases of other revolutionary movements. There was a brief period of violence and exaltation, when the new order was introduced, followed by a longer period of adjustment, disillusionment, and general deflation.

Probably no one expected the Negro would be permitted, without a struggle, to enjoy all his newly acquired civil rights; but it was hoped that, having the ballot, he would at least be able to enforce in the new social and political order a consideration that he had not received in the old.

---

[3] William Hannibal Thomas, *The American Negro: What He Was, What He Is, and What He May Become* (New York, 1901).

[4] The famous Hurricane Plantation, located on the river below Vicksburg and owned by Joseph Davis, brother of Jefferson, President of the Confederacy.

As it turned out, the interests of race and caste triumphed over the interests of class and party. With the rise of the so-called Solid South, at any rate, Negroes lost their representation not only in southern legislatures but in congress. They continued to share, to be sure, in the federal patronage, but they ceased to participate, in any effective way, in local politics.

Meanwhile, in the ensuing struggle to enforce the Negro's civil rights and to prevent a more or less complete nullification of the reconstruction legislation, by interpretation, qualification, and legal chiseling, the battle-ground shifted from the legislatures to the courts.

It is not enough, it seems, that laws, like New York's resolutions, be solemnly proclaimed and inscribed on the statute books. They must, eventually, be enforced. In no other way can they be so effectively incorporated in the habits of a people and in the customs of a country as to be, relatively at least, self-enforcing. The courts must complete the work of the legislature, and until the law, as interpreted and enforced, has brought about what the psychologists might describe as a "reconditioning" of the people for whom it was enacted, one cannot say that the political process is complete.

The task of securing the enforcement of the Negro's civil rights was eventually taken up by the emerging Negro intelligentsia, led by men like Burghardt Du Bois, supported by the Society for the Advancement of Colored People, of which he was the founder. This society inherited the idealism and the radicalism of the abolitionists, but radicalism, at this time, amounted to no more than an insistence that the Negro should have, here and now, the rights which the new order promised but in practice postponed.

Meanwhile the masses of the Negro people, where they were permitted to vote at all, continued to support the Republican party. In this way they were acting in accordance with, if not in response to, the admonition of their number one political leader, Frederick Douglass. "The Republican party," he once told them, "is the ship. All else is the open sea."

The migration to the northern cities, caused by the shortage of labor during the World War, has resulted in a renaissance in Negro politics. The character of this new Negro politics seems to have been largely determined by the fact that, like other immigrants, Negroes moving northward settled first where they encountered least opposition, either in the way of high rents or social prejudice, namely, in the slums.

In Chicago, for example, the first Negro settlement was on Dearborn Street in close proximity to the old red-light district of the First Ward. From there they moved southward, along State Street, and eastward, into more spacious and respectable quarters, in the direction of Lake Michigan. In New York Negroes were mainly settled in Greenwich Village as late as 1880. Later they were numerous in and around West Fifty-third Street and the San Juan Hill district, notorious for the riots which occurred there in 1900. At present the largest Negro settlement in New York is in Harlem, from north of 110th Street. Negro Harlem has been adequately characterized in Carl Van Vechten's novel, *Nigger Heaven,* and in Langston Hughes' volume of poems, *The Weary Blues.*

The slums of cities, where people live ordinarily from necessity rather than from choice, are in many respects the most democratic of all the territorial units into which the urban complex finally resolves itself. Here, where neighbors are mostly strangers, there is likely, if anywhere, to be some sort of equality and a general disposition to live and let live not characteristic of more highly organized communities. It was in the slums and the adjoining territories into which the Negro migrants moved that Negroes first achieved a voting preponderance that made them a political power to be reckoned with.

It is significant also, that the migration of the Negroes to the northern cities took place at a time when urban residents were abandoning their homes in the center of the city for the more spacious suburbs. As these suburbs multiplied the abandoned and the so-called "blighted" area surounding the central business core steadily expanded. These areas are now largely occupied by immigrants and Negroes. The result has been that by a singular turn of fortune the southern Negro, lately from the "sticks"—the man politically farthest down—now finds himself living in the center of a great metropolitan city where his vote is not only counted but where, in various ways and for various reasons, it counts.

IV

Not all Negro politicians of the new era got their political education in the slums. Some of them have merely held office and kept out of the dirt. But in the crowded Negro quarter, where most of the voters live, there is always a good deal of vice and disorder, and the men who owe their influence in politics to the fact that they have been able to get out the vote are likely to be on such intimate terms with the underworld that they are not received in colored society.

Some of them, like "Mushmouth" Johnson and "Teenan" Jones in Chicago, and R. R. Church, Sr., of Memphis, the boss of Beale Street, where the "blues" come from, who seem to have been political personalities before Negro politics achieved an organization, never quite emerged from the underworld in which they grew up.

Men who succeed in the jungle politics of a city slum are likely to be a hard-bitten, disillusioned, and cynical sort, not overscrupulous about police regulations, but faithful, on the whole, to their friends and respected by their enemies. Politics in the wards and among the lowly is more than elsewhere organized on a personal and a feudal basis.

In the case of Negroes, however, ward politics has assumed at times a dignity and importance it would not otherwise have had because it has been associated with the Negro's struggle for fundamental civil and political rights.

In any case, men of the sort here described, accustomed to the freedom and democracy of the city, are of a type different from the politicians of the reconstruction era, who grew up on the tradition of the anti-slavery movement and under the influence of the missionary schools.

They are, for one thing, not inhibited by the necessity of living at the same time in two different worlds, the world of the white man and the world of the black. Ward politicians are likely, in any case, to understand and feel at home among the people of whom they are the political shepherds.

If Negro politicians of the reconstruction era were, by temperament and training, idealists, the men who have recently come to power are realists. They are realists, for one reason, if not for others, because they are the products of the struggle to survive and live in a free and competitive world such as did not exist for most Negroes before emancipation. In this world, where every man is on his own, he is expected—whatever he may eventually do for the general good—at least to make an individual success.

From the Yankee school-ma'ams, who came South after the war to complete in the schools the emancipation of the Freedmen, Negroes learned, among other things, that they, like other Americans, were destined and expected to rise.

In the early days of freedom, when Negro schools and Negro colleges were springing up in every part of the South, General O. O. Howard, who as head of the Freedman's Bureau was more or less responsible for many if not most of them, visited Atlanta University. In concluding an address to the students he asked them what message he might take to the benefactors and well-wishers of the school in the North. Thereupon a small voice piped up: "Tell 'em," it said, "we'se aris'n."

The story, which has been repeated so often that it has become legendary, owes its wide currency at the time and since to the fact that it so aptly expresses the faith with which the Yankee teachers, more or less consciously, inspired their colored pupils.

"We'se aris'n" is, like the Declaration of Independence, an expression of the American spirit—the spirit most conspicuously manifest in the personalities, from Benjamin Franklin to Andrew Carnegie, of our so-called self-made men.

Nowhere has this American spirit—its optimism and its individualism—found a more complete embodiment than in the philosophy and the career of the author of *Up From Slavery*. At any rate, it is probable that no American was ever more convinced than Booker Washington that the main business of life was to rise and succeed. The future of the Negro—that was the substance of his teaching—rests finally on the ability of the individual Negro, each for himself, to make his way in the world. Only out of the struggle to rise will the race get the discipline that will make it master of its fate.

The secret of success for the man farthest down, is, as he put it, "to take advantage of his disadvantages."

The Negro politicians described by Gosnell, are, on the whole, men like that. They are, so to speak, self-made politicians. They are no longer obsessed with a sense of their dependence on Washington and the central government. They no longer regard themselves as the wards of the Republican party. They cherish no vain hopes and, like Margaret Fuller, they "accept the universe."

There is among the members of the Negro intelligentsia in New York and elsewhere a radical school of thought that gets its inspiration from Moscow. During the depression communist propaganda has made deep inroads in the ranks of the Negro proletariat. But the Negro politicians of Chicago are no more likely than Tammany Hall to go radical or indulge in romantic dreams about the future either of the country or the race.

The older generation of Negro politicians were very largely the descendants of old free Negro families, who have constituted, and still do, a colored aristocracy within the Negro race. But like most aristocracies they have been jealous of their privileged position, both within and without the race, and have been mainly interested in maintaining it.

Meanwhile, there has emerged a robust and vigorous middle class, men of the mental type of Booker Washington, and of the men of the Negro Business League which he organized. These men have more or less the attitudes of pioneers, men who have grown up on an advancing frontier—in this instance a racial frontier.

The Negro politicians who have risen in ward politics, as distinguished from those who still take their cue from Washington, seem to be, in most every case, of this type. They are not infrequently men of superior education and are active in promoting the interests of the race as they see them, but they act on the principle that the best way to solve the problem of the race as a whole is for each member to solve the problem as an individual. They are, in short, "We'se Arisers," who as a result of their conflict and competition with the white man have become race, rather than class, conscious.

What seems to be taking place in Negro politics, then, not only in Chicago but elsewhere, is a transfer of political power. A new generation and a new type of man has arisen within the ranks of the race, occupying a position between the traditional leaders and the masses of the Negro. It is upon this middle class that Negro political leadership has descended.

In sketching, by way of introduction to this study of Negro politics in Chicago, the story of the Negro's political adventures in the United States, I have sought, incidentally, to indicate the relation of Negro politics to some other aspects of Negro life which though significant are not so obvious and open to observation. In doing this I have been moved by the conviction that for most readers this volume [*Negro Politicians*] might have a double interest: First, because it illuminates the obscure region of local and racial politics; and second, because it adds another chapter in the career of the Negro race in America—a career which for sheer human interest, at any rate, is not equaled by that of any other element of our population, except the Jew.

CHAPTER 13

THE ETIQUETTE OF RACE RELATIONS IN THE SOUTH

A GOOD many years ago when I first became interested in the South and its problems I ran across in a little volume by John Spencer Bassett, entitled *Slavery in the State of North Carolina,* a reference to a legal decision by Chief Justice Ruffin of the Supreme Court of North Carolina, which set forth the character of the institution of slavery in such uncompromising terms that I have never since forgotten it, and I can still recall some of its more incisive phrases.

It was a decision, rendered in 1829, dismissing an indictment of a master for an assault upon his slave, the memorable thing about it being the Chief Justice's opinion affirming the master's right to inflict any kind of punishment upon his slave short of death. In support of this decision Justice Ruffin cited the fact that, in the whole history of slavery, there had been no such prosecution of a master for punishing a slave, and added, "against this general opinion in the community the court ought not to hold."

It had been said, the opinion continues, that the relation of master and slave was like that of parent and child. But this was a mistake. It was to the interest of the parent to give his son moral and intellectual instruction in order to fit him to live as a free man. The case of the slave was different. What sense could there be in addressing moral considerations to a slave?

The Chief Justice summed up his conception of the relations of

Being "Introduction" to Bertram W. Doyle, *The Etiquette of Race Relations in the South* (Chicago: University of Chicago Press, 1937), pp. xi-xxiv.

master and slave in these words: "The end [of slavery] is the profit of the master, his security, and the public safety; the subject, one doomed in his own person and his posterity to live without knowledge and without the capacity to make anything his own, and to toil that another may reap the fruits. What moral consideration shall be addressed to such a being to convince him, what it is impossible but that the most stupid must feel and know can never be true—that he is thus to labour upon a principle of natural duty, or for the sake of his own personal happiness. Such services can only be expected from one who has no will of his own, who surrenders his will in implicit obedience to that of another. Such obedience is the consequence only of uncontrolled authority over the body. There is nothing else which can operate to produce the effect. The power of the master must be absolute to render the submission of the slave perfect."

No harsher judgment, I can well believe, was ever passed upon the institution of slavery than that contained in this decision, and if I have ventured to quote it here at some considerable length it is partly because of its intrinsic historical interest but mainly because it seemed to contribute something, by way of contrast at least, to the present study of a very different aspect of slavery, and one which presents that institution in a more amiable light.

The very fact that there existed, in the South before the war, as the title of this volume suggests, a recognized social ritual and a code of etiquette regulating the personal relations of both races is evidence that the regime of slavery was not, everywhere and always, as inhuman as the laws defining the relations of master and slave might lead one to believe. Where there is custom there will always be some sort of justice and equity, and no individual will be wholly a law unto himself.

It is interesting, also, in this connection that having described with remorseless logic the nature of slavery, the Chief Justice should have felt moved to conclude his legal opinion with a personal comment which indicates how little he approved, in his private capacity as a citizen and a man, the institution which, in his public capacity as a lawyer and a judge, he felt compelled to support.

"I freely confess," he says, "my sense of the harshness of this proposition. I feel it as deeply as any one can and as a principle of right every person in his retirement must repudiate it. But in the actual condition of things it must be so; there is no remedy. This discipline belongs to the state of slavery. It constitutes the curse of slavery both to the bond and free portion of our population." [1]

There was always, it seems, a conflict in the minds, if not the counsels, of thoughtful southern people, between the demands of public policy, interested in the perpetuation of slavery, and the disposition of individual slaveholders who, for private and personal reasons, were disposed to emancipate their slaves. This was particularly true when, as often happened, emancipation seemed the only way to discharge an obligation which had been accumulating during a lifetime of intimate personal association and faithful service.

One evidence of this conflict was the uninterrupted increase in the number of free Negroes, particularly in Virginia, North Carolina, and the Border States, where the more intimate relations between masters and slaves tended to multiply emancipations, in spite of the efforts of legislators to discourage them. The motives of masters in freeing their slaves, in opposition to accepted public policy, are revealed in their testamentary statements where one encounters again and again the clause "in consequence of faithful service" such-and-such a one should be given his freedom. Not infrequently such provision for the emancipation of a faithful servant was made in final fulfilment of a promise made long before.

It is clear from these and other evidences that the actual position of the slave in the little world of the plantation, and his legal status in the world outside, were never in actual harmony; were finally, in fact, quite irreconcilable. The regime of slavery, constantly threatened from without, was at the same time steadily undermined and weakened from within; weakened by the claims of the slave, on the one hand, and the conscience of the master, on the other.

This contrast and conflict between slavery as a legal concept and as an actual working concern may be regarded perhaps as an instance of the normal reaction of living and conscious human nature against the formal and rational structure of the society which incloses it. We know how friendships sometimes corrupt politics. In a somewhat similar way the intimate association of master and slave may be said steadily to have corrupted the institution of slavery, and in so doing hastened it on its course to its predestined extinction.

---

[1] See John Spencer Basset, *Slavery in the State of North Carolina*, Johns Hopkins Studies in Historical and Political Science, pp. 23-24. Also *Judicial Cases Concerning American Slavery and the Negro*, Edited by Helen Tunnicliff Catterall. Vol. II. Cases from the Courts of North Carolina, South Carolina, and Tennessee.

Slavery came into existence to meet the demands of the frontier and plantation. The hard conditions that the system imposed upon the slaves were not essentially different from those imposed a little earlier upon indentured servants. In any case they responded to the necessities of the situation and the customs of the time and place. But "human relations," as a noted anthropologist, Malinowski, puts it, "do not rest merely or mainly on constraint coming from without. Men can only work with and for one another by the moral forces which grow out of personal attachments and loyalties."

Men come together ordinarily because they are useful to one another. Under these circumstances they may regard each other for a long time as mere utilities. But human beings do no live for long, like plants, in relations that are merely symbiotic. For men, unlike plants, communicate. In this way they come to know one another's minds and to be responsive to one another's attitudes and sentiments. They find themselves, eventually, living as it were, each in the mind of all his neighbors. It is in this way that a moral order grows up in which, under the happiest circumstances, the individual feels himself constrained only by those obligations which he freely accepts or imposes upon himself.

It is characteristic of such a moral order that it is nonrational. That means that it is not devised to protect any special interest, to serve any policy, and has no ulterior purposes of any sort. On the contrary, it arises in response to the natural claims which one individual makes upon another, as soon as he recognizes that other individual as human like himself.

I am reminded in this connection of an anecdote related of John Randolph, who was a slaveholder and abolitionist at a time when that combination did not seem as much like one of Oliver Hereford's mixed beasts as it did later. John Randolph was himself a great orator, and he had known Patrick Henry. Someone, knowing his reputation, asked him in the course of an interview whom, of all those he had ever heard speak in Congress or elsewhere, he regarded as the greatest orator.

"The greatest orator I ever heard," he replied, "was a woman. She was a slave and a mother and her rostrum was an auction block."

The anecdote illustrates the curious and unexpected ways in which men gain those moral insights which eventually undermine but humanize institutions. To make the record complete, one should know that John Randolph at his death emancipated all his slaves and settled them on free soil in the Northwest Territory, in what is now the state of Ohio.

Thus, long before emancipation had finally put an end to the regime of slavery, that institution was visibly breaking down under the tension of internal conflicts. At the same time, under the urge and pressure of sentiments and attitudes, which the lifelong association of master and slave evoked, one observed the burgeoning, within the framework of the old, of a new and more humane social order.

The emancipation of the slaves did not at once usher in a regime of free competition and democracy, in the sense of the Declaration of Independence, the Bill of Rights, and the laissez faire doctrines of Adam Smith and the Physiocrats.

On the contrary, the social order which emerged with the abolition of slavery was a system of caste—caste based on race and color. The plantation had been organized on the pattern of a familial and feudal, rather than of a civil and political, society. Caste was the form which race relations took under conditions which the plantation imposed.

So firmly was the system of caste fixed in the habits and custom— what Sumner calls the mores—of both races in the South that all the social disorganization incident to the Civil War and Reconstruction were not sufficient wholly or suddenly to destroy it.

Slavery is dead, and no one now defends it. But caste remains, and is still so much a part of the natural and expected order that few people in the South either question its right to exist or discuss its function. The North has never understood either the nature of race relations in the South or the fanaticism with which southern people have defended, wherever and whenever it has been attacked, the caste code in accordance with which these relations were regulated. The failure of reconstruction legislation to effect any fundamental change in the South's caste system is less an illustration of the recalcitrance of the Anglo-Saxon than of Sumner's dictum that it is not possible to reform the mores by law.[2]

People not reared in the southern tradition have sometimes assumed that southern people's insistence on racial segregation is evidence that they cherish some deep, instinctive antipathy for the Negro race. Anyone who accepts that conception of the matter is likely to be somewhat mystified when he learns that the Negro is

---

[2] See William Graham Sumner's *Folkways*, pp. 113-14. Boston, 1906.

quite all right in his place. And that place, like the place of everyone else, is the one to which tradition and custom has assigned him.

In 1906 Ray Stannard Baker came South to investigate the background of the Atlanta race riot. Later he recorded his observations in a volume entitled *Following the Color Line,* which is one of the very few books in which an author has succeeded in reporting race relations in the South with anything approaching disinterested objectivity. Baker made, in the course of his investigations, what amounted to an important discovery. He found that the "color line" was no mere incident of social life in the South. Rather it was an institution, the influence and ramifications of which entered into and pervaded all the life-relations of both races. The "color line" is, as a matter of fact, nothing more or less than a local variety of what students of society and human nature call caste. It is this institution to which southern people make oblique reference when they speak of "the doctrine of social equality." It is this institution, in what is sociologically, perhaps, its most important aspect—namely, its etiquette—which is the subject of Mr. Doyle's study.

Students of society are indebted to Herbert Spencer for directing attention to the importance of etiquette and social ritual as a form of government or social control, and, indeed, as a subject for sociological investigation. Etiquette—or "ceremonial observance," as he calls it—is not only, he points out, the earliest but the most pervasive form of social control, and for that reason, perhaps, has still "the largest share in regulating men's lives."

As every society that has achieved any sort of permanence has its traditions and customs, so every society has its etiquette. Social ritual is indeed a part of the social tradition, but it has its own special function. Something more in detail needs to be said here, perhaps, in regard to the origin and nature of etiquette. Its social function and the character of the control it actually enforces is amply illustrated in *The Etiquette of Race Relations in the South.*

Etiquette is concerned primarily with personal relations. It grows up in the first instance, perhaps, as the spontaneous expression of one person in the presence of another, of a sentiment of deference. Under ordinary circumstances such an attitude of propitiation of one individual implies and is likely to evoke a corresponding expression of benevolent recognition on the part of that other. Expression and response rather than stimulus and response are the natural termini of every instance of social interaction.

Forms of deference and recognition, repeated and imitated, soon crystallize into those conventional and obligatory forms of expression we call "etiquette," or social ritual. But ritual, as Sumner points out, "is not something to be thought or felt. It is something to be done." In fact, "ritual is strongest when it is perfunctory and excites no thought." It is for this reason that a social ritual which was originally the natural and unstudied expression of a social sentiment may serve finally as the masque behind which one controls and conceals his emotions rather than reveals them. Etiquette in that case becomes a kind of social device by which one does the expected thing but preserves his inner freedom.

Etiquette, so far as it can be conceived to be a form of government, or control, functions only in so far as it defines and maintains "social distances." Social distance is a phenomenon of a society that is based on primary or face-to-face relationships. In every such society, even in the most casual assembly, every individual will tend to be located at certain social distance in relation to every other. This means that, at a given time and place, every individual may be said to occupy a position, defined in terms of his psychical distance or intimacy, with respect to every other. What this distance may be at any time depends upon a number of things: upon the personality of the individual, for one thing; his office and function in the community, for another. It will depend in part, however, upon the number of persons present and the known relations of each to every other. The principle involved is stated in the aphorism, "Two is company but three is a crowd." In general one may say, therefore, that the larger the number the greater the distances.

A society or community of this sort may be said to have attained stable equilibrium when all the social distances are known and every individual is in his place. Thus etiquette turns out to be, at the same time, a principle of social order and an index of the stability of the society in which it exists. In such a society every individual is "all right," and quite acceptable, in his place and at his proper distance, even when that distance is only symbolically expressed.

Thus it was quite possible, on the plantation, and particularly in the case of the house servants and the master's family, to maintain the most intimate relationships between master and slave provided the social ritual defining and maintaining the caste relationship was maintained in its integrity.

There is a delightfully quaint and touching Negro spiritual of which the refrain is: "I want to be in heaven settin' down."

One misses the symbolic significance of this image of the perfect comfort of heaven if one fails to recognize its reference to a traditional racial etiquette. I suspect that the heaven here referred to is somehow identified in the mind of the singer with the image of the "Big House" on the plantation. When one went there, one did not ordinarily sit down. One stood and waited, on one's feet.

We are largely dependent upon the personal memories of travelers and the reports of writers of a reminiscent and nostalgic literature for our knowledge of the domestic life of the plantation. Margaret Mitchell's novel, *Gone with the Wind*, for example, is a veritable source book on race relations and racial etiquette. From these and other sources one learns that this plantation society, originally a mere *modus vivendi* to insure the co-operation of individuals of two divergent races, had achieved at the end of the era a social stability and a moral solidarity that enabled it to withstand the shock of a Civil War in which its very existence was involved.

In this society, it appears, every individual—from the carriage-driver to the field hand—each according to his office and function, had his place in the occupational hierarchy, and, in his place, each had a certain degree of security and independence. It was a security and an independence, to be sure, that disappeared outside of the limits of the plantation. Within these limits, however, the existing social order was sustained by tradition and a code of etiquette that was binding upon master and servant alike.

Etiquette is the very essence of caste, since the prestige of a superior always involves the respect of an inferior. But this respect is insured only when it manifests itself freely, either in a natural expression of deference or in some more conventional form of ceremonial observance, enforced by public opinion and the general expectation. Any relaxation by any individual of the rigors of the code is likely to involve a loss of prestige not merely to that individual but to the caste as a whole.

This fact explains at once the importance which etiquette assumed on the plantation before the Civil War and the fierce insistence of the southern people upon its observance afterward, when any sign of disrespect of any Negro for any white man was evidence that the whole structure of social life in the South was crumbling, and any toleration of a violation of the traditional code was likely to be resented as a concession to a political and social equality abhorrent to southern tradition.

The caste system as it had existed was maintained not by law but by a body of customs that was more or less self-enforcing. One evidence of the change in race relations, as a result of emancipation, was the efforts of the southern communities to enforce by statute racial distinctions and discriminations which it was difficult or impossible to maintain by custom and tradition.

Most of the racial conflicts and controversies in the southern states during Reconstruction and after seem to have had their origin in the caste system, and in the efforts to maintain it by law and force when it was no longer sustained by the inertia of tradition and the force of public opinion.

It was, I suspect, less the fear of the political domination of the Negro than opposition to any and every form of social equality that was responsible for the Solid South, one of the most notable if incidental consequences of Reconstruction. This solidarity was necessary to insure white supremacy, but it had one unexpected effect. It co-operated with other forces to bring about what has been sometimes described as the emancipation of the poor white man. It gave him an equality with the planter aristocracy he had never had under the old regime. It made him an enthusiastic defender of the ritual of a caste system in which he had once occupied a distinctly inferior position.

It has been the violent, often vituperative, and always tactless efforts of the New South, in which the poor white man has become the dominant figure, to enforce upon Negroes the ritual of a racial etiquette already obsolete that has been responsible for a good deal, including lynchings, of what we refer to as the "race problem" in the South. Negroes acquired in slavery the conviction that a poor white man was an inferior white man, and the course of events since emancipation has not increased the black man's respect for the white man as such.

In a certain sense we may say that the caste system, in so far as it has served anywhere to organize race relations, has been a solution of the race problem. It was when, after the abolition of slavery, the caste system broke down that the disorders and racial animosities that we ordinarily identify with the race problem began.

Generally speaking, there was no such thing as a race problem before the Civil War and there was at that time very little of what we ordinarily call race prejudice, except in the case of the free Negro.

The free Negro was the source and origin of whatever race problems there were. Because he was free he was at once an anomaly and a source of constant anxiety to the slaveholding population. He had no place in the system, and although exceptional individuals achieved a relatively high place in their community, and were respected by members of both races, free Negroes, as a class, were feared and often outrageously maligned.

Although caste still persists and serves in a way to regulate race relations, many things—education, the rise within the Negro community of a professional class (teachers, ministers, and physicians) and of an intelligentsia, seeking to organize and direct the Negro's rising race consciousness—have conspired not merely to undermine the traditional caste system but to render it obsolete.

Meanwhile, the slow but steady advance of the Negro, as a result of competition within and without the group, and the gradual rise of a Negro society within the limits of the white man's world have changed the whole structure of race relations in the United States, both in the North and in the South.

The restrictions on intermarriage still persist and continue to make of the Negro an endogamous social group, in much the same sense that the Jews, the Mennonites, and any of the more primitive religious sects are endogamous. On the other hand, in view of the fact that he has developed a society in which all the professions and many, if not most, occupations are represented, the Negro has an opportunity now, which he did not have earlier, to rise within the limits of the Negro world. Under those circumstances the Negro group has gradually ceased to exhibit the characteristics of a caste and has assumed rather the character of a racial or national minority.

The Jewish people have been described as "a permanent minority group," and by the same token the position of the Jew in Europe may be said to constitute a race problem in the same sense as the position of the Negro constitutes a race problem in the United States. But the Jewish people, if they may be described a minority group or nationality, cannot properly be described at the same time as a caste.

The change in the status of the Negro from that of a caste to minority group has not come about without some interesting changes and quaint compromises in the racial ritual, growing out of the contradiction between present conditions and the traditional attitudes of both races as they have become enshrined in the traditional racial etiquette. An anecdote told me years ago by Booker Washington will illustrate better than any exposition the point I am seeking to make.

One of the methods adopted by Washington to spread his gospel of education was to organize from time to time statewide educational campaigns. On such occasions he and his party traveled sometimes for a week in a special car visiting and speaking in every city and center of Negro population. On these occasions he was frequently visited by delegations of white folk from remote villages along the way who, attracted by the legendary reputation he had achieved, wanted to see this extraordinary man. Southern white people have always been interested in Negro prodigies.

On one of these occasions a delegation, headed by a lanky and rustic but enterprising member of the village intelligentsia, waited upon Mr. Washington at the station and introduced himself and his fellow-villagers in good-natured, backwoods fashion:

"Y'u know, Booker, I been hear'n about you, I been hear'n for a long time now, and I sure did want to see you. I been a tellin' my friends about y'u. I been tellin' them you was one of the biggest men in this country today. Yes, sir, one of the biggest men in the whole country."

At this time Theodore Roosevelt was at the height of his reputation, and Mr. Washington, somewhat at a loss for a reply, but thinking it well to discount the exuberance of his visitor replied, "Well, what do you think about President Roosevelt?"

"Oh! Hell, Roosevelt! Well, I used to be all for him until he let you eat dinner with him. That finished him far as I'm concerned."

This retort was not perhaps as naïve as it may at first appear, but it illustrates, at any rate, the curious and incongruous association of ideas and attitudes that arise out of the necessity of maintaining the customary caste distinctions in a world which is gradually outgrowing them.

In the daily newspaper that lies on my desk as I write this there is a more recent illustration, a little less comic, of a similar incongruity. Congressman Mitchell, the Negro Democratic congressman from Chicago, it appears is suing the Illinois Central and the Pullman Company for fifty thousand dollars damages because in Arkansas, in accordance with local custom and state law, he was compelled to leave the Pullman and go into the "Jim Crow" car.

This is an instance of caste a little less innocent and amiable than the casual mistake of addressing a bishop as "boy." However, if white folk have been disposed, in their intercourse with Negroes, to retain the intimate and familiar forms of address such as "uncle," "auntie," and "boy," which were appropriate to a familial and feudal society but sound rather quaint now, Negroes, on the other hand, are more and more disposed to reject any terms or any racial distinctions that reflect and tend to preserve the memories of an earlier inferior status.

There is, finally, one small but significant change in the ritual of race relations that, it seems to me, needs to be specially noted. The great majority of Negroes now, after a good deal of discussion and difference of opinion, have adopted the term "Negro" as a racial designation in preference to another more logical but less familiar expression like "Afro-American." Having adopted it, however, they spell it with a capital *N*.

CHAPTER 14

THE RACE RELATIONS CYCLE IN HAWAII

IT IS no longer a secret, even to the layman, that there are not now and probably never have been—not at any rate, in the sense in which that term is ordinarily understood,—any pure races. What we sometimes refer to as historic races, that is to say, races that have actually existed and had a history, are merely peoples who have acquired distinctive and distinguishing racial traits through long periods of isolation and continued inbreeding.

Although it is now generally recognized that there are no pure races it is not generally known to what extent the surviving peoples are of diverse racial origins. There has, as a matter of fact, been until very recently, little scientific interest in human hybrids or in the natural history of races. Races are supposed to be pure; even if individual human beings are notoriously mixed.

Of all European peoples the Jews, because they have by pretty constant inbreeding, succeeded in preserving, such as it is, their racial integrity and their tribal religion are, in the popular estimation, the classic example of racial purity. It is curious, in view of this fact, that Jews are almost the only one of "historic races" that have been interested in investigating the extent and conditions under which their racial stock has, at different times, been contaminated with gentile blood.[1]

Being "Introduction" to Romanzo Adams, *Interracial Marriage In Hawaii* (New York: The Macmillan Co., 1937), pp. vii-xiv.

[1] See Maurice Fishberg, "The Jew." A study of race and environment. London and New York, 1911.

Although there has been so little interest in the study of human hybrids the subject is nevertheless of real importance. It is important not merely because, in the long run, it is the mixed rather than pure races that survive, but because race relations have everywhere so largely determined the structure of human society.

It is probably not due to mere historical accident that society and civilization in India are everywhere dominated by the principle of caste, while in China, except perhaps between the Punte and Hakka peoples of South China, there is almost no trace of that institution. One explanation that suggests itself is this: In India the invading and conquering races were culturally as well as politically superior to the indigenous peoples. In China the reverse was the case. The result is that the Chinese have invariably absorbed and assimilated their conquerors, and race distinctions that might have once existed have disappeared. In India, on the other hand, the conquering peoples seem to have established a caste system, not merely to preserve their racial integrity, but to insure the permanence of a social order in which their dominance, having become customary, is now regarded as natural and right.

There is, however, another factor that invariably plays a role in race relations and that is visibility. In the case of India the invading races were of widely different physical types. They were so different, in fact, that even with all the miscegenation that has gone on since the earliest invasions the evidences of race mixture are everywhere evident to the most casual observer.

High visibility makes it easy to observe and to maintain race distinctions. On the other hand it is difficult,—particularly in a mobile society like our own, to maintain caste distinctions except—as in the case of the black man and the white—on the basis of obvious racial differences.

In China this situation did not exist. The Chinese empire and Chinese culture, partly by conquest and partly by the attraction which a higher civilization invariably exerts over less sophisticated peoples, have steadily extended their influence over the more primitive and tribal peoples on the margins of the Empire. Once these barbarians had acquired the Chinese language and Chinese customs, whether under the influence of Chinese merchants on the outer marches of the Empire, or, as in the case of the Mongols and Manchus, in the central cities, under the influence of Chinese officials with whose aid they ruled the Empire they had conquered, there were no very obvious racial marks to distinguish the foreign from the native peoples. Under these circumstances miscegenation, cultural assimilation and racial amalgamation, in a relatively short time, erased such racial and cultural differences as might otherwise have provided a basis for caste distinctions.

In any case whatever race problems the Chinese people may have encountered in the process of incorporating their tribal neighbors into the more complex matrix of a Chinese society, they were solved by the Chinese family system. The Chinese family seems to have included within the limits of its authority, at different times, a number of alien elements, including servants, slaves and concubines, and it is, apparently, under the influence of this familial authority that Chinese society has succeeded in assimilating the diverse racial elements of which, like every other higher civilization, it is composed.

If the caste system is characteristic of India, and the family system of China, then, in much the same fashion and to much the same extent, the territorial organization of society that we call the state, is characteristic of Europe. One of the functions of the state has been to provide a *modus vivendi* which would permit peoples of divergent races and cultures to live and work together within the limits of a single economy.

An examination of the population map of any European country today will reveal the existence of numerous little racial and cultural enclaves, where the language and tradition of some forgotten tribe or people, not yet wholly assimilated and absorbed, still persist in spite of the pressure imposed upon them by the enveloping economic and political order into which they are in process of being incorporated.

In this connection I am reminded of the fact that the Prussians, the most German of the German states, came into existence as the result of the imposition of a German upon a Slavic people. Prussia is, as a matter of fact, the name of Slavic people first subjugated and then assimilated by invading Germans.

One of the facts which is brought out into a clearer light by investigation of intermarriage in Hawaii, upon which Adams' work is based, is the intimate relations that exist here and elsewhere, between race and culture, and the extent to which in any society biological and social factors interact and influence one another.

If the diverse races of mankind are, so far as we can observe, the products of isolation and inbreeding, it is just as certain that human society and civilization are a consequence of the coming together of diverse races and peoples in intimate association and co-operation that we call society. Every society, every nation, and every civilization has been a kind of melting pot and has thus contributed to the intermingling of races by which new races and new cultures eventually emerge.

As I have said elsewhere:

Changes in race, inevitably follow, at some distance, changes in culture. The movements and mingling of peoples which bring rapid, sudden, and often catastrophic, changes in customs and habits are followed, in the course of time, as a result of interbreeding, by corresponding modifications in temperament and physique. There has probably never been an instance where races have lived together in the intimate contacts which a common economy enforces in which racial contiguity has not produced racial hybrids. However, changes in racial characteristics and in cultural traits proceed at very different rates, and it is notorious that cultural changes are not consolidated and transmitted biologically, or at least to only a very slight extent, if at all. Acquired characteristics are not biologically inherited.[2]

These are very general statements, so general in fact that they will hardly serve, as I hoped they might, either to suggest the theoretic interest of the problems with which this volume is concerned, or to indicate the conceptual limits of the field in which this and similar studies of race relations may be said to lie. I have, however, ventured to repeat here, what has been more fully and better said elsewhere, because it has seemed to me that a volume, dealing as this does with a case study of race mixture and acculturation, under conditions that are relatively unique, would perhaps be more impressive and gain significance if it were read in connection with some larger and more general statement of the historical process, of which it is itself at once an example and an integral part.

If then it happens that in this study of intermarriage in Hawaii, we seem to be brought, so to speak, into the very presence of the historical process, where we may observe civilization as it evolves under something like laboratory conditions, this is due, in part at least, to the advantages of islands for the purpose of sociological investigation.

In Sir J. M. Barrie's comedy, "The Admirable Crichton,"—a sort of whimsical version of the Swiss Family Robinson—the hero, who is

---

[2] Robert E. Park, "Human Migration and the Marginal Man," *The American Journal of Sociology*, Vol. XXXIII, May, 1928, No. 6, p. 883.

the family butler, facing the prospect of an indefinite sojourn on a desert island, makes this prescient remark: "You can't tell what will happen on an island." As might be expected succeeding events more than justify this prediction.

All kinds of things can and do happen on islands. One has only to know what has happened in the Hawaiian Islands since Captain Cook landed there in 1778, or to become acquainted with the extraordinary diversity of conditions existing in the different islands of the archipelago today to realize the justice of this observation. It is a far cry from the little island of Niihau with its population of two hundred natives, living almost in a state of nature, at any rate in well nigh complete isolation from the world about them, to the bustling, modern city of Honolulu. Honolulu, situated on the island of Oahu, at the crossroads of the Pacific where East meets West, is the news center of the Pacific, a kind of international listening post, responsive to every sign and signal that indicates a change in the political weather, so far, at least as this weather reflects relations between the Orient and Occident.

There are six other inhabited islands in the Hawaiian Archipelago besides Niihau and Oahu, but every one, in respect to climate, geography, population and social structure, is marked by individual differences. Every island is, in fact, likely to enclose within the limits of its coast line not merely another community but a different world, each with its own local traditions and way of life, and each more or less self-sufficing and complete in itself. Possibly these differences are not actually as great as they seem but the effect of isolation, which life on an island imposes, is to intensify personal intimacies and by so doing promotes the growth of local customs in response to local conditions. Insularity, in short, encourages individuality and in this sense, it is true that one cannot tell what will happen on an island.

On the other hand, it is just on an island, particularly a small island—and most of the Hawaiian islands are small,—rather than elsewhere that one can know what does go on. In these little island worlds, where the populations are small and everyone is neighborly, there is likely to be very little of that mystery and sentiment in regard to race which so readily springs up in more populous communities where local and occupational segregation so easily becomes the basis for the formation of hereditary classes, or castes.

Countries which encourage immigration are usually tolerant in respect to miscegenation, and where intermarriage is tolerated, there is ordinarily very little race prejudice. Immigrants are notoriously not addicted to ancestor worship. They are too busy getting on in the country. It is only later, after the invading peoples have settled down and the disproportion in sex ratio has declined that race prejudice—the sort of prejudice that may be said to be normal or latent in any racially mixed community—tends to assert itself.

What are popularly referred to as race relations ordinarily involve some sort of race conflict. Race relations conceived in this way, may be said to arise as a result of an extensive movement or mass migration of peoples. In such migrations males invariably arrive first and it is only gradually that the normal balance of the sexes is achieved. It is never fully achieved, in fact, until some time after any movement that could be described as mass migration has ceased. It is the earlier years of these migrations, and on what has been described as the racial frontier, that miscegenation and intermarriage goes on more rapidly. Later, as the disproportion in the sexes in the invading population is redressed, the pace at which intermarriage and race mixture proceeds will ordinarily decline.

The course of events, in such cases, is always more complicated than this statement of it indicates, and it is not possible to predict with any certainty the final outcome, except that one may expect, with a certain amount of assurance, that when stabilization is finally achieved race relations will assume one of three configurations. They will take the form of a caste system, as in India; they will terminate in complete assimilation as in China; or the unassimilated race will constitute a permanent racial minority within the limits of a national state, as is the case of the Jews in Europe.

What has been said suggests that race relations, like many if not most other relations among human beings, must be conceived as existing in three dimensions rather than, as we ordinarily conceive it, in two. Most human relations are a result of some sort of adjustment, and imply the existence, at any rate, of a *modus vivendi*, between individuals and between groups of individuals. But these adjustments are only partial and are themselves involved in a long term process of change, which frequently assumes, on closer examination, the form of an irreversible series or succession.

Changes may be, or seem to be, merely fortuitous. At other times they assume a cyclical or secular form. All three types of change are involved in the processes of growth and all three are more or less involved in what we may describe as the "race relation cycle." This means that race relations, at least the sort of race relations with which we are concerned in this volume, can best be interpreted if what they seem to be at any time and place is regarded merely as a phase in a cycle of change which, once initiated, inevitably continues until it terminates in some predestined racial configuration, and one consistent with an established social order of which it is a part.

Race relations in Hawaii today seem to be approaching the terminus of such a cycle as here described. The population of the islands has risen from the lowest level in 1875 to what it was at the time Cook visited it. The demand for foreign labor for the sugar and pineapple plantations has, apparently, ceased.

This involves a drastic change in the policy which has, within a period of sixty-two years, repeopled the islands with alien races. However, the result of this experiment is still in doubt and probably will remain so, at least until the normal ratio of the sexes has been re-established in the islands. One reason why it has been as successful as it actually has is the fact that owing to the control which the Hawaiian Planters' Association has exercised over its single important industry, Hawaii has had the advantage of a planned economy.

CHAPTER 15

The CAREER OF THE AFRICANS IN BRAZIL

DURING the years in which it has been a subject of discussion and investigation in the United States, the conception of what constitutes a race problem has undergone an extraordinary number of changes—one might say transfigurations. In recent years interest and research in the problematic aspects of race have centered about what is called technically "race relations." But new studies of race relations have invariably revealed new complexities in racial situations and have added new dimensions to the problem as originally conceived. The consequence is that with every new inquiry the conception of what constitutes race relations has steadily expanded until the term seems to include all or most human relations that have anywhere been defined and given formal recognition in the social sciences.

The most obvious and elementary of these relations are ecological and biological, that is, the territorial distribution of races and the inevitable miscegenation or interbreeding which changes in distribution inevitably bring about. The term also includes, by implication at least, all the special problems that emerge on every other level of social integration (i.e., economic, political, personal, or religious) as a consequence of the migration and mixture of races.

I say "personal" or "religious" because it is only within the fold of a family or of a religious society that human relations have anywhere assumed a character that can be described in any exclusive sense as personal and moral. Economic and political relations of indi-

Being "Introduction" to Donald Pierson, *Negroes In Brazil* (Chicago: University of Chicago Press, 1942), pp. xi-xxi.

viduals and of peoples are always relatively impersonal and external.

Meanwhile, a growing awareness of the complexities of the problem has been accompanied by a continuous expansion of what one may describe as "the racial horizon." As the world has grown smaller and our relations with other races and peoples more intimate, the race problem is no longer conceived either in the United States or elsewhere as a local problem or one that is limited to the Negro.

It is obvious today, as it possibly never was before, that race problems are neither a temporary nor an isolated phenomenon. On the contrary, it seems that, wherever European economic expansion has brought European peoples and the peoples or races of the world outside Europe into an association sufficiently intimate to produce a mixed-blood population, the resulting racial situation has inevitably constituted a race problem.

But race problems are not confined to colonial countries. Similar conditions, or at least conditions which make complete assimilation difficult or impossible, have produced in recent years, in Germany and elsewhere in Europe, a more conspicuous and more poignant instance of a race problem than the world outside of Europe has ever known. In fact, it is fair to say that if the race problem of the United States is pre-eminently the problem of Negroes, the race problem of Europe is and has been, ever since the Roman Empire first sought not only to conquer but to denationalize them, the problem of Jews.

Stated abstractly, and from the point of view of the Jewish people in Europe and the Negro people in the United States rather than from the point of view of the dominant majorities with whom they are associated, the race problem is that of a racial or cultural minority seeking to achieve, in a community in which it is regarded as in some sense and to some degree an alien, a status that is at once secure and unqualified by the stigma of any sort of inferiority. Elsewhere the race problem may take the form of a nationalistic struggle in which the native peoples, within the limits of an imperium where they have been conquered but not assimilated, are seeking, if not national independence, then some further measure of self-determination. This is the case of India. It may presently be, if the present German government succeeds in carrying out its program, the case of Europe.

The expansion of the racial horizon, which has changed and is changing current conceptions of the race problem in the United

States and elsewhere, has brought about—and this is particularly true of sociology and social anthropology—something like a reorientation of the social sciences, with respect to the race problem and to all that is ordinarily included under race relations.[1]

Social anthropology is, apparently, no longer regarded, to the extent that it once was, as a purely historical science, interested mainly in unraveling and tracing to their sources the varied threads that make up the cultural patterns of primitive societies.

Anthropology, as it has become "functional," has become less interested in cultural diffusion and more interested in acculturation and in the processes by which cultural traits have been not merely diffused but integrated into those larger and more complex cultural patterns we call civilizations.

Anthropology has begun, also, in recent years to turn its attention to contemporary social problems, including that of education. In England anthropologists have become technical advisers in colonial administration.[2] In the United States they are beginning to study "marginal peoples," that is to say, peoples who, under the influence of European culture, are now in the process, sometimes slowly but more often rapidly, of being assimilated and incorporated into an emerging world-society—the society which the expansion of Europe has brought into existence.[3]

The race problem has assumed new dimensions and new significance, likewise, with the recent researches of sociologists in the field of race and culture and in areas of observation and research immediately contiguous. Probably nothing has been more influential than the publication of the monumental work by W. I. Thomas and Florian Znaniecki, *The Polish Peasant*, in directing the attention of sociological students to the possibility and the importance of studies in the field of race and culture. Thomas and Znaniecki were the first, or almost the first, to call attention to the fact that the situation of the European immigrant in the United States can be defined in terms

---

[1] R. E. Park, "The Nature of Race Relations," in Edgar T. Thompson (ed.), *Race Relations and the Race Problem* (Durham, N.C.: Duke University Press, 1939), pp. 3-45.

[2] See G. Gordon Brown and A. McD. Bruce Hutt, *Anthropology in Action: An Experiment in the Iringa District of the Iringa Province, Tanganyika Territory* (London: International Institute of African Languages and Cultures; Oxford University Press, 1935). See also various papers on "Education and the Cultural Process," *American Journal of Sociology*, XLVIII, May, 1943, no. 6.

[3] See Robert Redfield, *The Folk Culture of Yucatan* (Chicago: University of Chicago Press, 1941).

that imply its logical relation to that of the Negro, even though the Negro, in the Americas, North and South and particularly in the West Indies, is not an alien or an immigrant but has become, in the course of some three hundred years' residence, an indigenous race intimately related by blood to the Indian who preceded him.

Perhaps I should add, now that I have mentioned the *Polish Peasant,* that it was the rather elaborate "methodological note" with which the authors prefaced that study which first defined "social attitudes" and indicated the way in which that concept could be used in characterizing local cultures as well as in measuring, in some fashion, cultural and institutional changes.[4]

If I have ventured by way of introduction to this study of race relations in Brazil to sketch the outlines of an expanding though as yet very little integrated field of sociological and anthropological research, it has been less with the purpose of reporting on the state of knowledge in that field at the moment than of indicating the context in which this study had been conceived and the place it seems to have in the sequence of studies that have preceded and which will presumably follow it.

In suggesting the possibility of future studies to follow this one, I am reckoning with two facts: (1) that Brazil is one of the more conspicuous melting-pots of races and cultures around the world where miscegenation and acculturation are obviously going on and (2) that a comparative study of the problematic aspects of race and culture is likely to have a special importance at this time when the structure of the existing world-order seems to be crumbling with the dissolution of the distances, physical and social, upon which that order seems to rest.

It has become fairly obvious that, in a world which in the midst of wars is steadfastly seeking peace, a stable political order can be erected only on a moral order that does not terminate at the boundaries of national states. The problem that emerges is this: How is it

---

[4] William I. Thomas and Florian Znaniecki, *The Polish Peasant in Europe and America* (1st ed.; Boston: Richard C. Badger, 1918-20; 2d ed.; New York: Alfred Knopf, 1927). Herbert Blumer, *Critiques of Research in the Social Sciences. I. An Appraisal of Thomas and Znaniecki's "The Polish Peasant in Europe and America"* (New York: Social Science Research Council, 1939). As an illustration of how "attitudes" have been used in measuring fundamental institutional changes see Alfred Winslow Jones, *Life, Liberty, and Property: A Story of Conflict and a Measurement of Conflicting Rights* (New York and London: J. B. Lippincott Co., 1941).

possible to establish and maintain an effective social order in a more or less completely urbanized, industrialized, and cosmopolitan world?

In the past it has been, in the main, the task of religion and more especially of Christian missions to create within the limits of an expanding world-economy a moral order and moral solidarity commensurate with the economic and political interdependence which the expansion of European commerce has brought about. But the totalitarian states have now apparently seceded from the ecumenical councils of international Christianity, and the task of re-creating a moral order that includes all mankind has assumed an importance that it did not have when it was regarded not merely as a religious but as a religious denominational enterprise.

It is obvious that studies of race and culture are destined to assume increasing importance in a world in which the ancient local and tribal cultures, as an ineluctable incident of the rise of the so-called "great society," are visibly going into the melting-pot.

One thing that makes the racial situation in Brazil interesting is the fact that, having a Negro population proportionally larger than the United States, Brazil has no race problem. This is, at any rate, what might be inferred from the occasional and apparently disinterested reports of visitors to that country who have ventured to inquire into the subject. Among these visitors there are two—James Bryce and Theodore Roosevelt—whose knowledge of conditions in the United States make their reports upon the situation in Brazil peculiarly interesting.

Viscount Bryce, whose "observations and impressions" of South America were first published in 1912, remarked that in Brazil, in contrast to the United States, the color line is nowhere sharply drawn and that "the fusion of whites and blacks by intermarriage goes steadily on." Mr. Roosevelt—Theodore and not Franklin Delano—who visited the country a few years later, is more explicit. He says: "If I were asked to name the one point in which there is a complete difference between the Brazilian and ourselves, I should say it was in the attitude to the black man."

This attitude manifests itself in the fact that in Brazil "any Negro or mulatto who shows himself fit is without question given the place to which his abilities entitle him." However, the most conspicuous difference—the "one real difference"—is "the tendency of Brazil to absorb the Negro." This tendency is, however, not merely a historical and biological fact; it is rather an expression of a national policy, in so far as Brazil can be said to have a policy with respect to the Negro.

Statistics of population, which are never very accurate in this matter of race and less so perhaps in Brazil than in the United States, indicate that the number of Africans of unmixed blood is growing steadily less so that "with two or more racial crossings"—so say those Brazilians who are conscious of the Negro or concerned about his future—"the Negro blood tends to disappear." This so-called Aryanization of the African, from the point of view of Brazilian national policy, is a thing, perhaps one should say *the* thing, to be desired. The policy of the United States, on the other hand, from the Brazilian point of view, particularly in so far as it counts every man a Negro who, to use the census definition, "is known to be a Negro in the community in which he lives," tends to perpetuate "a menacing element"—menacing not to the racial purity of the dominant race but to the political and cultural solidarity of the nation.

As a matter of fact the attitude of the Brazilian people to the race problem so far as concerns the Negro seems, on the whole, to be academic rather than pragmatic and actual. There is a certain ethnological and archeological interest in the survivals of the African fetish cults, the so-called *candomblés*, of which there seem to be an extraordinary number, especially in and about the cities of Bahia and Pernambuco. This archeological interest in the African is evidenced by two successive *Congressos Afro-brasileiros* which met in Recife and in Bahia in 1934 and 1937.

Since most of these *candomblés* are living and functioning forms of African religious practices, although obviously in process of assimilation to the ritual and mythology of local Catholicism, perhaps they should not be classed as survivals.

In any case it is a somewhat bizarre experience to a stranger in Bahia, walking along one of the ridges where *os ricos*, that is, the rich folk, live, to hear from the palm groves in the neighboring valleys where *os pobres*, the poor folk, live, the insistent boom of African drums. So narrow are the spatial distances that divide Europe on the ridges from Africa in the valleys that it is difficult to realize how wide the social distances are that separate them.

It is even more difficult for those of us whose conception of the Negro problem and of race relations generally has been formed in the United States to comprehend, in all its concreteness, the racial situation in a country with a different history and a different tradition.

Comprehension in these matters is not something that can be achieved, it seems, through the medium of any formal statement. Insight and understanding come only with intimate and firsthand acquaintance—and not even then if those barriers which race consciousness invariably raises are not removed. That is why little children are likely in these matters of race relations to be wiser than their elders.

This observation seems pertinent here because, after reading the manuscript and proofs of this volume [*Negroes in Brazil*], I have come to the conclusion that the difference between Brazil and the United States in respect to race is due to the fact that the people of Brazil have, somehow, regained that paradisaic innocence, with respect to differences of race, which the people of the United States have somehow lost. I mention this fact, but I shall not attempt to explain it. The situation is complex and the explanations are only partial and not wholly convincing. One circumstance mentioned by Donald Pierson, I am, however, disposed to underscore.

Brazil is a vast country and has been colonized, as has the United States, by a wide variety of peoples: Germans from northern Europe; Latins, particularly Italians, from southern Europe; not to mention the original settlers, the Portuguese. It has been colonized more recently by Orientals. There are possibly some two hundred thousand Japanese in Brazil today. With the exception of the Italians, these different peoples have settled in more or less closed communities in widely separated parts of a vast territory. Dependent upon water transportation rather more than upon rail to maintain economic and political unity, Brazil has been haunted by the fear that the country would some day fall apart. Under these circumstances it has seemed that the security and the solidarity of the nation depended upon its ability to assimilate and ultimately to amalgamate its different immigrant populations. From this point of view the Negro has not constituted a problem.

The first task of this, as of every other attempt to study the race problem rather than to solve it, has been to define the racial situation in the country and in the culture in which the problem exists. But the author of this volume has done something more, it seems, than that. He has, as he puts it, given an account of "the career of the Negro in Brazil," and he has made this account a chapter in the life-history of the Negro outside of Africa, in what one might, to use a term that has been usually applied to the Jewish people, call the Diaspora.

The term "diaspora" was first used by the Greeks to designate a nationality, or some part of it, dispersed among other nations but preserving its own culture. The Negro outside of Africa is neither a nation nor a nationality, and, with the exception of Brazil, there is no country outside of Africa, so far as I know, where a people of African origin has sought to preserve African customs or African culture. Nevertheless, the attitude of Europeans has imposed upon peoples of African origin under European domination, either in or outside of Africa, a certain degree of race consciousness and racial solidarity. It has tended to make them a nationality.

Living thus, as Booker Washington once said of the Negro in the United States, as "a nation within a nation," the Negro has been subjected to extraordinary changes of fortune but changes that are nonetheless typical not merely of Negroes abroad but of other peoples who, in the interest of European commercial expansion, have been dispersed to widely separated parts of the world.

The diaspora, however, is no longer what it once was—an area of dispersion merely. It has become rather an area of integration, economic and cultural. It is in this sense that this history, I might better say natural history, of the career of the African in·Brazil has sought to describe the processes by which the Negro has been assimilated and to measure the success he has had in finding a place in what was the diaspora but now is, to use Graham Wallas' term, *The Great Society*.

CHAPTER 16

R ACIAL ASSIMILATION
IN SECONDARY GROUPS[1]

With Particular Reference to the Negro

I

THE RACE PROBLEM has sometimes been described as a problem in assimilation. It is not always clear, however, what assimilation means. Historically the word has had two distinct significations. According to earlier usage it meant "to compare" or "to make like." According to later usage it signifies "to take up and incorporate."

There is a process that goes on in society by which individuals spontaneously acquire one another's language, characteristic attitudes, habits, and modes of behavior. There is also a process by which individuals and groups of individuals are taken over and incorporated into larger groups. Both processes have been concerned in the formation of modern nationalities. The modern Italian, Frenchman, and German is a composite of the broken fragments of several different racial groups. Interbreeding has broken up the ancient stocks, and interaction and imitation have created new national types which exhibit definite uniformities in language, manners, and formal behavior.

It has sometimes been assumed that the creation of a national type is the specific function of assimilation and that national solidarity is based upon national homogeneity and "like-mindedness." The extent and importance of the kind of homogeneity that individuals of the

[1] The distinction between primary and secondary groups used in this paper is that made by Charles H. Cooley.
Publication of the American Sociological Society, VIII (1913), pp. 66-83.

same nationality exhibit have been greatly exaggerated. Neither inter-breeding nor interaction has created, in what the French term "nationals," a more than superficial likeness or like-mindedness. Racial differences have, to be sure, disappeared or been obscured, but individual differences remain. Individual differences, again, have been intensified by education, personal competition, and the division of labor, until individual members of cosmopolitan groups probably represent greater variations in disposition, temperament, and mental capacity than those which distinguished the more homogeneous races and peoples of an earlier civilization.[2]

What then, precisely, is the nature of the homogeneity which characterizes cosmopolitan groups?

The growth of modern states exhibits the progressive merging of smaller, mutually exclusive, into larger and more inclusive social groups. This result has been achieved in various ways, but it has usually been followed, or accompanied, by a more or less complete adoption, by the members of the smaller groups, of the language, technique, and mores of the larger and more inclusive ones. The immigrant readily takes over the language, manners, the social ritual, and outward forms of his adopted country. In America it has become proverbial that a Pole, Lithuanian, or Norwegian cannot be distinguished, in the second generation, from an American born of native parents.

There is no reason to assume that this assimilation of alien groups to native standards has modified to any great extent fundamental racial characteristics. It has, however, erased the external signs which formerly distinguished the members of one race from those of another.

On the other hand, the breaking up of the isolation of smaller groups has had the effect of emancipating the individual man, giving him room and freedom for the expansion and development of his individual aptitudes.

What one actually finds in cosmopolitan groups, then, is a superficial uniformity, a homogeneity in manners and fashion, associated with relatively profound differences in individual opinions, sentiments, and beliefs. This is just the reverse of what one meets among primitive peoples, where diversity in external forms, as between different groups, is accompanied with a monotonous sameness in the men-

---

[2] F. Boas, *Journal of American Folk-Lore*, quoted by W. I. Thomas, in *Source Book for Social Origins*, p. 155.

tal attitudes of individuals. There is a striking similarity in the sentiments and mental attitudes of peasant peoples in all parts of the world, although the external differences are often great. In the Black Forest, in Baden, Germany, almost every valley shows a different style of costume, a different type of architecture, although in each separate valley every house is like every other and the costume, as well as the religion, is for every member of each separate community absolutely after the same pattern. On the other hand, a German, Russian, or Negro peasant of the southern states, different as each is in some respects, are all very much alike in certain habitual attitudes and sentiments.

What, then, is the rôle of homogeneity and like-mindedness, such as we find them to be, in cosmopolitan states?

So far as it makes each individual look like every other—no matter how different under the skin—homogeneity mobilizes the individual man. It removes the social taboo, permits the individual to move into strange groups, and thus facilitates new and adventurous contacts. In obliterating the external signs, which in secondary groups seem to be the sole basis of caste and class distinctions, it realizes, for the individual, the principle of *laissez-faire, laissez-aller*. Its ultimate economic effect is to substitute personal for racial competition, and to give free play to forces that tend to relegate every individual, irrespective of race or status, to the position he or she is best fitted to fill.

As a matter of fact, the ease and rapidity with which aliens, under existing conditions in the United States, have been able to assimilate themselves to the customs and manners of American life have enabled this country to swallow and digest every sort of normal human difference, except the purely external ones, like the color of the skin.

It is probably true, also, that like-mindedness of the kind that expresses itself in national types, contributes, indirectly, by facilitating the intermingling of the different elements of the population, to the national solidarity. This is due to the fact that the solidarity of modern states depends less on the homogeneity of population than, as James Bryce has suggested, upon the thorough-going mixture of heterogeneous elements.[3] Like-mindedness, so far as that term signifies

---

[3] "Racial differences and animosities, which have played a large part in threatening the unity of States, are usually dangerous when unfriendly races occupy different parts of the country. If they live intermixed, in tolerably equal numbers, and if in addition they are not of different religions, and speak the same tongue, the antagonism will disappear in a generation or two and especially by intermarriage. . . . . But in one set of cases no fusion is possible; and this set of cases

a standard grade of intelligence, contributes little or nothing to national solidarity. Likeness is, after all, a purely formal concept which of itself cannot hold anything together.

In the last analysis social solidarity is based on sentiment and habit. It is the sentiment of loyalty and the habit of what Sumner calls "concurrent action," that gives substance and insures unity to the state, as to every other type of social group. This sentiment of loyalty has its basis in a *modus vivendi*, a working relation and mutual understanding, of the members of the group. Social institutions are not founded in similarities any more than they are founded in differences, but in relations, and in the mutual interdependence of parts. When these relations have the sanction of custom and are fixed in individual habit, so that the activities of the group are running smoothly, personal attitudes and sentiments, which are the only forms in which individual minds collide and clash with one another, easily accommodate themselves to the existing situation.

It may, perhaps, be said that loyalty itself is a form of likemindedness, or that it is dependent in some way upon the likemindedness of the individuals whom it binds together. This, however, cannot be true, for there is no greater loyalty than that which binds the dog to his master, and this is a sentiment which that faithful animal usually extends to other members of the household to which he belongs. A dog without a master is a dangerous animal, but the dog that has been domesticated is a member of society. He is not, of course, a citizen, although he is not entirely without rights. But he has got into some sort of practical working relations with the group to which he belongs.

It is this practical working arrangement, into which individuals with widely different mental capacities enter as co-ordinate parts, that gives the corporate character to social groups and insures their solidarity.

It is the process of assimilation by which groups of individuals, originally indifferent or perhaps hostile, achieve this corporate character, rather than the process by which they acquire a formal likemindedness, with which this paper is mainly concerned.

The difficulty with the conception of assimilation which one ordinarily meets in discussions of the race problem, is that it is based on

---

forms the despair of statesmen. It presents a problem which no constitution can solve. It is the juxtaposition on the same soil of races of different color."—James Bryce, *Studies in History and Jurisprudence*, pp. 245-46.

observations confined to individualistic groups where the characteristic relations are indirect and secondary. It takes no account of the
kind of assimilation that takes place in primary groups where relations are direct and personal—in the tribe, for example, and in the
family.

Thus Charles Francis Adams, referring to the race problem in an
address at Richmond, Va., in November, 1908, said:

> The American system, as we know, was founded on the assumed basis
> of a common humanity, that is, absence of absolutely fundamental racial
> characteristics was accepted as an established truth. Those of all races were
> welcomed to our shores. They came, aliens; they and their descendants
> would become citizens first, natives afterward. It was a process first of
> assimilation and then of absorption. On this all depended. There could be
> no permanent divisional lines. That theory is now plainly broken down.
> We are confronted by the obvious fact, as undeniable as it is hard, that the
> African will only partially assimilate and that he cannot be absorbed. He
> remains an alien element in the body politic. A foreign substance, he can
> neither be assimilated nor thrown out.

More recently an editorial in the *Outlook*, discussing the Japanese
situation in California, made this statement:

> The hundred millions of people now inhabiting the United States must
> be a united people, not merely a collection of groups of different peoples,
> different in racial cultures and ideals, agreeing to live together in peace
> and amity. These hundred millions must have common ideals, common
> aims, a common custom, a common culture, a common language, and com-
> mon characteristics if the nation is to endure.[4]

All this is quite true and interesting, but it does not clearly recognize the fact that the chief obstacle to the assimilation of the Negro
and the Oriental are not mental but physical traits. It is not because
the Negro and the Japanese are so differently constituted that they do
not assimilate. If they were given an opportunity the Japanese are
quite as capable as the Italians, the Armenians, or the Slavs of acquiring our culture, and sharing our national ideals. The trouble is not
with the Japanese mind but with the Japanese skin. The "Jap" is not
the right color.

The fact that the Japanese bears in his features a distinctive racial
hallmark, that he wears, so to speak, a racial uniform, classifies him.
He cannot become a mere individual, indistinguishable in the cosmopolitan mass of the population, as is true, for example, of the Irish

---

[4] *Outlook*, August 2, 1913.

and, to a lesser extent, of some of the other immigrant races. The Japanese, like the Negro is condemned to remain among us an abstraction, a symbol, and a symbol not merely of his own race, but of the Orient and of that vague, ill-defined menace we sometimes refer to as the "yellow peril." This not only determines, to a very large extent, the attitude of the white world toward the yellow man, but it determines the attitude of the yellow man toward the white. It puts between the races the invisible but very real gulf of self-consciousness.

There is another consideration. Peoples we know intimately we respect and esteem. In our casual contact with aliens, however, it is the offensive rather than the pleasing traits that impress us. These impressions accumulate and reinforce natural prejudices. Where races are distinguished by certain external marks these furnish a permanent physical substratum upon which and around which the irritations and animosities, incidental to all human intercourse, tend to accumulate and so gain strength and volume.

II

Assimilation, as the word is here used, brings with it a certain borrowed significance which it carried over from physiology where it is employed to describe the process of nutrition. By a process of nutrition, somewhat similar to the physiological one, we may conceive alien peoples to be incorporated with, and made part of, the community or state. Ordinarily assimilation goes on silently and unconsciously, and only forces itself into popular conscience when there is some interruption or disturbance of the process.

At the outset it may be said, then, that assimilation rarely becomes a problem except in secondary groups. Admission to the primary group, that is to say, the group in which relationships are direct and personal, as, for example, in the family and in the tribe, makes assimilation comparatively easy, and almost inevitable.

The most striking illustration of this is the fact of domestic slavery. Slavery has been, historically, the usual method by which peoples have been incorporated into alien groups. When a member of an alien race is adopted into the family as a servant, or as a slave, and particularly when that status is made hereditary, as it was in the case of the Negro after his importation to America, assimilation followed rapidly and as a matter of course.

It is difficult to conceive two races farther removed from each other in temperament and tradition than the Anglo-Saxon and the Negro, and yet the Negro in the southern states, particularly where he was adopted into the household as a family servant, learned in a comparatively short time the manners and customs of his master's family. He very soon possessed himself of so much of the language, religion, and the technique of the civilization of his master as, in his station, he was fitted or permitted to acquire. Eventually, also, Negro slaves transferred their allegiance to the state, of which they were only indirectly members, or at least to their masters' families, with whom they felt themselves in most things one in sentiment and interest.

The assimilation of the Negro field hand, where the contact of the slave with his master and his master's family was less intimate, was naturally less complete. On the large plantations, where an overseer stood between the master and the majority of his slaves, and especially on the Sea Island plantations off the coast of South Carolina, where the master and his family were likely to be merely winter visitors, this distance between master and slave was greatly increased. The consequence is that the Negroes in these regions are less touched today by the white man's influence and civilization than elsewhere in the southern states. The size of the plantation, the density of the slave population, and the extent and character of the isolation in which the master and his slave lived are factors to be reckoned with in estimating the influence which the plantation exerted on the Negro. In Virginia the average slave population on the plantation has been estimated at about ten. On the Sea Islands and farther south it was thirty; and in Jamaica it was two hundred.[5]

As might be expected there were class distinctions among the slaves as among the whites, and these class distinctions were more rigidly enforced on the large plantations than on the smaller ones. In Jamaica, for example, it was customary to employ the mulattoes in the lighter and the more desirable occupations about the master's house. The mulattoes in that part of the country, more definitely than was true in the United States, constituted a separate caste midway between the white man and black. Under these conditions the assimilation of the masses of the Negro people took place more slowly and less completely in Jamaica than in the United States.

In Virginia and the border states, and in what was known as the

---

[5] *Documentary History of American and Industrial Society*, Vol. I, "Plantation and Frontier": Introduction, pp. 80-81.

Back Country, where the plantations were smaller and the relation of the races more intimate, slaves gained relatively more of the white man's civilization. The kindly relations of master and slave in Virginia are indicated by the number of free Negroes in that state. In 1860 one Negro in every eight was free and in one county in the Tidewater Region, the county of Nansemond, there were 2,473 Negroes and only 581 slaves. The differences in the Negro population which existed before the Civil War are still clearly marked today. They are so clearly marked, in fact, that an outline of the areas in which the different types of plantation existed before the War would furnish the basis for a map showing distinct cultural levels in the Negro population in the South today.

The first Negroes were imported into the United States in 1619. At the beginning of the nineteenth century there were 900,000 slaves in the United States. By 1860 that number had increased to nearly 4,000,000. At that time, it is safe to say, the great mass of the Negroes were no longer, in any true sense, an alien people. They were, of course, not citizens. They lived in the smaller world of the particular plantation to which they belonged. It might, perhaps, be more correct to say that they were less assimilated than domesticated.

In this respect, however, the situation of the Negro was not different from that of the Russian peasant, at least as late as 1860. The Russian noble and the Russian peasant were likely to be of the same ethnic stock, but mentally they were probably not much more alike than the Negro slave and his matser. The noble and the peasant did not intermarry. The peasant lived in the little world of the *mir* or commune. He had his own customs and traditions. His life and thought moved in a smaller orbit and he knew nothing about the larger world which belonged exclusively to the noble. The relations between the serf and the proprietor of the estate to which he was attached were, perhaps, less familiar and less frank than those which existed between the Negro slave and his master. The attitude of the serf in the presence of the noble was more abject. Still, one could hardly say that the Russian peasant had not been assimilated, at least in the sense in which it has been decided to use that term in this paper.

A right understanding of conditions in the South before the War will make clear that the southern plantation was founded in the different temperaments, habits, and sentiments of the white man and the black. The discipline of the plantation put its own impress upon, and largely formed the character of, both races. In the life of the plantation white and black were different but complementary, the one bred to the rôle of a slave and the other to that of master. This, of course, takes no account of the poor white man who was also formed by slavery, but rather as a by-product.

Where the conditions of slavery brought the two races, as it frequently did, into close and intimate contact, there grew up a mutual sympathy and understanding which frequently withstood not only the shock of the Civil War, but the political agitation and chicane which followed it in the southern states.

Speaking of the difference between the North and the South in its attitude toward the Negro, Booker T. Washington says: "It is the individual touch which holds the races together in the South, and it is this individual touch which is lacking to a large degree in the North."

No doubt kindly relations between individual members of the two races do exist in the South to an extent not known in the North. As a rule, it will be found that these kindly relations had their origin in slavery. The men who have given the tone to political discussion in southern states in recent years are men who did not own slaves. The men from the mountain districts of the South, whose sentiments found expression in a great antislavery document, like Hinton Helper's *Impending Crisis*, hated slavery with an intensity that was only equaled by their hatred for the Negro. It is the raucous note of the Hill Billy and the Red Neck that one hears in the public utterances of men like Senator Vardaman, of Mississippi, and Governor Blease, of South Carolina.

III

The Civil War weakened but did not fully destroy the *modus vivendi* which slavery had established between the slave and his master. With emancipation the authority which had formerly been exercised by the master was transferred to the state, and Washington, D.C., began to assume in the mind of the freedman the position that formerly had been occupied by the "big house" on the plantation. The masses of the Negro people still maintained their habit of dependence, however, and after the first confusion of the change had passed, life went on, for most of them, much as it had before the War. As one old farmer explained, the only difference he could see was that in slavery he "was working for old Marster and now he was working for himself."

There was one difference between slavery and freedom, nevertheless, which was very real to the freedman. And this was the liberty to move. To move from one plantation to another in case he was discontented was one of the ways in which a freedman was able to realize his freedom and to make sure that he possessed it. This liberty to move meant a good deal more to the plantation Negro than one not acquainted with the situation in the South is likely to understand.

If there had been an abundance of labor in the South; if the situation had been such that the Negro laborer was seeking the opportunity to work, or such that the Negro tenant farmers were competing for the opportunity to get a place on the land, as is so frequently the case in Europe, the situation would have been fundamentally different from what it actually was. But the South was, and is today, what Nieboer called a country of "open," in contradistinction to a country of "closed" resources. In other words there is more land in the South than there is labor to till it. Land owners are driven to competing for laborers and tenants to work their plantations.

Owing to his ignorance of business matters and to a long-established habit of submission the Negro after emancipation was placed at a great disadvantage in his dealings with the white man. His right to move from one plantation to another became, therefore, the Negro tenant's method of enforcing consideration from the planter. He might not dispute the planter's accounts, because he was not capable of doing so, and it was unprofitable to attempt it, but if he felt aggrieved he could move.

This was the significance of the exodus in some of the southern states which took place about 1879, when 40,000 people left the plantations in the Black Belts of Louisiana and Mississippi and went to Kansas. The masses of the colored people were dissatisfied with the treatment they were receiving from the planters and made up their minds to move to "a free country," as they described it. At the same time it was the attempt of the planter to bind the Negro tenant who was in debt to him, to his place on the plantation, that gave rise to the system of peonage that still exists in a mitigated form in the South today.

When the Negro moved off the plantation upon which he was reared he severed the personal relations which bound him to his master's people. It was just at this point that the two races began to lose touch with each other. From this time on the relations of the black man and the white, which in slavery had been direct and personal, became every year, as the old associations were broken, more and more indirect and secondary. There lingers still the disposition on the part of the white man to treat every Negro familiarly, and the disposition on the part of every Negro to treat every white man respectfully. But these are habits which are gradually disappearing. The breaking down of the instincts and habits of servitude, and the acquisition, by the masses of the Negro people, of the instincts and habits of freedom have proceeded slowly but steadily. The reason the change seems to have gone on more rapidly in some cases than others is explained by the fact that at the time of emancipation 10 per cent of the Negroes in the United States were already free, and others, those who had worked in trades, many of whom had hired their own time from their masters, had become more or less adapted to the competitive conditions of free society.

One of the effects of the mobilization of the Negro has been to bring him into closer and more intimate contact with his own people. Common interests have drawn the blacks together, and caste sentiment has kept the black and white apart. The segregation of the races, which began as a spontaneous movement on the part of both, has been fostered by the policy of the dominant race. The agitation of the Reconstruction Period made the division between the races in politics absolute. Segregation and separation in other matters have gone on steadily ever since. The Negro at the present time has separate churces, schools, libraries, hospitals, Y.M.C.A. associations, and even separate towns. There are, perhaps, a half-dozen communities in the United States, every inhabitant of which is a Negro. Most of these so-called Negro towns are suburban villages; two of them, at any rate, are the centers of a considerable Negro farming population. In general it may be said that where the Negro schools, churches, and Y.M.C.A. associations are not separate they do not exist.

It is hard to estimate the ultimate effect of this isolation of the black man. One of the most important effects has been to establish a common interest among all the different colors and classes of the race. This sense of solidarity has grown up gradually with the organization of the Negro people. It is stronger in the South, where segregation is more complete, than it is in the North where, twenty years ago, it would have been safe to say it did not exist. Gradually, imperceptibly, within the larger world of the white man, a smaller world, the world of the black man, is silently taking form and shape.

Every advance in education and intelligence puts the Negro in possession of the technique of communication and organization of the white man, and so contributes to the extension and consolidation of the Negro world within the white.

The motive for this increasing solidarity is furnished by the increasing pressure, or perhaps I should say, by the increasing sensibility of Negroes to the pressure and the prejudice without. The sentiment of racial loyalty, which is a comparatively recent manifestation of the growing self-consciousness of the race, must be regarded as a response and "accommodation" to changing internal and external relations of the race. The sentiment which Negroes are beginning to call "race pride" does not exist to the same extent in the North as in the South, but an increasing disposition to enforce racial distinctions in the North, as in the South, is bringing it into existence.

One or two incidents in this connection are significant. A few years ago a man who is the head of the largest Negro publishing business in this country sent to Germany and had a number of Negro dolls manufactured according to specifications of his own. At the time this company was started Negro children were in the habit of playing with white dolls. There were already Negro dolls on the market, but they were for white children and represented the white man's conception of the Negro and not the Negro's ideal of himself. The new Negro doll was a mulatto with regular features slightly modified in favor of the conventional Negro type. It was a neat, prim, well-dressed, well-behaved, self-respecting doll. Later on, as I understand, there were other dolls, equally tidy and respectable in appearance, but in darker shades with Negro features a little more pronounced. The man who designed these dolls was perfectly clear in regard to the significance of the substitution that he was making. He said that he thought it was a good thing to let Negro girls become accustomed to dolls of their own color. He thought it important, as long as the races were to be segregated, that the dolls, which like other forms of art, are patterns and represent ideals, should be segregated also.

This substitution of the Negro model for the white is a very interesting and a very significant fact. It means that the Negro has begun to fashion his own ideals and in his own image rather than in that of the white man. It is also interesting to know that the Negro doll company has been a success and that these dolls are now widely sold in every part of the United States. Nothing exhibits more clearly the extent to which the Negro has become assimilated in slavery or the extent to which he has broken with the past in recent years than this episode of the Negro doll.

The incident is typical. It is an indication of the nature of tendencies and of forces that are stirring in the background of the Negro's mind, although they have not succeeded in forcing themselves, except in special instances, into clear consciousness.

In this same category must be reckoned the poetry of Paul Lawrence Dunbar, in whom, as William Dean Howells has said, the Negro "attained civilization." Before Paul Lawrence Dunbar, Negro literature had been either apologetic or self-assertive, but Dunbar "studied the Negro objectively." He represented him as he found him, not only without apology, but with an affectionate understanding and sympathy which one can have only for what is one's own. In Dunbar, Negro literature attained an ethnocentric point of view. Through the medium of his verses the ordinary shapes and forms of the Negro's life have taken on the color of his affections and sentiments and we see the black man, not as he looks, but as he feels and is.

It is a significant fact that a certain number of educated—or rather the so-called educated—Negroes were not at first disposed to accept at their full value either Dunbar's dialect verse or the familiar pictures of Negro life which are the symbols in which his poetry usually found expression. The explanation sometimes offered for the dialect poems was that "they were made to please white folk." The assumption seems to have been that if they had been written for Negroes it would have been impossible in his poetry to distinguish black people from white. This was a sentiment which was never shared by the masses of the people, who, upon the occasions when Dunbar recited to them, were fairly bowled over with amusement and delight because of the authenticity of the portraits he offered them. At the present time Dunbar is so far accepted as to have hundreds of imitators.

Literature and art have played a similar and perhaps more important rôle in the racial struggles of Europe than of America. One reason seems to be that racial conflicts, as they occur in secondary groups, are primarily sentimental and secondarily economic. Literature and art, when they are employed to give expression to racial sentiment and form to racial ideals, serve, along with other agencies, to mobilize the group and put the masses *en rapport* with their leaders and with each other. In such case art and literature are like silent drummers which summon into action the latent instincts and energies of the race.

These struggles, I might add, in which a submerged people seek to rise and make for themselves a place in a world occupied by superior and privileged races, are not less vital or less important because they are bloodless. They serve to stimulate ambitions and inspire ideals which years, perhaps, of subjection and subordination have suppressed. In fact, it seems as if it were through conflicts of this kind, rather than through war, that the minor peoples were destined to gain the moral concentration and discipline that fit them to share, on anything like equal terms, in the conscious life of the civilized world.

IV

The progress of race adjustment in the southern states since the emancipation has, on the whole, run parallel with the nationalist movement in Europe. The so-called "nationalities" are, for the most part, Slavic peoples, fragments of the great Slavic race, that have attained national self-consciousness as a result of their struggle for freedom and air against their German conquerors. It is a significant fact that the nationalist movement, as well as the "nationalities" that it has brought into existence, had its rise in that twilight zone, upon the eastern border of Germany and the western border of Russia, and is part of the century-long conflict, partly racial, partly cultural, of which this meeting-place of the East and West has been the scene.

Until the beginning of the last century the European peasant, like the Negro slave, bound as he was to the soil, lived in the little world of direct and personal relations, under what we may call a domestic régime. It was military necessity that first turned the attention of statesmen like Frederick the Great of Prussia to the welfare of the peasant. It was the overthrow of Prussia by Napoleon in 1807 that brought about his final emancipation in that country. In recent years it has been the international struggle for economic efficiency which has contributed most to mobilize the peasant and laboring classes in Europe.

As the peasant slowly emerged from serfdom he found himself a member of a depressed class, without education, political privileges, or capital. It was the struggle of this class for wider opportunity and better conditions of life that made most of the history of the previous

century. Among the peoples in the racial borderland the effect of this
struggle has been, on the whole, to substitute for a horizontal organization of society—in which the upper stratum, that is to say the
wealthy or privileged class, was mainly of one race and the poorer
and subject class was mainly of another—a vertical organization in
which all classes of each racial group were united under the title of
their respective nationalities. Thus organized, the nationalities represent, on the one hand, intractable minorities engaged in a ruthless
partisan struggle for political privilege or economic advantage and,
on the other, they represent cultural groups, each struggling to
maintain a sentiment of loyalty to the distinctive traditions, language,
and institutions of the race they represent.

This sketch of the racial situation in Europe is, of course, the
barest abstraction and should not be accepted realistically. It is intended merely as an indication of similarities, in the broader outlines, of the motives that have produced nationalities in Europe and
are making the Negro in America, as Booker Washington says, "a
nation within a nation."

It may be said that there is one profound difference between the
Negro and the European nationalities, namely, that the Negro has had
his separateness and consequent race consciousness thrust upon him,
because of his exclusion and forcible isolation from white society.
The Slavic nationalities, on the contrary, have segregated themselves
in order to escape assimilation and escape racial extinction in the
larger cosmopolitan states.

The difference is, however, not so great as it seems. With the
exception of the Poles, nationalistic sentiment may be said hardly
to have existed fifty years ago. Forty years ago when German was
the language of the educated classes, educated Bohemians were a
little ashamed to speak their own language in public. Now nationalist
sentiment is so strong that, where the Czech nationality has gained
control, it has sought to wipe out every vestige of the German language. It has changed the names of streets, buildings, and public
places. In the city of Prag, for example, all that formerly held
German associations now fairly reeks with the sentiment of Bohemian
nationality.

On the other hand, the masses of the Polish people cherished very
little nationalist sentiment until after the Franco-Prussian War. The
fact is that nationalist sentiment among the Slavs, like racial sentiment
among the Negroes, has sprung up as the result of a struggle against

privilege and discrimination based upon racial distinctions. The movement is not so far advanced among Negroes; sentiment is not so intense, and for several reasons probably never will be. One reason is that Negroes, in their struggle for equal opportunities, have the democratic sentiment of the country on their side.

From what has been said it seems fair to draw one conclusion, namely: under conditions of secondary contact, that is to say, conditions of individual liberty and individual competition, characteristic of modern civilization, depressed racial groups tend to assume the form of nationalities. A nationality, in this narrower sense, may be defined as the racial group which has attained self-consciousness, no matter whether it has at the same time gained political independence or not.

In societies organized along horizontal lines the disposition of individuals in the lower strata is to seek their models in the strata above them. Loyalty attaches to individuals, particularly to the upper classes, who furnish, in their persons and in their lives, the models for the masses of the people below them. Long after the nobility has lost every other social function connected with its vocation the ideals of the nobility have survived in our conception of the gentleman, genteel manners and bearing—gentility.

The sentiment of the Negro slave was, in a certain sense, not merely loyalty to his master, but to the white race. Negroes of the older generations speak very frequently, with a sense of proprietorship, of "our white folk." This sentiment was not always confined to the ignorant masses. An educated colored man once explained to me "that we colored people always want our white folks to be superior." He was shocked when I showed no particular enthusiasm for that form of sentiment.

The fundamental significance of the nationalist movement must be sought in the effort of subject races, sometimes consciously, sometimes unconsciously, to substitute, for those supplied them by aliens, models based on their own racial individuality and embodying sentiments and ideals which spring naturally out of their own lives.

After a race has achieved in this way its moral independence assimilation, in the sense of copying, will still continue. Nations and races borrow from those whom they fear as well as from those whom they admire. Materials taken over in this way, however, are inevitably stamped with the individuality of the nationalities that appropriate them. These materials will contribute to the dignity, to the prestige, and to the solidarity of the nationality which borrows them, but they will no longer inspire loyalty to the race from which they are borrowed. A race which has attained the character of a nationality may still retain its loyalty to the state of which it is a part, but only in so far as that state incorporates, as an integral part of its organization, the practical interests, the aspirations and ideals of that nationality.

The aim of the contending nationalities in Austria-Hungry at the present time seems to be a federation, like that of Switzerland, based upon the autonomy of the different races composing the empire.[6] In the South, similarly, the races seem to be tending in the direction of a bi-racial organization of society, in which the Negro is gradually gaining a limited autonomy. What the ultimate outcome of this movement may be it is not safe to predict.

---

6 Aurel C. Popovici, *Die Vereinigten Staaten von Gross-Oestreich, Politische Studien zur Lösung der nationalen Fragen u. staatsrechtlichen Krisen in Oestreich*, Leipzig, 1906.

PART III *Racial Attitudes*

CHAPTER 17

RACE PREJUDICE AND JAPANESE-AMERICAN RELATIONS

THERE is a conviction, widespread in America at the present time, that one of the most fruitful sources of international wars are racial prejudice and national egotism. This conviction is the nerve of much present day pacifism. It has been the inspiration of such unofficial diplomacy, for example, as that of the Federal Council of the Churches of Christ in its effort to bring about a better understanding between the Japanese and America. This book [*The Japanese Invasion*] is an attempt to study this phenomenon of race prejudice and national egotism, so far as it reveals itself in the relations of the Japanese and the Americans in this country, and to estimate the rôle it is likely to play in the future relations of the two countries.

So far as I know, an investigation of precisely this nature has not hitherto been made. One reason for this is, perhaps, that not until very recent times did the problem present itself in precisely this form. So long as the nations lived in practical isolation, carrying on their intercourse through the medium of professional diplomats, and knowing each other mainly through the products they exchanged, census reports, and the discreet observations of polite travellers, racial prejudice did not disturb international relations. With the extension of international commerce, the increase of immigration, and the interpenetration of peoples, the scene changes. The railway, the steamship, and the telegraph are rapidly mobilizing the peoples of the earth. The

Being "Introduction" to J. F. Steiner, *The Japanese Invasion* (Chicago: A. C. McClurg, 1917), pp. vii–xvii.

nations are coming out of their isolation, and distances which separated the different races are rapidly giving way before the extension of communication.

The same human motives, which have led men to spread a network of trade-communication over the whole earth, in order to bring about an exchange of commodities, are now bringing about a new distribution of populations. When these populations become as mobile as the commodities of commerce there will be practically no limits—except those artificial barriers, like the customs and immigration restrictions, maintained by individual states—to a world wide economic and personal competition. Furthermore, when the natural barriers are broken down, artificial barriers will be maintained with increasing difficulty.

Some conception of the extent of the changes which are taking place in the world under the influence of these forces may be gathered from the fact that in 1870 the cost of transporting a bushel of grain in Europe was so great as to prohibit its sale beyond a radius of two hundred miles from a primary market. By 1883 the importation of grains from the virgin soil of the Western prairies in the United States had brought about an agricultural crisis in every country in Western Europe.

One may illustrate, but it is scarcely possible to estimate the economic changes which have been brought about by the enormous increase in ocean transportation. In 1840 the first Cunard liner, of 740 horsepower with a speed of 8.5 knots per hour, was launched. In 1907, when the Lusitania was built, ocean-going vessels had attained a speed of 25 knots an hour and were drawn by engines of 70,000 horsepower.

It is difficult to estimate the economic changes which have been brought about by the changes in ocean transportation represented by these figures. It is still less possible to predict the political effects of the steadily increasing mobility of the peoples of the earth. At the present time this mobility has already reached a point at which it is often easier and cheaper to transport the world's population to the sources of raw materials than to carry the world's manufactures to the established seats of population.

With the progressive rapidity, ease, and security of transportation, and the increase in communication, there follows an increasing detachment of the population from the soil, and a concurrent concentration in great cities. These cities, in time, become the centers of vast numbers of uprooted individuals, casual and seasonal laborers, tenement and apartment house dwellers, sophisticated and emancipated urbanites, who are bound together neither by local attachment nor by ties of family, clan, religion, or nationality. Under such conditions it is reasonable to expect that the same economic motive which leads every trader to sell in the highest market and to buy in the lowest will steadily increase and intensify the tendency, which has already reached enormous proportions of the population in overcrowded regions, with diminished resources, to seek their fortunes, either permanently or temporarily, in the new countries of undeveloped resources.

Already the extension of commerce and the increase of immigration have brought about an international and interracial situation that has strained the inherited political order of the United States. It is this same expansive movement of population and of commerce, together with the racial and national rivalries that have sprung from them, which first destroyed the traditional scheme of international control which rested on it. Whatever may have been the immediate causes of the world war, the more remote sources of the conflict must undoubtedly be sought in the great cosmic forces which have broken down the barriers which formerly separated the races and nationalities of the world, and forced them into new intimacies and new forms of competition, rivalry, and conflict.

Since 1870 the conditions which I have attempted to sketch have steadily forced upon America and the nations of Europe the problem of assimilating their heterogeneous populations. What we call the race problem is an incident of this process of assimilation, and is an evidence of its failure.

The present volume [*The Japanese Invasion*] touches but does not deal with the general situation which I have briefly sketched. It is, as its title suggests, a study in "racial contacts," and is an attempt to distinguish and trace to their sources the attitudes and the sentiments—that is to say, mutual prejudices—which have been and still are a source of mutual irritation and misunderstanding between the Japanese and American peoples.

Fundamentally, prejudice against the Japanese in the United States is merely the prejudice which attaches to every alien and immigrant people. The immigrant from Europe, like the immigrant from Asia, comes to this country because he finds here a freedom of individual action and an economic opportunity which he did not find at home.

It is an instance of the general tendency of populations to move from an area of relatively closed to one of relatively open resources. The movement is as inevitable and, in the long run, as resistless as that which draws water from its mountain sources to the sea. It is one way of redressing the economic balance and bringing about an economic equilibrium.

The very circumstances under which this modern movement of population has arisen implies then that the standard of living, if not the cultural level, of the immigrant is lower than that of the native population. The consequence is that immigration brings with it a new and disturbing form of competition, the competition, namely, of peoples of a lower and of a higher standard of living. The effect of this competition, where it is free and unrestricted, is either to lower the living standards of the native population; to expel them from the vocations in which the immigrants are able or permitted to compete; or what may, perhaps, be regarded as a more sinister consequence, to induce such a restriction of the birth rate of the native population as to insure its ultimate extinction. The latter is, in fact, what seems to be happening in the New England manufacturing towns where the birth rate in the native population for some years past has fallen below the death rate, so that the native stock has long since ceased to reproduce itself. The foreign peoples, on the other hand, are rapidly replacing the native stocks, not merely by the influence of new immigration but because of a relatively high excess of births over deaths.

It has been assumed that the prejudice which blinds the people of one race to the virtues of another, and leads them to exaggerate that other's faults, is in the nature of a misunderstanding which further knowledge will dispel. This is so far from true that it would be more exact to say that our racial misunderstandings are merely the expression of our racial antipathies. Behind these antipathies are deep-seated, vital, and instinctive impulses. These antipathies represent collision of invisible forces, the clash of interests, dimly felt but not yet clearly perceived. They are present in every situation where the fundamental interests of races and peoples are not yet regulated by some law, custom, or any other *modus vivendi* which commands the assent and the mutual support of both parties. We hate people because we fear them; because our interests, as we understand them at any rate, run counter to theirs. On the other hand, good will is founded in the long run upon cooperation. The extension of our so-called altruistic sentiments is made possible only by the organization of our otherwise conflicting interests and by the extension of the machinery of co-operation and social control.

Race prejudice may be regarded as a spontaneous, more or less instinctive defense-reaction, the practical effect of which is to restrict free competition between races. Its importance as a social function is due to the fact that free competition, particularly between people with different standards of living, seems to be, if not the original source, at least the stimulus to which race prejudice is the response.

From this point of view we may regard caste, or even slavery, as one of those accommodations through which the race problem found a natural solution. Caste, by relegating the subject race to an inferior status, gives to each race at any rate a monopoly of its own tasks. When this status is accepted by the subject people, as is the case where the caste or slavery systems become fully established, racial competition ceases and racial animosity tends to disappear. That is the explanation of the intimate and friendly relations which so often existed in slavery between master and servant. It is for this reason that we hear it said today that "the Negro is all right in his place." In his place he is a convenience and not a competitor. Each race being in its place, no obstacle to racial cooperation exists.

The fact that race prejudice is due to, or is in some sense dependent upon, race competition is further manifest by a fact which Mr. Steiner has emphasized, namely, that prejudice against the Japanese is nowhere uniform throughout the United States. It is only where Japanese are present in sufficient numbers to actually disturb the economic status of the white population that prejudice has manifested itself to such a degree as to demand serious consideration. It is an interesting fact, also, that prejudice against the Japanese is now more intense than it is against any other oriental people. The reason for this, as Mr. Steiner has pointed out, is that the Japanese are more aggressive, more disposed to test the sincerity of that statement of the Declaration of Independence which declares that all men are equally entitled to "life, liberty, and the pursuit of happiness"—a statement, by the way, which is merely a forensic assertion of the *laissez-faire* doctrine of free and unrestricted competition as applied to the relations of individual men.

The Japanese, the Chinese, they too would be all right in their place, no doubt. That place, if they find it, will be one in which they do not greatly intensify and so embitter the struggle for existence of the white man. The difficulty is that the Japanese is still less disposed than the Negro or the Chinese to submit to the regulations of a caste system and to stay in his place. The Japanese are an organized and morally efficient nation. They have the national pride and the national egotism which rests on the consciousness of this efficiency. In fact it is not too much to say that national egotism, if one pleases to call it such, is essential to national efficiency, just as a certain irascibility of temper seems to be essential to a good fighter.

Another difficulty is that caste and the limitation of free competition is economically unsound, even though it be politically desirable. A national policy of national efficiency demands that every individual have not merely the opportunity but the preparation necessary to perform that particular service for the community for which his natural disposition and aptitude fit him, irrespective of race or "previous condition."

Finally, caste and the limitation of economic opportunity is contrary, if not to our traditions, at least to our political principles. That means that there will always be an active minority opposed on grounds of political sentiment to any settlement based on the caste system as applied to either the black or the brown man. This minority will be small in parts of the country immediately adversely affected by the competition of the invading race. It will be larger in regions which are not greatly affected. It will be increased if immigration is so rapid as to make the competition more acute. We must look to other measures for the solution of the Japanese problem, if it should prove true, as seems probable, that we are not able or, for various reasons, do not care to hold back permanently the rising tide of the oriental invasion.

I have said that fundamentally and in principle prejudice against the Japanese in America today was indentical with the prejudice which attaches to any immigrant people. There is, as Mr. Steiner has pointed out, a difference. This is due to the existence in the human mind of a mechanism by which we inevitably and automatically classify every individual human being we meet. When a race bears an external mark by which every individual member of it can infallibly be identified, that race is by that fact set apart and segregated. Japanese, Chinese, and Negroes cannot move among us with the same freedom as the members of other races because they bear marks which identify them as members of their race. This fact isolates them. In the end, the effect of this isolation, both in its effects upon the Japanese themselves, and upon the human environment in which they live, is profound. Isolation is at once a cause and an effect of race prejudice.

It is a vicious circle—isolation, prejudice; prejudice, isolation. Were there no other reasons which urge us to consider the case of the Japanese and the oriental peoples in a category different from that of the European immigrant, this fact, that he is bound to live in the American community a more or less isolated life, would impel us to do so.

I have called what I have here written an introduction. It is perhaps less an introduction than an interpretation. As such, however, it may serve its purpose, which has been to add, if possible, something to the significance of this study [*The Japanese Invasion*] by a review of the larger situation, in which its special problem lies.

In conclusion, I may perhaps say in a word what seems to me the practical bearing of Mr. Steiner's book. Race prejudice is a mechanism of the group mind which acts reflexly and automatically in response to its proper stimulus. That stimulus seems to be, in the cases where I have met it, unrestricted competition of peoples with different standards of living. Racial animosities and the so-called racial misunderstandings that grow out of them cannot be explained or argued away. They can only be affected when there has been a readjustment of relations and an organization of interests in such a way as to bring about a larger measure of cooperation and a less amount of friction and conflict. This demands something more than a diplomacy of kind words. It demands a national policy based on an unflinching examination of the facts.

CHAPTER 18

THE BASES OF RACE PREJUDICE

PREJUDICE, even race prejudice, no matter how reprehensible in itself, is a profoundly human phenomenon. As such, it deserves, perhaps, to be defended against those who inveigh against it, as if it were not a common human weakness in which we all, more or less, share. It is not, however, in precisely this sense that President John Grier Hibben, of Princeton, wrote some years ago his "Defense of Prejudice." He sought to show that prejudice was, as he says, "a natural factor in any thinking, and not to be regarded in any sense as an abnormal and disturbing element."

DEFENSE OF PREJUDICE

When the matter is stated in this fundamental way, it serves merely to call attention to the fact that primarily men are practical creatures; that thought is, after all, merely an incident of action, and that reflection arises, and gets its justification, in our efforts to achieve ends. We are biased by our own purposes, and in the final analysis, knowledge is relative to them. The fact is, we come into the world with certain predispositions, and we acquire others. Tradition into which we are born, and which we imbibe with our mothers' milk, is infused with prejudices. "There is," as President Hibben puts it, "no thought, however original, that does not rest upon a credit basis." A man without prejudices is a man without conviction, and ultimately without character.

Common sense, "that diffuse sagacity which eludes all attempt at definition," is a tissue of hunches and prejudices that have not been, and in most cases cannot be, justified on general and rational grounds. Our friendships, our hobbies, our amiable but irrational predilections for certain places and certain persons all are manifestations of what, under certain circumstances, we are likely to condemn as prejudices. It is notorious, for example, that friendships corrupt politics. The situation has been defined in the phrase, "What is the constitution among friends?" What, indeed, is the constitution or any other formal principle of action in the presence of the elementary claims of friendship, and the personal prejudices which such friendships imply?

As it seems impossible to conceive of a world without friendships, so it seems improbable, in such a world, that life should go on without enmities, for these two things are, in some sense and in some degree, correlative, so that the bias with which we view the qualities of our friends makes it difficult if not impossible to do justice to the virtues of our enemies and theirs. There is always and everywhere the inevitable dichotomy between those who call each other "we," and the outsiders whom one refers to as "they." As William Graham Sumner puts it,

The relation of comradeship and peace in the "we-group" and that of hostility and war toward the "other-groups" are correlative to each other. . . . Sentiments are produced to correspond. Loyalty to the group, sacrifice for it, hatred and contempt for outsiders, brotherhood within, warlikeness without—all grow together, common products of the same situation.

All our sentiments, love, loyalty, patriotism, homesickness, contempt, arrogance, hate, are based upon and supported by prejudices. Furthermore, mankind is incurably sentimental, and sentiments and prejudices are part of the stuff from which our human life is made.

The thing reduces itself to this, that prejudice, defined in this broad and inclusive way, has its source and origin in the very nature of men and their relation to one another. It gets itself fixed and sublimated in the habits of individuals, and enters into the very structure of society. In short, prejudice is an attitude, a social attitude.

RACE PREJUDICE

There is no reason to believe that attitudes based upon race are fundamentally different from any other attitudes. Race prejudice is like class and caste prejudices—merely one variety of a species. So far as it can be described in these terms, race prejudice may be regarded as a phenomenon of status. Most of us are familiar with the fact that thought, particularly scientific thought, proceeds by the method of classification. According to the rules of Aristotelian logic—which is the logic of common sense—we may be said to know a thing when we are able to classify it. We have not always recognized that the thinking of the ordinary man proceeds, if less consciously, still substantially, in the same manner.

We are all dependent, to a degree that we do not recognize, upon our categories, and this is true in a very special sense with respect to our knowledge of human beings. Every individual we meet inevitably finds a place in our minds in some category already defined. He is either a friend, a neighbor, a mere acquaintance, or, as we often say, a complete stranger. The category into which he falls determines, more or less automatically, and with very little conscious reflection on our part, the attitude we assume toward each individual figure in the changing scene of our daily experiences. Furthermore, our attitudes, our fundamental attitudes at any rate, are substantially alike. Each of us has, of course, his own preferences and his own opinions, and we are all likely to be a little proud of our independence of thought. On the other hand, any very marked divergence from the generally accepted opinion is invariably shocking, and frequently quite unintelligible. Most of our "opinions" are merely justifications and apologies for what are, after all, rather slight deviations from views that are orthodox in the society in which we happen to live. Opinions are individual, but the attitudes upon which they are based are collective.

On the whole and in the large, in every society, things have very much the same meaning. That is merely to say that every society has its own universe of discourse, and that is what Walter Lippmann means when he says that the public thinks only in stereotypes. There is, in fact, no other way in which the public can think. Where there is substantial agreement as to the categories, as there is bound to be in every stable society, there the status of every individual is defined by the class in which, by tradition or general consensus, he happens to find himself. The individual who is in no class at all is a pariah and an outlaw. The man who seeks to rise, or who rises suddenly, from a lower to a higher class is an upstart and a parvenu. The man who loses his status and sinks to a lower class is what the French describe as *déclassé*.

The point is that every change in status, whether of an individual or of a group, involves a change in social organization. Prejudice—that is caste, class and race prejudice—in its more naïve and innocent manifestations, is merely the resistance of the social order to change. Every effort of the Negro—to take the most striking example—to move, to rise and improve his status, rather than his condition, has invariably met with opposition, aroused prejudice and stimulated racial animosities. Race prejudice, so conceived is merely an elementary expression of conservatism.

As a matter of fact, changes in status are constantly taking place in every society. Certain individuals and certain classes rise and invade the higher levels of society. As a consequence the prestige of other individuals and other classes is diminished, with the result that they are forced to decline and to accept a lower position. In America, where changes in underlying conditions proceed more rapidly than they do elsewhere, changes in status are correspondingly rapid. There seems, under ordinary conditions, to be no barrier in America to advancement—except failure to succeed. Lindbergh, a small town boy from the Middle West, flies across the Atlantic and becomes a national hero. Gene Tunney, yesterday a prize fighter, today moves in the most exclusive circles. Prohibition has created a new generation of plutocrats, composed of retired "bootleggers." The spectacle of American life is amazing and inspiring. No man, it seems, is so far down that he cannot hope to rise. Every boy born in America may aspire to be president, even if he be a Catholic.

It may strike the disinterested observer as a little strange that in America, where, humanly speaking, there are no class distinctions, there is still so much race prejudice, particularly when we consider that as far as race relations are concerned, racial minorities are merely social classes. What is the answer?

First of all we ordinarily confuse racial prejudice with racial antagonism. There is probably less racial prejudice in America then elsewhere, but there is more racial conflict and more racial antagonism. There is more conflict because there is more change, more progress. The Negro is rising in America and the measure of the antagonism he encounters is, in some very real sense, the measure of his progress. The fact seems to be that racial prejudices do not always and everywhere express themselves in racial animosities. Animosities arise in conflict, and racial animosities are an incident of the struggles in which racial classes are formed. When, however, conflict ceases; when some sort of accommodation of the contending is achieved, animosities subside. In that case the sentiments change. They are no longer hostile, or are only potentially so. On the other hand, the racial prejudices, which are the basis of this hostility, may and often do persist.

RACE RELATIONS

Where there are social classes there will invariably be corresponding attitudes and sentiments. Racial distinctions, when they exist, will always be supported by racial prejudices. But where distinctions based on class, caste, and race, are part of the established social order, as they invariably are in a static society, each caste and class lives within the limitations of its own world and accepts the definition imposed upon it as if it were a part of the order of nature. Under such circumstances each class and caste, having its own internal organization, maintains its own norms of conduct, and each expects and demands that every individual will live up to the standards of his own class. So far as this normal expectancy is maintained, good-will will exist, and each class will respect the other.

Something approaching this condition existed in the southern states before the Civil War, particularly in the far South, where slavery was firmly established and race relations, especially the relation of master and slave, assumed that fixed and irrevocable character which simulated the permanence of physical nature.

It was, however, during this period, and under the influences of the associations thus established, that those intimate and friendly relations between master and slave were established which are still so unintelligible to those who have looked upon slavery as if it were, always and everywhere, something inhuman and monstrous.

It was, nevertheless, during this same period that there grew up, out of the daily experience of master and slave, that conception of the Negro, according to which he was predestined by God and Nature, to be forever a hewer of wood and a drawer of water, "a servant of servants unto his brethren."

There is evidence to show that, on the whole, the black man accepted the position to which the white man assigned him. Negro servants spoke habitually in a proprietary sense of their masters' families as "our white folks." And, on the other hand, the masters' families thought of the slaves on their plantations as "our Negroes." In short, the plantation population, in spite of differences of race and status, constituted what I have described as a we-group. This was conspicuously the case of the members of the families and the house servants, between whom a lifelong intimacy existed.

Every large plantation in the South tended to assume the character of a little feudal state, each relatively independent of the others. In the intimacy of that isolated life, racial antipathy, such as existed elsewhere, and especially in the North, disappeared. Nathaniel S. Shaler, who knew this life intimately, says:

It is an interesting fact, if my observations on the matter are correct, that the instinctive dislike to the Negro disappears more quickly than prejudices against others less remote in quality of body from ourselves. I have never known an instance in which it persisted, provided contacts were intimate.[1]

On the other hand, race and class distinctions within this feudal society were rigidly enforced. Writing of the plantation overseer, John Spencer Bassett says:

It was not even his fortune to be esteemed for what he did. He was patronized by the benign planters and condemned by the heedless. He might belong to the same church with the planter, but he usually preferred some plain form of worship, as in the churches of Methodists or Baptists. If the two found themselves worshiping in the same place they sat apart quite distinctly. Their children did not visit one another nor intermarry. Each was a class in society, and between them in social matters was a frozen ocean.

When there was illness in the overseer's family there was much kindness for him in the mansion. The mistress on a Southern plantation knew no caste in time of distress. . . . But she knew, and the overseer knew, that her visits of mercy were not visits of social equality. And he suffered nothing in his mind because of his lower place on the ladder. He was born to it. His wife was born to it. His children would never have aught else so far as the existing environment was concerned. Being a sensible man, he was not discontented. He took the best he could get of what life offered to overseers, finding his wife and marrying off his children in the ranks of such people as himself. If he did not like this prospect, and sometimes he was in revolt against it, he might turn to the frontier, which always had a welcome for a man with courage and industry.[2]

[1] N. S. Shaler, *The Neighbor: The Natural History of Human Contacts,* Boston, 1904, p. 166.

[2] John Spencer Bassett, *The Southern Plantation Overseer,* Northampton, Mass., 1925, pp. 2-3.

One may suspect that the distances which separated the families of the planter and the overseer, if they were not so great as those between master and slave, were more rigidly maintained. However, the very definiteness with which the position of the overseer was defined within the plantation hierarchy, is an indication of the solid character of the institution. The structure within which master and slave had lived for two hundred and fifty years was not at once dissolved by the publication of the Emancipation Proclamation. The old order, which was fixed in the habits and customs of both races, persisted long after the institution of slavery had been deprived of its legal sanctions. In many of its characteristic features it exists today, but it is crumbling.

EFFECTS OF SOCIAL DISSOLUTION

The effect of the gradual dissolution of the traditional social order was to release interests and passions which, on the plantation if not in the cities, had achieved something like a stable equilibrium. The resulting struggles and conflicts, with the incidental disorganization, released all the latent animosities in the old social order, and created antipathies and prejudices between the races which previously did not exist.

Prejudices against the Negro in the South were, and are still, prejudices in favor of an order that is changing or no longer exists. "The Negro," Southern people were wont to say, "is all right in his place." On the whole, and so far as one may make any general statement of the matter, race prejudice in the southern states is caste prejudice. If the Negro were content to remain in a subordinate position to which the white man's prejudices—prejudices which have grown up through long and intimate association—assigned him, racial animosities would probably not exist.

As far as the South is concerned, it is where racial prejudices, and the social order which they perpetuated, are breaking down, that racial animosities are most intense. It is when the Negro invades a new region that race riots occur; it is when he seeks a place in a new occupation or a new profession that he meets the most vigorous opposition; it is when he seeks to assume a new dignity that he ceases to be quaint and becomes ridiculous.

The Negro achieved in slavery a definite position in the social organization and the cultural life of the South. In the South the black man is a native and has his roots in the soil; he has a place in tradition and is a figure in literature. The folk-songs of the South are Negro songs. Tradition assigns him a place in the social order, and race prejudice has made it difficult for him to get out of it.

Not so in the North. There, until very recently, the Negro has been, in the main, a sojourner and a stranger. He has had more freedom, but his status is precarious and undefined. It is true that, in the more liberal atmosphere of the Northern cities, the Negro has contributed something of his tradition to literature, and something of his temperament to the stage. On the other hand, as a serious figure either in literature or on the stage, he is still a good deal of a novelty and his contributions to our culture have the interest of something exotic.

Antagonism to the Negro in the North is different from that which he meets in the South. In the North it is less prejudice than antipathy, which is something more elementary and more insidious.

Racial antipathies, in a somewhat more positive sense than is true of racial prejudices, have their sources in fundamental human nature. This does not mean, however, that any particular prejudice nor the antipathies with which it is so often associated are instinctive; that is to say, biologically fixed and inalterable, so that the individual who grows up without the customary and expected race consciousness and the corresponding race prejudice, is to be regarded as in some sense abnormal—an aberrant individual.

Race consciousness, like the racial reserves, antipathies, and tabus in which it finds expression, is invariably, as far as observation goes, an acquired trait, quite as much as the taste for olives or the mania for collecting stamps. Children do not have it. They take the world of human beings in which they find themselves as part of the order of nature and respond to a black or yellow face as readily as they do to a white, depending upon the character and intimacy of the association. In the South it is a mark of distinction to have had a "black mammy," and the lasting affections which have so frequently grown out of that early intimacy are unquestionably the normal and natural consequences of human associations of this description everywhere.

RACE INSTINCTIVENESS

The fact seems to be that what we ordinarily regard as instinctive, and biologically determined in our behavior and attitudes toward peoples and races other than our own, is merely, in the first instance at least, the spontaneous response of most sentient creatures—including men and dogs—to what is strange and unfamiliar. We are always keenly conscious of whatever in our experience is novel and undefined, and we are invariably interested in other creatures like ourselves, especially if they are at the same time different. Man is notoriously the most unstable and unpredictable element in the environment. Nature, physical nature, is changing and moody; but behind those brooding human faces that men wear, and particularly behind those faces that we do not know, who can tell what things are going on?

On the whole, we may define the situation in which races meet, as one of vague apprehension tinged with and qualified by curiosity. The first effect is to provoke in us a state of tension—a more vivid awareness and readiness to act—and with that a certain amount of reserve and self-consciousness which is incident to every effort at self-control. In all this there is so far neither prejudice nor antipathy, but merely expectancy. The strange new creature may prove to be attractive, even fascinating. The reports of the first meetings of primitive peoples with Europeans are instructive on this point. The first Europeans to reach Mexico were received ceremonially and regarded as superior beings.

On the other hand, if we seek to get at the very core of this so-called instinctive element in race prejudice, it seems to have its locus just here. If the strange creature approach too suddenly, or if on further acquaintance he seems to behave in outlandish and incalculable ways, we may retain our interest, but we maintain our distance. In that case, anything approaching intimacy may leave us with a vague sense of insecurity and malaise which effectually limits intercourse and understanding.

It is in such situations, I suspect, that those antipathies arise which seem to constitute the most irrational, and at the same time the most invincible, elements in racial prejudice. The sense of insecurity which the presence of the stranger inspires, when not dispelled by more intimate acquaintance, crystallizes into an attitude. Sentiments grow about it which give it substance and support. The racial mark becomes a symbol of these sentiments, the core of which is a sense of insecurity. We do not know what, under certain circumstances, a creature so unlike ourselves will do. Even after a prolonged and rather intimate acquaintance with an individual of another race, there usually remains a residue of uncertainty and vague apprehension, particularly if the stranger maintains a reserve that we cannot fully penetrate. Under such circumstances it is inevitable that rumors and legends will arise and gain general currency which purport to describe and explain racial differences, but in fact serve merely to give support to apprehensions and vague terrors for which there is no real ground in fact. Anything that tends to make a mystery of divergent and alien races, even biological theories which suggest remote and ill-defined dangers of contact and intimacy, tends to intensify antipathies and lend support to racial prejudices. For racial differences in which we are ultimately interested are not the obviously physical and biological marks by which one race is distinguished from another, but the less obvious mental and moral traits of which these physical characters are assumed to be an index and a symbol. The more obvious the differences in physical traits, the greater the presumption of fundamentally divergent moral characteristics.

ANTIPATHIES

Racial antipathies are intensified by anything which arouses disgust. For this reason we tend to contract many of our racial antipathies, so to speak, through the nose. Some writers have gone so far as to suppose that the sense of smell is in some subtle way, a guide to moral differences in individuals.[3] At any rate, it seems to be a fact that races and individuals have each a distinctive smell, and this odor becomes, in certain cases, the sensuous basis for racial antipathies. The Hindu, for example, who are so meticulous about their contacts with aliens, as well as with members of the different castes of their own people, profess a special abhorrence to the smell of the Anglo-Saxon. A few years ago a Hindu acquaintance of mine, in explaining the opposition of his family to his marriage to an American woman, confessed that his father had written him saying he hoped, if no other considerations were sufficient, that the smell of an Anglo-Saxon would be sufficient to prohibit such a mesalliance. W. H. Hudson, in his volume *A Hind in Richmond Park*, discussing the sense of smell in animals, devotes a chapter to the explanation of the fact that those who have a nose for these things are sensitive to the smell of other races, but quite oblivious to the odor of their own. He relates an incident, by way of illustration, which I quote in his own words:

---

[3] W. H. Hudson, *A Hind in Richmond Park*, New York, 1923, pp. 77 ff.

Many and curious are the tricks our olfactories play us. . . . A young army doctor in India and at Bombay zealously set himself to win a good private practice. He made himself well known in the society of the place, and his servant had strict instructions to come always into the church where he attended Sunday morning service to call him out to a supposed urgent case.

The natives just then were in a state of political excitement, and he was desirous of finding out all he could about their aspirations, intentions, and so on. One day he told his servant that he wished to attend a big meeting about to be held in a quarter of the town he was not well acquainted with, to listen to the speeches of the orators, and he asked his man to take him there and get him admitted. Accordingly they went on an oppressively hot evening, and he sat in a huge densely-packed hall for about half an hour, then came out. After taking a few deep breaths he exclaimed: "What a relief to get out! In another ten minutes I should have collapsed. The smell!"

To which his servant promptly replied: "Ah, Sahib, *now* you will understand what I suffer every Sunday when I have to go right to the middle of the church to call you out! . . ."

The extraordinary readiness, the candour, the spontaneity, and even the glee, with which he brought out his words made it impossible for his master to doubt his perfect sincerity. He had taken it for granted that his master *would* understand, and after his own unhappy experience at the native meeting would be ready to sympathise with his servant's sufferings in the performance of that painful Sunday duty. . . . And what did it mean? Why, that we white-skinned Westerns, lords of creation, have our smell just as the blacks and bi-colored races and the lower animals have theirs; that we are unconscious of this fact with regard to ourselves—our own race—but are quite conscious of it with regard to the others.[4]

It is because smell is so definitely associated with the organic reactions that it is the least intellectual of the senses. For the same reason, no doubt, it is so intimately related to the antipathies and the sentiments generally. At any rate, racial antipathies are frequently concerned with touch and smell. If these antipathies have, as many persons contend, a biological significance, it is because they seem to inhibit intimate and ultimately sexual contacts. They are a bar to miscegenation. There seems to be just as good reason for adopting as some writers do, the opposite view. It is the strange woman who is sexually the more stimulating; and it is the man from abroad to whom the most romantic interest attaches. This is one explanation of exogamy.

The facts seem to indicate that racial antipathies and tabus have a conventional rather than a natural and instinctive origin. The man

---

[4] W. H. Hudson, *op. cit.*, pp. 76-7.

who arrives with a strange, new, pungent odor may arouse disgust, but he may, under other circumstances, evoke a sentiment of awe and respect. We are most of us familiar with the odor of sanctity that attaches to saints and sacred edifices. It seems, therefore, that antipathy and prestige may, and perhaps often do, rest on the same sensuous basis. To a Hindu, the mere thought of eating meat is disgusting. The Japanese are shocked to see men and women embrace in public. Whether a stranger entering an unfamiliar society will be treated with consideration or contempt, is apparently uncertain, except in so far as the situation is controlled by ceremonial and etiquette. It is notorious that representatives of every race and color have been received at one time and another in the most select and intimate circles. Marco Polo was received with distinction at the court of Kubla Khan, and Booker T. Washington dined with President Roosevelt at the White House. It seems as if there were no instinctive racial antipathies that cannot be overcome by scrupulous adherence to etiquette.

CEREMONIAL AND SOCIAL RITUAL

While etiquette and ceremonial are at once a convenience and a necessity in facilitating human intercourse, they serve even more effectively to maintain social distances and to preserve the rank and order of individuals and classes, which seems to be essential to social organization and effective collective action. This is the significance of the ceremonial and social ritual so rigidly enforced in the South, by which racial distinctions are preserved amid all the inevitable changes and promiscuity of an expanding industrial and democratic society. Thus white folk and colored, in the small town at any rate, eat at the same restaurant, if it is conducted by a Negro, but not at the same tables.

A colored nurse may ride, without objection, in a Pullman coach if she has a white baby in her arms. On the other hand, if a white nurse should appear in the same car with a colored baby, no one knows what would happen. There is no provision in the social ritual for the unprecedented.

Southern people have difficulty in addressing a colored man as "Mr.," even though he may have achieved an eminent position in the world. In that case it is possible to avoid the difficulty, as one man is reported to have done in the case of Booker Washington, by calling him "Professor." A distinguished clergyman in the Southern Episcopal Church, after some mental conflict, announced a few years ago that he had resolved that thenceforth when a colored woman was decently married, to address her as "Mrs.," "out of respect," as he explained, "for the holy estate of matrimony."

On the other hand, in a little Negro town in Oklahoma, Boley, where at the time no separate provision was made for white visitors, a traveling salesman appealed to the Negro hotel keeper to give him a table apart, because, as he said, with a certain amount of pathos in his voice, "I am from Mississippi, and I just can't eat with you niggers."

These are illustrations of what Ogburn calls "cultural lag." The situation changes, but the cultural form persists.

There exists in the South, and in the North too, for that matter, a great body of materials which no student of race problems has, so far as I know, seen fit or found time to collect and interpret. These are the legends, anecdotes, and racial myths current in the South in which each race, in perfect good faith, and often with very real insight, has characterized the follies and foibles, and occasionally the more excellent qualities, of the other. These materials, because they do not get into print, are a kind of folklore, a form of verbal literature which passes sometimes for history, and sometimes for scientific fact. In this as in every other form of literature, the wishes—and particularly the conflicting wishes—of the two races are unconsciously reflected. As might be expected, the stories which circulate among white people concerning Negroes tend to support the traditional social order, which assigns every Negro to a position inferior to that of every white man. On the other hand the stories which circulate among Negroes are those which show that the old order is cracking or exhibit the traditional racial distinctions in some paradoxical or logically untenable and ridiculous form.

For example, a white farmer in Alabama, one of the so-called "poor whites," became greatly interested in the farm demonstration work which a colored agent was carrying on among the Negroes. The white man invited the colored agent to come over and look at his place and advise him about his crops. Eventually he invited him to stay to dinner. He arranged the matter simply. The colored man sat at one table, and the white man at another, close enough to continue their discussions. The white man's wife waited upon them both. This was merely reversing the situation in which a white man visits a Negro planter and perhaps remains all night. In that case the white man eats in the dining room, and the colored man more than likely eats in the kitchen. In both cases the social amenities are served, and what amounts, in these cases, to caste distinctions are preserved. They are part of the etiquette which makes intercourse and coöperation among the races in the South possible.

CHANGE IN RACE RELATIONS

Originally race relations in the South could be rather accurately represented by a horizontal line, with all the white folk above, and all the Negro folk below. But at present these relations are assuming new forms, and in consequence changing in character and meaning. With the development of industrial and professional classes within the Negro race, the distinction between the races tends to assume the form of a vertical line. On one side of this line the Negro is represented in most of the occupational and professional classes; on the other side of the line the white man is similarly represented. The situation *was* this:

All white
_____
All colored

It is *now* this:

White	Colored
Professional occupation	Professional occupation
Business occupation	Business occupation
Labor	Labor

The result is to develop in every occupational class professional and industrial bi-racial organizations. Bi-racial organizations preserve race distinction, but change their content. The distances which separate the races are maintained, but the attitudes involved are different. The races no longer look up and down; they look across. These bi-racial organizations, so far as I know, are a unique product of the racial struggle in this country; they do not exist outside the United States.

CHAPTER 19

BEHIND OUR MASKS

PRESENT differences between the Orient and the Occident are largely concerned with what the Chinese call "face."

In China's earlier negotiations with Europe, Chinese diplomacy invariably emerged with a sense of triumph whenever it was possible to find a formula which saved China's face, no matter what the material loss. But in her more recent encounters with foreign devils, China has suffered losses that no diplomatic formulae can explain away. The shock and humiliation of repeated defeats is reflected in the rising tide of nationalism.

The whole present situation between Japan and the United States, likewise, is largely a matter of etiquette. Japan had lost the battle in America before the passage of the Exclusion Law of 1924. The position of the Japanese in America had been completely undermined by the passage of the Alien Land Law. Not only that, but under the influence of the continued irritation and agitation the social status of the Japanese in America was steadily declining. The drift of legislation and of court decisions had gone steadily against the Oriental. All the deeper currents, the undertow of public sentiment, were carrying the Japanese in the United States, in spite of every effort to conciliate American public opinion, into the same sort of racial ghetto in which the Chinese before them had found refuge.

At the same time a new caste was slowly emerging on the Pacific Coast, a caste in which the Oriental was destined to occupy as definite

Survey Graphic, LVI (May, 1926), pp. 135-139.

a position in American society as the Negro, who, even though he be legally a citizen, has been socially an outcast. These subterranean forces in American life would have made the position of the Oriental in America untenable, even had there been no exclusion law, and at the moment exclusion was inevitable. Japanese statesmen were certainly not wholly unaware of this. They were, in fact, preparing to accept a modification of the Immigration Law that would have amounted, in practice, to exclusion. What they hoped for, apparently, was an opportunity to retire, without loss of dignity, from a struggle in which they had lost everything else. What they sought to maintain was not so much a principle as an attitude.

It is a little difficult to believe that in the minds of Japanese statesmen there were no other and more substantial interests involved in the exclusion legislation than those of international courtesy; but the Japanese people were undoubtedly shocked less by the act than by the gesture by which it was performed. And what was their reply? An unknown man committed suicide on the site of the American Embassy. Something like an epidemic of suicides ensued. This characteristically oriental protest was followed by other demonstrations, directed not so much against America as against the cult of America that had grown up in Japan, the most outrageous manifestations of which were the popularity of American dances and of the American cinema.

America, however, missed the significance, as well as the pathos, of Japan's tragic gesture. It was not the act, but the spirit that animated it, against which Japan protested, and sought, in this dramatic way, to defend herself. It was in this way that the Japanese people sought to appeal their case to a higher court; to the future; to the conscience of mankind; to whatever gods there be that rule the destinies of nations. The whole incident is illuminating, since it indicates to what an extent, for the Oriental, this whole matter lies in the region of the so-called imponderables, in the realm of spirit.

Such a conception of things is quite foreign to the customary American manner of thinking. All the more so because in this controversy neither our national honor nor our national prestige—nothing but our material interests—was, or seemed to be, involved in the contentions of those elements in our population who in sum have shaped our national frontage toward the Orient. We do not want competition at home, but we should like to have it abroad. We do not want Japanese farmers in California, but our business groups would like to have an open door in China. Add these together and we have the program of the Pacific coast as stated succinctly and accurately by George Wheeler Hinman, one of the trumpets through which Mr. Hearst, of the Examiners, has essayed to proclaim the voice of the people all over our broad land:

First, no more Japanese immigration, because "Americans do not intend to be disinherited in their own country."

Second, fair treatment to the Japanese already here.

Third, equal rights and privileges in the business and commercial development of East Asia.

If human relations could be reduced to the simple and rational term of popular economics, life would be much less complicated and very much less interesting than it actually is. But economic relations are always more or less involved with the stubborn and incalculable factors of human nature. Furthermore, the plain, practical interests of the economic man, theoretically so permanent and calculable, are always complicated with sentiments that change in what seem quite irrational ways, and in ways that are quite beyond our control. It is, on the whole, in the region of the sentiments rather than of the interests, it seems to me, that the problem of race relations in the Pacific mainly lies.

In his interesting little volume, *The Neighbor*, Nathaniel Shaler, who was one of our first and keenest of human naturalists, pointed out that when strangers meet it is not the individual that they see in one another first, but the type. Knowledge proceeds by classification, and this is as true of persons as of material objects. It is the strange, and in human beings, the outlandish, that first fixes and fascinates our attention. Where racial differences are great, the individual is often quite unseen.

Why is it that to the average American all Chinese, like all Negroes, look alike? It is because the individual man is concealed behind the racial type. The individual is there, to be sure, but we do not meet him. Where racial characteristics are marked, and where the social distances that separate the races are great, it sometimes happens that he is not discovered at all. Under these circumstances, as Shaler points out, the stranger remains strange; a representative of his race, but not a neighbor.

These racial traits and racial differences that constitute the racial type and conceal the individual man are not always or altogether physical. Physical differences are emphasized and reenforced by differences of dress, of manner, of deportment, and by characteristic expressions of the face.

It is not, according to Fishberg, because Jews are a race, in the anthropological sense, that in so many parts of the world they are so easily identified. It is because they have a history. "Centuries of confinement in the ghetto, ceaseless sufferings under the ban of abuse and persecution have been instrumental in producing a characteristic, psychic type, which manifests itself in his cast of countenance, which is considered peculiarly Jewish."

The Jew, however, emerges finally from the ghetto and with the natural vivacity and intellectual virtuosity which is his heritage, enters into all the varied interests of this modern cosmopolitan life. The old, haunting memories of his racial history grow dim. He loses his characteristic type, his cast of countenance, and sometimes even his soul. In the vast tide of cosmopolitan life the Jewish racial type does not so much disappear as become invisible. When he is no longer seen, anti-Semitism declines. For race prejudice is a function of visibility. The races of high visibility, to speak in naval parlance, are the natural and inevitable objects of race prejudice.

The emancipation of the Jews has not taken place without internal struggle and external conflict. Jewry itself has been swept repeatedly by cross currents of sentiment. When the forward, outward movement of the race has been too rapid, it has invariably provoked a racial reaction in the outer Gentile world, and Jewish life has been thrown back upon itself. What then happens is that the Jewish community contracts and withdraws into itself. Shadows of the old ghetto walls arise. Jewry returns to the sources of its inspiration and its strength; and becomes conscious of itself as a people set apart, a chosen people, a people with a destiny and a mission.

Among those Jews who, because they have lived among us all longer, have departed farthest from the ancient heritage and penetrated deepest into the life of the outer Gentile world, these recurring outbursts of racial prejudice and the resulting revulsions of Jewish life inevitably provoke profound moral disturbances. It is not easy, in the long run it is impossible, for those who have once gone out, ever to return, even though the ghetto walls are no longer visible. The result is, however, that they are obsessed with a sense of moral isolation; they feel themselves not quite at home either in the Gentile or the Jewish world. Life goes on outwardly as it did before, but they are possessed by insatiable restlessness, and "a secret anguish" gnaws at the core of their existence.

In view of this history, the old legend of the wandering Jew finds a new interpretation, since it is impossible to be at ease in a world where one is not wanted, and the Jew, it sometimes seems to him, is not wanted anywhere, not even in Jerusalem. In this twentieth century it is the Jew's fate to be a cosmopolitan in a world which is still dominated by an intransigent nationalism.

What has happened more than once in the history of the Jewish people, is precisely what has happened to the Oriental on the Pacific coast; what is happening, in a very special sense, to the second and third generation of Orientals. It is, in fact, only by comparisons such as these that we can make the present position of the Oriental in America intelligible.

I recently had the curious experience of talking with a young Japanese woman who was not only born in the United States, but was brought up in an American family, in an American college town, where she had almost no association with members of her own race. I found myself watching her expectantly for some slight accent, some gesture or intonation that would betray her racial origin. When I was not able, by the slightest expression, to detect the oriental mentality behind the oriental mask, I was still not able to escape the impression that I was listening to an American woman in a Japanese disguise.

A few months later I met this same young woman after she had returned from her first, and perhaps her last, visit to Japan. She was unusually reticent about her experiences, but explained that it was impossible for her to remain longer in Japan, although she had had every intention of doing so. She had found herself at a peculiar disadvantage there, because, though she looked like a Japanese, she was unable to speak the language; and besides, her dress, her language, everything about her, in fact, betrayed her American origin. The anomaly struck the Japanese public as something scandalous, almost uncanny. When she appeared on the streets, crowds followed her. They resented, perhaps even more at the time because of the recent passage of the Alien Land law, the appearance of a Japanese woman in the masquerade of an American lady.

Many of the earlier Japanese immigrants who came to California and settled with their families on the land, entertained rather romantic notions about America. They came with the deliberate purpose of casting in their lot with the American people, and rearing their children to be Americans. This was particularly true of the little Christian colony at Livingston, which is described elsewhere in this number. Now, however, these Japanese pilgrims are restless and uncertain about their future. Many of them would like to return to Japan, but their children prefer to stay here.

Meanwhile, something extraordinary is taking place in these same children. They are growing up to be Americans, and, as such, are more or less disposed to accept the estimates of Japanese, and of all Orientals, which are current in the communities in which they live. Children acquire the prevailing attitudes in the community by a kind of moral infection, but even the adults are not immune, and there are moments when they are not wholly able to overcome that "sickening sense of inferiority" which overtakes most of us at times; moments when they could say, what members of other racial minorities have sometimes said: "I hate my race! I hate myself!"

In this way the conflict between the Orient and the Occident, which presents itself in one of its aspects as external and international, assumes, in another aspect, the character of an internal and moral conflict. It becomes a conflict of loyalty; a struggle to knit together the strands of a divided self, to find a place to live, and preserve one's moral integrity in a world in which one can hardly hope for understanding or recognition. For the Oriental who is born in America and educated in our western schools is culturally an Occidental, even though he be racially an Oriental, and this is true to an extent that no one who has not investigated the matter disinterestedly and at first hand is ever likely to imagine.

It is probably no mere historical accident that the word person, in its first meaning, is a mask. It is rather a recognition of the fact that everyone is always and everywhere, more or less consciously, playing a rôle. We are parents and children, masters and servants, teachers and students, clients and professional men, Gentiles and Jews. It is in these rôles that we know each other; it is in these rôles that we know ourselves.

Our very faces are living masks, which reflect, to be sure, the changing emotions of our inner lives, but tend more and more to conform to the type we are seeking to impersonate. Not only every race, but every nationality, has its characteristic "face," its conventional mask. As Emerson points out in *English Traits:*

> Every religious sect has its physiognomy. The Methodists have acquired a face, the Quakers a face, the nuns a face. An Englishman will point out a dissenter by his manner. Trades and professions carve their own lines on faces and forms.

In a sense, and in so far as this mask represents the conception we have formed of ourselves—the role we are striving to live up to—this mask is our truer self, the self we would like to be. In the end, our conception of our role becomes second nature and an integral part of our personality. We come into the world as individuals, achieve character, and become persons.

Now, one striking difference between oriental and occidental people is that the former are more conscious, more conventional, in their behavior than we. They are more elaborate in their manners, and more meticulous in preserving social forums. Etiquette is an immensely more serious matter with the oriental than it is with the occidental peoples. That is the reason why the Chinese go to such elaborate lengths to save their face. "To save your face" is to preserve an attitude, and to maintain self-control.

It is not so many years ago, according to Lafcadio Hearn, that the Japanese regarded a breach of etiquette as a crime, even a sin. There was a time when a Samurai might kill an individual of the inferior classes who was guilty of rudeness, and as a rude fellow was defined as "an-other-than expected person," to commit an offense worthy of death it was only necessary to act "in an unexpected way."

Etiquette is not a characteristic trait of an individualistic society like our own. Democracy is impatient of forms. The social distances that are still maintained in Japan, where etiquette has become a fine art, are quite incomprehensible to the average American. On the other hand, the impatient directness, the disconcerting candor of our speech and manner, the lack of reserve which we everywhere display, strikes the thoroughbred Oriental, I suspect, not only as indecent, but almost obscene.

Orientals live more completely behind the mask than the rest of us. Naturally enough we misinterpret them, and attribute to disingenuousness and craft what is actually conformity to an ingrained convention. The American who is flattered at first by the politeness of his Japanese servant will later on, perhaps, cite as a reproach against the race the fact that "we can never tell what a Japanese is thinking about." "We never know what is going on in their heads."

All this changes, however, in the second generation. The contrast between the Chinese-born in this country and their parents is sometimes startling. The native sons are likely to be brusque and familiar. If they enter your house at all, they use the front door, not the back. They haven't the slightest ambition to follow in the steps of their parents, and they are likely to speak with a certain amount of contempt of the "grinning subservience" of those faithful Chinese servants of the older generation to whom the people of the Pacific coast refer affectionately and regretfully, now that they have gone.

In the case of the Japanese, the break between the older and the younger generation is usually not so abrupt and so complete, but the native-born Japanese will probably not remain on the farm, even in cases where they are able to realize the ambitions of their parents and become proprietors. It is not merely that they are infected with what we sometimes call the American spirit, but they cannot endure the isolation of a rural community. The same forces that have driven the Jew into the freer air of the city, are making of the Japanese farmer a city man. With this change in residence and ideals, there has been an abrupt mutation in racial characteristics. It is probably true of the Oriental, as of other immigrant peoples, that in the process of Americanization, only superficial traits are modified, but *most of the racial traits that determine race relations are superficial.*

The facts indicating the nature and extent of the changes that are taking place in the manners and character of the younger generation of Orientals are probably the most significant that our Race Relations Survey on the Pacific coast has thus far disclosed. They tend to emphasize and reenforce a growing conviction among students of human nature that the most important, if not the most fundamental, differences between nations and peoples, aside from physical characteristics, are reflected in their manners, in their etiquette, and in the conceptions which they form of themselves. The characteristic traits of people are, in other words, not so much innate qualities as conventions.

But conventions change. They have changed in Europe since the war. Mussolini has set a new fashion in Italy, and the Italian character is apparently changing under the influence of a new national ideal. The Germans have assumed in Europe a decidedly different rôle from that which they sought to play before the war. And the German character—all the superficial features of that character, at any rate—is changing.

Nothing which our recent studies in individual psychology and psychiatry has disclosed in regard to human behavior is more interesting and more surprising than the sudden changes which take place in personality under the influence of a persistent mood, particularly when that mood becomes the basis of the individual's new conception of himself. When such changes of mood take place in a whole people, and the mood of individuals is reenforced and sustained by the contagious influence of other individuals, manners and customs, art and literature, all the natural forms of expression reflect the change in attitude and orientation.

Physical traits, however, do not change. The Oriental in America experiences a profound transfiguration in sentiment and attitude, but he cannot change his physical characteristics. He is still constrained to wear his racial uniform; he cannot, much as he may sometimes like to do so, cast aside the racial mask.

The physical marks of race, in so far as they increase the racial visibility, inevitably segregate the races, set them apart, and so prolong and intensify the racial conflict. If it is true that it is the type, the abstraction and not the individual, that we see in the stranger first, it is just as true that it is the individual and not the type that we see in our friends. It is a curious thing about human faces that when we look at them, abstractly and disinterestedly, most of them are ugly, some of them uncanny, and all of them are more or less caricatures. It is only as we become aware of the feelings, the passions, and the curiously changing moods which they reflect, that faces become interesting. It is, in fact, only as faces become expressive that the persons behind these living masks assume for us the character of human beings.

It is curious and interesting that this character that we call human should be so intimately connected with expressiveness. Human interest, as we ordinarily use that phrase, attaches to anything that is "expressive"; that is, to anything that suggests, symbolizes or reveals sentiments and passions in others of which we are immediately conscious in ourselves. The faces we know have no secrets for us. For that reason, if for no other, we feel secure and at home with them as we do not among less familiar faces. Probably the most expressive, the most human face we ever know, is that of a mother; or it may be that of an old nurse, even that of an old black mammy.

One of the first and most important discoveries the one who meets an alien people for the first time is likely to make, is that, different as they seem, most strange people, when you come to know them, turn out to be human like ourselves. It always requires an effort of imagination to realize this. It is because their faces are for us not expressive; and we, in turn, do not respond to sentiments whose expression we are not able to read.

When we say, as we often do, that human nature is fundamentally everywhere and always the same, we mean simply that when we are able to penetrate to the motives behind customs and conduct which at first seemed strange, outlandish and forbidding, they inevitably turn out to be motives such as might have moved us under similar circumstances.

"To comprehend all," as the old French proverb puts it, "is to forgive all." On the other hand, failure to comprehend opens the way to sinister as well as romantic interpretations. We are very likely to attribute something sinister to conduct the motive for which we do not understand. In fact, it is only to the extent that we are able to enter imaginatively into the lives and experience of others that we regard them as human like ourselves.

One reason why our immigrant populations seem alien and different is because they are more self-conscious and reserved with us than they are with one another. On the other hand, they are self-conscious and reserved because they are alien and different. It is a vicious circle. The more marked the racial differences, the more intense is the racial self-consciousness, and the greater the *social distance* that separates the alien from the native peoples.

In time, however, what was strange becomes familiar. We discover the same human motives and wishes reflected in the manners of other people of which we are conscious in ourselves. Conduct that formerly struck us as queer becomes familiar and intelligible. Faces once impenetrable become expressive and human.

The race problem turns out, then, in one of its aspects at least, to be a problem of communication. The barriers to communication are not differences of language and of culture merely, but more particularly of self-consciousness, race consciousness, and consciousness of kind; not physical distances merely, but social distances. Whenever representatives of different races meet and discover in one another— beneath the differences of race—sentiments, tastes, interests, and human qualities generally that they can understand and respect, racial barriers are undermined and eventually broken down. Personal relations and personal friendships are the great moral solvents. Under their influence all distinctions of class, of caste, and even of race, are dissolved into the general flux which we sometimes call democracy.

It was a minor statesman who said: "What is the Constitution between friends?" As the embodiment of a moral doctrine, this question, with its implications, is subject to grave qualifications, but as a statement of psychological fact it has to be reckoned with. What, between friends, are any of our conventions, moral codes, and political doctrines and institutions? It is personal friendships that corrupt politics. Not only politics, but all our formal and conventional relations are undermined by those elemental loyalties that have their roots in personal attachments. There is no way of preserving existing social barriers, except by preserving the existing animosities that buttress them.

We must reckon with the fact that for good or for ill, under the conditions of modern life, these personal friendships are steadily increasing. Trade, travel, literature, every form of communication, multiply them. Furthermore, our churches, missions, and Christian associations, among other agencies, are systematically seeking not only to increase but to institutionalize them. In their efforts to do this, they may create new prejudices, but at any rate they are undermining old ones. It is indeed in the very nature of the religious enterprise that it should run counter to every movement that seeks to stabilize society on the basis of race.

At the conclusion of the session of the Institute of Pacific Relations at Honolulu last summer, a member of the Japanese delegation summed up the results of that unique gathering in one casual but illuminating remark: "Well," he said, speaking for himself and for the Japanese delegation, "our attitudes have been profoundly changed, but our opinions remain the same." The discussions, and even more, perhaps, the intimate and friendly relations established, undeniably changed the sentiments, even though they did not change the program, of every member of the conference. A good deal of that sense of injury which has so frequently poisoned international and interracial relations evaporated during the progress of the discussions.

Issues that had previously been maintained as matters of principle and of national honor passed over, in this friendly atmosphere, into the category of matters for negotiation. The Institute was described, in fact, as "an adventure in friendship."

The purpose of the Race Relations Survey on the Pacific coast may be described in much the same terms. It has sought to gain a knowledge which will not so much change opinion as attitudes. It was not the purpose of the survey to crystalize opinion on either side of an issue, but rather to provide a context in which issues could be discussed in a friendlier spirit; create a situation in which the common, as over against sectarian, party, and racial interests, might receive a more deliberate and intelligent consideration. An impartial investigation of the facts, it seemed, would at least reduce the inflammation and purge the situation of some of its bitterness.

It has been necessary to review the facts and the issues, but our survey sought to go behind the opinions and the programs of parties and sects, to the sources of public opinion—the concrete experiences, the personal sentiments and private feelings of individual men, compared with which the forensic display of arguments and propaganda is, after all, a kind of masquerade. From the point of view of the Race Relations Survey, the situation on the Pacific coast is not so much a problem of politics, in the ordinary sense of that word, as a problem of behavior—*collective behavior*. It is in this sense, and with this purpose, that the Oriental number of *The Survey* has been conceived.

CHAPTER 20

THE CONCEPT OF SOCIAL DISTANCE

As Applied to the Study of Racial Attitudes and Racial Relations

I

SOCIAL DISTANCE DEFINED

THE concept of "distance" as applied to human, as distinguished from spacial relations, has come into use among sociologists, in an attempt to reduce to something like measurable terms the grades and degrees of understanding and intimacy which characterize personal and social relations generally.

We frequently say of A that he is very "close" to B, but that C is distant and reserved, but that D, on the other hand, is open-minded, sympathetic, understanding, and generally "easy to meet." All these expressions describe and to some extent measure "social distance."

We do not, it must be confessed, know all the factors that enter into and determine what we call social distance. We know, to be sure, that in many cases "reserve" is an effect of timidity and self-consciousness. We know, also, that under certain circumstances reserves may be "broken down" and that with this break-down social distances dissolve and the most intimate understandings are frequently established.

The point is that we are clearly conscious, in all our personal relationships, of degree of intimacy. A is closer to B than C and the *degree of this intimacy measures the inflence which each has over the other.*

Journal of Applied Sociology, VIII (1924), pp. 339-344.

The fact that we can so easily distinguish degrees of intimacy suggests that we may be able eventually to measure "distance" in the sense in which that word is here used, quite as accurately as we now measure intelligence, since we do not know all the factors that determine intelligence any more than we know all the factors that determine intimacy.

The native human impulse that leads us to enter imaginatively into the other persons' minds, to share their experience and sympathize with their pains and pleasures, joys, and sorrows, hopes and fears, may be blocked by self-consciousness, by vague fears, by positive self-interest, etc., and all these are matters that need to be reckoned with in seeking to measure "distances."

Now it is not only true that we have a sense of distance toward individuals with whom we come into contact but we have much the same feeling with regard to classes and races. The terms "race consciousness" and "class consciousness," with which most of us are familiar, describe a state of mind in which we become, often suddenly and unexpectedly conscious of the distances that separate, or seem to separate us, from classes and races whom we do not fully understand.

Not only is it true that we have this sense of distance with reference to whole groups of persons but it is also true that "race" and "class" consciousness frequently interferes with, modifies and qualifies personal relations; relations which, under other circumstances, it seems, might become of the most intimate and understanding sort.

For example, the lady of the house may be on the most intimate personal relations with her cook, but these intimate relations will be maintained only so long as the cook retains her "proper distance." There is always some sort of social ritual that keeps the cook in her place, particularly when there are guests. This is one of the things that every woman knows.

The same is true in the relations of races. The Negro is "all right in his place" and the same is probably true of every other race, class or category of persons towards whom our attitudes have become fixed, customary, and conventionalized. Every one, it seems, is capable of getting on with every one else, provided each preserves his proper distance.

The importance of these personal and racial reserves, which so invariably and inevitably spring up to complicate and, in some measure, to fix and conventionalize our spontaneous human relations, is that they get themselves expressed in all our formal social and even our political relations.

It is characteristic of democracy that, relatively speaking and in theory, there are no "social distances." Walt Whitman, who interpreted democracy mystically and poetically, refused to shut out any human creature from the circle of his cordial understanding and sympathy. In his famous lines addressed *To a Common Prostitute*, he said: "Not until the sun excludes you will I exclude you." And in that inclusive phrase he seemed to include in a wide fraternal embrace everything human and living which the rain wet and the sun warmed. But he did not profess to make no distinction at all between human beings.

Democracy abhors social distinctions but it maintains them. The difference between democracy and other forms of society is that it refuses to make class or race, i.e., group distinctions. Distinctions and distances must be of a purely individual and personal nature. In an individualistic society like ours, every man theoretically is treated on his merits as an individual.

Aristocratic society, on the other hand, maintains itself by an insistence on social distinctions and differences. The obeisances, condescensions, and ceremonial taboos which characterize a highly stratified society exist for the express purpose of enforcing the reserves and social distances upon which the social and political hierarchy rests.

The ideals of democratic society, as we know them, are a heritage of the frontier. On the frontier, where there are, generally speaking, no traditions, no condescensions, and no obeisances, every man is master of his own immortal soul. Under these circumstances social distances disappear and social relations are more direct, candid, and informal than they are likely to be under any other circumstances.

But the frontier has passed or is passing. Besides, the very existence of frontier life assumed conditions that no longer obtain. In any case, the frontier has its own peculiar prejudices. The characteristic prejudice of the frontier was directed not against the stranger, but against the man who acted strangely, who stood aloof or assumed superiority, who did not fraternize and mix. Any sort of reserve was likely to be looked on with suspicion. Under these conditions the melting pot was effective and democracy flourished.

With the coming of the Oriental, however, the situation changed. He looked strange, he spoke a quaint language, and he developed habits of industry and thrift that were intolerable to those who had to compete with him. On this point democratic society broke down. It was no longer possible to treat the Orientals as individuals. They did not assimilate. One looked at them without being able to tell what was going on in their heads. They were "foreign devils." As Bret Harte expressed it, "For ways that are dark and tricks that are vain, the heathen Chinee is peculiar." Competition, which had been personal, became racial, and race competition became race conflict.

As a result of this conflict we have had the rise of a new "race consciousness," so called, a consciousness based on "color." *The Rising Tide of Color*, which makes the title of Lothrop Stoddard's book, is a description of the circumstances and conditions under which that new consciousness has arisen. Because group consciousness usually grows out of group conflict it invariably brings with it group prejudice.

What we ordinarily call prejudice seems then to be more or less instinctive and spontaneous disposition to maintain social distances. Those distances, in our democratic society tend to assume a purely individual character. We say we are without prejudice, but we choose our company. On the frontier, before the coming of the Chinaman, and in our village communities where every one called every one else by his first name, we succeeded fairly well in maintaining a society without race or class distinctions. But in the cities we have become "class conscious," just as, with the emancipation of the Negro and the invasion of the European and Asiatic immigrants, we have become "race conscious."

Prejudice, in this broad conception of the term, seems to be an incident of group consciousness just as reserve seems to be an incident of self-consciousness. The child at first has no reserves; knows nothing either of pride, humility, gratitude, nor of any of the other excitements and the sufferings of self-consciousness.

The child has no class or race prejudices either. Except in precocious children these manifestations of group consciousness that we call "class" and "race" consciousness do not ordinarily appear until shortly before the age of puberty. When they do arrive, however, they bring with them all the traditional prejudices by which the class and race distinctions and the traditional social distances are maintained.

It is not intended, in what has been said, to suggest that consciousness, race consciousness, prejudice, and all the personal and social distinctions related to social distance, are in any sense identical with it.

As a matter of fact self-consciousness usually arises out of some sort of personal conflict and the personal reserves that spring up as a consequence of past conflicts and the anticipation of new ones, serve the purpose of preserving the individual's private, personal life from intrusion, misinterpretation, and censorship.

Prejudice, on the other hand, seems to arise when, not our economic interests, but our social status is menaced. Prejudice and race prejudice are by no means to be identified by social distance, but arise when our personal and racial reserves are, or seem to be, invaded. Prejudice is on the whole not an aggressive but a conservative force; a sort of spontaneous conservation which tends to preserve the social order and the social distances upon which that order rests.

One purpose of a racial study is to measure, not our prejudices, but those vaguer, subtler taboos and inhibitions which persist even in so mobile and changing an order as our own, and represent the stabilizing, spontaneous, and instinctive and conservative forces upon which social organization rests.

CHAPTER 21

EDUCATION IN ITS RELATION TO THE CONFLICT AND FUSION OF CULTURES

With Special Reference to the Problems of the Immigrant, the Negro, and Missions

I. THE PROBLEM STATED

IT HAS long been a cardinal problem in sociology to determine just how to conceive in objective terms so very real and palpable a thing as the continuity and persistence of social groups. Looked at as a physical object society appears to be made up of mobile and independent units. The problem is to understand the nature of the bonds that bind these independent units together and how these connections are maintained and transmitted.

Conceived of in its lowest terms the unity of the social group may be compared to that of the plant communities. In these communities, the relation between the individual species which compose it seems at first wholly fortuitous and external. Cooperation and community, so far as it exists, consists merely in the fact that, within a given geographical area, certain species come together merely because each happens to provide by its presence an environment in which the life of the other is easier, more secure, than if they lived in isolation. It seems to be a fact, however, that this communal life of the associated plants fulfils, as in other forms of life, a typical series of changes, which correspond to growth, decay, and death. The plant community comes into existence, matures, grows old, and eventually dies. In doing this,

Publication of the American Sociological Society, XIII (1918), pp. 38-63.

however, it provides by its own death an environment in which another form of community finds its natural habitat. Each community thus precedes and prepares the way for its successor. Under such circumstances the succession of the individual communities itself assumes the character of a life-process.[1]

In the case of the animal and human societies we have all these conditions and forces and something more. The individuals associated in an animal community not only provide, each for the other, a physical environment in which all may live, but the members of the community are organically pre-adapted to one another in ways which are not characteristic of the members of a plant community. As a consequence, the relations between the members of the animal community assume a much more organic character. It is, in fact, a characteristic of animal society that the members of a social group are organically adapted to one another and therefore the organization of animal society is almost wholly transmitted by physical inheritance.

In the case of human societies we discover not merely organically inherited adaptation, which characterizes animal societies, but, in addition, a great body of habits and accommodations which are transmitted in the form of social inheritance. Something that corresponds to social tradition exists, to be sure, in animal societies. Animals learn by imitation from one another, and there is evidence that this social tradition varies with changes in environment. In man, however, association is based on something more than habits or instinct. In human society, largely as a result of language, there exists a conscious community of purpose. We have not merely folkways, which by an extension of that term might be attributed to animals, but we have mores and formal standards of conduct.

In a recent notable volume on education, John Dewey has formulated a definition of the educational process which he identifies with the process by which the social tradition of human society is transmitted. Education, he says in effect, is a self-renewing process, a process in which and through which the social organism lives.

With the renewal of physical existence goes, in the case of human beings, the re-creation of beliefs, ideals, hopes, happiness, misery and practices. The continuity of experience, through renewal of the social group is a literal fact. Education, in its broadest sense, is the means of this social continuity of life.[2]

---

[1] Frederic E. Clemens, *Plant Succession: An Analysis of the Development of Vegetation.* Published by the Carnegie Institution of Washington, 1916, p. 6.
[2] *Education and Democracy*, pp. 2-3.

Under ordinary circumstances the transmission of the social tradition is from the parents to the children. Children are born into the
society and take over its customs, habits, and standards of life simply,
naturally, and without conflict. But it will at once occur to anyone
that the physical life of society is not always continued and maintained in this natural way, i.e., by the succession of parents and
children. New societies are formed by conquest and by the imposition
of one people upon another. In such cases there arises a conflict of
cultures, and as a result the process of fusion takes place slowly and
is frequently not complete. New societies are frequently formed by
colonization, in which case new cultures are grafted onto older ones.
The work of missionary societies is essentially one of colonization in
this sense. Finally we have societies growing up, as in the United
States by immigration. These immigrants, coming as they do from all
parts of the world, bring with them fragments of divergent cultures.
Here again the process of assimilation is slow, often painful, not
always complete.

In the case where societies are formed and maintained by adoption,
that is, by immigration, the question arises: How is it possible for a
people of a different race and a different culture to take over the
traditions and social inheritance of another and an alien people? What
are the conditions which facilitate this transmission and, in general,
what happpens when people of different races and cultures are
brought together in the intimate relations of community life?

These questions have already arisen in connection with the education of the Negro in America and with the work of foreign missions.
If the schools are to extend and rationalize the work they are already
doing in the Americanization of the immigrant peoples, questions of
this sort may become actual in the field of pedagogy. This paper is
mainly concerned with the Negro, not because the case of the Negro
is more urgent than or essentially different from that of the immigrant, but because the materials for investigation are more accessible.

Much has been said and written in the past about the intellectual
inferiority of the Negro. Attempts have been made to demonstrate
this inferiority on the basis of general anthropological, ethnological,
and even theological grounds. The history of these efforts has produced some curious and sociologically interesting literature. But this
literature is valuable mainly for what it reveals of the distortion of

sentiment and opinion which the racial conflict has produced in the black man and the white.[3]

More recently efforts have been made to determine the relative intellectual capacity of the Negro and the white man by psychological measurements of the achievements of Negro school children as compared with white. The result of these investigations is still highly speculative and, on the whole, inconclusive.[4] On the basis of all the evidence at hand the question remains where Boas left it when he said that the black man was little, if any, inferior to the white man in intellectual capacity and, in any case, racial as compared with individual differences were small and relatively unimportant.[5]

Admitting, as the anthropologists now seem disposed to do, that the average native intelligence in the races is about the same, we may still expect to find in different races certain special traits and tendencies which rest on biological rather than cultural differences. For example, over and above all differences of language, custom, or historic tradition it is to be presumed that Teuton and Latin, the Negro and the Jew—to compare the most primitive with the most sophisticated of peoples—have certain racial aptitudes, certain innate and characteristic differences of temperament which manifest themselves especially in the objects of attention, in tastes, and in talents. Is the Jewish intellectual, for example, a manifestation of an original and peculiar endowment of the Jewish race or is he rather a product of traditional interest and emphasis characteristic of Jewish people—a characteristic which may be explained as an accommodation to the long-continued urban environment of the race? [6]

Is the Negro's undoubted interest in music and taste for bright colors, commonly attributed to the race, to be regarded as inherent and racial traits or are they merely the characteristics of primitive people?

Is Catholicism to be regarded as the natural manifestation of the Latin temperament as it has been said that Protestanism is of the Teutonic?

Here are differences in the character of the cultural life which can

---

[3] Charles Carroll, *The Negro a Beast*, American Book and Bible House, 1890.

[4] George Oscar Ferguson, Jr., "The Psychology of the Negro: An Experimental Study," *Archives of Psychology*, No. 36, April, 1916.

[5] Franz Boas, *The Mind of Primitive Man*, 1911, p. 269.

[6] Robert E. Park, "The City: Suggestions for the Investigation of Human Behavior in the City Environment," *American Journal of Sociology*, XX (March, 1915), 589.

scarcely be measured quantitatively in terms of gross intellectual capacity. Historical causes do not, it seems, adequately account for them. So far as this is true we are perhaps warranted in regarding them as modifications of transmitted tradition due to innate traits of the people who have produced them. Granted that civilization, as we find it, is due to the development of communication and the possibility of mutual exchange of cultural materials, still every special culture is the result of a selection, and every people borrows from the whole fund of cultural materials not merely that which it can use but which, because of certain organic characteristics, it finds stimulating and interesting.

The question then resolves itself into this: How far do racial characteristics and innate biological interests determine the extent to which one racial group can and will take over and assimilate the characteristic features of an alien civilization? How far will it merely take over the cultural forms, giving them a different content or a different inflection?

This problem, so far as it is related to the lives of primitive peoples, has already been studied by the ethnologists. Rivers, in his analysis of the cultures of Australian people, has found that what has hitherto been regarded as primitive cultures are really fusions of other and earlier forms of culture.[7] The evidence of this is the fact that the fusion has not been complete. In the process of interchange it frequently happens that what Rivers calls the "fundamental structure" of the primitive society has remained unchanged while the relatively formal and external elements of the culture only have been taken over.

There are indications also that where cultural borrowings have taken place the formal elements have a different meaning for the people who have taken them over than they had for the people from whom they were borrowed. W. J. McGee, in an article entitled "Piratical Acculturation," has given an interesting illustration of this fact.[8]

McGee's observations of the Seri Indians go to show that they imitated the weapons of their enemies but that they regarded them as magical instruments and the common people did not even know their names. There are numerous other illustrations of this so-called "piratical acculturation" among the observations of ethnologists. It

---

[7] W. H. R. Rivers, "Ethnological Analysis of Cultures," *Nature*, Vol. 87, 1911
[8] W. J. McGee, "Piratical Acculturation," *Am. Anthropologist*, V. No. 11 pp. 243-49.

is said that the Negroes, when they first came into possession of the white man's guns, regarded them as magical instruments for making a noise and used them, as the Germans used the zeppelins and the newspapers, merely to destroy the enemy's morale.

No doubt the disposition of primitive peoples is to conceive everything mystically, or animistically, to use the language of ethnology, particularly where it concerns something strange. On the other hand, when the primitive man encounters among the cultural objects to which civilization has introduced him something which he can make immediately intelligible to himself, he at once forms a perfectly rational conception of it.

Some years ago at Lovedale, South Africa, the seat of one of the first successful industrial mission schools, there was an important ceremony to which all the native African chiefs in the vicinity were formally invited. It was the introduction and demonstration of the use of the plow, the first one that had ever been seen in those parts. The proceedings were followed with great interest by a large gathering of natives. When the demonstration was finished one old chief turned to his followers and said with great conviction: "This is a great thing which the white man has brought us. One hoe like that is worth as much as ten wives." An African chief could hardly have expressed appreciation of this one fundamental device of our civilization in more pragmatic or less mystical terms. The wise old chief grasped the meaning of the plow at once, but this was because he had been pre-adapted by earlier experience to do so.

It is in general the subjective, historic, and ultimately, perhaps, racial and temperamental factor in the lives of peoples which makes it difficult, though not impossible, perhaps, to transmit political and religious institutions to people of a different racial type and a different social tradition. William James's essay "On a Certain Blindness in Human Beings," in which he points out how completely we are likely to miss the point and mistake the inner significance of the lives of those about us unless we share their experience, emphasizes this fact.

If then the transmission and fusion of cultures is slow, incomplete, and sometimes impossible it is because the external forms, the formulas, technical devices of every social tradition, can be more easily transmitted than the aims, the attitudes, sentiments, and ideals which attach to them, which are embodied in them. The former can be copied and used; the latter must be appreciated and understood.

II. AFRICAN HERITAGE OF THE AMERICAN NEGRO

For a study of the acculturation process there are probably no materials more complete and accessible than those offered by the history of the American Negro. No other representatives of a primitive race have had so prolonged and so intimate an association with European civilization and still preserved their racial identity. Among no other people is it possible to find so many stages of culture existing contemporaneously.

It has been generally taken for granted that the Negro brought a considerable fund of African tradition and African superstition from Africa to America. One not infrequently runs across, in the current literature and even in standard books upon the Negro, references to voodoo practices among the Negro in the southern states. As a matter of fact the last authentic account which we have of anything approaching a Negro nature worship in the United States took place in Louisiana in 1884. It is described by George W. Cable in an article on "Creole Slave Songs" which appeared in the *Century Magazine* in 1886. In this case it seems to have been an importation from the West Indies. I have never run across an account of a genuine instance of voodoo worship elsewhere in the United States, although it seems to have been common enough in the West Indies at one time.

My own impression is that the amount of African tradition which the Negro brought to the United States was very small. In fact there is every reason to believe, it seems to me, that the Negro, when he landed in the United States, left behind him almost everything but his dark complexion and his tropical temperament. It is very difficult to find in the South today anything that can be traced directly back to Africa. This does not mean that there is not a great deal of superstition, conjuring, root doctoring, and magic generally among the Negroes of the United States. What it does mean is that the superstitions we do find are those which we might expect to grow up anywhere among an imaginative people living in an intellectual twilight such as exists on the isolated plantations of the southern states. Furthermore this is in no way associated as it is in some of the countries of Europe, southern Italy for example, with the Negroes' religious beliefs and practices. It is not part of Negro Christianity. It is with him, as it is with us, folk-lore pure and simple. It is said that there are but two African words that have been retained in the English language. One of these words is "Buckra," from which the name

Buchra Beach in Virginia comes. This seems remarkable when we consider that slaves were still brought into the United States clandestinely up to 1862.[9]

The explanation is to be found in the manner in which the Negro slaves were collected in Africa and the manner in which they were disposed of after they arrived in this country. The great markets for slaves in Africa were on the west coast, but the old slave trails ran back from the coast far into the interior of the continent and all the peoples of Central Africa contributed to the stream of enforced emigration to the New World. In the West Indies a great deal was known among slave-traders and plantation owners about the character and relative value of slaves from different parts of Africa, but in the United States there was less knowledge and less discrimination. Coming from all parts of Africa and having no common language and common tradition, the memories of Africa which they brought with them were soon lost.

There was less opportunity in the United States, also, than in the West Indies for a slave to meet one of his own people because the plantations were considerably smaller, more widely scattered, and especially because as soon as they were landed in this country slaves were immediately divided and shipped in small numbers, frequently no more than one or two at a time, to different plantations. This was the procedure with the very first Negroes brought to this country. It was found easier to deal with the slaves if they were separated from their kinsmen.

On the plantation they were thrown together with slaves who had already forgotten or only dimly remembered their life in Africa. English was the only language of the plantation. The attitude of the plantation slave to each fresh arrival seems to have been much like that of the older immigrant toward the greenhorn. Everything that marked him as an alien was regarded as ridiculous and barbaric.[10] Furthermore the slave had in fact very little desire to return to his

---

[9] There is or was a few years ago near Mobile a colony of Africans who were brought to the United States as late as 1860. It is true, also, that Major R. R. Moten, who has succeeded Booker T. Washington as head of Tuskegee Institute, still preserves the story that was told him by his grandmother of the way in which his great-grandfather was brought from Africa in a slave ship.

[10] Mrs. Carmichael, *Domestic Manners and Social Condition of the White, Coloured and Negro Population of the West Indies*, Vol. I, p. 251. London: Wittaker, Treacher and Co. "Native Africans do not at all like it to be supposed that they retain the customs of their country and consider themselves wonderfully civilized by being transplanted from Africa to the West Indies. Creole

native land. I once had an opportunity to talk with an old man living just outside of Mobile who was a member of what was known as the African colony. This African colony represented the cargo of one of the last slave ships that was landed in this country just at the opening of the war. The old man remembered Africa and gave me a very interesting account of the way in which he was captured and brought to America. I asked him if he had ever wished to return. He said that a missionary had visited them at one time who had been in their country and spoke their language. This missionary offered to send them back to Africa and even urged them to go. "I told him," said the old man, "that I crossed the ocean once but I made up my mind then never to trust myself in a boat with a white man again."

The fact that the Negro brought with him from Africa so little tradition which he was able to transmit and perpetuate on American soil makes that race unique among all peoples of our cosmopolitan population. Other people have lost, under the disintegrating influence of the American environment, much of their cultural heritages. None have been so utterly cut off and estranged from their ancestral land, traditions, and people.

It is just because of this that the history of the Negro offers exceptional materials for determining the relative influence of temperamental and historical conditions upon the process by which cultural materials from one racial group are transmitted to another. For, in spite of the fact that the Negro brought so little intellectual baggage with him, he has exhibited a rather marked ethnical individuality in the use and interpretation of the cultural materials to which he has had access.

III. RELIGION OF THE SLAVE

The first, and perhaps the only distinctive, institution which the Negro has developed in this country is the Negro church, and it is in connection with this religion that we may expect to find, if anywhere, the indications of a distinctive Afro-American culture.

The actual conditions under which the African slaves were converted to Christianity have never been adequately investigated. We know, in a general way, that there was at first considerable opposition to admitting the Negro into the church because it was feared that it would impair the master's title to his slaves. We know, however,

---

Negroes invariably consider themselves superior people, and lord it over the native Africans."

that the house servants were very early admitted to churches and that in many cases masters went to considerable pains to instruct those servants who shared with them the intimacy of the household.

The Society for the Propagation of the Gospel in Foreign Parts was founded in 1701, and the efforts to Christianize the Negro were carried on with a great deal of zeal and with some success. It was not, however, until the coming of the new, free, and evangelistic types of Christianity, the Baptists and the Methodists, that the masses of the Negro people, i.e., the plantation Negroes, found a form of Christianity that they could make their own.

How eagerly and completely the Negro did make the religion of these two denominations his own may be gathered from some of the contemporary writings, which record the founding of the first Negro churches in America. The first Negro church in Jamaica was founded by George Liele, shortly after the close of the Revolutionary War. George Liele had been a slave in Savannah, Ga., but his master, who seems to have been a Tory, emigrated to Jamaica after the war. The following excerpt from a missionary report indicates the way in which Liele entered upon his self-appointed ministry.

Being "called by grace" himself, George began to discover his love to other Negroes, on the same plantation with himself, by reading hymns among them, encouraging them to sing, and sometimes by explaining the most striking parts of them.[11]

Andrew Bryan in Savannah was one of Liele's congregation. He was converted, according to the contemporary record, by Liele's exposition of the text "You must be born again!" About eight months after Liele's departure, Andrew began to preach to a Negro congregation, "with a few whites." The colored people had been permitted to erect a building at Yamacraw, but white people in the vicinity objected to the meetings and Bryan and some of his associates were arrested and whipped. But he "rejoiced in his whippings" and holding up his hand declared "he would freely suffer death for the cause of Jesus Christ." Bryan's master interceded for him and "was most affected and grieved" at his punishment. He gave Bryan and his followers a barn to worship in, after Chief Justice Osborne had given them their liberty. This was the origin of what was probably the first Negro church in America. George Liele and Andrew Bryan were

---

[11] "Letters Showing the Rise and Progress of the Early Negro Churches of Georgia and the West Indies," *Journal of Negro History*, I (1916), 70.

probably not exceptional men even for their day. The Rev. James Cook wrote of Bryan: "His gifts are small but he is clear in the grand doctrines of the Gospel. I believe him truly pious and he has been the instrument of doing more good among the poor slaves than all the learned doctors in America." [12]

The significant thing is that, with the appearance of these men, the Negroes in America ceased to be a mission people. At least, from this time on, the movement went on of its own momentum, more and more largely under the direction of Negro leaders. Little Negro congregations, under the leadership of Negro preachers, sprang up wherever they were tolerated. Often they were suppressed, more often they were privately encouraged. Not infrequently they met in secret. The following description is written of one of these churches by an English visitor to the United States in 1835:

I learned that in the afternoon there would be worship at the African church, and I resolved to go. . . . . The building, called a church, is without the town, and placed in a hollow so as to be out of sight; it is, in the fullest sense, "without the gate." It is a poor log-house, built by the hands of the Negroes, and so placed as to show that they must worship by stealth. It is, perhaps, 20 by 25, with boarding and rails breast high, run around three sides, so as to form galleries. To this is added a lean-to, to take the overplus, when the fine weather should admit of larger numbers. There were three small openings besides the door, and the chinks in the building, to admit light and air. . . . . By the law of the State, no coloured persons are permitted to assemble for worship, unless a white person be present and preside. On this account the elders of Mr. Douglas' church attend in turn, that the poor people may not lose the privileges they prize. . . . . One of the blacks . . . . gave out Dr. Watt's beautiful psalm "Show pity, Lord; O Lord, forgive," etc. They all rose immediately. They had no books, for they could not read; but it was printed on their memory, and they sang it off with freedom and feeling. There is much melody in their voice; and when they enjoy a hymn, there is a raised expression of the face, and an undulating motion of the body, keeping time with the music, which is very touching. . . . . Much has been said, and is still said, about the essential inequality of the races. That is a question which must be settled by experiment. Here the experiment was undoubtedly in favour of the blacks. In sense and in feeling, both in prayer and address, they were equal to the whites; and in free and pointed expression much superior. Indeed I know not that while I was in America, I listened to a peroration of an address that was superior to the one I have briefly noted to you.[13]

---

[12] *Journal of Negro History*, I (1916), 70.

[13] Andrew Reed, D.D., and James Matheson, D.D., *A Narrative of the Visit to the American Churches by the Deputation from the Congregational Union of England and Wales*, Vol. I. London: Jackson and Walford, 1235.

In 1787 Richard Allen and Absalom Jones had formed in Philadelphia the Free African Society, out of which four years later in 1790 arose the first separate denominational organization of Negroes, the African Methodist Episcopal Church. George Liele, Andrew Bryan, Richard Allen, and the other founders of the Negro church were men of some education as their letters and other writings show. They had had the advantage of life in a city environment and the churches which they founded were in all essentials faithful copies of the denominational forms as they found them in the churches of that period.

The religion of the Negroes on the plantations was then, as it is today, of a much more primitive sort. Furthermore there were considerable differences in the cultural status of different regions of the South and these differences were reflected in the Negro churches. There was at that time, as there is today, a marked contrast between the Upland and the Sea Island Negroes. Back from the coast the plantations were smaller, the contact of the master and slave were more intimate. On the Sea Islands, however, where the Negroes were and still are more completely isolated than elsewhere in the South, the Negro population approached more closely to the cultural status of the native African.

The Sea Islanders were taken possession of in the first years of the war by the federal forces, and it was here that people from the North first came in contact with the plantation Negro of the lower South. They immediately became interested in the manners and customs of the Island Negroes, and from them we have the first accurate accounts of their folk-lore and songs.

The Sea Island Negroes speak a distinct dialect and retain certain customs which are supposed to be of African origin. It is, however, in their religious practices that we have the nearest approach to anything positively African. The following description of a "shout" is interesting in this connection:

There is a ceremony which the white clergymen are inclined to discountenance, and even of the colored elders, some of the more discreet try sometimes to put on a face of discouragement; and, although if pressed for Biblical warrant for the "shout" they generally seem to think, "he in de Book," or "he dere-da in Matchew," still it is not considered blasphemous or improper if "de chillen" and "dem young gal" carry it on in the evening, for amusement's sake, and with no well-defined intention of "praise." But the true "shout" takes place on Sundays, or on "praise" nights through the week, and either in the praise-house or in some cabin in which a regular religious meeting had been held. Very likely more than half the population of a plantation is gathered together. Let it be the evening, and a light wood-fire burns red before the door of the house and on the hearth. For some time one can hear, though at a good distance, the vociferous exhortation or a prayer of the presiding elder or of the brother who has a gift that way and is not "on the back seat"—a phrase the interpretation of which is "under the censure of the church authorities for bad behavior"—and at regular intervals one hears the elder "dealing" a hymnbook hymn, which is sung two lines at a time and whose wailing cadences, born on the night air, are indescribably melancholy.

But the benches are pushed back to the wall when the formal meeting is over, and old and young, men and women, sprucely dressed young men, grotesquely half-clad field hands, the women generally with gay handkerchiefs twisted about their heads and with short skirts, boys with tattered shirts and men's trousers, young girls bare-footed, all stand up in the middle of the floor, and when the "sperichil" is struck up, begin first walking and by and by shuffling around, one after the other, in a ring. The foot is hardly taken from the floor and the progression is mainly due to a jerking, hitching motion which agitates the entire shouter and soon brings out streams of perspiration. Sometimes they dance silently, sometimes as they shuffle they sing the chorus of the spiritual, and sometimes the song itself is also sung by the dancers. But more frequently a band, composed of some of the best singers and of tired shouters, stand at the side of the room to "base" the others, singing the body of the song and dropping their hands together or on their knees. Song and dance are alike extremely energetic and often, when the shout lasts into the middle of the night, the monotonous thud, thud of the feet prevents sleep within half a mile of the praise-house.[14]

This has undoubtedly the characteristics of primitive ritual. But this does not mean that it is African in origin. It seems to me more likely that it is to be interpreted as a very simple and natural expression of group emotion, which is just beginning to crystalize and assume formal character. The general tone of these meetings is that of a religious revival in which we expect a free and uncontrolled expression of religious emotion, the difference being that in this case the expression of the excitement is beginning to assume a formal and ritualistic character.

In the voodoo practices, of which we have many accurate records, the incantations that were pronounced by the priests contain strange, magic words, scraps of ancient ritual, the meanings of which are forgotten. Lafcadio Hearne, who knew the Negro life of Louisiana and

---

[14] Henry Edward Krehbiel, *Afro-American Folksongs. A Study in Racial and National Music*, p. 33. New York and London: G. Schirmer. Quotation taken from *The Nation*, May 30, 1867.

Martinique intimately and was keen on the subject of Negro folk-lore, has preserved for us this scrap from an old Negro folk-song in which some of these magic words have been preserved. Writing to his friend Edward Krehbiel he says:

> Your friend is right, no doubt about the
> > "Tig, tig, malabon
> > La Chelerna che tanog
> > Redjoum!"

I asked my black nurse what it meant. She only laughed and shook her head. "Mais c'est voodoo, ça; je n'en sais rien!" "Well," said I, "don't you know anything about voodoo songs?" "Yes," she answered, "I know voodoo songs; but I can't tell you what they mean." And she broke out into the wildest, weirdest ditty I ever heard. I tried to write down the words; but as I did not know what they meant I had to write by sound alone, spelling the words according to the French pronunciation.[15]

So far as I know there are, among the plantation hymns, no such remains of ancient ritual, mystical words whose meanings are unknown, no traces whatever of African tradition. If there is anything that is African about the Negroes' Christianity it is not African tradition but the African temperament which has contributed it. I assume, therefore, that what we find in the most primitive form of Negro Christianity is not the revival of an older and more barbaric religion but the inception of a new and original form of Christianity.

An interesting fact in regard to the religious practices of the Negroes of the Sea Islands, which has not so far as I know been recorded in any of the descriptions of that people, is the existence among them of two distinct religious institutions, namely the church and the "praise house." The praise house is the earlier institution and represents apparently a more primitive and more characteristically Negro or African type. In slavery days, the church was the white man's place of worship. Negroes were permitted to attend the services and there was usually a gallery reserved for their use. Churches, however, were few and not all the slaves on the plantation could attend at any one time. Those who did attend were usually the house servants. On every large plantation, however, there was likely to be, and this was characteristic of the Sea Island plantations, a "praise house" where the slaves were permitted to worship in their own peculiar way. It was here that the "shout" took place. After the Civil War, churches were erected and regular congregations of the Negro

---

[15] Henry Edward Krehbiel, *op. cit.*, p. 37. From a letter of Lafcadio Hearne.

denominations were formed. The Negro churches, however, never wholly displaced the praise houses on Port Royal and some of the other islands. It is a singular fact that today, among the Negroes of Port Royal, at any rate, no one is converted in church. It is only in the praise houses that Negroes get religion. It is only through the praise house that one enters the church. The whole process involves, as I have been informed, not merely an "experience," the precise nature of which is not clear, but also an examination by the elders to determine whether the experience is genuine, before candidates are admitted in good standing as members of the congregation.

IV. THE NEGRO "SPIRITUALS"

On the whole the plantation Negro's religion was a faithful copy of the white man's. It was content rather than the form which suffered sea-change in the process of transmission from the white man to the black. What this content was, what new inflection and color the Negro slave imparted to the religious forms which he borrowed from his master, we may, perhaps, gather from a study of the plantation hymns. These folk-songs represent, at any rate, the naïve and spontaneous utterance of hopes and aspirations for which the Negro slave had no other adequate means of expression.

The first and most interesting account we have of these Negro spirituals is that of Col. Thomas Wentworth Higginson in his *Army Life in a Black Regiment*.[16] He collected them from the lips of his own black soldiers as they sung them about the campfire at night. He was almost the first to recognize that these rude plantation hymns represented a real literature, the only real literature the American Negro has produced, until very recent times.

Col. Higginson has compared the Negro spirituals to the Scotch ballads and to the folk-songs of other races. It is, however, not so much their similarities as their differences which are interesting and significant. Negro folk-songs are ruder and more primitive. The verses, often but not always rhymed, are composed almost entirely of single phrases, followed by a refrain, which is repeated again with slight modifications, ending, not infrequently, in an exclamation.

---

[16] Thomas Wentworth Higginson, *Army Life in a Black Regiment*. Boston: Fields, Osgood & Co., 1870.

An' I couldn't hear nobody pray,
      O Lord!
Couldn't hear nobody pray.
      O—way down yonder
      By myself,
I couldn't hear nobody pray.

In the valley,
      Couldn't hear nobody pray,
On my knees,
      Couldn't hear nobody pray,
With my burden,
      Couldn't hear nobody pray,
An' my Saviour,
      Couldn't hear nobody pray.

      O Lord!
I couldn't hear nobody pray,
      O Lord!
Couldn't hear nobody pray.
      O—way down yonder
      By myself,
I couldn't hear nobody pray.

Chilly waters,
      Couldn't hear nobody pray,
In the Jerdan,
      Couldn't hear nobody pray,
Crossing over,
      Couldn't hear nobody pray,
Into Canaan,
      Couldn't hear nobody pray.

In Negro folk-songs the music and expression are everything. The words, often striking and suggestive to be sure, represent broken fragments of ideas, thrown up from the depths of the Negroes' consciousness and swept along upon a torrent of wild, weird, and often beautiful melody.

One reason the verses of the Negro folk-songs are so broken and fragmentary is that the Negroes were not yet in secure possession of the English language. Another explanation is the conditions under which they were produced. The very structure of these verses indicates their origin in the communal excitement of a religious assembly. A happy phrase, a striking bit of imagery, flung out by some individual was taken up and repeated by the whole congregation. Naturally the most expressive phrases, the lines that most adequately voiced the deep, unconscious desires of the whole people, were remembered longest and repeated most frequently. There was, therefore, a process of natural selection by which the best, the most representative verses, those which most adequately expressed the profounder and more permanent moods and sentiments of the Negro, were preserved and became part of the permanent tradition of the race.

Negro melodies still spring up on the plantations of the South as they did in the days of slavery. The Negro is, like the Italian, an improviser, but the songs he produces today have not, so far as my knowledge goes, the quality of those he sang in slavery. The schools have introduced reading, and this, with the reflection which writing enforces, are destroying the folk-songs of the Negro, as they have those of other races.

Not only are the Negro folk-songs more primitive, in the sense I have indicated, than the folk-songs of other peoples with which we are familiar, but the themes are different. The themes of the Scotch ballads are love and battles, the adventures and tragedies of a wild, free life. The Negro songs, those that he has remembered best, are religious and otherworldly.

It is a singular fact that very few secular songs, those which are referred to as "reel tunes," "fiddle songs," "corn songs," and "devil songs," for which slaves generally expressed a deep abhorrence, though many of them no doubt were used to stimulate them while in the fields, have been preserved while "shout songs" and other "speritchils" have been kept alive by the hundred.[17]

If it is the plantation melodies that, by a process of natural selection, have been preserved in the traditions of the Negro people, it is probably because in these songs they found a free and natural expression of their unfulfilled desires. In the imagery of these songs, in the visions which they conjure up, in the themes which they again and again renew, we may discern the reflection of dawning racial consciousness, a common racial ideal.

The content of the Negro folk-songs has been made the subject of a careful investigation by Howard Odum in his *Study of the Social and Mental Traits of the Negro.*

The Negro's fancies of "Heaven's bright home" are scarcely exceeded by our fairy tales. There are silver and golden slippers, crowns of stars,

[17] Krehbiel, *Afro-American Folksongs*, p. 16.

jewels and belt of gold. There are robes of spotless white and wings all bejeweled with heavenly gems. Beyond the Jordan the Negro will outshine the sun, moon and stars. He will slip and slide the golden street and eat the fruit of the trees of paradise. . . . . With rest and ease, with a golden band about him and with palms of victory in his hands and beautiful robes, the Negro will indeed be a happy being. . . . . To find a happy home, to see all the loved ones and especially the Biblical characters, to see Jesus and the angels, to walk and talk with them, to wear robes and slippers as they do, and to *rest forever,* constitute the chief images of the Negro's heaven. He is tired of the world which has been a hell to him. Now on his knees, now shouting, now sorrowful and glad, the Negro comes from "hanging over hell" to die and "set by de Fadder's side!" [18]

In the imagery which the Negro chooses to clothe his hopes and dreams, we have, as in the musical idiom in which he expresses them, reflections of the imagination and the temperament of Africa and the African. On the other hand, in the themes of this rude rhapsodical poetry, the House of Bondage, Moses, the Promised Land, Heaven, the apocalyptic visions of Freedom, but freedom confined miraculously and to another world, are the reflections of the Negro's experience in slavery.

The Negro's songs of slavery have been referred to by Du Bois in his *Souls of Blackfolk* as "sorrow songs," and other writers have referred to the fact that all the songs of the slaves were in a plaintive minor key. As a matter of fact, investigation has shown that actually less than 12 per cent of Negro songs are in a minor.[19] There are no other folk-songs, with the exception of those of Finland, of which so large a percentage are in the major mood. And this is interesting as indicating the racial temperament of the Negro. It tends to justify the general impression that the Negro is naturally sunny, cheerful, optimistic. It is true that the slave songs express longing, that they refer to hard trials and great tribulations, but the dominant mood is one of jubilation. "Going to sing, going to shout, going to play all over God's heaven."

Otherworldliness is not peculiar to the region of the slave. It is a trait which the slave encountered in the religion of his master. But in the Negro's conception of religion it received a peculiar emphasis. In fact these ecstatic visions of the next world, which the Negro slave songs portrayed with a directness and simplicity that is at once quaint

---

[18] Howard W. Odum, Ph.D., "Social and Mental Traits of the Negro," *Studies in History, Economics, and Public Law.* Edited by The Faculty of Political Science of Columbia University, XXXVII (New York, 1910), 91.

[19] Krehbiel, *Afro-American Folksongs.*

and pathetic, are the most significant feature of the Negro's songs of slavery.

It is interesting to note in this connection that nowhere in these songs do we discover the slightest references to Africa. They reflect no memories of a far-off happier land. Before the Negro gained his emancipation Africa had, so far as he was concerned, almost ceased to exist. Furthermore, the whole tone and emphasis of these songs and of all other religious expressions of the American Negro are in marked contrast with the tone and emphasis of African religious ideas. The African knew of the existence of another world but he was not interested in it. The world, as the African understood it, was full of malignant spirits, diseases, and forces with which he was in constant mortal struggle. His religious practices were intended to gain for him immunity in this world rather than assurance of the next. But the Negro in America was in a different situation. He was not living in his own world. He was a slave, and that, aside from the physical inconvenience, implied a vast deal of inhibition. He was, moreover, a constant spectator of life in which he could not participate; excited to actions and enterprises that were forbidden to him because he was a slave. The restlessness which this situation provoked found expression, not in insurrection and rebellion—although of course there were Negro insurrections—but in his religion and in his dreams of another and freer world. I assume, therefore, that the reason the Negro so readily and eagerly took over from the white man his heaven and apocalyptic visions was because these materials met the demands of his peculiar racial temperament and furnished relief to the emotional strains that were provoked in him by the conditions of slavery.

So far as slavery was responsible for the peculiar individuality of the Negro's religion we should expect that the racial ideals and racial religion would take on another and different character under the influence of freedom. This, indeed, is what seems to me is taking place. New ideals of life are expressed in recent Negro literature and slowly and imperceptibly those ideas are becoming institutionalized in the Negro church and more particularly in the cultural ideals of the Negro school. But this makes another chapter in the history of Negro culture in America.

V. TEMPERAMENT, TRADITION, AND NATIONALITY

I have sought in this brief sketch to indicate the modifications, changes, and fortune which a distinctive racial temperament has undergone as a result of its encounters with an alien life and culture. This temperament, as I conceive it, consists in a few elementary but distinctive characteristics, determined by physical organizations and transmitted biologically. These characteristics manifest themselves in a genial, sunny, and social disposition, in an interest and attachment to external, physical things rather than to subjective states and objects of introspection; in a disposition for expression rather than enterprise and action.

The changes which have taken place in the manifestations of this temperament have been actuated by an inherent and natural impulse, characteristic of all living beings, to persist and maintain itself in a changed environment. Such changes have occurred as are likely to take place in any organism in its struggle to live and to use its environment to further and complete its own existence.

The result has been that this racial temperament has selected out of the mass of cultural materials, to which it had access, such technical, mechanical, and intellectual devices as met its needs at a particular period of its existence. It has clothed and enriched itself with such new customs, habits, and cultural forms as it was able, or permitted to use. It has put into these relatively external things, moreover, such concrete meanings as its changing experience and its unchanging racial individuality demanded. Everywhere and always it has been interested rather in expression than in action; interested in life itself rather than in its reconstruction or reformation. The Negro is, by natural disposition, neither an intellectual nor an idealist, like the Jew; nor a brooding introspective, like the East African; nor a pioneer and frontiersman, like the Anglo-Saxon. He is primarily an artist, loving life for its own sake. His *métier* is expression rather than action. He is, so to speak, the lady among the races.

In reviewing the fortunes of the Negro's temperament as it is manifested in the external events of the Negro's life in America, our analysis suggests that this racial character of the Negro has exhibited itself everywhere in something like the rôle of the *wish* in the Freudian analysis of dream life. The external cultural forms which he found here, like the memories of the individual, have furnished the materials in which the racial wish, i.e., the Negro temperament, has clothed itself. The inner meaning, the sentiment, the emphasis, the emotional color, which these forms assumed as the result of their transference from the white man to the Negro, these have been the Negro's own. They have represented his temperament—his temperament modified, however, by his experience and the tradition which he has accumulated in this country. The temperament is African, but the tradition is American.

I present this thesis merely as a hypothesis. As such its value consists in its suggestion of a point of view and program for investigation. I may, however, suggest some of the obvious practical consequences. If racial temperament, particularly when it gets itself embodied in institutions and in nationalities, i.e., social groups based upon race, is so real and obdurate a thing that education can only enrich and develop it but not dispose of it, then we must be concerned to take account of it in all our schemes for promoting naturalization, assimilation, Americanization, Christianization, and acculturation generally.

If it is true that the Jew, as has been suggested, just because of his intellectuality is a natural-born idealist, internationalist, doctrinaire, and revolutionist, while the Negro, because of his natural attachment to known familiar objects, places, and persons, is pre-adapted to conservatism and to local and personal loyalties—if these things are true, we shall eventually have to take account of them practically. It is certain that the Negro has uniformly shown a disposition to loyalty during slavery to his master and during freedom to the South and the country as a whole. He has maintained this attitude of loyalty, too, under very discouraging circumstances. I once heard Keely Miller, the most philosophical of the leaders and teachers of his race, say in a public speech that one of the greatest hardships the Negro suffered in this country was due to the fact that he was not permitted to be patriotic.

Of course all these alleged racial characteristics have a positive as well as a negative significance. Every race, like every individual, has the vices of its virtues. The question remains still to what extent so-called racial characteristics are actually racial, i.e., biological, and to what extent they are the effect of environmental conditions. The thesis of this paper, to state it again, is (1) that fundamental temperamental qualities, which are the basis of interest and attention, act as selective agencies and as such determine what elements in the cultural environment each race will select; in what region it will seek and find its vocation in the larger social organization; (2) that, on the other hand, technique, science, machinery, tools, habits, discipline, and all the intellectual and mechanical devices with which the civilized man lives and works remain relatively external to the inner core of significant attitudes and values which constitute what we may call the will of the group. This racial will is, to be sure, largely social, that is, modified by social experience, but it rests ultimately upon a complex of inherited characteristics, which are racial.

It follows from what has been said that the individual man is the bearer of a double inheritance. As a member of a race, he transmits by interbreeding a biological inheritance. As a member of society or a social group, on the other hand, he transmits by communication a social inheritance. The particular complex of inheritable characters which characterizes the individuals of a racial group constitutes the racial temperament. The particular group of habits, accommodations, sentiments, attitudes, and ideals transmitted by communication and education constitute a social tradition. Between this temperament and this tradition there is, as has been generally recognized, a very intimate relationship. My assumption is that temperament is the basis of the interests; that as such it determines in the long run the general run of attention, and this, eventually, determines the selection in the case of an individual of his vocation, in the case of the racial group of its culture. That is to say, temperament determines what things the individual and the group will be interested in; what elements of the general culture, to which they have access, they will assimilate; what, to state it pedagogically, they will learn.

It will be evident at once that where individuals of the same race and hence the same temperament are associated, the temperamental interests will tend to reinforce one another, and the attention of members of the group will be more completely focused upon the specific objects and values that correspond to the racial temperament. In this way racial qualities become the basis for nationalities, a nationalistic group being merely a cultural and, eventually, a political society founded on the basis of racial inheritances.

On the other hand, when racial segregation is broken up and members of a racial group are dispersed, the opposite effect will take place. This explains the phenomena which have frequently been the subject of comment and observation, that the racial characteristics manifest themselves in an extraordinary way in large homogeneous gatherings. The contrast between a mass meeting of one race and a similar meeting of another is particularly striking. Under such circumstances characteristic racial and temperamental differences appear that would otherwise pass entirely unnoticed.

When the physical unity of a group is perpetuated by the succession of parents and children, the racial temperament, including fundamental attitudes and values which rest in it, is preserved intact. When, however, society grows and is perpetuated by immigration and adaptation, there ensues, as a result of miscegenation, a breaking up or the complex of the biologically inherited qualities which constitute the temperament of the race. This again initiates changes in the mores, traditions, and eventually in the institutions of the community. The changes which proceed from modification in the racial temperament will, however, modify but slightly the external forms of the social traditions, but they will be likely to change profoundly their content and meaning. Of course other factors, individual competition, the formation of classes, and especially the increase of communication, all co-operate to complicate the whole situation and to modify the effects which would be produced by racial factors working in isolation. All these factors must be eventually taken account of, in any satisfactory scheme of dealing with the problem of Americanization by education. This is, however, a matter for more complete analysis and further investigation.

I may, then, on the basis of the present discussion, venture one practical suggestion. It seems to me that the real problem of the foreigner, so far as education is concerned, is to devise means to transmit to him the content as well as the external form of American life. This would suggest that we should encourage the study of American history. This will help, no doubt. But America, in view of all the races and peoples which we have incorporated into our body politic, lies in the future rather than in the past. As the ends of the earth have come together in America, we have become, against our wills, a world's melting-pot. For us the international situation has now become a domestic problem. It would, therefore, seem quite as important that we should, through schools and in the course of the educational process, make ourselves acquainted with the heritages and backgrounds of the foreign peoples, as it is important that immigrants should become acquainted with our national history. So far as Americanization is undertaken by the schools, effort should be directed, it would seem, toward maintaining and creating a mutual understanding among our peoples rather than toward perpetrating, as we have been disposed to do in the past, a sentimental and ceremonial patriotism based on a reverent and uncritical contemplation of our national heritages which, as compared with those of other peoples, the Jews, for example, are not likely to impress the unbiased outsider as having great value.

CHAPTER 22

NEGRO RACE CONSCIOUS-NESS AS REFLECTED IN RACE LITERATURE

I

ROBERT T. KERLIN, head of the English Department of the Virginia Military University, in a recent paper on Contemporary Poetry of the Negro, makes the following interesting observation: "A people that is producing poetry is not perishing, but is astir with life, with vital impulses, with life-giving visions. A people's poetry, therefore, affords the most serious subject of study to those who would understand the people—that people's soul, that people's status, that people's potentialities."

Mr. Kerlin is a literary man. He has been studying the recent literature of the Negro and, as it seems to me, to some purpose. He writes of it, not exactly with enthusiasm, but with profound appreciation. Something in the quality of this literature, the themes that inspire it, the wistful and pathetic yearning which it reflects, the occasional ominous flashes of prophecy—"the sternness of rebuke and the yearning for things that should be"—these I suspect are the qualities in this poetry that would and should attract and interest the student of literature.

My interest in this poetry is not that of a student of literature, but of a student of human nature. I cannot and shall not attempt to speak in the language of literary criticism. But I am disposed to accept quite literally, not as a figure of speech, but as a matter of

_____
American Review I (September, October, 1923), pp. 505-516.

fact, Mr. Kerlin's statement that a "people that is producing poetry is not perishing, but astir with life, with vital impulses and life-giving visions." It certainly is true, also, more true if possible of the Negro than of any other people, that the Negro poetry is a transcript of Negro life.

The Negro has always produced poetry of some sort. It has not always been good poetry, but it has always been a faithful reflection of his inner life. Expression is, perhaps, his *métier*, his vocation.

First, most characteristic, and best remembered are the songs of slavery, particularly the "spirituals." Sorrow songs, Mr. Du Bois called them, "weird old songs in which the soul of the black slave spoke to men."

The Negro folk songs are the Negroes' literature of slavery. They reflect life as he saw it and felt it at that time. Sixty years ago travelers on the lower Mississippi were invariably attracted by the rude chanteys of the Negro deckhands on the tow boat. Some fragments of these, as well as the work songs, say, of the mowers, of the rowers, and the cornhuskers have been preserved. The love songs of the Louisiana Creoles, with their plaintive melodies and their quaint, exotic sentiments are part of this same tradition. There are besides rhymes and jingles, sung when the slaves danced at evening around the cabin fire and the songs of longing, sad, dreaming airs, describing the more sorrowful pictures of slave life, and sung in the dusk when the slaves were returning home from their day's work. It is perhaps the ghosts of these songs that haunt us in familiar ballads like "Swanee River" and "Massa's in the Cold, Cold Groun'." This is one of which a fragment has been preserved.

> Mother, is Massa goin' to sell, sell us tomorow?
> Yes, my child! Yes, my child! Yes, my child!
> Going to sell us down in Georgia?
>   Yes, yes, yes!
> Going to sell us way down in Georgia?
>   Yes, yes, yes!
>   Oh! Watch and pray!

> Fare you well Mother,
> I must leave you,
> Fare you well,
> Fare you well Mother,
> I must leave you,
> Fare you well.
> Oh! Watch and pray!

These songs are no longer sung. They have been supplanted by others, more personal and less naïve. Only the religious songs of the Negro, the spirituals, have outlived the occasions that called them forth.

Colonel Thomas Wentworth Higginson, who was the first, so far as I know, to make a serious study of the Negro spirituals, compared them to the Scottish ballads. The comparison is interesting, less for the similarities than the differences that it brings out. The tragic little episodes commemorated in the Scottish ballads have very little in common, at least so far as their themes are concerned, with the rude hymns of the Negro slaves.

Negro folk songs also are more primitive and less articulate. The best of them, those that touch us most deeply, are not composed; they are merely uttered. The verses are often mere disconnected phrases, interrupted with a shout and a groan, but rendered dramatic and expressive by the melody and the chorus which accompanied them.

An' I couldn't hear nobody pray,
     O Lord!
Couldn't hear nobody pray.
     O—way down yonder
     By myself,
I couldn't hear nobody pray.

In the valley,
     Couldn't hear nobody pray,
On my knees,
     Couldn't hear nobody pray,
With my burden,
     Couldn't hear nobody pray
 An' my Savior
     Couldn't hear nobody pray.

     O Lord!
I couldn't hear nobody pray,
     O Lord!
Coudn't hear nobody pray
     O—way down yonder
     By myself,
I couldn't hear nobody pray.

Chilly waters,
     Couldn't hear nobody pray
In the Jordan,
     Couldn't hear nobody pray,

Crossing over,
    Couldn't hear nobody pray
Into Canaan,
    Couldn't hear nobody pray.

The Negro had been taught, and he had it from the Bible, too, that the curse of Canaan had made him black and condemned him forever to be a hewer of wood, a drawer of water, and servant to his brother, the white man. One can imagine that there were some dark moments, when the sense of his helplessness, under the burden of this ancient ancestral curse, must have quite overwhelmed the black man. But what words could more eloquently express the feeling of a slave at such a moment than these simple lines from an old slave song:

O Lord! O my Lord!
O my good Lord!
Keep me from sinking down!

Whatever may have been the origin of his other songs we know that the spirituals arose spontaneously out of the communal excitements of a religious meeting—a revival or a "shout." The best of these were remembered, repeated and handed down by oral tradition. The songs that were most often repeated were those that most completely and adequately voiced the deep unconscious wishes of those who sang them. Thus by a process of natural selection the songs that circulated widest and lived longest were those which reflected the profounder and more permanent moods and sentiments of the race. It was through the medium of these religious songs which were sung all over the South, wherever slave plantations existed, that the Negro achieved in slavery, if not, as one writer has finely put it, race consciousness, at least a consciousness of his race.

These rude hymns of the slave, crude and elemental as they were, nevertheless, like every other literature in which men's hopes and fears and faiths have found expression, embodied a scheme of life.

The sinner on the mourner's bench, "down in the valley," despairing of this world, with its troubles, its disappointments, and its insecurity, found consolation in the bright vision of another world, almost visible over there beyond Jordan; a world where all troubles vanished, where every day was Sunday, and where the souls redeemed walked in majesty with long white robes and golden slippers, talked familiarly with the angels, with Peter and Paul—and there was no more **work.**

Recent psychology has been much concerned with the interpretation of dreams. Dreams are a sort of compensation for the inadequacies and the imperfections of a real world. When the world denies us the fulfillment of our wishes we seek refuge in dreams. But poetry, like dreams, is a product of the phantasy. The Negro's poetry is a racial dream. The slave's ecstatic visions of "bright mansions above" are manifestly a compensation for a real existence in which so many of his human wishes were unfulfilled.

This other-worldliness, with its practical implications, patience, humility, resignation in this life, mitigated by the expectations of a glorious riot in the next—this is the Negroes' philosophy of life as expressed in the songs of slavery.

With the dawn of freedom we observe the onset of a profound change in the Negro ethos. The old scheme of life did not lose its hold at once upon the masess of the Negro people. The older generation have remained for the most part "respectable and humble," as Southern people phrase it. The Negroes on the plantations still sang the old hymns, but they sang them with less conviction. The younger generation, particularly the ambitious, newly educated of the race, refused to sing them at all. They wanted to put behind them everything that reminded them of slavery and of the past.

The Negro still sings; and still, when the occasion arises, new melodies blossom on the southern plantations, but the folk songs that the Negro produces today do not have the quality of those he sang in slavery.

Howard Odum, who has studied Negro folk songs extensively and at first hand, says that the religious songs of today are different in several specific ways from the songs of slavery days. The songs of recent origin have more rhymed words and less meaning. There is more emphasis on the form; meanings are often sacrificed to make rhyme, or make the song fit into a tune, to emphasize a well sounding word. There is, in short, less conviction and more conscious striving for effects.[1]

The recent folk songs are not only less spontaneous, but they show in other ways the blighting effects of deliberate artifice. They are very likely to be cluttered up with moral casuistry and theological reflection. The refrain of one of these songs, as I recall it, is something like this:

---

[1] "Religious Folk-Songs of the Southern Negroes," *The American Journal of Religious Psychology and Education*, July, 1909, p. 274.

Ain't it a shame to gamble on Sunday?
There's Monday, Tuesday, Wednesday,
Thursday, Friday, Saturday.
Ain't it a shame to gamble on Sunday?

Still another song turns about the interesting question: "What is the Soul?"

Oh, pray will someone tell me,
What is the Soul of man?

Folk songs are the literature of an illiterate people. The first effect of the introduction of reading and writing among an illiterate folk is to destroy the sources of their songs. Writing enforces reflection. Reflection makes the writer self-conscious and destroys that natural spontaneity which is the essence of folk poetry.

Negroes did not cease to produce poetry after they learned to read and write. But for a long time this poetry was turgid stuff. Much of the poetry of the newly educated Negro, written before he had full possession of the new poetic idiom, was pedantic and dull. Some of it was atrocious. Here is a gem from a volume called *Priceless Jewels*.[2]

"THERE'S HOPE IN BREAST OF HAM."

Regardless of all the Prejudice,
　Regardless jim-crow cars!
Though law and justice fail to stand
　Behind the pleading bars.
Though all the World may wrongfully
　Hold back him in command;
Amid trials and temptations
　There's hope in breast of Ham.

The're heavy clouds of grief sometimes,
　Rise o'er this distant way.
His shaking head with discourage
　At time waits justice sway.
But facing hopes of victory
　With Jesus, the World's Lamb,
In hardest strife with all his foe;
　There's hope in breast of Ham.

Old Ethiopia did Pay well,
　The price of Slavery's chain.
She bore the toil in mournful songs,
　And then endured the Pain.

---

[2] *Priceless Jewels* was printed in 1911, but it is fairly representative of much that was written and printed earlier and much more that was never printed at all.

How God was pleased! Then said to her,
"Ye shall stretch forth your hand!"
Though Powers may rise against her
There's hope in breast of Ham.

This represents, so to speak, the dark ages of Negro poetry; the period of transition from the natural simplicity of the folk songs to the conscious art of written verse. Poetry of the type of *Priceless Jewels* is representative of the period of conscious imitation, when the Negro, not yet race conscious, in the sense in which that expression is used by recent writers, was nevertheless acutely, often morbidly, conscious of himself. This is indicated by the naïve and pathetic striving for recognition and for distinction. The Negro was trying at this period to prove to himself and the world that he was a man like other men; that he could think the white man's thoughts and practice the white man's arts.

It was not until the appearance, in the early nineties, of Paul Laurence Dunbar that the Negro in America produced a poet who was able to command the respectful attention of the world. W. D. Howells said that it seemed to him that the American Negro "had come to its most modern consciousness" in Dunbar "whose unique achievement was to have studied the American Negro objectively and to have represented him as he found him to be, with humor, with sympathy and yet with what the reader must instinctively feel to be entire truthfulness." [3]

To say that Dunbar described the Negro objectively, without apology and without prejudice, is to define precisely the nature of his achievement. But Dunbar's description of the Negro, if objective, is at the same time superficial. The period, from 1892 when Dunbar began to publish until 1906 when he died, was for the Negro one of storm and stress, of conflict and contention. The Negro ethos was confused, distracted, and divided within itself. The old order, with its other worldliness, and its Christian counsels of patience, humility, and resignation, was passing away. The new order, as Negro radicals conceived it, at any rate, was distinctly of this world. The men who represented what Mr. Kerlin calls "the renaissance of the Negro soul," were militant, insistent, repudiating compromise, rejecting any paradise of hopes deferred. They dreamed of a world in which the

---

[3] Quoted in the Introduction to the *Life and Works of Paul Lawrence Dunbar*, p. 1.

Negro should have freedom, equality, and justice, not in some dim distant future, but presently, here and now.

Of all this turmoil there are almost no intimations in Dunbar's poetry. In two poems only—the "Ode to Ethiopia" and "We Wear the Mask"—does Dunbar refer to things with which the Negro people of his day were most deeply concerned.

> We wear the mask that grins and lies,
> It hides our cheeks and shades our eyes—
> This debt we pay to human guile;
> With torn and bleeding hearts we smile
> And mouth with myriad subtilties.[4]

Emancipation had made the Negro free, but it had not made him, in the full sense of the word, a citizen. His status was still undefined, different in the northern and in the southern states, but different, in some respects, in every different community. Every day the Negro was compelled to face anew the problem how to be at once a Negro and a citizen. This has been and is still the enigma of the Negro's existence.

To America.

> How would you have us—as we are,
>   Or sinking 'neath the load we bear?
> Our eyes fixed forward on a star?
>   Or gazing empty at despair?
> Rising or falling? Men or things?
>   With dragging pace, or footsteps fleet?
> Strong, willing sinews in your wings?
>   Or tightening chains about your feet? [5]

The history of the American Negro, according to Mr. Du Bois, is the history of this struggle "to make it possible for a man to be both a Negro and an American."

This sense of endless striving to reconcile irreconcilable ideals has found a classic expression in Du Bois' *Souls of Black Folk:*

It is a peculiar sensation, this double-consciousness, this sense of always looking at one's self through the eyes of others, of measuring one's soul by the tape of a world that looks on in amused contempt and pity. One feels his two-ness—an American, a Negro; two souls, two thoughts, two unreconciled strivings; two warring ideals in one dark body, whose dogged strength alone keeps it from being torn asunder.

---

[4] *Life and Works,* p. 184.
[5] James W. Johnson.

It is this double consciousness of the Negro, always looking at himself through the eyes of others, that has made it difficult for Negro poetry to achieve a sincere expression of Negro life. Dunbar's reference to the "mask" with which the Negro covers his deeper feelings; Du Bois' description of the "veil" through which the Negro, as by a sort of second sight, reads all the secrets of the white man's life, even as it hides his own soul from the understanding of the white man, are merely different accounts of an experience that comes sometime in life to every Negro.

"The Negro," says Du Bois, "is a sort of seventh son, born with a veil, and gifted with second sight in this American world—a world which yields him no true self-consciousness, but only lets him see through the revelation of the other world." [6]

MY PEOPLE.

> My people laugh and sing
> And dance to death—
> None imagining
> The heartbreak under breath.[7]

This introspective mood, this recognition of the conflict in his own soul is itself the manifestation of a new race-consciousness. It is an indication that the Negro had already begun to reflect upon his own experience and consciously to redefine the aims of his racial life. Two poems written about the time of the fiftieth anniversary of emancipation indicate this changed attitude of the Negro towards himself and his past, James Weldon Johnson's *Black and Unknown Bards* and Kelly Miller's *I See and Am Satisfied.*

O BLACK AND UNKOWN BARDS.

> * * * *
>
> O black slave singers, gone, forgot,—unfamed,
> You—you alone, of all the long, long line
> Of those who've sung untaught, unknown, unnamed,
> Have stretched out upward, seeking the divine.
>
> * * * *
>
> You sang far better than you knew, the songs
> That for your listeners' hungry hearts sufficed
> Still live—but more than this to you belongs:
> You sang a race from wood and stone to Christ.[8]

---

[6] W. E. Burghardt Du Bois, *The Souls of Black Folk,* p. 3. 9th Ed., 1911.
[7] Charles Bertram Johnson.
[8] James W. Johnson, *Century Magazine,* November, 1908.

What impresses me about these two poems is the serenity with which they accept the past and the confidence they seem to feel in the future. It is as if the Negro, at the end of his first fifty years of freedom, had paused to look back upon his past and forward upon his future. These two poems, perhaps, better than others mark the change that has been taking place in the attitudes of the Negro towards the world and himself. From this time forward, judging not merely by their literature, but by the attitudes of individual men, Negroes have been less interested in demonstrating their right as individuals to participate in the common cultural life about them; they have been more concerned, on the other hand, in defining their own conception of their mission and destiny as a race.

Most Negroes, at one time, probably looked forward to a day when all racial marks that now divide the races would disappear or at least be forgotten. Amalgamation, many Negroes as well as whites thought, must eventually solve the Negro problem. A very recent poem dwells on the pathos of that isolation which racial barriers impose.

THE BARRIER.

I must not gaze at them although
  Your eyes are dawning day;
I must not watch you as you go
  Your sun-illumined way;

I hear but I must never heed
  The fascinating note,
Which, fluting like a river reed,
  Comes trembling from your throat;

I must not see upon your face
  Love's softly glowing spark;
For there's the barrier of race,
  You're fair and I am dark.[9]

In America, where the census definition of a Negro is a person who passes for a Negro in the community where he lives, it has been, as might be expected, the mulattos and the mixed bloods, themselves the products of the mingling of the races, who have looked forward most hopefully to the ultimate fusion of the races.[10] No doubt Ne-

---

[9] Claude McKay.

[10] It is an interesting fact that in other countries than our own the mixed blood, the coloured men, is a separate caste. It is true, however, that caste lines are more stiffly drawn in English than in the French and Spanish colonies.

groes are still influenced by this, as by every other motive or trend that has dominated the race at any period of its history. The disposition of the Negro in America today, however, no matter how slightly tinged with African blood, is to accept the racial designation that America has thrust upon him and identify himself with the people whose traditions, status, and ambitions he shares.

THE MULATTO TO HIS CRITICS.

Ashamed of my race?
And of what race am I?
I am many in one.
Through my veins there flows the blood
Of Red Man, Black Man, Briton, Celt and Scot,
In warring clash and tumultuous riot.
I welcome all,
But love the blood of the kindly race
That swarthes my skin, crinkles my hair,
And puts sweet music into my soul.

It is the necessity for collective action, the necessity that Negroes should cooperate to win for themselves the place and the respect in the white man's world that the Constitution could not give them, that has created among the Negroes of the United States a solidarity that does not exist elsewhere. Race consciousness is the natural and inevitable reaction to race prejudice.

The new literacy movement, what Mr. Kerlin calls "the renaissance of the Negro soul," is in some sense also a response of the Negro to prejudice and opposition. It is more than that, however. It is the natural expression of the Negro temperament under all the conditions of modern life. The Negro has learned to write; and as he feels life keenly, he expresses it emotionally.

The Negro has not ceased to sing nor to value the old slave hymns, but the latter have no message for the present day. The songs of slavery were songs of surrender and resignation.

"This world almost done;"
"One more river:"
"I want to go home:"
"Give me Jesus and take all this world."

These were themes of the spirituals.

The new poetry, the poetry of the Negro renaissance, is distinctly of this world. It is characteristically the poetry of rebellion and self-assertion.

If We Must Die.

If we must die, let it not be like hogs
Hunted and penned in an inglorious spot,
While round us bark the mad and hungry dogs,
Making their mock at our accursed lot.
If we must die, oh, let us nobly die
So that our precious blood may not be shed
In vain: then even the monsters we defy
Shall be constrained to honor us, though dead!

Oh, kinsmen! We must meet the common foe;
Though far outnumbered, let us still be brave,
And for their thousand blows deal one deathblow!
What though before us lies the open grave?
Like men we'll face the murderous, cowardly pack,
Pressed to the wall, dying, but—fighting back! [11]

The new poetry is not irreligious. No poetry that seeks to express, define and justify the deepest emotions of men can be called irreligious. It is, however, radical.[12]

Credo.

I am an Iconoclast.
I break the limbs of idols
And smash the traditions of men.
I am an Anarchist,
I believe in war and destruction—
Not in the killing of men,
But the killing of creed and custom.
I am an Agnostic.
I accept nothing without questioning.
It is my inherent right and duty
To ask the reason why.
To accept without a reason
Is to debase one's humanity
And destroy the fundamental process
In the ascertainment of Truth.
I believe in Justice and freedom.
To me Liberty is priestly and kingly;
Freedom is my Bride,
Liberty my Angel of Light,
Justice my God.

---

[11] Claude McKay.

[12] There is a very good collection of it in the Report of the Department of Justice, 66 Congress, First Session, Document 153, Investigations Activities of the Department of Justice, Washington, 1919.

　　　　　　I oppose all laws of state or country,
　　　All creeds of church and social orders,
　　　All conventionalities of society and system
　　　Which cross the path of the light of Freedom
　　　Or obstruct the reign of Right.[13]

There is a vein of cynicism in some of this more radical poetry that seems quite foreign to the traditional attitudes of Negroes. In the following poem the victim of a "Christian mob," as the author calls it, is represented as reciting the horrors of his own lynching:

　　　　* * * And it was on a Sabbath day
　　　While men and women went to pray,
　　　I passed the crowd in humble mode
　　　In going to my meek abode;
　　　From out the crowd arose a cry,
　　　And epithets began to fly;
　　　And thus like hounds they took my track—
　　　My only crime—my face was black.
　　　And so this Christian mob did turn
　　　From prayer to rob, to rack and burn.
　　　A victim helpless I fell
　　　To tortures truly kin to hell;
　　　They bound me fast and strung me high,
　　　Then cut me down lest I should die
　　　Before their savage zeal was spent
　　　In torturing to their hearts' content.
　　　They tore my flesh and broke my bones,
　　　And laughed in triumph at my groans;
　　　They chopped my fingers, clipped my ears,
　　　And passed them round for souvenirs.
　　　And then round my quivering frame;
　　　They piled the wood, the oil and flame;
　　　And thus their Sabbath sacrifice
　　　Was wafted upward to the skies.
　　　A little boy stepped out the crowd,
　　　His face was pale, his voice was loud;
　　　"My ma could not get to the fun,
　　　And so I came, her youngest son,
　　　To get the news of what went on."
　　　He stirred the ashes, found a bone—
　　　(A bit of flesh was hanging on)
　　　He bore it off, a cherished prize,
　　　A remnant of the sacrifice. * * *

　　　O, heathen minds on heathen strand,
　　　What think you of Christian land,

---

[13] Walter Everette Hawkins.

Where men and boys and women turn
From prayer to lynch, to rob, and burn,
And oft their drowsy minds refresh
Through sport in burning human flesh?
Yet none dare tell who led the band;
And this was in a Christian land.[14]

This probably is not good poetry, but it gives a vivid picture. It probably represents very accurately the images in which the Negro thinks, sometimes, of the race problem.

What now, finally, have been the sources and what is the practical outcome of this new movement and this new orientation of Negro life?

1. The Negro is now, to an extent that was never before true, awake. The Negro race, for good or for ill, is coming out of its isolation, and entering a world where it is exposed to all the contagious influences of modern life. The unrest which is fermenting in every part of the world, has gotten finally under the skin of the Negro. The Negro is not only becoming radical, but he is becoming Bolshevist, at least in spots.
2. The Negro, particularly during and since the war, is learning to live in cities. The traditions and habits acquired in slavery, which have been embalmed and preserved to a very considerable extent, under the conditions of southern rural life, vanish as soon as the Negro enters into the vivid, restless, individualistic life of cities.
3. The Negro in the cities is learning to read. The art of reading and the use of books which was regarded as a luxury in the rural community becomes a necessity to the city. The Negro publishes at present more than two hundred papers in the United States, some of them with large circulations and wide influence.
4. The Negroes in Africa are learning to read and are beginning to publish, sometimes in European languages, sometimes in native dialects, their native newspapers. The more enterprising Negro editors in America read their African exchanges and comment from time to time upon events of common interest.

The whole world is becoming literate and under the influence of these newly acquired habits, a new intimacy is growing up between colored races in the most distant portions of the world.

It is an interesting comment on the present state of the world that native life in Central Africa has begun to respond to the price of raw rubber on the London market. It was strange, likewise, to read in the newspapers of a few months ago of the election of Marcus Garvey, leader of a great, popular back-to-Africa and Africa-for-the-

---

[14] This poem is quoted in the report of the Department of Justice, November 17, 1919, as a specimen of Negro radical literature. The author's name is not given.

Africans movement, to the presidency of an African Republic not yet born.

A recent copy of the *Crisis*, the organ of the National Association for the Advancement of Colored People, of which Mr. Du Bois is editor, publishes the manifesto of the second Pan African Congress held last August in London and Brussels and Paris.

The American Negro no longer conceives his destiny as bounded by the limits of the United States. He is seeking alliances and creating loyalties that transcend the boundaries of our American commonwealth. The Negro in his racial relationship at least, is internationalist. He is becoming a citizen of the world.

So much for the general social conditions, under which the new Negro poetry, and the new vision which inspires it, have come into existence. These, however, are the same conditions under which new literary movements have sprung up, within a period of a hundred years, among all the disinherited races of Europe.

The great nations have arisen in Europe by the imposition of their institutions and their languages upon lesser peoples, whom they conquered but never fully assimilated. The dominant peoples established their cultures in the cities, but in the rural regions the native languages and the primitive cultures persisted.

The struggles of these racial and cultural minorities to maintain their historical traditions and lift their folk speech to the dignity of literary language has, one might almost say, made the history of Europe during the last seventy-five years.

Every nationalist movement in Europe from that of the Catalonians in Spain to that of the Norse in Norway has been at the same time a linguistic and a literary movement.

Irrespective of time, place and historical circumstances, all the general features of these movements have been the same. Nationalist movements, whether they occur in Ireland or Slovakia, whether they are called Zionism among the Jews, Irredentism among the Italians, or socialism among the Finns, all have the same natural history.

1. They are the struggles of a predominantly rural population to maintain their cultural existences in competition with populations and cultures predominantly urban. They are, in a sense, the struggles of the rural populations to get to the city and appropriate the cultures of the cities for their own uses.
2. They have invariably been the struggles of the disinherited, neglected, if not oppressed, peoples to emancipate themselves culturally and eco-

nomically, and so gain for themselves a status in the world which had been denied them by the dominant races.

3. They have invariably resulted in a general expansion of the people, geographical as well as cultural, accompanied by a marked elevation and intensification of the lives of the individuals and of the peoples as a whole. It is a perfectly accurate statement to say that these movements have invariably had the general character of a renaissance, a nationalist, or racial rebirth.

A people that is producing poetry, as has already been said, is not a people that is perishing. On the contrary, it is a people that is astir with vital impulses, a people inspired by life-giving visions.

All nationalist struggles in Europe and elsewhere, seem to have had a history not unlike that which has been described as the Negro renaissance. This fact makes the Negro movement, as I have been describing it, somewhat less unique, but, at any rate, a little more intelligible.

If now we ask what have been the fundamental human motives or trends—as the new psychology would say—in all these different racial and nationalist movements, I can answer best perhaps, by quoting from George Santayana's *Winds of Doctrine*.

"Man," he says, "is certainly an animal that, when he lives at all, lives for ideals. Something must be found to occupy his imagination, to raise pleasure and pain into love and hatred and change the prosaic alternative between comfort and discomfort into the tragic one between happiness and sorrow."

Santayana goes on to add that, nowadays, when religion is "for the most part so vague and accommodating," nationality, "the one eloquent, public, intrepid illusion" which modern life has left us, has taken the place of religion in the lives of modern men. Not only Nationalism, but Socialism, Bolshevism, Christian Science, and many another "ism" which we have taken as a "mystical essence" or "an ultimate good," has taken the place of religion in the minds of modern peoples.

Wherever the old ideals of life, for any reason, have ceased to interest us, have lost for us their sense of reality, or for any reason no longer seem an adequate description of anything real, anything in which we can wholeheartedly believe, we have sought, if not a new religion, at any rate, some new definition of life's ultimate values, something men must have that will "change the prosaic alternative between comfort and discomfort into the tragic one between happiness and sorrow."

What has happened to other peoples in this modern world, has happened, is happening, to the Negro. Freedom has not given him the opportunity for participation in the common life of America and of the world that he hoped for. Negroes are restless and seeking. We are all restless, as a matter of fact.

In some respects, however, it seems to me the Negro, like all the other disinherited peoples, is more fortunate than the dominant races. He is restless, but he knows what he wants. The issues in his case, at least, are clearly defined. More than that, in this racial struggle, he is daily gaining not merely new faith in himself, but new faith in the world. Since he wants nothing except what he is willing to give to every other man on the same terms he feels that the great forces that shape the destinies of peoples are on his side. It is always a source of great power to any people when they feel that their interests, so far from being antagonistic, are actually identified with the interests of the antagonists. We of the dominant, comfortable classes, on the other hand, are steadily driven to something like an obstinate and irrational resistance to the Negro's claims, or we are put in the position of sympathetic spectators, sharing vicariously in his struggles but never really able to make his cause wholeheartedly our own.

Much of the poetry that Negroes write today is like much of our own—interesting but unconvincing. It has form but not conviction. Negro writers, however, have the inspiration of a great theme, and occasionally, when their songs arise spontaneously out of a deep racial experience, they speak with an authority of deep conviction, and with a tone of prophecy.

CHAPTER 23

RACE IDEOLOGIES

PUBLIC OPINION AND REVOLUTION

SOME months ago—August 16, 1942, to be exact—the *New York Times,* commenting on the anniversary of the Atlantic Charter, pointed out that the tragic events of the preceding twelve months had served as a commentary on and an interpretation of that historic document, making its words and phrases seem, as the writer put it, more significant and more acceptable in 1942 than they had been in 1941.

The experience to which the *Times* editorial refers is one which most of us have doubtless shared. Great changes have taken place and more are impending. In the course of an incredibly brief space things that were once familiar have begun to look strange and eventualities that seemed remote are now visibly close at hand. We are all of us, it seems, in somewhat the situation of the expectant traveler, who, as he approaches his destination in some new and strange country, sees the dim and visionary outlines of a distant landscape slowly rise above the horizon and assume, in the measure that he approaches it, the form and substance of an actual world. At the same time, as a result of the rapidity with which events have moved, the world in which we have lived is, as it appears, visibly receding. Nevertheless, we are still far from our destination, and the shape of things to come is still obscure.

In William F. Ogburn (ed.), *American Society In Wartime* (Chicago: University of Chicago Press, 1943), pp. 165-183.

Far-reaching changes are taking place in every aspect of social life, economic, political, and cultural, owing directly to advances in science and technology but indirectly to the urgent demands of a world war. The war has given unprecedented impetus—to cite a single instance—to invention and discovery in the field of chemistry, and this has brought about in turn something like a renaissance in all related sciences. So rapid have been the advances that, as one writer puts it, "already our world of 1940 is so distant in the past that it has become an antiquity, as seen through scientific eyes." [1]

Some of the revolutionary changes taking place, however, are in men's minds. Here are some of them as described in the *Times* editorial to which I have referred:

> The concept of nationality is being limited by universal necessity.
> We no longer believe that small nations can be sovereign or that the sovereignty of large nations can include the right to expand by force.
> We realize that freedom of commerce is not a negative thing, the result of noninterference, but a positive result of international effort.
> We begin to understand that peace is not possible without some supernational agency capable of making economic, political, and military decisions.
> This world war is also a world revolution. . . . . The word "revolution" need not alarm the timid. . . . . It can be a revolution not of destruction but of reconstruction.

I have quoted the *Times* on war and revolution, not because I am, at the moment, interested in specific statements of editorial opinion or creed but because these particular comments on the current scene seem to indicate the direction and the progress of the nation's adjustment to the national emergency and to be an index of changes in the public mind more fundamental than those registered from day to day by the Gallup poll in its effort to keep the public informed in regard to public opinion and national morale.

Changes in public opinion are, in the strict sense of that term, never revolutionary, because, for one thing, public opinion is concerned with what is in process and therefore problematic and debatable. Public opinion is the public mind in unstable equilibrium. The changes to which the *Times* refers, on the other hand, as far as they are indices of anything that could properly be described as revolutionary, are changes not so much in opinion as in orientation and point

---

[1] Dr. Charles M. A. Stine, in an address before the general session of the American Chemical Society, Buffalo, N. Y., September 7, 1942, entitled "Molders of a Better Destiny" (*Science*, October 2, 1942).

of view. They seem to reflect changes that have arisen in the public mind not in response to something in prospect but in response to *faits accomplis*. They indicate, perhaps, the efforts of the public mind to keep up with events and to achieve what one may describe, in the language of W. I. Thomas, as a new "definition of the situation" and a new point of view.

Differences of "definition," in the sense in which Thomas uses that term, are differences in the folkways and mores. As these differences are not ordinarily or obviously the product of discussion, they are not ordinarily discussable. To say that folkways are not debatable and hence nonrational, is, however, no more than to say that they are matters of custom and common sense. Possessing them, we respond to familiar situations with much the same spontaneity and unreflecting assurance that we would if folkways were instincts. This spontaneity and assurance with which we perform familiar and customary acts are, nevertheless, sometimes quite mistaken. Anyone who has witnessed the fanatical devotion with which a setting hen will sit on a glass egg will realize that, with all the assurance and conviction a hen may display, she is sometimes terribly and pathetically wrong. The fact is that neither instincts, folkways, or common sense—all of which are characteristically nonrational—can be trusted outside the situations and the habitats to which they are adapted.

If folkways are nonrational, there is, nevertheless, some wisdom or, as Sumner put it, some philosophy implicit in them. Thus custom, when interpreted by the courts, tends to assume the character of a principle or rule of law. In much the same way the will and the wisdom, implicit in the customs of peoples, emerge from the conflicts and controversies which more intimate association of races, peoples, and cultural groups provokes. They emerge in the form of creeds, doctrines, or, to use a term that has suddenly acquired a new and wide currency in the United States, ideologies.

IDEOLOGIES AND THE HISTORICAL PROCESS

What students of society and politics know about ideologies and about revolutions seems to have its source, for the most part, in the literature inspired by Karl Marx and by the writers who inherited the Marxian tradition. Darwin had described the historical process by which the manifold types of animal life were evolved as a struggle for existence in the course of which the earlier and less competent individuals and species were superseded by later and fitter forms. Marx seems to have adopted the Darwinian thesis, but with important qualifications as far as it applied to man, under the conditions imposed by human society. In the case of human beings the historical process, as he conceived it, has ceased to be a struggle of individuals and of species for existence in a purely natural economy, such as exists among plants and animals living together in a common habitat. It has become rather a struggle of economic or functional classes for social status in a social hierarchy.

The situation is not essentially different, as far as I can see, if the conflict is racial rather than economic, the classes, in that case, being castes and the dominant group a majority instead of a minority. In fact, racial conflicts where they occur are perhaps more elementary and logically, if not historically, earlier in the historical sequence.[2] In any case, the point is that the conflict of classes, or of races, in becoming forensic and political, ceases to be a mere clash of blind, brute force and assumes a form and character that Herr Hitler has described as "spiritual," that is, a kind of psychic warfare in which the weapons are words, slogans, so-called "vital lies" and other forms of propaganda, not excluding the news and the editors' and columnists' interpretations of it.

Ultimately, however, the historical process, as Marx conceives it, tends to assume the character of a prolonged Socratic dialogue or discussion, in the course of which not only a new, more inclusive, and presumably more tenable point of view emerges but a new social order. The new point of view and the assumptions on which it is based constitute in that case the logical structure of the new social order. The process, which is at once social and logical, Marx, using the language of Hegel and Plato, called "dialectic."

Revolutions and ideologies seem to be a characteristic of modern or at any rate of civic life. They arose historically, with the decline of tribal societies and the rise of cities. Among the things we miss in primitive society is anything that corresponds with what we ordinarily understand by either public opinion, ideology, or revolution. Organized public discussion and public opinion seem to have first come into existence when the market place was converted into a public forum. It was, apparently, in these forums that men's beliefs began to assume the form of creeds, and the myths which grew up to

---

[2] "The Nature of Race Relations," in *Race Relations and the Race Problem,* ed. Edgar T. Thompson (Durham, N.C.: Duke University Press, 1939), pp. 43-45.

support traditional beliefs assumed under these circumstances a rational and an ideological character.

Actually the way in which a new society and a new social order grows up within the shell of the old is not, even as Marx conceived it, as simple and intelliglible a process as this summary statement suggests. The point is, however, that social change and social revolution, under human conditions, always involve not only competition but conflict; not always the clash of physical forces, as in the case of wars or strikes, but of the ideas and of the ideologies by which the contending forces are inspired and directed. Thus every war tends to become an ideological conflict, i.e., tends to become a revolution.

THE SOCIOLOGY OF KNOWLEDGE AND THE "COLLECTIVE MIND"

Recently a new school of sociological thought, if not a new science—the sociology of knowledge—has risen above the intellectual horizon of Europe. Seeing in the current social myths and in the "collective dreams," as well as more rational forms of knowledge which emerge in the course of social revolutions, a significant social phenomenon, it has undertaken to study empirically the function of ideologies and utopias in the evolutionary process.[3] Thus the sociology of knowledge turns out to be a study of the nature of the collective mind, provided one means by "mind," either in the individual or in the group, what historians mean when they refer to "the mind of an age" or "the mind of an epoch," namely, the mental patterns, traditional ways of thinking, including the memories, mores, and, in general, the common sense which men in any society ordinarily employ in judging the value of objects, the importance of actions, and the credibility of current interpretations of events. In short, a mind is the instrument with which men think; and, according to the sociologists of knowledge, this instrument is very largely, if not wholly, a social and socialized product.[4] This is necessarily true, since we think with what we know, and knowledge is science only when it is verified and verifiable.

---

[3] Karl Mannheim, "Utopia," *Encyclopaedia of the Social Sciences*, XV, 200-203.

[4] Robert Redfield, *Tepoztlán: A Mexican Village* (Chicago: University of Chicago Press, 1930), pp. 222-23. Also Henry Osborn Taylor, *The Medieval Mind* (5th ed., 1938); and James Harvey Robinson, *The Making of the Modern Mind* (New York, 1923).

Collective thinking, where it goes on at all, invariably takes the form of a dialectic process or discussion in which individuals, and groups, having different interests and different points of view, seek to achieve some sort of understanding and some sort of agreement or at least some statement of their differences that is consistent and intelligible. What we ordinarily describe as public opinion arises where the issues are political and pragmatic rather than theoretic and ideological. One of the conditions of any sort of public opinion is the existence of (1) a public and a forum where criticism is tolerated and of (2) what is called in academic parlance a "universe of discourse," that is, a fund of fundamental ideas and assumptions which are understood and taken for granted but not, under ordinary circumstances, debatable. It is within the limits of such a universe of discourse that the discussions out of which public opinion emerges ordinarily take place. When, as often happens, in the course of a discussion, participants find they are not in the same universe of discourse, the discreet thing to do is undoubtedly to permit the discussion to subside before it reaches an embarrassing impasse. If it is to continue without violence either in word or in deed, an understanding may perhaps be reached by redefining the terms, making explicit the assumptions upon which differing points of view rest. But this is a kind of game which is not easy for experts and is practically impossible for ordinary human beings and politicians, that is, people who have real interests at stake. Political debates are fruitful when they are confined to discussing the means by which ends are to be achieved rather than ideologies by which ends are justified and legitimatized.

As a matter of fact, fundamental points of view and the assumptions on which they are based do not ordinarily get into public discussion either in the societies or communities where they are, so to speak, indigenous and generally accepted or in the societies and communities in which, in the light of generally accepted notions, they are likely to appear quaint, irrational, and generally unintelligible. Discussion, like other forms of communication, goes on easily and amiably when it is not concerned with fundamentals. Nonetheless, the fundamental assumptions continue to influence attitudes and get, in obscure, sublimated, and symbolic forms, some sort of overt expression, even where they are not discussed and not discussable.

The case of the Negro is an instance. Those who know the Negro spirituals will readily recognize in them the expression of the messianic hopes of the Negro slaves, and anyone who has heard Negro voices sing "Go down, Moses, way down in Egypt's land, tell old Pharaoh let my people go" cannot mistake the import of that hymn. Now that Negroes are free and have become race, if not class, conscious, they are in a position to state their case in more articulate fashion. However, the authors of the Declaration of Independence and the United States Constitution have provided them with a ready-made ideology.

Obviously much goes on in the collective mind that is not articulate and cannot be construed in the form of a dialogue or conversation. There is always in every culture and every society what William Graham Sumner called a "strain for consistency"—a consistency that is effectively achieved, perhaps, only in primitive communities but that is not altogether lacking in more complex and more sophisticated societies. This strain for consistency, which goes on ordinarily below the level of clear thinking, tends to impose uniformities on the meanings and mentalities of peoples and classes even in those instances where interests are so divergent that discussion of them in parliament, press, public forum, or anywhere that public opinion is ordinarily formed, is difficult or impossible.

For example, there is invariably a tendency within a public, parliamentary, or other discussion group to polarize opinions and form parties to support them. When that tendency persists to the point of creating within a public or a parliament irreconcilable and intransigent blocs, then discussion may be said to cease and war begins.

Conflicting and fundamental points of view are likely, however, to remain, if not suppressed, at least submerged, as long as the conventions are maintained intact and social routine not greatly interrupted. They force themselves into public consciousness and demand recognition, however, in times of crisis. In such case, anything that tends to heighten the tension makes communication, even for the purposes of ordinary intercourse, difficult, and public discussion, as a means of clarifying issues, ceases to function.

In such a case, the difficulty is not that people have differences of opinion about specific issues but rather that they look at things from fundamentally different points of view. Points of view give perspective to our thinking, and when they are defined by doctrines and assume the character of ideologies, they insure (1) consistency in the collective acts of societies, sects, and social classes and (2) integrity to the life-policies of the individuals who compose them. This seems, in fact, to be the peculiar function of ideologies.

It is characteristic of men that, when they undertake to act consistently and on principle, they measurably lose their capacity to respond to events in terms of equity and mere common sense. There is, as I recall, a rule of law that declares it is more important that the law be consistent than that it be just. I can see why this should be true. We must know what to expect of our laws, and we cannot do so unless courts are consistent. This explains, I suspect, the fact that the strategy of labor, in its disputes with capital, has been to appeal to public opinion by picketing or by strikes rather than submit its dispute to arbitration or to the adjudication of the courts. Public opinion is more likely than law to decide issues on the merits of the individual case. A court of arbitration inevitably interprets issues in accordance with tradition and recognized principle. The principle is conceived retrospectively in terms of an order, that is. The strikers, on the other hand, view the case prospectively in terms of what they hope for.

The whole point of this discussion, I might say, is based on the difference between public opinion and law, ideology or doctrine.

RACE RELATIONS AND RACIAL IDEOLOGIES

Much has been happening to race relations in the South in the course of the present war. They are not so cordial as they were. In the movement and changes which the national emergency has occasioned, the racial structure of society seems to be cracking, and a *modus vivendi* that survived the Civil War seems to be under attack at a time and under conditions when it is particularly difficult to defend it.

But great changes in race relations, mostly for the better, have been going on over a considerable period in recent years. These changes have come about in response to (1) improvement in Negro education and education generally in the southern states; (2) the rise of a responsible and conservative Negro middle class; (3) Negro migration from the rural South to the industrial cities of the North; (4) a marked decrease if not in interracial homicide at least in mob violence,[5] and (5) the rise of a Negro intelligentsia able to state the case of the Negro to Negroes in an increasingly influential Negro press and to the world at large in a growing body of literature which

---

[5] Lynch law is no longer tolerated in the southern states as it once was. Opposition to the institution, if one may so describe it, in becoming active in the South, has ceased to be sectional.

is always interesting, sometimes eloquent, and often disturbing in its revelations.

As a result of these changes it has seemed that the status of the Negro in the North, if not in the South, had been approximating that of other racial and cultural minority groups. Nevertheless, racial ideology and the point of view from which people in the South and in the North look at race relations seem to have changed but little if at all, and the conflict that is going on today in the South seems to be the expression of the determined efforts of southern white people of all classes to maintain at any cost the traditional racial etiquette and the traditional symbols which reflect the traditional racial structure of southern society.

Some twenty-eight years ago Thomas Pearce Bailey, in a volume entitled *Race Orthodoxy in the South,* made a statement of the racial creed and the racial doctrines of the southern people. The accuracy and authenticity of that statement, as far as I know, have never been questioned. This statement was neither an attack nor a defense. It was rather an exposition and explanation in the course of which the author expressed the conviction that, whatever else one might say about the racial doctrines of the southern people, they are inexorable historical facts and probably represent the only terms upon which the two races can continue to live together. Racial attitudes, according to Bailey, are, I might add, not instinctive but traditional. They are, in the South, at least, a part of the religious culture. Here are the items of this creed:

1. "Blood will tell."
2. The white race must dominate.
3. The Teutonic peoples stand for race purity.
4. The Negro is inferior and will remain so.
5. "This is a white man's country."
6. No social equality.
7. No political equality.
8. In matters of civil rights and legal adjustments give the white man, as opposed to the colored man, the benefit of the doubt; and under no circumstances interfere with the prestige of the white race.
9. In educational policy let the Negro have the crumbs that fall from the white man's table.
10. Let there be such industrial education of the Negro as will best fit him to serve the white man.
11. Only Southerners understand the Negro question.
12. Let the South settle the Negro question.

13. The status of peasantry is all the Negro may hope for, if the races are to live together in peace.

14. Let the lowest white man count for more than the highest Negro.

15. The above statements indicate the leadings of Providence.[6]

What Bailey has described as racial orthodoxy in the South is merely a more vigorous local expression of the racial ideology of the United States as a whole. It can all be summed up in one or, at most, two pregnant phrases: "This is a white man's country." "The Negro is all right in his place."

The first phrase, though it was coined in the South and is rarely heard in the North, seems to me to characterize pretty fairly America's attitude North and South, East and West, toward colored peoples, including the Indians, particularly when they came to this country from Mexico. The second phrase applies only to Negroes and characterizes the peculiar attitude of the southern white population toward the Negro. The difference is that in the South the Negroes have a place, if only they would stay in it; in the North, as far as there is any racial doctrine that could be described as orthodox, the Negro, the Indian, and the Asiatic have no place at all. They are merely more or less tolerated aliens.

The racial doctrines with which we are familiar in the United States are obviously the product of the controversies provoked by the racial problem. While the attitudes of the American people North and South, East and West, differ in emphasis and in detail, they are, it seems to me, fundamentally the same. Back of these racial doctrines is the whole history of the South and of the United States. One is able to record and read these racial creeds, but it is impossible to understand them unles one knows intimately the people in whose minds they grew up. For racial ideologies are no mere logical artifacts, formulas, or general conceptions; they are rather the historical products of long-continued conflict and controversy.

The southern people have been obsessed with this problem of race relations all their lives. It has been a source of a lively interest and anxiety for three hundred years. Needless to say, it has been during this time a concern of Negroes also. The whole history of the United States, North and South, has forced upon Negroes in slavery and in freedom a race consciousness that has slowly created out of individual men and women without history and without tradi-

---

[6] Thomas Pearce Bailey, *Race Orthodoxy in the South* (New York: Neale Publishing Co., 1914), p. 93.

tions a people conscious of common destiny; in short, a self-conscious minority with a cause and an ideal if not an ideology.

It is obvious that a doctrine and ideology that is deeply rooted in the geography, the economy, and the intimate personal relations and etiquette of the races of the South is not something to be swept away by anything short of war or revolution. As a matter of fact, the Civil War and the revolution that accompanied it in the period of reconstruction did not change, fundamentally and at once, the relations of races in the South or elsewhere.

Nevertheless, changes have taken and are taking place. These changes began when the freedmen first realized that they were free to change masters, so to speak, and to move from one plantation to the next. It changed profoundly when Negroes began to leave the plantation altogether and make their home in the slums of the cities, where they had a freedom that exists nowhere else except on the frontiers of settlement and civilization. It has continued to change with the progress of Negro education in the South and with the migration of the Negro population to the North, where they have in the public schools the same opportunities to get an education as the immigrant and all the other national and racial groups of which the American population is made up.

The most profound changes in race relations, if not in racial ideology, have come about with the rise of a hierarchy of occupational classes within the limits of the Negro race, so that Negroes can and do rise to some sort of occupational and professional equality with other races and peoples who have not been handicapped by the segregations and institutions of a caste system. The class system, as it exists in the United States at least, does permit individuals and eventually races to rise. At present, at least in the northern cities, to which the Negroes in recent years have migrated in such large numbers, the status of the Negro population is no longer that of a caste. It is rather that of a racial and cultural minority; like the Jews, the Japanese, and perhaps, the Indian and Mexican.

RACE RELATIONS AND NATIONAL SOLIDARITY

Owing, no doubt, to regional diversities of the country and of the peoples who settled it, the United States has always had the problem of maintaining national solidarity. In the early days of the Republic this problem took the form of sectionalism. Sectionalism, and the divergence of interests and ideologies that grew up as a result of these regional differences, rather than differences in national or racial origins, was responsible for the Civil War. Since that time, with the advent of the so-called new immigration from more distant countries and culturally diverse peoples, and particularly with the emergence of the Negroes as one of America's national and racial minorities, the problem of national solidarity has assumed a new and increasing importance. At present time, although there is little or no immigration and the different races and peoples of which our population is made up have been pretty thoroughly distributed and culturally assimilated, they still cherish, nevertheless, their ancestral traditions and still look with nostalgic interest to the lands and the peoples from which they and their ancestors sprung. The world wars, in which America has been involved, have inevitably intensified this consciousness of kind and have tended to make the United States less a federation of territorial than of racial and cultural units. This sense of difference is maintained by the fact that peoples of the same racial stock, even when they marry in their class, marry nevertheless in their own racial and national group, so that the United States tends to become a congeries of racial and national groups. The problem of national solidarity today is not one of sectionalism but one of racialism.

Meanwhile, with the progress of the war, the issues involved are becoming clarified, and the points of view of the contending parties, the Axis and the Allies, are obviously in process of redefinition. The war, which began as a struggle for living space between the "haves" and the "have-nots," has become a struggle between the master-races and the rest of the world; the former to gain the political and cultural hegemony of the world, and the latter to achieve a new social order that will insure at least a measure of freedom, independence, and security to individuals and peoples, irrespective of race, such as they have not hitherto enjoyed. In short, the issues which were economic and political have become racial and cultural.

The entrance of the United States into World War II has given the American public a new orientation and a new issue. With American soldiers fighting on every front in every part of the world, the political and cultural horizon of the American people has suddenly expanded and become like the war—global. Americans are now, more than ever before, finding themselves living not merely in America but in the world. Under the conditions which this war has imposed, isolation as a geographical and geopolitical fact has ceased to exist and isolationism as a doctrine and policy has become obsolete.

All this has resulted in sudden if not profound changes in our attitudes toward those peoples, white and colored, with whom we are now allied and with those others all over the world whose fate seems somehow bound up with our own. We have hitherto maintained toward the peoples of India, China, Japan, and Africa a curious attitude of complacency verging on contempt. Toward peoples of a different color we have usually acted as a benevolent "master-race," possessing all the wisdom and therefore entitled to impose our political and religious institutions and social practices upon both lands and peoples.

But now that we find ourselves fighting on the same battlefields for the same cause, all this seems to be an anachronism. Faith in a democratic social order which asserts that all men are or should be brothers rather than masters and servants is more contagious when men find themselves fighting together in a life-and-death struggle for a common cause. Under these circumstances we have begun to conceive of ourselves as possibly living on terms of neighborly intimacy and mutual understanding hitherto undreamed of with peoples all over the world. This is the good-neighbor policy, as we have learned to interpret it, since we have come to think of the peoples of South America as allies rather than as customers. But it is inevitable that the good-neighbor policy must eventually extend to all the peoples with whom we are now allied and whose cooperation we must have in winning the war and carrying into operation the terms of the peace. The good-neighbor policy involves, apparently, not merely an alliance of governments but an understanding of peoples.

Under these circumstances many people in the United States have become suddenly conscious of the limited and parochial view which our previous isolation has fostered and are now apparently in a way to revise their opinions of alien peoples and to improve, at least, our international and interracial manners.

Few Americans are as yet prepared to go as far as Lawrence K. Frank would have them. In a recent number of *Free World*, under the title, "World Order and Cultural Diversity," he has stated the racial issues of the present war in a way which reveals, to be sure, their international importance but makes our responsibility for them almost personal and moral rather than collective and political merely. "What Hitler, with his assertion of a German master race has done," he says, "is to reveal, in all its stark ruthlessness and self-centered, almost paranoid, distortion, what Western European culture has accepted as the major premise of its international relations."

In spite of the new orientation and the sudden awakening which the war has brought about, it has not, thus far at least, profoundly changed the mind and the mentality with which the American people look at this matter of race. In the nature of things it could not. There is too much race consciousness to permit it. There are still relatively few people in the United States who are able, even if they wished to do so, to treat a Negro democratically, that is, on his merits as an individual rather than as a representative of his race. This is where the racial policy of the Anglo-Saxon American differs from the racial policy of Latin America. This is likewise the point at which people of the United States cease to be intelligible to the people of Brazil.⁷ On the other hand, it is just here that the racial policy of the United States is identical with that of Australia and South Africa, whose racial ideologies must be reckoned with in winning the war and making the peace. And then there is India, Mother India, with her mélange of unassimilated races and peoples! Should India decide, at the conclusion of the war, to participate in organizing the peace, how will she reconcile her caste system at home with democracy abroad?

It seems obvious, to an increasing number of people in the United States, that the ability of the United Nations to win the peace will depend upon their ability to achieve a new, profoundly different, perhaps one might describe it as revolutionary, change in their attitudes toward alien and particularly colored and colonial peoples.

It is obvious, however, that ideologies, since they are basic, since they reflect the point of view from which we look at the world and the point of view from which we interpret events as they occur, do not and cannot change with every change in opinion and every wind of doctrine. It is these ideologies rather than public opinion that represent the public mind, as far as the public can be said to have a mind. They are rooted in the memories, the tradition, and the mores of the particular community or society in which each of us lives; they reflect the mentality and habits of thought with which any society and the individuals who compose it determine not only what is right or wrong but what things we hear—rumor, propaganda, or news—are credible. Things that happen, which from the customary point of view are quite unconscionable, cannot be reported even in

---

⁷ Donald Pierson, *Negroes in Brazil* (Chicago: University of Chicago Press, 1942).

a press as free as we have in America and could not be discussed if they were.

I might add that, with all its recent realism, and in spite of the success that propaganda experts have had in measuring opinion, in improving or undermining morale, it seems doubtful whether political science has thus far discovered any technical devices capable of bringing about changes in the public mind that can properly be described as revolutionary. Revolutions are the product not of changes in opinion but of changes in ideology and in those common understandings and assumptions which make differences of opinion communicable and public discussion possible.

What the war has done thus far has been to make race relations an international rather than a local and national problem. We may expect, therefore, no matter how great the changes the war brings, that racial and cultural conflicts will continue in some form or other in the future as in the past. Nevertheless, the issues of the world war and the world peace will be very largely determined by the progress and outcome of this ideological conflict.

Furthermore, in the prosecution of the war and in the organization of the peace, racial diversities of the American population will be either a national handicap or a national asset, depending upon our ability to make our racial policies and our racial ideology conform to our national interests. We have not succeeded in doing that yet. A revolution in race relations in the United States may be impending, but it has not yet arrived. The war has changed the nature of the race problem, but it has not changed fundamentally the mind of the American people.

I can bring this discussion to no better conclusion than by quoting the words of Winston Churchill's latest broadcast. "It is not much use pursuing these speculations further at this time, for no one can possibly know what the state of Europe or the world will be when the Nazi and Fascist tyrannies are finally broken."

One thing, however, seems certain: the races and peoples which fate has brought together in America and within the limits of the larger world economy will continue, in the emerging world society, their struggle for a political and a racial equality that was denied them in the world that is passing. As far as this prediction turns out to be true, it will be, perhaps, because the historical process, as it operates among human beings, is determined finally not merely by biological but by ideological forces, and not by what men have or are merely but what they hope for and believe.

CHAPTER 24

EDUCATION AND THE CULTURAL CRISIS

JOHN DEWEY introduces his notable book, *Democracy and Education*, with an impressive statement of a fact which most of us take for granted, namely, that education is a process by which a cultural heritage is transmitted from one generation to the next. It is, at the same time, a process by which a society renews and perpetuates its existence, for society, as Dewey has said elsewhere, exists in and through communication, and communication is precisely the means by which the cultural, as distinguished from the biological, heritage is transmitted. Formal education is, therefore, merely a rational procedure for carrying on and completing, in the schoolroom, a task that began spontaneously with the child in the home.

In order to emphasize the importance of this process of cultural transmission and renewal, Dewey invites his readers to consider the possibility that by some strange chance an older generation should come to an untimely end, so that there would be a complete break in the cultural succession. In that case a new, naïve, and unsophisticated generation, abandoned in the midst of this complex civilization of ours, unable to read or even to talk, would have great difficulty digging out of books, artifacts, and other archeological remains the insights that would enable it to recover its lost inheritance.

This is, in some sense and to some degree, what happens any day when young folk leave home to seek their fortunes in the city. This is what happens to a younger generation of immigrants, particularly

American Journal of Sociology, XLVIII (May 1943), pp. 728-736.

if it grows up in an immigrant community such as exists on the East Side in New York City or the West Side in Chicago. A rather complete and informing literature, consisting mainly of immigrant biographies, has been written on this theme.

To this second generation of immigrants, because the new world, which is strange and foreign to their parents, is the only world they know, strange things happen of which they are scarcely aware; things the significance of which only a psychiatrist would, perhaps, fully understand. Strange things happen to the older generation, also, when they learn, as they sometimes do, that they and their ways seem queer to their children.

What happens in such cases is a more or less complete break in the cultural succession. The tradition which the immigrant family brings with it is rooted in a different milieu and is part of a local and national culture different from that in which the family is living in the country of its adoption. To be sure, the difference between one culture and another is not very great as long as both are European or as long as they are local cultures which are integral parts of one of those more inclusive cultural units we call "civilization."

Even so, any interruption of the cultural process may have profound consequences which involve the whole educational process —not only that which goes on normally in the home and in the schoolroom but that which is continued outside, in the workshop and on the playground, and, finally, in all the adventures which the theater, the dance hall, and the city streets eventually provide.

When, however, the immigrant is not of European origin (as, for example, in the case of the Japanese and Chinese), then the break in the cultural succession is likely to be more complete and more devastating. Particularly is this true in a region or in a community— like that of the Hawaiian Islands—where the population is so largely made up of peoples of different racial stocks, each living in the isolation of a more or less completely closed community. There the break between the first and the second generation is likely to be much greater and its effects more profound. In Hawaii, where there is a great deal of intermarriage between the migrant and the native population, it sometimes happens that neither parent learns to speak the language of the other and they are therefore able to communicate with each other and with their children only through the medium of English, which is, naturally, the lingua franca of the island and, like every other franca, only imperfectly understood by the people who use it.

Some of the consequences referred to are so obvious and so marked that they have produced in the second generation a recognizable personality type sometimes described as "the marginal man," i.e., the man who lives on the margin of two cultures—that of the country of his parents and that of the country of his adoption, in neither of which he is quite at home. We know, in a general way, for reasons that are not at present wholly intelligible, that this so-called "marginal man" is likely to be smart, i.e., a superior, though sometimes a superficial, intellectual type.

On the other hand, the immigrants, whether of the first or the second generation, if they continue to live in the isolation of an immigrant community, are likely to sink to a cultural level in the country of their adoption lower than that of the national or racial stock in the country of their origin. This is true not merely in the United States but also, conspicuously so, in Brazil, where European countries have attempted to colonize and to maintain in the New World environment an Old World language and culture.

We ordinarily think of the problems that arise, in the course of such cultural diffusion and acculturation as have been described, as problems of personality. They are, however, at the same time, whether they arise in the home, in the school, or in the community, pedagogical problems—problems that grow out of the difficulties of transmitting a cultural tradition from one generation to another or from one cultural unit to another. As it appears in the schoolroom, the problem is likely to be that of rote learning; as it appears in the family or the local community, on the other hand, it is that of the problem child.[1]

What we do not know is just what is involved in this process of transmission of a tradition from one generation to another and from one cultural group to another. Especially is this true where the two cultural groups are as different as are, for example, those of the American Indian and the European, where, under ordinary circumstances, the two races live together, to be sure, but in more or less complete cultural isolation—i.e., in relations that are symbiotic rather than social. One need not, however, go so far afield for an illustration as the American Indian. An equally outstanding illustration of cultural

---

[1] Robert E. Park, "A Memorandum on Rote Learning," *American Journal of Sociology*, XLIII (1938), 23.

*i*solation is that of the Mennonites in Pennsylvania, the so-called Pennsylvania Dutch, or the so-called "Cajuns" (Acadians) of Louisiana.

In such cases as these, isolation may measuredly preserve and perpetuate an existing culture; but some sort and some degree of break or change in the culture is bound to take place in every case in the course of the educational process. Some modification of the tradition is necessary to preserve not merely the form but also the content of the cultural tradition; for a tradition is not merely a treasure to be preserved, but, like the society of which it is a part, it is an organism to be renewed and perpetuated. That is why we have continually to re-write our histories; to redefine our laws and renew, in the light of a later experience, our faith in our traditional ways of life. That is why education, when successful, is a more or less creative process in which the culture is, in course of transmission, re-created in the mind of the student and of the community.

Not only do societies and cultures change, but they sometimes change so rapidly that one generation so far loses contact with the next that it is with difficulty that the cultural tradition is transmitted. This has certainly happened more than once in America. It has happened since 1914 in the case of the younger and older generations of women in the United States. It has taken place more than once in Russia. It is, interestingly enough, the theme of Turgenev's famous novel *Fathers and Sons,* written sixty years ago, and of other less notable works of fiction, dealing with European life, written since that time.

At other times and under other conditions societies expand territorially so rapidly that they are not able, even where the economic organization continues to function, to maintain cultural contacts. In fact, as we shall see later, sectionalism in a political society, like sectarianism in a religious society, is one characteristic way in which cultural crises arise. In such cases the common understandings, or mores, by which personal and political relations are ordinarily regulated and effective political and moral order maintained, are dissolved, and understanding gives way to confusion and disorder.

Society, it seems, has at least two dimensions: (1) a temporal and (2) a spatial or territorial. If it is the function of education to perpetuate the life of society in time, by renewing and transmitting the cultural tradition from one generation to the next, it is, by the same token, the function of education (if not of the school) to perpetuate its existence in space by renewing the understandings by which different sections, classes, and races in the community not only carry on a common economy but are able to maintain a degree of political and moral solidarity which makes effective collective action possible.

Crises, it seems, may arise in several different ways and on more than one level of integration. If I speak here and now of different levels of integration, that is merely a recognition of the fact that society, as we know it, is actually a hierarchy of relatively independent levels of association—economic, political, and religious. For each of these levels of association, with their institutions, there exist distinct and more or less independent social sciences. Furthermore, with the emergence of our totalitarian states and the existence of total war it is perhaps more obvious today than ever before that these different levels of social integration are not so independent of one another as they have sometimes seemed. It is inevitable that, in a society more completely integrated, changes and crises which occur on the economic level, where human relations are relatively abstract and impersonal, must bring about repercussions on every other level, including that occupied by the family and the church, where associations are more intimate and more personal and hence more controlled by imperatives that are traditional and nonrational rather than explicit and formal.

It may not be so obvious that these different levels of societal integration represent a hierarchy in which the economic order, at the base of the social triangle, supports the political, which, in turn, supports the personal and moral, the order characteristic of familial and religious societies.

Nevertheless, when changes on the economic level are more rapid than changes on the political and religious levels, the solidarity and efficiency of society on every other level are inevitably affected. This is the phenomenon ordinarily referred to as "cultural lag." We have cultural lag when customs and creeds no longer conform to the actual functioning of the social process and no longer control or direct them. As a matter of fact, any movement or disturbance of an existing order, if long continued, may bring about a social crisis.

Since Malthus wrote his treatise on population, there has been no question of the fact that the mere increase and aggregation of populations, or their movements and migrations from one cultural milieu to another, may have consequences on every other level of integration.

One of the more remarkable instances of disintegration of the moral order as a result of migration is reported by Pauline V. Young in her volume, *The Pilgrims of Russian-Town*.[2] In this instance a primitive religious sect of German origin, the so-called "Molokans," or "milk-drinkers," migrated to America from central Russia, where they had lived for many years in more or less complete cultural, if not economic, isolation. They settled on the outskirts of Los Angeles and attempted to maintain there the religious practices and moral discipline to which they had been accustomed in Russia. The results were disastrous, not merely to the religious community, but to the personal careers of many of its members, particularly to those of the second generation.

Recently my attention was attracted to an item in the *Nashville Tennessean* entitled " 'Sudeten Problem' Has Baptists Fighting Civil War Over Again."[3] It was an account of a prolonged debate over the petition of three thousand Southern Baptists, living in California, for admission to the Southern Baptist Convention then in session in San Antonio, Texas. The petitioners had found it impossible, they said, to work in harmony with the Northern Baptists. Living in California, they were territorially northerners, but in their customs and traditions they were southerners still. The petition was received with sympathy and understanding, but it raised a constitutional question. It was opposed on the ground that it would offend the California Northern Baptists and would, as the opposition put it, "constitute an action similar to Hitler's assumption that Czecho-Slovakia was German because some Germans lived there." However, human nature prevailed finally over logic, and the California exiles were taken into full fellowship in the Southern Convention. The case suggests the following comments.

1. It is extraordinary what difficulties a difference of local customs can make, even among Baptists. The differences between the Northern and Southern Baptists were due, it was said, to "certain practices such as open communion." However, as I recall John Steinbeck's account—in his novel, *Grapes of Wrath*—of the migration of the "Okies" and "Arkies" to the fruit farms of California, I suspect this is, to say the least, an understatement.

2. It is interesting, too, that the case of Hitler and the Sudeten Irredentists was cited as a precedent to characterize and define a

---

[2] Chicago: University of Chicago Press, 1932.
[3] Tuesday, May 19, 1942.

constitutional issue in a Baptist convention in San Antonio. It suggests that our traditional policy of national isolation is weakening in places where we might least expect it.

3. My interest in this incident is in the fact that the trouble between Northern and Southern Baptists in California was due to a cultural conflict—a conflict which arose as a consequence of a migration. However, a migration, if one does not take its ultimate consequences into the reckoning, is no more than a change in the territorial distribution of a population. If my diagnosis be correct, the incident may be regarded as a symptom of a condition by no means peculiar to California. It is rather, I suspect, a minor indication of a condition which exists there more obviously perhaps than in most other parts of the United States, except in our great metropolitan centers like New York and Chicago.

For some years past, during a period when migration from abroad has almost ceased, internal migration in the United States, and particularly the westward movement of population, has continued. California with its glamorous landscape has been the haven toward which everything that was human and mobile, it seems, has gravitated. During the last three decades the population of California has increased more rapidly than that of any other state in the Union.

California has been at once the gateway and the barrier to migration from the Orient. When the gates were open and migration was encouraged, considerable numbers of Chinese, Japanese, Filipinos, and Koreans poured into the country, largely by way of Hawaii. When the gates were closed, they nevertheless continued to filter in.

The demand for labor to till California's vast fruit and vegetable gardens did not cease with the restrictions that excluded Japanese immigrants. The demand was temporarily supplied by seasonal laborers from Mexico. Every year, in response to the seasonal demand, the tide of immigration that crossed the border left behind in the course of its recession a permanent deposit of Mexican Indians and mestizos and formed in this way a kind of population delta extending northward from the Imperial Valley.

Later, when the combined effects of the drought and the depression had completed the ruin of the farmers on the marginal lands in the Southwest, there poured out of that dust bowl a flood of migratory laborers to recruit the army of fruit tramps who follow the harvest from the Imperial Valley to the Canadian border.

Meanwhile, to add to the cultural complexity of California's cosmopolitan population, there has been a steady drift, westward and northward to the coast cities, of Negroes from the Southwest, destined to fill in the niches in the expanding industrial organization of the West Coast cities.

All this migration has had a marked effect upon the social structure of California society. For one thing, it has dotted the Pacific Coast with Chinatowns and Little Tokyos, not to mention the large Mexican colony in Los Angeles and the transient fruit camps all up and down the valley. Here a large part of California's population, which comes from such diverse and distant places, lives in more or less closed communities, in intimate economic dependence, but in more or less complete cultural independence of the world about them.

But the disposition of racial and cultural minorities to settle in colonies and to cherish, in the seclusion and security of their own communities, different traditions and peculiar folkways is true of other sections of California's population which are also, in some sense, alien, alien at least to those who count everyone a foreigner who was not born in the state. California is celebrated for its residential suburban cities—cities like Pasadena, where the rich and retired live in a seclusion so complete and so silent that in some of the residential hotels, it is said, one scarcely hears anything but the ticking of the clock or the hardening of one's arteries.

And then there is Hollywood, where, to be sure, the seclusion is perhaps maintained but the silence is absent. Hollywood is a sort of legendary place, visible but remote, where, from the distance that the public sees them, our film favorites live like the gods on Mount Olympus, carefree and unconcerned about anything except their family troubles.

I mention Pasadena because Professor Thorndike of Columbia, in his search for statistical indices of the good life in American cities, found that Pasadena ranks first among the first 10 which have more radios, telephones, bathtubs, and dentists, in proportion to their populations, than any of the 295 others.[4] Professor Thorndike's statistics are based on thirty-seven such indices. I mention four which seem fairly representative of the values of what Professor Sorokin characterizes as our "sensate civilization." Professor Sorokin has meanwhile published, under the title *The Crisis of Our Age*, a critique of our modern urban civilization in which he says, in effect, that it is

---

[4] E. L. Thorndike, *Your City* (New York: Harcourt, Brace & Co., 1939).

a civilization based on gadgets rather than on ideas and ideals.[5] Obviously one evidence of the cultural crisis is the fact that such distinguished scholars could differ so widely with respect to the indices of the good life.

The fact that California, with its Hollywood, residential suburbs, Little Tokyos, and Chinatowns, has, like some of our metropolitan cities, become a congeries of culturally insulated communities, suggests that America has already measurably achieved the communistic ideal of a classless society—that is, a society without any hierarchical structure or, one might almost say, a society with no structure at all.

But this would by no means be a complete description of California, or of any of our great cities where changes have been going on at a comparable pace. California not only has its closed communities, but it has its proletariat. It has its "Okies" and its "Arkies," its mobile, foot-loose, and dispossessed—victims alike of wanderlust and the great depression, as these have affected the population in those great open spaces we used to call "God's country." With these one should include the large numbers of people from the Middle West who, before the depression and since, have gone to the Pacific Coast to enjoy the sunshine and the luxury of a suburban fruit farm where, with an automobile, one may have all the spacious freedom of the country and the intellectual emancipation of the city.

These varied elements of a population, already pretty thoroughly mixed, meeting and mingling again in the expansive atmosphere of this last frontier, have created a milieu and provided a soil in which a wild, weedy growth of political isms and religious cults has sprung up. But that is something that has always happened, it seems, on the frontier in America. It is, as Tolstoy has pointed out, one of the fruits of enlightenment.[6]

I have cited California because it is one of the conspicuous spots in which the diverse races and cultures of our cosmopolitan population have been thrown, so to speak, into the crucible: a crucible in which, perhaps, a new civilization is brewing and a new indigenous race is in the making.

One cannot, of course, be certain what will ultimately come out of the crucible, except as we are able to compare it with what has

---

[5] Pitirim Alex Sorokin, *The Crisis of Our Age: The Social and Cultural Outlook* (New York: E. P. Dutton & Co., Inc., 1941).

[6] Lev Nikolaevich Tolstoy, *The Fruits of Enlightenment* (Boston: W. H. Baker, 1901).

taken place in similar situations, earlier and elsewhere. Gilbert
Murray, in his volume, *The Rise of the Greek Epic*,[7] has described
in convincing detail the invasion and conquest by the northern
barbarians of the Aegean world of 1100 B.C. This invasion was at
once the source of the Homeric legends and of the ancient Greek
civilization which arose on the ruins of the earlier Aegean. The time
was some three thousand years ago, but the process, though it
proceeded at a slower pace, was not unlike that we seem to be witnessing in the world today. "It is almost a rule of history," says Murray,
"that before any definite invasion of a new territory there is a long
period of peaceful penetration. In the beginning it is not an army
that comes to invade. It is some adventurers or traders who come and
settle; some mercenaries who are invited in."

I cannot repeat the whole story. It impresses one, on the whole, as
something with which one is not unfamiliar. The historical context
is different, but the consequences are the same. While there is room
for both races there is little fighting. But a time comes when there is
violence: violence which terminates in confusion and chaos, "a chaos
in which an old civilization is shattered into fragments, its laws set
at naught." It is a time when, to state it in one of the happiest descrip-
tive phrases with which I am familiar, "that intricate web of normal
expectation which forms the very essence of human society [has
been] torn so often and so utterly by continued disappointment that
there ceases to be any normal expectation at all."[8]

It is the "intricate web of normal expectation" which is torn and
rent likewise when peoples migrate anywhere in large numbers or
when the pace of economic change is too much quickened. Professor
Herman Clarence Nixon of Vanderbilt University has recently published the annals of a little community in the hills of northern Alabama, called Possum Trot. Since it is the story of his home town,
Professor Nixon's account is autobiographical and personal, but by
no means less instructive for that reason. *Possum Trot* interested me
for several reasons, but mainly because it gave me a detailed historical
account of another and different aspect of the migration which has
been responsible for prosperity and the present condition of California and some other parts of the country that have been similarly
blessed.

If the racial and cultural situation of California, as it exists today,

[7] (2d ed.; Oxford: Clarendon Press, 1911), p. 67.
[8] *Ibid.*, p. 78.

is the result of a current of population flowing into a growing center, then Possum Trot, as it exists today, is the result of a corresponding movement of dispersion. One of the first things that is likely to strike the sophisticated reader of Mr. Nixon's description of Possum Trot is its earlier isolation. Culture, like race, is, or was originally, a local phenomenon, the product of isolation. Civilization, on the other hand, as Spengler and others have observed, is a product of the city. In the modern world of city-dwellers the rural community is a place to be born but is not a place to live. The tragedy of life in the country, we are told, is its isolation. But Possum Trot in the last forty years has been gradually emerging from its isolation, and that seems to Professor Nixon the only really tragic thing about it. This is what he says:

> Possum Trot is not more isolated than it used to be. It is less isolated than it used to be. It is closely connected with the world by economic ties. It is connected with urban "5 and 10 cent" stores. It is connected with cotton warehouses in Anniston. It is connected with the government's A.A.A. office in the county. It is connected with the courthouse in Anniston, and a few Possum Trotters can frequently be seen sitting on the low retaining wall around the courthouse lawn. Sitting there and talking. Sitting there passing the time away. Sitting there waiting for bus time.
>
> Possum Trot is no longer either an economic or a social unit, though it once was both. Possum Trot, the population of Possum Trot, the economy of Possum Trot, is now just an integral part of a larger and unpredictable economic unit.
>
> But Possum Trot is only slightly connected in any conscious social way with the rest of the world. It is an economic part of Anniston, but not a social part of Anniston. It is an economic part of Jacksonville, but not a social part of Jacksonville. It is an economic part of Piedmont, but not a social part of Piedmont. The economic world has absorbed Possum Trot. The social world has largely passed Possum Trot by. For Anniston, Piedmont, Jacksonville, Alabama, and the United States, the Possum Trot men, to a large extent, are just economic men. Here is then a social lag. Social change is not keeping up with economic change. Economic life goes on changing; but socially something is lost and not yet replaced. The community, no longer isolated, is an aggregation of individuals who are culturally more isolated than ever.

Possum Trot is no longer isolated. It has been incorporated into the national and into the world economy. It no longer has the control it once had, or seemed to have when people were more interested in politics than they are today, over its own destiny. Meanwhile, somehow, life in Possum Trot has lost its meaning and its zest. Something new has been added, no doubt. There are more things to buy in the stores, if one has the money. That means the standard of living is higher. But, as the author puts it, socially something has been lost. The social world, the old familiar world of personal and neighborly relations, has somehow disappeared. What remains of Possum Trot is, in the drastic language of the author, "an aggregation of economic men."

Not only in Possum Trot but in every other part of the world the economic necessities of an emerging and more inclusive social order have undermined the ancient local, tribal, and familial loyalties which once bound men together. At the same time, and as an incident of the growth of a world economy, the mechanization and rationalization of what was traditional and customary have banished the old superstitions and the old creeds by which men formerly regulated their lives. Everywhere individual men, in pursuing and achieving a new economic freedom and a new economic independence in the expanding markets of the world, have measurably ceased to be persons and neighbors and have become, in Nixon's language, "economic men."

The question that emerges from this wide-ranging discussion is this: What can education do about it? What can education do about Possum Trot? What can it do about the world? This is obviously not a problem for technology. No gadgets or scientific formulas can re-create the understandings or revitalize the institutions that have disintegrated, largely under the influence of scientific analysis and of technological changes.

Institutions are not artifacts, not even legal artifacts. They cannot be created either by discussion or by legislation. On the contrary, they are the product of what Sumner describes as "concurrent action," operating over considerable periods of time. They are the product of growth and of education, assuming that education is, as Dewey described it, a process by which society renews and perpetuates itself. There is, as far as I can see, no other means by which a society or an institution can perpetuate itself, i.e., continue in some form or other to live—except as individuals acquire, as a result of their continued participation in the conscious life of the nation and of the race, the accumulated experience and traditions of the society and institutions of which they are a part.

In the new and more inclusive society which is emerging, we shall be living—particularly if it is to be a free and democratic society —in a new intimacy with all the peoples of the world, not only with our allies but with our enemies. In this situation, what will be? What is the task of the schools?

We shall need, as never before, to know human geography and, perhaps, geopolitics. We shall need to know—not all of us, but some of us—all the languages. We must have institutes, such as they have long had in Germany, France, and England, for the study of the languages and cultures of the peoples outside of Europe, in Asia and Africa. We must, in short, prepare ourselves as never before to live not merely in America but in the world.

The most important task of the schools, including high schools and colleges, has been and will continue to be, I believe, to make Americans literate—literate in a large way, of course, making them capable, for one thing, of reading newspapers intelligently. News, like other forms of knowledge, comes to us, for the most part, in little items. To read these items intelligently involves the conscious or unconscious sorting of them and integrating of them with some precious fund of knowledge, i.e., knowledge which has accumulated in our minds about some one or the other of our permanent interests.

Integration, in the sense that I use the term here involves interpretation of the new in terms of the old. It is, in fact, only in this way that what we read becomes intelligible. To interpret the news we must supply, from our own resources, a background that will make the news and the current events it records significant. This business of sorting out and classifying the news is done for us in a rather imperfect way by the daily newspaper when it prints its items on the particular page where its readers are accustomed to look for them. News magazines, like *Time* and *Fortune*, do the same thing but do it better. They not only classify the news, but they supply, from their records of current events and other sources, a background for the understanding of news which the average reader cannot command.

One of the outstanding characteristics of the world today is the extraordinary amount of news that is published, not merely in the daily press, but in other periodicals and in what publishers designate as current books. Furthermore, writers of current books who, like Kaltenborn, are editing the news, have turned more and more to history to find materials that enable them to interpret current events. Thus a recent writer in the *Saturday Review of Literature* (Elmer Davis, I believe) announces that two books above all others—Hitler's *Mein Kampf* and Thucydides' *History of the Peloponnesian War*—

should be required reading today. Current events are never wholly intelligible except as we see them in perspective and as incidents of long-term changes in social institutions. These long-term, so-called "secular" trends represent what is really going on in the world rather than just what seems to have happened.

High schools and colleges, in preparing students to live in the world rather than in their special occupations, should prepare them to read literature. Our modern world seems to be falling apart and disintegrating, largely because men—rather than women—are so profoundly interested in their vocations that they have ceased to read literature. At any rate, they have ceased to read Shakespeare and the classics. They read instead the news, particularly the news in their special fields of interest.

William James, in an essay the full import of which seems to have escaped most professional students of human nature and society, calls attention to what he calls "a certain blindness in human beings" with which we are more or less afflicted and which makes us insensible to the feelings of creatures and people different from ourselves. This blindness is due to the fact that all values are originally individual and subjective. It is only as men and women learn to participate in common enterprises, like war or the rearing of a family, and only as these common enterprises become institutionalized, that values that were individual and subjective become objective and social.

One problem of our modern world, perhaps at the moment the greatest problem, has arisen from the necessity of curing ourselves, as far as that is humanly possible, of every form of blindness which makes it difficult for us to communicate, to achieve understandings, and to act effectively with others in the interest of a common cause. That is essentially the problem of morale—national and international. If anything—except a continued, intimate, and personal association—is measurably to cure the "blindness" of which James writes, it will be done, I believe, through the medium of literature—literature and the expressive arts.

Literature and art are, in the language of Tolstoy, "forms of human activity consisting in this, that one man consciously, by means of certain signs, hands over to others feelings he has lived through, and that other people are infected and also experience them." [9] What Tolstoy's statement amounts to, it seems to me, is this. The function

---

[9] Lev Nikolaevich Tolstoy, *What Is Art?* (New York: Oxford University Press, 1930).

—perhaps I might be more specific and say the social function—of art is to communicate not ideas but sentiments, incidentally, perhaps, creating and sustaining in this way a mood in which, for a space, one's sense of individual and personal differences is lessened and one's sense of mutual understanding and moral solidarity is enhanced. At any rate, something like this is with most of us, I am sure, a familiar experience.

Implicit in Tolstoy's statement and in his creed is the notion that art no more than science exists for itself alone. It has some more important function than that of providing an entertainment, merely, or a momentary escape from reality. "Nothing," says Santayana, "is so poor and melancholy as an art that is interested in itself and not in its subject." The same thing may be said of a science that is interested in its method rather than in its discoveries.

If, then, the function of education is, as has been said, to transmit, renew, and so perpetuate the cultural heritage, then the task of the schools in a period of cultural crisis does not differ; it is merely more difficult than it would otherwise be under normal conditions of life. That task of the schools is, in any case, to prepare students to read the news at a time when news is more disturbing and when there is more of it than usual; to prepare them to read and understand literature—the literature of great writers, whose wisdom constitutes perhaps the most important part of tradition—and to read in addition the literature of contemporary life in so far as it serves to reveal what gives significance to other, and particularly other alien, lives in regard to which, as James insists, our judgments are likely to be obscure, unjust, and stupid.[10]

---

[10] William James, *Talks to Teachers on Psychology and to Students on Some of Life's Ideals* (New York: Henry Holt & Co., 1914).

CHAPTER 25

Missions and the Modern World

What have missions done, and what can missions do to create a moral solidarity among races and peoples which will achieve and insure international and interracial peace?

I

During the last hundred years the external conditions of civilized life have been transformed by a series of inventions which have abolished the old limits to the creation of mechanical force, the carriage of men and goods, and communication by written and spoken words. One effect of this transformation is a general change of social scale. Men find themselves working and thinking and feeling in relation to an environment which, both in its world-wide extension and in its intimate connection with all sides of human existence, is without precedent in the history of the world.

Economists have invented the term the "Great Industry" for the special aspect of this change which is dealt with by their science and sociologists may conveniently call the whole result the "Great Society."

II

In those countries in which the transformation first began, a majority of the inhabitants already lived either in huge commercial cities or in closely populated industrial districts threaded by systems

American Journal of Sociology L (November 1944), pp. 177-183.

of mechanical traction and covering hundreds of square miles. Cities and districts are only parts of highly organized national states, each with fifty or a hundred million inhabitants; and these states are themselves every year drawn more effectively into a general system of international relationships.

Every member of the Great Society, whether he be stupid or clever, whether he have the wide curiosity of the born politician and trader or the concentration on what he can see and touch of the born craftsman, is affected by this ever extending and ever tightening nexus. A sudden decision by some financier whose name he has never heard may, at any moment, close the office or mine or factory in which he is employed, and he may either be left without a livelihood or be forced to move with his family to a new center. He and his fellows can maintain their standard wage or any measure of permanency in their employment only if the majority of them judge rightly on different questions put to them by national political parties and national or international trade-unions. Even in those English villages into which the Great Industry may seem to have scarcely penetrated the change of scale is already felt. The widow who takes in washing fails or succeeds according to her skill in choosing starch or soda or a wringer under the influence of half-a-dozen competing world schemes of advertisement. The boys playing football on the village green think of themselves as possible members of a champion English team. The spectacled young schoolmaster who looks on is brooding, with all his future happiness consciously at stake, on his chances of advancement in the Transvaal or West Australia or on the relation between his own religious opinion and an analysis of Hebrew eschatology by a German professor.

The English factory girl who is urged to join her union, the tired old Scotch gatekeeper with a few pounds to invest, the Galician peasant when the emigration agent calls, the artisan in a French provincial town whose industry is threatened by a new invention—all know that unless they find their way successfully among world-wide facts which reach them only through misleading words they will be crushed. They may desire to live the old life among familiar sights and sounds and the friends whom they know and trust, but they dare not try to do so. To their children, brought up in the outskirts of Chicago or the mean streets of Tottenham or Middlesborough, the old life will have ceased to exist, even as an object of desire.

III

The core of this Great Society is naturally Europe. The Great Society and the new world order have come into existence with the continued expansion of Europe and European civilization. European commerce has brought the whole world within the limits of a single economy. The world wars have revealed the fact that this new world is potentially a political, as well as an economic, unit and that it must become an actual and effectively organized political unit if it is to maintain international peace.

Furthermore, within the framework of the existing world economy which European commerce and European industry have imposed upon the rest of the world, there is growing up a body of custom and social practices which are now more or less understood and accepted by all the diverse races and peoples that have come within the sphere of their influence. These constitute a culture or a civilization that is no longer local but world wide and destined, it seems, to inherit the cultural traditions of all earlier and simpler peoples, so that there is now probably no racial minority and no local culture that has not made its contribution to the cultural resources of this Great Society.

IV

Fifty years ago the practical men who were bringing the Great Society into existence thought, when they had time to think at all, that they were thereby offering an enormously better existence to the whole human race. Men were rational beings and, having obtained limitless power over nature, would certainly use it for their own good. In 1867, for instance, Bernard Cracroft, in *Essays on Reform* described the intense optimism of the typical English manufacturer of his time:

> The mercantile feeling and fever, the ardent faith in progress, the belief . . . . in a mercantile millennium, to be obtained partly by the boundless development of human energy striving like fire ever upwards, partly by unforeseen but probable discoveries, which at any moment may throw additional millions into the lap of human comfort, and so raise humanity another stage above the gulf of wretchedness and want.

The Great Society, even if it should deprive men of some of the romance and intimacy of life, must, they thought, at least give them such an increase of security as would be far more than an equal return.

Famine would be impossible when any laborer could buy flour and bacon from the world market in his village shop. Wars would be few and short if they meant disaster to an international system of credit.

V

Now, however, that the change has come, hardly anyone thinks of it with the old undoubting enthusiasm. Actual famine has, it is true, disappeared from the Great Society, but there remains the constant possibility of general and uncontrollable depression of trade. The intervals between great wars are apparently becoming longer, but never has the expenditure on armaments been so great or the fear of war so constant.

But wars and commercial crises may be thought of as merely accidental interruptions to a social development which steadily advances in spite of them. The deeper anxiety of our time arises from a doubt, more or less clearly realized, as to whether that development is itself proceeding on right lines. Coming back to London after a visit to a place where a simpler form of life is still in some degree possible, we notice from a fresh point of view the men and women who hurry with us out of the trains or bend over ledgers in banks and offices or stand, tired and vacant, outside factories at the dinner-hour. We see some few who seem to have found an environment that fits them. One has perhaps been taken on as an assistant porter at King's Cross and is irradiated, not only with confidence in his own future but with a glorious sense of identity between himself and the Great Northern Railway. Such faces are, however, rare exceptions. Of the rest, not many are consciously unhappy, but there are strangely few signs of that harmony of the whole being which constitutes happiness. Even the parks and picture galleries and libraries and the other mitigations of the new environment, for which during the rest of the year we are working and voting, seem to us, for the moment, to be tragically inadequate.

Those who have watched the more rapid change from the old to the new in the East describe themselves as having the same feeling in a sharper form. A Hindu peasant, who exchanges the penury and uncertainty of village agriculture for the steadier work and better pay of a Bombay cotton factory, never looks, they say, as if he had thereby attained greater satisfaction for the inner needs of his nature. Lafcadio Hearn wrote in 1894, when the resolute determination of the Japanese to enter the Great Society was already beginning to take effect, "The new Japan will be richer and stronger and in many things wiser, but it will neither be so happy nor so kindly as the old."

VI

Our fathers, under the influence of Herbert Spencer and the popular science of 1850, could trust that, even if the members of a single generation should find it difficult to adapt their nervous structure to the new conditions, yet that adaptation, when once it had been achieved by habit, would be handed on to succeeding generations by biological inheritance. The biologists of our time, however, have forced us to realize that such "acquired characteristics" are not inherited. Each generation, except in so far as we create, by selective breeding, a somewhat different human type, will start, we are told, in essentials, not where their fathers left off, but where their fathers began. Why should we expect a social organization to endure which has been formed in a moment of time by human beings whose bodies and minds are the result of age-long selection under far different conditions?

The problem of the Great Society has not been solved by the vast increase in wealth which trade and a world-wide division have produced. Neither the cash nexus nor the right to vote are sufficient to hold together the widely dispersed social units of which the modern world is composed.

VII

Social organization on a large scale is not a wholly new thing. For certain restricted purposes—chiefly, the levying of taxes and the gathering of armies—the empires of Assyria, Persia, and Rome organized men on a scale not less than that of a modern state. Any one of those empires, at the moment of its greatest efficiency, must have seemed to the statesmen who were directing it from the center to fulfil all the conditions of permanency. Each of them possessed not only irresistible military power but a monopoly of all means of rapid communication and the control of the only important body of accumulated wealth in the world which they knew. Yet the systems which created these powerful cohesive forces created, at the same time, disruptive forces which proved even more powerful. As the ancient empires became larger, they became too distant and too unreal to stimulate the affection or pride of their subjects. The methods of their agents became more mechanical and inhuman, and the passions which grouped themselves around smaller units, local or racial or religious, produced an ever increasing inner strain.

VIII

Are there any signs of such an inner strain resulting from the size and impersonal power of the Great Society? Has the invention of representative government, as its advocates used to argue, prevented the forces of class or race or religion or self from ever again thrusting against the larger cohesion of the state? Not one who tries to interpret the obscure feelings of half-articulate men and women will say so. France is a representative republic, and that republic is supported by a stronger feeling of political solidarity than is to be found in any other European nation. But who can be sure that the forces represented by the "sabotage" of the French railway servants or the turbulence of the vinegrowers are declining? In America the racial and class feeling of the new immigrants shows itself unexpectedly resistant to the dissolving force of national consciousness. In England the "particularism" of trades and professions and the racial feeling of Wales or Ulster, of Scotland or Catholic Ireland, seem to be growing stronger and not weaker.

More threatening still to the cohesion of the Great Society are the motives openly avowed by some of the American and European masters of concentrated capital—the men who direct enormous social power without attempting to form a social purpose, who smash working-class unions with no idea of any system to take their place, who boast that their trade is their politics and corrupt whole parties merely to increase the personal wealth which they will waste in making or buying things they hardly desire. The "cash nexus" has, no more than the "voting nexus," insured that common membership of the Great Society shall mean a common interest in its solidarity.

If one looks from the forces acting within the separate states to the forces which bear upon that relation between states without which world industry and world commerce cannot exist, one sees there, too, that the men who claim to voice in England or in Germany the living human passions stand not for European unity but for European disruption.

When, indeed, one gets behind the mechanical arrangements of railways and telegraphs or of laws and treaties and elections, what are the real forces on which our hopes of national or international solidarity depend? One remembers afternoons spent conversing on the streets of a modern city, and the words and looks which showed how weak are the feelings which attach the citizen to a society whose power he dimly recognizes but which he often seems to think of merely with distrust and dislike.

And if, once more, we turn away from Europe and the United States to the beginning of the Great Society in South America or China, the question as to whether the new system is creating sufficient cohesive force to insure its own permanence becomes even more difficult to answer with confident hope.

But, owing to the very complexity of the relations which bind us to the Great Society, we stand to lose much more by any failure in its cohesion than did the subjects of the ancient empires. Up until our own time the vast majority of the inhabitants of the world lived in little, almost self-supporting villages. If an empire broke up, some of these villages might be wasted by war, but the rest, like the cells of a divided rotifer, grouped themselves easily enough as part of a new body. If, at the capital of the empire, a population had been brought together which depended on a more intricate form of social organization, that population was destroyed or scattered. Some day the Assyriologists will reconstruct for us the industrial and financial system which enabled the inhabitants of Nineveh or Babylon to be fed and employed, and we shall then be able to imagine the sufferings which left those cities mere piles of ruins surrounded by a few peasants' huts. When the corn-ships of Egypt and the tribute-money of Gaul and Spain ceased to come to Rome, the population of that city declined from about a million to perhaps a third of that number. But now, thirty-five out of the forty-five million inhabitants of the United Kingdom depend for their food upon a system of world relations far more complex than that which was built up by Assyria or Rome for the supply of their capitals.

It is by imagining the effect of an actual dissolution of this Great Society that we can make most clear to ourselves the nature of our fears for its future. But, even if the forces of cohesion and dissolution remain as evenly balanced as they are now, our prospects are dark enough. The human material of our social machinery will continue to disintegrate just at the points where strength is most urgently required. Men whom we are compelled to trust will continue to prefer the smaller to the larger good. The director will sacrifice the interest of his shareholders to his own or that of his family; the statesman will sacrifice his country to his party or his constituency or his church; the Concert of Europe will remain helpless because each of its constituent nations refuses to work for the good of the whole. And the results of a system which we are not strong enough either to remodel or to control will continue to be seen in the slum and the sweatshop, the barracks and the base hospitals.

Throughout the politics and literature of the twentieth century one traces this fear, conscious or half-conscious, lest the civilization which we have adopted so rapidly and with so little forethought may prove unable to secure either a harmonious life for its members or even its own stability. The old delight in the "manifest finger of destiny" and "the tide of progress"—even the newer belief in the effortless "evolution" of social institutions—is gone. We are afraid of the blind forces to which we used so willingly to surrender ourselves. We feel that we must reconsider the basis of our organized life because, without reconsideration, we have no chance of controlling it. Our philosophers are toiling to refashion for the purposes of social life the systems which used so confidently to offer guidance for individual conduct. Our poets and playwrights and novelists are revolutionizing their art in the attempt to bring the essential facts of the Great Society within its range.

All these efforts run counter to the intellectual habits in which our generation was brought up. On its intellectual side the Great Society was the work of specialists. During its formation we and our fathers learned to admire the leaders of specialized sciences—the chemists who are "wakeful to make clean the furnace" and the biologists "whose discourse is of the stock of bulls." Each of them became "wise in his own work."

We are forced, however, now to recognize that a society whose intellectual direction consists only of unrelated specialisms must drift and that we dare not drift any longer. We stand, as the Greek thinkers stood, in a new world. And because that world is new, we feel that neither the sectional observations of the special student nor the ever accumulating records of the past nor the narrow experience of the practical man nor the technological devices of science—not even the techniques of this new social science—can suffice us.

The task of missions has been to create from the existing social and cultural units a common culture and a moral solidarity in which all can share. Incidentally, they have made themselves the intermediaries and the interpreters of the peoples in the Great Society to one another.

In learning the languages and constructing the grammar of the widely dispersed peoples of the earth they have removed the most important barrier to those common understandings which are the essence of cultures, and they have thus laid the foundation for a moral order that includes all peoples, since the existence of such common tradition and its transmission from one people to another and from one generation to another depends upon intimate and personal communication.

What seems to have held the ancient empires together, enabling them to survive the external shocks and the internal convulsions which threatened their existence, was less the wisdom or the prestige of the ruling caste which directed their destinies than the possession by the diverse nations and peoples involved of a body of common customs and fundamental beliefs in accordance with which they sought to direct their individual and collective lives—that is to say, a common culture and a common religion.

The English schools and the English church perform similar functions for the British Empire, the same function that the Mikado and Shintoism perform for the Japanese people. In each case the political organization of the empires has been sustained in the past by their religious, moral, and cultural order, which insures a common understanding and a loyalty to the common purpose and program.

The process by which the ancient empires were finally dissolved has been variously described as one of urbanization or of secularization. In the course of this process what had once been sacred ceased to be inspiring, and the loyalties and the moral solidarity which held these great societies dissolved.

In the present state of the world the Christian religion seems predestined to perform for Europe and the Great Society, of which it is the center and the core, what it once performed for the Roman world when that world was similarly disturbed and disrupted by the conflicts and disorders which the expansion of the Roman Empire had brought about.

In this situation the task of Christian missions seems to have been to create a moral solidarity among the nations and peoples that will permit European civilization and the Great Society which it has brought into existence to survive.

Christian missions have already done something to achieve this end, it seems, incidental to the propaganda which different forms of European Christianity have carried on in the effort to extend the influence of the various branches of Christianity to all other parts of the world.

IX

Missions have already done something to relieve the tensions of the Great Society and to create a solidarity that would enable it to survive the convulsions through which it is now passing.

1. Modern civilization, merely because of the size of the social unit it has created, has effectively changed the functioning not only of economic institutions but of every other type of social institution.

One consequence of the size of the Great Society is this: As the web of human relations has become more extensive, mobility has increased, and personal and moral relations have become more casual, promiscuous, and secular. Everywhere the diffusion of European culture has been accompanied by an increasing relaxation of the familial and tribal bonds which formerly, in some fashion, held society together and maintained, without the benefit of police or the courts, some sort of discipline.

Everywhere the diffusion of European culture has tended to plow under the local and traditional religious beliefs and to substitute a secular for a religious social order.

The little religious sects which have sprung up so spontaneously and in such great numbers on the frontiers of European civilization, in the United States, and elsewhere it seems have, in some sense and to some degree, performed in the modern world the function of the clan, the tribal unit in more primitive societies.

These new sects seem to represent in most cases the pathetic attempts of lost souls to renew and recover a religious faith which they have somehow lost. Where they have found difficulty or failed, it seems to be because they have been, for the most part, recruited by converts from racially and culturally heterogeneous groups. They are, like the Mormons or the Seventh-Day Adventists or the Christian Scientists, recruited from peoples of essentially the same class rather than of the same race. The result is that the bonds which hold them together are ideological rather than those of race and kinship.

Nevertheless, in so far as they have been successful in bringing together these heterogeneous peoples into an effective society, they have measurably solved the race problem in the communities in which they were established. What the Baptists have accomplished in Burma is, perhaps, not wholly typical, but it represents what other missions have measurably achieved.

2. Missionaries have learned the languages of the peoples and have established schools in which they have made many or most of the so-called preliterate peoples literate in their mother-tongues. In this way they have given them access to the knowledge of literate peoples, lack of which has been mainly responsible for their so-called backwardness. This, alone, has done more than any other one thing to make the world which Mr. Willkie recently discovered to be so economically, politically, and culturally one.

This new literacy which the missionaries are responsible for has also brought into existence a considerable secular press among the so-called colonial peoples. Through this press these peoples have begun to pass their own independent comments upon the world in which they find themselves, and this is possibly a necessary preparation for any active co-operation on their part in the affairs of the world-after-the war, into which we seem to be moving very rapidly. The secular press and the incipient nationalism to which it seems to give expression are topics that must inevitably be touched upon in any discussion of missions in the modern world.

3. Missions have established not only schools but hospitals. This has given to a very large part of mankind the benefits of modern surgery and scientific medicine. The recent volume, *Burma Surgeon*, is a commentary on what missionaries, through their hospitals, are doing to bring about understanding in the modern world, in addition to whatever other services they may be performing. Through these agencies they are creating the sort of moral solidarity which seems to be the most pressing need of a Great Society.

4. These mission stations scattered all over the world have become through their schools and through their hospitals and other social units which they have established, what Mr. Willkie described them to be, outposts of European civilization where anyone and everyone may find people of good will and understanding, people who are capable of interpreting the colonial peoples of the world to the Europeans under whose cultural and political domination they so largely live.

The result of these and other missionary activities has made missions the instruments of a good-neighbor policy that is no longer continental merely but world wide.

PART IV *The Marginal Man*

Human MIGRATION AND THE MARGINAL MAN

STUDENTS of the great society, looking at mankind in the long perspective of history, have frequently been disposed to seek an explanation of existing cultural differences among races and peoples in some single dominating cause or condition. One school of thought, represented most conspicuously by Montesquieu, has found that explanation in climate and in the physical environment. Another school, identified with the name of Arthur de Gobineau, author of *The Inequality of Human Races*, has sought an explanation of divergent cultures in the innate qualities of races biologically inherited. These two theories have this in common, namely, that they both conceive civilization and society to be the result of evolutionary processes—processes by which man has acquired new inheritable traits —rather than processes by which new relations have been established between men.

In contrast to both of these, Frederick Teggart has recently restated and amplified what may be called the catastrophic theory of civilization, a theory that goes back to Hume in England, and to Turgot in France. From this point of view, climate and innate racial traits, important as they may have been in the evolution of races, have been of only minor influence in creating existing cultural differences. In fact, races and cultures, so far from being in any sense identical—or even the product of similar conditions and forces—are perhaps to be set over against one another as contrast effects, the

The American Journal of Sociology XXXIII (May, 1928), no. 6, pp. 881-893.

results of antagonistic tendencies, so that civilization may be said to flourish at the expense of racial differences rather than to be conserved by them. At any rate, if it is true that races are the products of isolation and inbreeding, it is just as certain that civilization, on the other hand, is a consequence of contact and communication. The forces which have been decisive in the history of mankind are those which have brought men together in fruitful competition, conflict, and co-operation.

Among the most important of these influences have been—according to what I have called the catastrophic theory of progress—migration and the incidental collisions, conflicts, and fusions of people and cultures which they have occasioned.

"Every advance in culture," says Bücher, in his *Industrial Evolution*, "commences, so to speak, with a new period of wandering," and in support of this thesis he points out that the earlier forms of trade were migratory, that the first industries to free themselves from the household husbandry and become independent occupations were carried on itinerantly. "The great founders of religion, the earliest poets and philosophers, the musicians and actors of past epochs, are all great wanderers. Even today, do not the inventor, the preacher of a new doctrine, and the virtuoso travel from place to place in search of adherents and admirers—notwithstanding the immense recent development in the means of communicating information?"[1]

The influences of migrations have not been limited, of course, by the changes which they have effected in existing cultures. In the long run, they have determined the racial characteristics of historical peoples. "The whole teaching of ethnology," as Griffith Taylor remarks, "shows that peoples of mixed race are the rule and not the exception."[2] Every nation, upon examination, turns out to have been a more or less successful melting-pot. To this constant sifting of races and peoples, human geographers have given the title "the historical movement," because, as Miss Semple says in her volume *Influences of Geographic Environment*, "it underlies most written history and constitutes the major part of unwritten history, especially that of savage and nomadic tribes."[3]

Changes in race, it is true, do inevitably follow, at some distance,

---

[1] Carl Bücher, *Industrial Evolution*, p. 347.

[2] Griffith Taylor, *Environment and Race: A Study of the Evolution, Migration, Settlement, and Status of the Races of Men*, p. 336.

[3] Ellen Churchill Semple, *Influences of Geographic Environment*, p. 75.

changes in culture. The movements and mingling of peoples which bring rapid, sudden, and often catastrophic, changes in customs and habits are followed, in the course of time, as a result of interbreeding, by corresponding modifications in temperament and physique. There has probably never been an instance where races have lived together in the intimate contacts which a common economy enforces in which racial contiguity has not produced racial hybrids. However, changes in racial characteristics and in cultural traits proceed at very different rates, and it is notorious that cultural changes are not consolidated and transmitted biologically, or at least to only a very slight extent, if at all. Acquired characteristics are not biologically inherited.

Writers who emphasize the importance of migration as an agency of progress are invariably led to ascribe a similar rôle to war. Thus Waitz, commenting upon the rôle of migration as an agency of civilization, points out that migrations are "rarely of a peaceful nature at first." Of war he says: "The first consequence of war is that fixed relations are established between peoples, which render friendly intercourse possible, an intercourse which becomes more important from the interchange of knowledge and experience than from the mere interchange of commodities." [4] And then he adds:

> Whenever we see a people, of whatever degree of civilization, not living in contact and reciprocal action with others, we shall generally find a certain stagnation, a mental inertness, and a want of activity, which render any change of social and political condition next to impossible. These are, in times of peace, transmitted like an everlasting disease, and war appears then, in spite of what the apostles of peace may say, as a saving angel, who rouses the national spirit, and renders all forces more elastic.[5]

Among the writers who conceive the historical process in terms of intrusions, either peaceful or hostile, of one people into the domain of another, must be reckoned such sociologists as Gumplowicz and Oppenheimer. The former, in an effort to define the social process abstractly, has described it as the interaction of heterogeneous ethnic groups, the resulting subordination and superordination of races constituting the social order—society, in fact.

In much the same way, Oppenheimer, in his study of the sociological origin of the state, believes he has shown that in every instance the state has had its historical beginnings in the imposition, by

---

[4] Theodor Waitz, *Introduction to Anthropology*, p. 347.
[5] *Ibid.*, p. 348.

conquest and force, of the authority of a nomadic upon a sedentary and agricultural people. The facts which Oppenheimer has gathered to sustain his thesis show, at any rate, that social institutions have actually, in many instances at least, come into existence abruptly by a mutation, rather than by a process of evolutionary selection and the gradual accumulation of relatively slight variations.[6]

It is not at once apparent why a theory which insists upon the importance of catastrophic change in the evolution of civilization should not at the same time take some account of revolution as a factor in progress. If peace and stagnation, as Waitz suggests, tend to assume the form of a social disease; if, as Sumner says, "society needs to have some ferment in it" to break up this stagnation and emancipate the energies of individuals imprisoned within an existing social order; it seems that some "adventurous folly" like the crusades of the middle ages, or some romantic enthusiasm like that which found expression in the French Revolution, or in the more recent Bolshevist adventure in Russia, might serve quite as effectively as either migration or war to interrupt the routine of existing habit and break the cake of custom. Revolutionary doctrines are naturally based upon a conception of catastrophic rather than of evolutionary change. Revolutionary strategy, as it has been worked out and rationalized in Sorel's *Reflections on Violence*, makes the great catastrophe, the general strike, an article of faith. As such it becomes a means of maintaining morale and enforcing discipline in the revolutionary masses.[7]

The first and most obvious difference between revolution and migration is that in migration the breakdown of social order is initiated by the impact of an invading population, and completed by the contact and fusion of native with alien peoples. In the case of the former, revolutionary ferment and the forces which have disrupted society have ordinarily had, or seem to have had, their sources and origins mainly if not wholly within, rather than without, the society affected. It is doubtful whether it can be successfully maintained that every revolution, every *Aufklärung*, every intellectual awakening and renaissance has been and will be provoked by some invading population movement or by the intrusion of some alien cultural agency. At least it seems as if some modification of this view is necessary, since

    [6] Franz Oppenheimer, *The State: Its History and Development Viewed Sociologically* (1914).

    [7] Georges Sorel, *Reflections on Violence* (New York, 1914).

with the growth of commerce and communication there is progressively and relatively more movement and less migration. Commerce, in bringing the ends of the earth together, has made travel relatively secure. Moreover, with the development of machine industry and the growth of cities, it is the commodities rather than men which circulate. The peddler, who carries his stock on his back, gives way to the traveling salesman, and the catalogue of the mail order house now reaches remote regions which even the Yankee peddler rarely if ever penetrated. With the development of a world-economy and the interpenetration of peoples, migrations, as Bücher has pointed out, have changed their character:

The migrations occurring at the opening of the history of European peoples are migrations of whole tribes, a pushing and pressing of collective units from east to west which lasted for centuries. The migrations of the Middle Ages ever affect individual classes alone; the knights in the crusades, the merchants, the wage craftsmen, the journeymen hand-workers, the jugglers and minstrels, the villeins seeking protection within the walls of a town. Modern migrations, on the contrary, are generally a matter of private concern, the individuals being led by the most varied motives. They are almost invariably without organization. The process repeating itself daily a thousand times is united only through the one characteristic, that it is everywhere a question of change of locality by persons seeking more favourable conditions of life.[8]

Migration, which was formerly an invasion, followed by the forcible displacement or subjugation of one people by another, has assumed the character of a peaceful penetration. Migration of peoples has, in other words, been transmuted into mobility of individuals, and the wars which these movements so frequently occasioned have assumed the character of internecine struggles, of which strikes and revolutions are to be regarded as types.

Furthermore, if one were to attempt to reckon with all the forms in which catastrophic changes take place, it would be necessary to include the changes that are effected by the sudden rise of some new religious movement like Mohammedanism or Christianity, both of which began as schismatic and sectarian movements, and which by extension and internal evolution have become independent religions. Looked at from this point of view, migration assumes a character less unique and exceptional than has hitherto been conceived by the writers whom the problem has most intrigued. It appears as one, merely, of a series of forms in which historic changes may take place.

---

[8] Carl Bücher, *op. cit.*, p. 349.

Nevertheless, regarded abstractly as a type of collective action, human migration exhibits everywhere characteristics that are sufficiently typical to make it a subject of independent investigation and study, both in respect to its form and in respect to the effects which it produces.

Migration is not, however, to be identified with mere movement. It involves, at the very least, change of residence and the breaking of home ties. The movements of gypsies and other pariah peoples, because they bring about no important changes in cultural life, are to be regarded rather as a geographical fact than a social phenomenon. Nomadic life is stabilized on the basis of movement, and even though gypsies now travel by automobile, they still maintain, comparatively unchanged, their ancient tribal organization and customs. The result is that their relation to the communities in which they may at any time be found is to be described as symbiotic rather than social. This tends to be true of any section or class of the population—the hobos, for example, and the hotel dwellers—which is unsettled and mobile.

Migration as a social phenomenon must be studied not merely in its grosser effects, as manifested in changes in custom and in the mores, but it may be envisaged in its subjective aspects as manifested in the changed type of personality which it produces. When the traditional organization of society breaks down, as a result of contact and collision with a new invading culture, the effect is, so to speak, to emancipate the individual man. Energies that were formerly controlled by custom and tradition are released. The individual is free for new adventures, but he is more or less without direction and control. Teggart's statement of the matter is as follows:

As a result of the breakdown of customary modes of action and of thought, the individual experiences a "release" from the restraints and constraints to which he has been subject, and gives evidence of this "release" in aggressive self-assertion. The overexpression of individuality is one of the marked features of all epochs of change. On the other hand, the study of the psychological effects of collision and contact between different groups reveals the fact that the most important aspect of "release" lies not in freeing the soldier, warrior, or berserker from the restraint of conventional modes of action, but in freeing the individual judgment from the inhibitions of conventional modes of thought. It will thus be seen [he adds] that the study of the *modus operandi* of change in time gives a common focus to the efforts of political historians, of the historians of literature and of ideas, of psychologists, and of students of ethics and the theory of education.[9]

---

[9] Frederick J. Teggart, *Theory of History*, p. 196.

Social changes, according to Teggart, have their inception in events which "release" the individuals out of which society is composed. Inevitably, however, this release is followed in the course of time by the reintegration of the individuals so released into a new social order. In the meantime, however, certain changes take place—at any rate they are likely to take place—in the character of the individuals themselves. They become, in the process, not merely emancipated, but enlightened.

The emancipated individual invariably becomes in a certain sense and to a certain degree a cosmopolitan. He learns to look upon the world in which he was born and bred with something of the detachment of a stranger. He acquires, in short, an intellectual bias. Simmel has described the position of the stranger in the community, and his personality, in terms of movement and migration.

"If wandering," he says, "considered as the liberation from every given point in space, is the conceptual opposite of fixation at any point, then surely the sociological form of the stranger presents the union of both of these specifications." The stranger stays, but he is not settled. He is a potential wanderer. That means that he is not bound as others are by the local proprieties and conventions. "He is the freer man, practically and theoretically. He views his relation to others with less prejudice; he submits them to more general, more objective standards, and he is not confined in his action by custom, piety or precedents."

The effect of mobility and migration is to secularize relations which were formerly sacred. One may describe the process, in its dual aspect, perhaps, as the secularization of society and the individuation of the person. For a brief, vivid, and authentic picture of the way in which migration of the earlier sort, the migration of a people, has, in fact, brought about the destruction of an earlier civilization and liberated the peoples involved for the creation of a later, more secular, and freer society, I suggest Gilbert Murray's introduction to *The Rise of the Greek Epic*, in which he seeks to reproduce the events of the Nordic invasion of the Aegean area.

What ensued, he says, was a period of chaos:

A chaos in which an old civilization is shattered into fragments, its laws set at naught, and that intricate web of normal expectation which forms the very essence of human society torn so often and so utterly by continued disappointment that at last there ceases to be any normal expectation at all. For the fugitive settlers on the shores that were afterwards

Ionia, and for parts too of Doris and Aeolis, there were no tribal gods or tribal obligations left, because there were no tribes. There were no old laws, because there was no one to administer or even to remember them; only such compulsions as the strongest power of the moment chose to enforce. Household and family life had disappeared, and all its innumerable ties with it. A man was now not living with a wife of his own race, but with a dangerous strange woman, of alien language and alien gods, a woman whose husband or father he had perhaps murdered—or, at best, whom he had bought as a slave from the murderer. The old Aryan husbandman, as we shall see hereafter, had lived with his herds in a sort of familiar connexion. He slew "his brother the ox" only under special stress or for definite religious reasons, and he expected his women to weep when the slaying was performed. But now he had left his own herds far away. They had been devoured by enemies. And he lived on the beasts of strangers whom he robbed or held in servitude. He had left the graves of his fathers, the kindly ghosts of his own blood, who took food from his hand and loved him. He was surrounded by the graves of alien dead, strange ghosts whose names he knew not, and who were beyond his power to control, whom he tried his best to placate with fear and aversion. One only concrete thing existed for him to make henceforth the centre of his allegience, to supply the place of his old family hearth, his gods, his tribal customs and sanctities. It was a circuit wall of stones, a *Polis;* the wall which he and his fellows, men of diverse tongues and worships united by a tremendous need, had built up to be the one barrier between themselves and a world of enemies.[10]

It was within the walls of the *polis* and in this mixed company that Greek civilization was born. The whole secret of ancient Greek life, its relative freedom from the grosser superstitions and from fear of the gods, is bound up, we are told, with this period of transition and chaos, in which the older primitive world perished and from which the freer, more enlightened social order sprang into existence. Thought is emancipated, philosophy is born, public opinion sets itself up as an authority as over against tradition and custom. As Guyot puts it, "The Greek with his festivals, his songs, his poetry, seems to celebrate, in a perpetual hymn, the liberation of man from the mighty fetters of nature." [11]

What took place in Greece first has since taken place in the rest of Europe and is now going on in America. The movement and migration of peoples, the expansion of trade and commerce, and particularly the growth, in modern times, of these vast melting-pots of races and

---

10 Gilbert Murray, *The Rise of the Greek Epic*, pp. 78-79.
11 A. H. Guyot, *Earth and Man* (Boston, 1857), cited by Franklin Thomas, *The Environmental Basis of Society* (New York, 1921), p. 205.

cultures, the metropolitan cities, has loosened local bonds, destroyed the cultures of tribe and folk, and substituted for the local loyalties the freedom of the cities; for the sacred order of tribal custom, the rational organization which we call civilization.

In these great cities, where all the passions, all the energies of mankind are released, we are in position to investigate the processes of civilization, as it were, under a microscope.

It is in the cities that the old clan and kinship groups are broken up and replaced by social organization based on rational interests and temperamental predilections. It is in the cities, more particularly, that the grand division of labor is effected which permits and more or less compels the individual man to concentrate his energies and his talents on the particular task he is best fitted to perform, and in this way emancipates him and his fellows from the control of nature and circumstance which so thoroughly dominates primitive man.

It happens, however, that the process of acculturation and assimilation and the accompanying amalgamation of racial stocks does not proceed with the same ease and the same speed in all cases. Particularly where peoples who come together are of divergent cultures and widely different racial stocks, assimilation and amalgamation do not take place so rapidly as they do in other cases. All our so-called racial problems grow out of situations in which assimilation and amalgamation do not take place at all, or take place very slowly. As I have said elsewhere, the chief obstacle to the cultural assimilation of races is not their different mental, but rather their divergent physical traits. It is not because of the mentality of the Japanese that they do not so easily assimilate as do the Europeans. It is because

the Japanese bears in his features a distinctive racial hallmark, that he wears, so to speak, a racial uniform which classifies him. He cannot become a mere individual, indistinguishable in the cosmopolitan mass of the population, as is true, for example, of the Irish, and, to a lesser extent, of some of the other immigrant races. The Japanese, like the Negro, is condemned to remain among us an abstraction, a symbol—and a symbol not merely of his own race but of the Orient and of that vague, ill-defined menace we sometimes refer to as the "yellow peril." [12]

Under such circumstances peoples of different racial stocks may live side by side in a relation of symbiosis, each playing a rôle in a common economy, but not interbreeding to any great extent; each

---

[12] "Racial Assimilation in Secondary Groups," *Publications of the American Sociological Society*, Vol. VIII (1914), p. 71.

maintaining, like the gypsy or the pariah peoples of India, a more or less complete tribal organization or society of their own. Such was the situation of the Jew in Europe up to modern times, and a somewhat similar relation exists today between the native white and the Hindu populations in Southeast Africa and in the West Indies.

In the long run, however, peoples and races who live together, sharing in the same economy, inevitably interbreed, and in this way if in no other, the relations which were merely co-operative and economic become social and cultural. When migration leads to conquest, either economic or political, assimilation is inevitable. The conquering peoples impose their culture and their standards upon the conquered, and there follows a period of cultural endosmosis.

Sometimes relations between the conquering and the conquered peoples take the form of slavery; sometimes they assume the form, as in India, of a system of caste. But in either case the dominant and the subject peoples become, in time, integral parts of one society. Slavery and caste are merely forms of accommodation, in which the race problem finds a temporary solution. The case of the Jews was different. Jews never were a subject people, at least not in Europe. They were never reduced to the position of an inferior caste. In their ghettos in which they first elected, and then were forced, to live, they preserved their own tribal traditions and their cultural, if not their political, independence. The Jew who left the ghetto did not escape; he deserted and became that execrable object, an apostate. The relation of the ghetto Jew to the larger community in which he lived was, and to some extent still is, symbiotic rather than social.

When, however, the walls of the medieval ghetto were torn down and the Jew was permitted to participate in the cultural life of the peoples among whom he lived, there appeared a new type of personality, namely, a cultural hybrid, a man living and sharing intimately in the cultural life and traditions of two distinct peoples; never quite willing to break, even if he were permitted to do so, with his past and his traditions, and not quite accepted, because of racial prejudice, in the new society in which he now sought to find a place. He was a man on the margin of two cultures and two societies, which never completely interpenetrated and fused. The emancipated Jew was, and is, historically and typically the marginal man, the first cosmopolite and citizen of the world. He is, par excellence, the "stranger," whom Simmel, himself a Jew, has described with such profound insight and understanding in his *Sociologie*. Most if not all the characteristics of the Jew, certainly his pre-eminence as a trader and his keen intellectual interest, his sophistication, his idealism and lack of historic sense, are the characteristics of the city man, the man who ranges widely, lives preferably in a hotel—in short, the cosmopolite. The autobiographies of Jewish immigrants, of which a great number have been published in America in recent years, are all different versions of the same story—the story of the marginal man; the man who, emerging from the ghetto in which he lived in Europe, is seeking to find a place in the freer, more complex and cosmopolitan life of an American city. One may learn from these autobiographies how the process of assimilation actually takes place in the individual immigrant. In the more sensitive minds its effects are as profound and as disturbing as some of the religious conversions of which William James has given us so classical an account in his *Varieties of Religious Experience.* In these immigrant autobiographies the conflict of cultures, as it takes place in the mind of the immigrant, is just the conflict of "the divided self," the old self and the new. And frequently there is no satisfying issue of this conflict, which often terminates in a profound disillusionment, as described, for example, in Lewisohn's autobiography *Up Stream.* But Lewisohn's restless wavering between the warm security of the ghetto, which he has abandoned, and the cold freedom of the outer world, in which he is not yet quite at home, is typical. A century earlier, Heinrich Heine, torn with the same conflicting loyalties, struggling to be at the same time a German and a Jew, enacted a similar rôle. It was, according to his latest biographer, the secret and the tragedy of Heine's life that circumstance condemned him to live in two worlds, in neither of which he ever quite belonged. It was this that embittered his intellectual life and gave to his writings that character of spiritual conflict and instability which, as Browne says, is evidence of "spiritual distress." His mind lacked the integrity which is based on conviction: "His arms were weak"—to continue the quotation—"because his mind was divided; his hands were nerveless because his soul was in turmoil."

Something of the same sense of moral dichotomy and conflict is probably characteristic of every immigrant during the period of transition, when old habits are being discarded and new ones are not yet formed. It is inevitably a period of inner turmoil and intense self-consciousness.

There are no doubt periods of transition and crisis in the lives of most of us that are comparable with those which the immigrant experiences when he leaves home to seek his fortunes in a strange country. But in the case of the marginal man the period of crisis is relatively permanent. The result is that he tends to become a personality type. Ordinarily the marginal man is a mixed blood, like the Mulatto in the United States or the Eurasian in Asia, but that is apparently because the man of mixed blood is one who lives in two worlds, in both of which he is more or less of a stranger. The Christian convert in Asia or in Africa exhibits many if not most of the characteristics of the marginal man—the same spiritual instability, intensified self-consciousness, restlessness, and *malaise*.

It is in the mind of the marginal man that the moral turmoil which new cultural contacts occasion, manifests itself in the most obvious forms. It is in the mind of the marginal man—where the changes and fusions of culture are going on—that we can best study the processes of civilization and of progress.

CHAPTER 27

PERSONALITY AND CULTURAL CONFLICT

A SURVEY of current conceptions of personality indicates that they fall, roughly, into three categories: (1) the physiological, (2) the psychological, (3) the sociological or sociopsychological, according as they envisage and emphasize one or another of the various aspects in which personalities present themselves to our observation.

Physiologically, the personality seems to be identical with organism, in so far, at least, as the organism is integrated and organized for action. Child, for example, in his volume *The Physiological Foundations for Behavior*, describes "organismic behavior," in terms that are identical with those Watson uses to describe what he regards the proper subject of psychological study, namely, "the behavior of the organism of the whole, as distinguished from the behavior of single parts."

The behaviorist, says Watson, "is interested in the behavior of the whole man," and the whole man, he adds, "is an assembled organic machine ready to run." "Personality is but the end-product of our habit systems." [1]

Personality as conceived by traditional as well as by medical and clinical psychology tends to identify personality with the ego and the self. Behavior, from the psychologist's point of view, becomes "self-expression." The organism, thus conceived, is not merely condi-

---

Publication of the American Sociological Society, Vol. XXV (May, 1931), pp. 95-110.
[1] J. B. Watson, *Behaviorism* (New York, 1930), pp. 15-69, 274.

tioned but controlled. The ego surveys its past, reflects upon it, and projects itself into the future.

"If I know the goal of a person," says Adler, "I know, in a general way what will happen. . . . If I am acquainted only with the causes, know only the reflexes, the reaction times, the ability to repeat, and such facts, I am aware of nothing that actually takes place in the soul of man." [2]

Man, as contrasted with the lower animals, lives in a world of time. He is, as has been said, a "time-binding animal." His actions are controlled, not merely by reflections upon his past, but by his hopes of his future; by his fear of hell and his hope of heaven. Memory, imagination, and phantasy add, in the case of man as contrasted with the lower animals, a new dimension to the world in which he lives.

Man is not merely conscious, but he is self-conscious, and the conception which the individual makes of himself becomes eventually the most important constituent of his personality. It becomes, for one thing, the object of what McDougall calls his "self-regarding sentiments." Honor, reputation, and self-respect, status, in short, become to him, finally, more important than life itself.

It is this conception that man forms of his self, furthermore, which seems to constitute what Freud has described as the "censor." This censorship is responsible, on the one hand, for the "repressions" with which the psychoanalysts are mainly concerned, and, on the other hand, for the "dissociations" to which Janet and his associates have almost exclusively devoted their attention.[3]

The sociological conception of personality, so far as sociologists have formulated any independent conceptions of their own, may be said to take its departure from the observations of Thomas and Znaniecki that "personality is the subjective aspect of culture." The customs of the community inevitably become the habits of the individuals who compose it. The individual invariably incorporates, in his own personality, the purposes and aims that find expression in the institutions by which the individual's conduct is controlled. In other words, the individual is not born human but the character we describe as human is for each of us a personal achievement. Each one of us acquires a personality in his effort to find a place and play a rôle in

---

[2] Alfred Adler, *The Practice and Theory of Individual Psychology* (New York, 1929), p. 3.

[3] R. E. Gordon, *The Neurotic Personality* (New York, 1927), p. 50.

some society, and in the various and more or less integrated social groups of which that society is composed—first of all in the family and the local community and later in the larger, freer, and more impersonal world of politics and of professional and business affairs.

What may be described as the processes of socialization—competition, conflict, accommodation, and assimilation—are therefore not merely the processes by which an individual is incorporated into a society, but they are the processes by which the individual, in achieving social status, becomes not merely a human being but a person. That is to say, an individual, conscious of rights and duties and more or less concerned about the common welfare of the group to which he belongs.

It is evident that the person as here described is more or less of an artifact, an ideal construction and, in short, a conceptual rather than an empirical entity. But it is just the possession of this conception that makes the behavior of individuals differ from that of the lower animals. It is just this that makes the difference between the personality of human beings and the personality of animals, if, indeed, we are willing to attribute personality to brutes.

There seems to be no reason to deny the existence in animals of many, if not most, of the traits, that are ordinarily regarded as human. In fact, any organism may be said to exhibit personality traits if we limit the term personality to its purely physiological aspects. Certain animals seem to have, as a matter of fact, a certain degree of self-consciousness. The peacock and the turkey gobbler, for example, when they are naïvely sunning themselves in their reflection of their own glory, are the very image of that self-regarding sentiment called vanity. Most of us who are intimately acquainted with dogs are able to recognize differences in the behavior of individuals that we are disposed to describe as differences of personality, although these differences seem, on the whole, to be the traits of a variety or a species rather than of individual animals.

If the humbler creatures do have personalities, they can, nevertheless, hardly be described as persons because they have no aims in life, no ideals, ambitions; they are neither self-respecting nor respected, are concerned neither about their reputations nor their souls. In fact, we may say of the lower animals what we sometimes say of a certain class of Bohemians and artists, that they have temperament but no character. Inconsistency, according to Thomas and Znaniecki, is the essential feature of the Bohemian's activity.⁴ Character, on the other hand, is nothing if not consistent.

A character, as the term is here used, is not identical with habit. The essence of character, as Robach defines it, is consistency.⁵ But Robach describes consistency as the "ability to perform acts and to refrain from them in accordance with rational principles." It is character and consistency which distinguishes man from the lower animals.

It is this that permits us to say of man that he not only lives, as do the lower animals, from hand to mouth and from day to day, but he may, and in most cases does, achieve a career. Not only are his impulses controlled with reference to the individual acts, but his acts are controlled and directed toward some goal that exists in his imagination and is based upon his memory of past acts. Consistent behavior, in the sense in which Robach uses that term, may be described as conduct.

Conduct, as distinguished from the more general term behavior, has a moral connotation. Sociology, so far as its interests are theoretic rather than practical, is not concerned with morals as such. It is, however, peculiarly interested in behavior that is sanctioned and that has, as I have said, a moral connotation. Most human actions—even so natural and irresistible an action as sneezing—are sanctioned in some society—and relatively few of man's actions are wholly natural and naïve.

We may express the matter by saying that human beings, as distinguished from the lowlier creatures, are sophisticated. There is always an element of convention, sophistication, and artifice in the behavior of human beings. This is probably due to the fact that human beings habitually live in two worlds, an actual and an ideal, a present and a future; because the individual's conception of himself invariably assumes a more or less conventional pattern, and is based quite as much on conditions that are prospective and hoped for as upon conditions that are actual and present. The result is that the individual is always consciously or unconsciously playing a rôle. He is an actor, with one eye always on the gallery. In the society of other members of the species, he puts on a front, acquires manners and a style and dresses for the part he is expected to play.

---

⁴ W. I. Thomas and Florian Znaniecki, *The Polish Peasant in Europe and America* (Boston, 1919), III, p. 29.

⁵ A. A. Robach, *The Psychology of Character* (New York, 1927), pp. 158, 192.

It is part of the art of life, particularly in a stable and ceremonious society, to maintain under all circumstances the appropriate attitudes; to preserve at all hazards the social conventions; and to behave always and everywhere in the expected manner. Thus the conventions of society enter into the very fiber of the individual's personality. It is therefore a mistake, as Dewey says, to think of the individual's personal habits as his private possession. "Personal traits are functions of social situations." [6]

Considering that man lives so largely in the minds of other men, and is so responsive to the attitudes and emotions of those about him, it is nevertheless true that he is rather less dependent upon his environment, that is to say, the world to which he is oriented, than other animals. He maintains, as over against other individuals—their attitudes and their claims—a certain degree of reserve. It is only in states of exultation and of ecstasy that he lets himself go completely, and yields himself wholly to the occasion and to the influences of the persons about him.

Ordinarily he is able by means of his rationalizations, his cynicism, and his casuistry, to defend himself against the psychic assaults which the presence of other persons makes upon him. He can, when he chooses, make his manners a cloak and his face a mask, behind which he is able to preserve a certain amount of inner freedom even while mingling freely with other persons. He can withdraw from the world on occasion, and men have always consciously and unconsciously devised means for maintaining social distances and of preserving their independence of thought even when they were unable to maintain their independence of action. And this fact is just as significant and as characteristic a trait of human behavior as is the opposite disposition to respond to every change in the social atmosphere of the world about him.

It is for this reason, as much as for any other, that man invariably builds himself somewhere and at some time a home, a retreat, a refuge, where, surrounded by his family and his friends, he can relax and, so far as it is possible for so gregarious a creature, be wholly at home and at ease, and in more or less complete possession of his own soul. This is no more than to say that most men and some women possess a sales resistance which not even the magic of the new salesmanship can always overcome. [7]

---

[6] John Dewey, *Human Nature and Conduct* (New York, 1922), pp. 16, 20.
[7] See William James, *Psychology* (New York), I, p. 312.

The fact, that every individual, with any personality at all, is able to maintain a certain amount of personal reserve and to offer some resistance to the claims of other persons, does not alter the fact that he is at the same time under the necessity of integrating his actions and making them consistent with some recognized rule of life, not only in response to the expectations of other individuals and to the conventions of the society in which he lives, but also in the interest of the ends that he as an individual chooses to pursue.

Consistency and conformity is naturally in the interest of social solidarity and peace, even if it is not favorable to intellectual life and social progress. It is, at any rate, of first importance, if indivduals are to live together, that they should know what to expect of one another. The normal expectation of mankind is finally the basis of all law and order, and that is no doubt the justification for that maxim of Anglo-Saxon law which says that it is more important that the law should be consistent than that it should be just. On the other hand, it is just this necessity for consistency in human behavior under the conditions of a changing communal and social life that is responsible for those internal conflicts, mental worries, and perils of the soul, so characteristic of human beings but unknown to the other species.

The psychoanalysts are probably quite right when they say that "neurosis is one of man's ways of meeting various difficulties in his relations to his fellow-man" and that study of these pathological conditions in the individual cannot be undertaken "without throwing light also on the inner nature and meaning of the social institutions themselves in regard to which the difficulties have arisen." [8]

One of the institutions which the study of pathological conditions in the individual seems to illuminate is the family. It was an anthropologist, by the way, who seems to have been the first to call attention to the importance of this fact. Malinowski, in his volume, *Sex Repression in Savage Society*, describes the psychoanalytic doctrine as "essentially a theory of the influence of family life on the mind." [9] He likewise makes the pertinent observation that "if family life is so fateful for human mentality, its character deserves more attention. For the fact is the family is not the same in all human societies." It does not therefore exercise its influence in the same way.

---

[8] Ernest Jones, *Abnormal and Social Psychology in Problems of Personality* (edited by C. MacFee Campbell and others; New York, 1925), p. 23.
[9] Malinowski, *Sex Repression in Savage Society* (New York, 1927), p. 2.

It is significant also that the psychoanalysts should have discovered their explanation of the neuroses in the conditions which the intimacies and inhibitions of the familial organization imposes, for it is in the family and the primary group, according to Cooley, that most of the traits that we ordinarily describe as human have their origin. If the family is the institution to which first and last we owe the domestication of mankind, it is, according to Freud, to the conflicts which domestication, in each succeeding generation, involves that most of the neuroses and psychoses of later life owe their origin.

The family, moreover, for most of the civilized world, is the last refuge of the mores. It is the one form of society which not only children but adults enter at a time and under conditions when they are most in need of protection and least able to protect themselves, namely, when they are born and when they are in love. It remains today, in the midst of an individualistic and secular world, the prototype and living example of an authoritative and sacred society in which every one has duties and no one has rights, and in which the personal interests of the individual, even in the most intimate and personal matters of conduct, are completely subject to the communal interests and authority of the group.

Outside of the family, it is only within the narrow limits of the little and socially isolated religious sects that there exists a society which imposes upon its individual members a code, a discipline, and mode of life which often seems, at least, to run counter to all man's instinctive, spontaneous, and natural impulses.[10]

In reviewing recently Janet's *History of Psychological Healing*, I have been struck by the extraordinary number of cases in which the treatment of the neuroses makes it necessary for the psychotherapist to deal with a family situation, or at any rate with a situation involving intimate and personal relationships of some sort. This treatment, to use Janet's language, makes it necessary to take account, on the one hand, of "the fatigue which human beings produce in one another, the expenditure demanded by social relations, the impoverishing action exercised by antipathetic individuals, and on the other, of the stimulating influence of social life, of enrichment by guidance, and of the advantages of association with sympathetic persons." "Few people," says Janet, "realize how numerous are the moral problems opened by the simplest psychiatric studies; few realize what a wealth

---

[10] Cf. W. I. Thomas and Florian Znaniecki, *op. cit.*, pp. 35-36.

of interesting details is furnished even by the most superficial study of mental disorder." [11]

Among the exhausting actions Janet includes such things as the first communion, the entry into life. "It is so exhausting," says one patient, "to cogitate about life, about one's career, about the world which one cannot avoid seeing and which one hates." [12]

Other exhausting actions are social functions, college life, examinations, rest, and holidays. "Many persons are less capable of resting than of working. They become depressed because they are incompetent to perform the special actions which go by the name of inaction." [13]

Then there are the "occupational psychoses"; the obsessions and phobias to which lawyers, doctors, dressmakers, and barbers are likely to succumb, and the costs in mental energy necessary "to adapt oneself to those who form the family circle, to live on satisfactory terms with parents, friends, and intimate associates." Finally there are the difficulties that arise from changes in environment. "I could write," says Janet, "a whole treatise on the pathology of housemoving, so amazing and serious are the illnesses brought about by such an upheaval of the house." [14]

What impresses one in reviewing those cases of mental distress, subject to psychological and even sociological treatment, is that, on the whole, they seem to be due less to the rigor with which the tribal mores and the family discipline are enforced than to the general lack of direction and the new responsibilities which have come in with the new freedom, that is to say, with the individualization of the person, the secularization of social life. [15]

Functional derangements of the mental life seem to be due less to the nature and severity of the inhibition which the family and the community impose upon the individual than to the fact that they are no longer consistently enforced.

Under the older familial system the individual was so completely submerged in the family organization that he was not expected to choose his career and make his own way in the world. He was not

---

[11] Pierre Janet, *History of Psychological Healing* (New York, 1925), I, 19.

[12] *Ibid.*, p. 417.

[13] *Ibid.*, p. 419.

[14] *Ibid.*, p. 422.

[15] W. I. Thomas and Florian Znaniecki, *op. cit.*, p. 79; W. I. Thomas, *The Unadjusted Girl* (Boston, 1923), chap. iii, "The Individualization of Behavior," pp. 70–97.

even held responsible for selecting his own wife. Rather the family insisted on performing that service for him. He was not expected to found a family and make a career. He was merely called upon to take his place in a family already established and fit himself to carry on the family fortunes and uphold the family honor in accordance with a long-standing tradition.

In the modern world this is all changed. The individual is less concerned about the family honor and the family fortune than he is in preparing himself to become an efficient cog in the economic system and a conspicuous figure in a society that is no longer local or even national. Not duty, nor conformity, but efficiency is what the modern world demands and rewards.

It is under conditions such as these that the modern form of the *tedium vitae*, which the psychiatrists call neurasthenia, seems to occur. But it is significant that "the brain fag," "mental exhaustion," and undefined *malaise* of which so many patients complain is not due, apparently, to overwork, in the ordinary sense of that word. In fact, work which makes some new demands upon attention and interest of the individual may alleviate the patient's condition. This condition is due, according to Janet, to the effort necessary to maintain tension on a higher level than that which the individual is accustomed or has the capacity to sustain.[16]

If one asks what, in general, are the acts which, as Janet says, are costly, and for that reason, so frequently result in mental and moral bankruptcy, they are actions which arouse conflicts; actions which require deliberation under conditions where, for various reasons, it is difficult to reach a decision.[17] In many cases "the basic disorder is the depression caused by struggle with a difficult moral problem." [18]

In other words, mental exhaustion is due not so much to the effort to act, as to the effort to act in conformity with the accepted social code and in a manner consistent with the individual's conception of himself in a social situation or in a society. In that case, the patient may be cured by falling in love, by religious conversion, by going abroad, or by seeking adventure in some new region of experience. He may finally take up golf. In other words, the neurasthenic may be improved if not cured by rest, by isolation, by excitation, and what Janet calls liquidation, that is, by psychoanalysis; by anything, in fact,

---

[16] Pierre Janet, *op. cit.*, p. 244.
[17] *Ibid.*, p. 450.
[18] *Ibid.*, p. 480.

that lowers tension and reduces what one might describe as the overhead costs of living.

Mental conflicts, however they may arise, do not always terminate in a neurosis or in any other condition that would ordinarily be considered pathological. As conflicts arise because the individual finds it difficult to live in the world in which he finds himself, he may solve his problem by contriving a means of escape. He may get a divorce, or go on a pilgrimage, as was customary in the Middle Ages, or he may, like St. Anthony and the hermits of the fourth century, withdraw from the world altogether.

One of the ways in which men and women escape from the world in modern times is by joining or founding a religious sect, where they live, like the Mormons, the Mennonites, and others, in more or less complete isolation from the world. One may solve his problems as the Christian Scientists have sought to do, by reading the *Christian Science Monitor*, where nothing disturbing is recorded, neither crime, disease, nor death, and in general, by denying the existence of anything that should not happen.

Religion has always been concerned with the problem of evil but the solution which Christian Science offers is at the same time the most recent and, in some respects, the most naïve. At any rate, it is facts of this sort that justify a statement of Ernest Jones, in his discussion of the relations of abnormal and social psychology, that "the social institutions studied by the one discipline are the products of the same forces that create the neurotic manifestations with which the other is concerned: they are simply alternative modes of expression."[19]

Mental conflicts often have their sources in cultural conflicts. The man or class that seeks to rise from a lower to a higher cultural level; the immigrant who seeks to settle in a foreign community, meets with discrimination and prejudice because he is identified with a race or nationality which is regarded by the native peoples as inferior—inferior mainly because different. The stranger, though he may be accepted as a utility, is rejected as a citizen, a neighbor, and a "social equal." A social equal, as ordinarily defined in America, is one that you will be willing to have your daughter marry.

The criterion of social equality would be defined in more liberal terms if social equals were defined as those whom daughters and particularly sons, sometimes contrary to the wishes of their parents

---

[19] Ernest Jones, *Problems of Personality*, p. 24.

and in face of the general disapproval, do actually marry. At any rate, it is at the point where marriage is interdicted that caste begins. It is when peoples of divergent races and cultures seek to live within the limits of a cosmopolitan society and escape the limitations of class and caste that, under the conditions of modern life, what we call cultural conflicts take place.

Miller, in his interesting volume, *Races, Nations, and Classes,* has pointed out that most nationalist movements have their origin in the difficulties and the frustrations of a struggle for status, the consequence of which he describes as an "oppression psychosis." "The outstanding result of the oppression psychosis is to create a group solidarity which is far stronger than could be created by any other means." [20]

As a matter of fact, most cultural conflicts and the racial and nationalist movements in which they find expression, whatever their ultimate source and origin may be, are precipitated by the fact that some exceptional and otherwise amiable individual was snubbed and ill-treated, not because of his individual deserts, but simply because he was identified with some racial and cultural minority regarded as inferior—all right in its place, perhaps, but constituting in the eyes of the dominant people an inferior caste. Having experienced in his own person the ignominy and the wrong to which his fellow nationals were subjected, he makes their cause his own.

Gandhi, the Indian patriot and prophet, is a conspicuous instance. It was his long and bitter struggle for the liberties of the Indian settlers in South Africa that made him the most influential and intransigent leader of the Indian nationalist movement. No doubt he found at home, as other nationalist leaders who have made the same pilgrimage abroad have found, a seething mass of discontent to which he could appeal and which gave a moral backing to what was at first a purely personal sense of injury. But this is an episode which has been repeated again and again in the history of racial and national movements in every part of the world. It is an incident of the process of socialization by which the individual identifies himself with and becomes incorporated in the group.

It is interesting to note in this connection that most nationalist

---

[20] Herbert Adolphus Miller, *Races, Nations, and Classes,* (Lippincott, 1924), p. 36; see also H. A. Miller, *Race and Class Parallelism,* The Annals, Vol. CXXX, *The American Negro* (Philadelphia; November, 1928).

movements have had their origin abroad.[21] Many of them, notably the Irish and Lithuanian, may be said to have had their birth in America.

"There are in the United States," wrote Miller in 1924, "more than twenty million people who are more or less psychopathic on account of one or all of the forms of oppression previously or at present active in Europe." [22] This estimate is probably based upon the number of people either foreign-born or of foreign parents in the United States. This number in 1920 was 29,407,293. Subtracting the Nordics, whose psychosis, if any, is different, the number remaining might well amount to the twenty million of Miller's estimate. Even if this estimate of the number of persons in America whose national sympathies and loyalties were aroused by the war in Europe were true, one may still question the accuracy of Miller's statement of their state of mind.[23] It was very doubtful whether the mental state of the most ardent national minorities in the United States can be described as in any real sense pathological at this or any other time.

Looked at from the point of view of their ultimate consequences, the efforts of minority groups to assert themselves in response to the prejudices which they invariably encounter in a foreign country may be regarded on the whole as beneficial if not beneficent. In any case, the disposition of immigrant peoples to unite, in order that as Agaton Giller, a Polish patriot put it, they may "be morally and nationally raised" and thus better qualified to represent their native land abroad, is not in itself something to be deplored.[24]

The rise of nationalist and racial movements within the limits of a state, like the rise of sects and religious orders within the limits of a church, strike me as a natural and wholesome disturbance of the social routine, the effect of which is to arouse in those involved a lively sense of common purpose and to give those who feel themselves oppressed the inspiration of a common cause.

At bottom what we have in these so-called cultural conflicts is the

---

[21] Robert E. Park, *The Immigrant Press and Its Control* (New York, 1922), pp. 49-50.

[22] Miller, *Races, Nations, and Classes,* p. 38.

[23] See C. C. Playne, *The Neuroses of the Nation,* for a more extended statement of the mental condition of the people of Europe at the period of the outbreak of the World War.

[24] See Robert E. Park and Herbert A. Miller, *Old World Traits Transplanted* (New York, 1921), pp. 135-36.

struggle of socially handicapped or culturally inferior peoples to improve their status. The effect of this struggle is to increase the solidarity and improve the morale of the "oppressed" minority. Oppression is always more or less of a subjective matter and it is doubtful if the conflicts to which it gives rise would be as fruitful as they usually are if they were not accompanied by the incidental animosities which such struggles inevitably provoke. This sense of inferiority which seems to be identical with the so-called "oppression complex" is probably a more or less inevitable incident of the cultural process everywhere.

It seems that, if the oppressed minority is to rise and take possession of its own soul, some one must do the oppressing. The oppressors as I have known them, in the Philippines and in Korea, for example, strike me as a harassed, overworked, and, on the whole, as a well-intentioned type of person. A great deal is expected of them and they get very little appreciation for what they do accomplish.

Furthermore, the oppressed nationalities, like persecuted sects, have certain compensations. As individuals they have within the limits of their sect or their nationality a sense of security and dignity that they do not have outside. At the worst, the sectarian or the nationalist may become either a religious martyr or a national hero. Finally, a new religious order within the church and the new nationality within the imperium of the state tend, in most cases, to create a new society with a code and a culture peculiarly their own. Each may be regarded as a new bud on the old trunk of the social organism. It is in such conflicts as these that society renews its life and preserves its existence.

On the other hand, cultural conflicts when they do not provoke mass movements are likely to manifest themselves in family disorganization, in delinquency, and in functional derangement of the individual psyche.

Evidence which has been accumulating from many different sources indicates that it is difficult for individuals to maintain a stable personality except on the basis of a stable society. The delinquent boy is frequently a product of a broken home. Studies of delinquent children made by the Institute of Juvenile Research in Chicago and under the auspices of the Judge Baker Foundation in Boston indicate that one reason for juvenile delinquency, particularly among immigrant peoples, is the difficulty of maintaining family discipline in a "mixed community," that is to say, in a community where the family mores are not supported by the custom and tradition of the community.[25]

The life history documents of immigrant peoples, many of which have been published in recent years, have revealed the manner and extent of the inner moral conflicts to which immigrants and frequently immigrant children are subjected in making the transition from the cultural tradition of the home country to that of the new. All these facts indicate the intimate relationship which exists between the personality of the individual and the cultural tradition of the community and the people among whom he has found himself.

Cultural conflict seems to be an incident of cultural assimilation and the result is that those persons who are, so to speak, in transit become the melting pot or melting pots in which the cultural processes take place. This is the case in a peculiar sense of the so-called marginal man, i.e., the individual who finds himself on the margins of two cultures and not fully or permanently accommodated to either.

The typical marginal man is a mixed blood, an Eurasian, mestizo, or mulatto, i.e., a man who by the very fact of his racial origin is predestined to occupy a position somewhere between the two cultures represented by his respective parents. If, in addition to this, the two races of which he is a product are so different in their physical characteristics that he bears on his face, as is true of the mulatto and the Eurasian, the evidence of his mixed origin; and if, in addition to that, the mixed blood occupies, as he always tends to do, a separate caste or class—in such a situation all the factors are present to produce a specific type of mentality—i.e., intellectual and moral qualities, which are characteristic of the cultural hybrid or the marginal man.[26]

Much the same consequences ensue, however, in the case of the individual who is the product of parents representing two widely different cultures, particularly if the two groups are endogamous and do not intermarry as in the case of the Jew and the Gentile or even Catholics and Protestants.

Studies now in progress in Hawaii, where there has been a great deal of intermarriage between Europeans, Asiatics, Malays from the

---

[25] See, for example, Case 17, Series I, of the Judge Baker Foundation Studies: "Stasia and Stanley Andrews" (Boston, 1923). See also W. I. Thomas and Florian Znaniecki, *op. cit.* (Boston, 1920), Vol. V, *Organization and Disorganization in America.*

[26] Robert E. Park, "Human Migration and the Marginal Man," *American Journal of Sociology*, XXXIII (May, 1928), 881-93.

Philippines, and the native Polynesians exhibit in a very interesting way conflicts in culture and changes in personality which take place in the opposite situation. In this case conflicts arise in the family as a consequence of intermarriage of individuals representing different traditions and cultures. In all these different situations, changes in mood, temperament, and outlook on life, though they do not ordinarily express themselves in behavior that is ordinarily regarded as pathological, do represent changes that are profound and significant and suggest that studies in clinical psychology may be of very real importance to the understanding of social and cultural changes. They suggest also that the investigation of cultural changes and cultural conflicts may throw some light upon the functional disorders of the individual psyche.

CHAPTER 28

CULTURAL CONFLICT
AND THE MARGINAL MAN

WILLIAM GRAHAM SUMNER, in what is probably the most frequently quoted passage in the *Folkways,* tells us that we should conceive primitive society as a congeries of small ethnocentric groups scattered over a territory. In such a society each group thinks of itself in the first person and regards itself as "the center of everything." It is a "we-group." Others are outsiders. They are part of the landscape.

The size of such a group is determined "by the conditions of the struggle for existence, and its internal organization corresponds to its size but is further conditioned by its relations with all the others. This is because order and discipline in each 'we-group' or 'in-group' depends upon the exigences of war and peace with the 'other-groups' or 'out-groups.'" Thus society, primitive society at least, turns out to be "a group of groups," in which the normal relation of each to every other is "one of war and plunder, except so far as agreements have modified it." Under these circumstances "the relation of comradeship and peace in the we-group and that of hostility and war towards others-groups are correlative to each other." The loyalties that bind together the members of the little world—the world of the family, the clan and the tribe—are in direct proportion to the intensity of the fears and hatreds with which they view their enemies and rivals in the larger intertribal and international world outside.

In the course of the long historical process from which the modern

Being Introduction to E. V. Stonequist, *The Marginal Man* (New York: Charles Scribner's Sons, 1937), pp. xiii-xviii.

world has emerged this picture of primitive society has been progressively altered. Now that the aeroplane has wellnigh abolished the distances that once separated the nations and peoples and the radio has converted the world into one vast whispering gallery, the great world—intertribal, interracial, and international—the world of business and politics—has grown at the expense of the little world, the world of intimate, personal loyalties in which men were bound together by tradition, custom, and natural piety.

Nevertheless the general patterns of primitive society still persist and human nature is, on the whole, what it has been. It is still in the family and under the influence of the tribe, the sect or the local community, as Cooley insisted, that the individual acquires those habits, sentiments, attitudes and other personality traits that characterize him as human.

On the other hand, it was and is in the market place where men from distant places come together to chaffer and bargain, that men first learn the subtleties of commerce and exchange; the necessity for cool calculation, even in human affairs, and the freedom to act, as individuals, in accordance with interests, rather than sentiments. It is with the expansion of the market, as a matter of fact, that intellectual life has prospered and local tribal cultures have been progressively integrated into that wider and more rational social order we call civilization.

Thus the vast expansion of Europe during the last four hundred years has brought about changes more devastating than in any earlier period in the world's history. Europeans have invaded every part of the world, and no part of the earth has escaped the disturbing, even if vivifying, contacts of European commerce and culture. The movements and migrations incident to this expansion have brought about everywhere an interpenetration of peoples and a fusion of cultures. Incidentally it has produced, at certain times and under certain conditions, a personality type, a type which if not wholly new is at any rate peculiarly characteristic of the modern world. It is a type to which some of us, including the author of this volume [Stonequist], have given the title "The Marginal Man."

The marginal man, as here conceived, is one whom fate has condemned to live in two societies and in two, not merely different but antagonistic, cultures. Thus, the individual whose mother is a Jew and whose father is a Gentile is fatally condemned to grow up under the influence of two traditions. In that case, his mind is the crucible in which two different and refractory cultures may be said to melt and, either wholly or in part, fuse. One runs across individuals who are caught in this conflict of cultures in the most unlikely places.

Readers of George Santayana's *The Last Puritan* will hardly fail to discover—even if the subtitle, "A Memoir in the Form of a Novel," did not advertise the fact—that the story it tells, if not an autobiography, is nevertheless, in some subtle and symbolic way, autobiographical. Obviously the two leading characters, Oliver and Mario, are the symbols of the two cultures, which the author united in his own person, and the almost mystical friendship which, in spite of differences of temperament and tradition, unites them indicates how intimately the traditions they represent were related in the mind of the author.

In the epilogue the author refers to this novel as a "fable," and Mario, with whom he represents himself as discussing the import of the fable, adds, that "perhaps there is a better philosophy in it than in your other books."

Perhaps the best philosophy is one that achieves, as in the case of Plato, its fullest and happiest expression in fables. In any case a man's philosophy is always an aspect, if not an integral part, of his personality, and Santayana's philosophy reflects the effect, upon a mind conscious of a conflict in its natural loyalties, of an effort to achieve an inner harmony and consistency; such a harmony and consistency as is essential to that "life of reason" which he has so persuasively set forth in the volumes he has written under that title.

Santayana was born in Spain of Spanish parents, but fate ordained that he should get his education and live most of his life in America and England. It is evident from his account of life in Boston, that he lived there with his mother, as he did in fact in Spain with his father, more or less as an alien, always conscious of a different tradition and of intimate and indissoluble connections with another and a different world. In fact his life in both Spain and America seems to have been that of the typical "stranger," as described by Simmel in his *Sociology;* that is, one who lives in intimate association with the world about him but never so completely identified with it that he is unable to look at it with a certain critical detachment. In Santayana's case this detachment has become, as Edman expresses it, an intimate but "compassionate understanding" of his world.[1]

---

[1] See Irwin Edman's Introductory Essay to his volume of Selections from Santayana's Works, *The Philosophy of Santayana*, Introduction, p. lvi.

In an article, contributed to a symposium on the subject of contemporary American philosophy, Santayana[2] has described "the mixed associations" under which his "opinions" came into existence, subjected as they were to the strain of his "complex allegiances." He says: "My philosophy may be regarded as a synthesis of these various traditions, or an attempt to view them from a level from which their several deliverances may be justly understood."

Of himself a little later, he adds: "I felt like a foreigner in Spain, more acutely so than in America, although for more trivial reason. . . . English had become my only possible instrument, and I deliberately put away everything that might confuse me in that medium. English, and the whole Anglo-Saxon tradition in literature and philosophy, have always been a medium to me rather than a scholarship, and learning of any sort seemed to me a means, not an end. . . . Thus in renouncing everything else for the sake of English letters I might be said to have been guilty, quite unintentionally, of a little stratagem, as if I had set out to say plausibly in English as many un-English things as possible." [3]

The Last Puritan, whether it be an "indirect memoir" of the author, as Edman assumes, or a philosophy in the form of a fable, as Santayana himself suggests, is in any case for the student of human nature a human document in which the conflict and fusion of cultures, as it actually takes place under certain circumstances and in certain minds, is clearly reflected.

The fundamental notion upon which this present study of the so-called marginal man is based is, I should say, the conviction that the individual's personality, while based on instincts, temperament and the endocrine balance, achieves its final form under the influence of the individual's conception of himself. The conception which each individual inevitably forms of himself is determined by the rôle which fate assigns to him in some society, and upon the opinion and attitude which persons in that society form of him—depends, in short, upon his social status. The individual's conception of himself is, in this sense, not an individual but a social product.

The marginal man is a personality type that arises at a time and a place where, out of the conflict of races and cultures, new societies, new peoples and cultures are coming into existence. The fate which

---

[2] Irwin Edman, *op. cit.*, pp. 1-20.

[3] *Philosophy of Santayana*, Selections from the Complete Works of George Santayana, pp. 4-5.

condemns him to live, at the same time, in two worlds is the same which compels him to assume, in relation to the worlds in which he lives, the rôle of a cosmopolitan and a stranger. Inevitably he becomes, relatively to his cultural milieu, the individual with the wider horizon, the keener intelligence, the more detached and rational viewpoint. The marginal man is always relatively the more civilized human being. He occupies the position which has been, historically, that of the Jew in the Diaspora. The Jew, particularly the Jew who has emerged from the provincialism of the ghetto, has everywhere and always been the most civilized of human creatures.

From what has been said one may infer that the marginal man is an incidental product of a process of acculturation, such as inevitably ensues when peoples of different cultures and different races come together to carry on a common life. He is, as I have suggested, an effect of imperialism, economic, political and cultural; an incident of the process by which civilization, as Spengler has said, grows up at the expense of earlier and simpler cultures.[9]

The Marginal Man is concerned finally and fundamentally less, as the title might suggest, with a personality type, than with a social process, the process of acculturation. The distinction is that, in the latter case, the author has chosen to investigate the process less from the point of view of the person than of the society of which he is a part; less from the point of view of custom and culture than from habit and personality.

---

[4] See Oswald Spengler's *The Decline of the West* (translated) (1926).

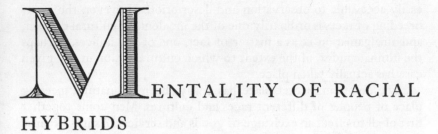

CHAPTER 29

MENTALITY OF RACIAL HYBRIDS

I. HYBRIDIZATION

RACIAL hybrids seem to be one of the invariable accompaniments and consequences of human migration. Hybridization is probably, therefore, a mathematical function of the geographic mobility of peoples. At any rate, miscegenation seems to take place, other things being equal, more rapidly than elsewhere on the frontiers of an advancing civilization; in seaport cities, and in commercial centers, where people of divers cultures meet and mingle with more than ordinary freedom; and where, under the influence of a mobile, changing, and cosmopolitan population, custom is relaxed and the traditional distinctions of class and caste not rigorously enforced.[1]

An address delivered at the Fourth Pacific Science Congress, held at Batavia-Bandoeng, Java, May 16 to 25, 1929. Reproduced in *The American Journal of Sociology*, XXXVI (January, 1931), pp. 534-551.

[1] See Dr. Arthur Ruppin, *The Jews of Today* (New York, 1913), chap. x, "Intermarriage."

It is true that marital statistics in the United States seem to support the opposite thesis. They indicate that, so far as European immigrants are concerned, intermarriage of the immigrant and native population is taking place more rapidly in rural communities than in cities. This is due in part to the fact that the so-called "new immigration," in which biological assimilation takes place slowly, is very largely located in the cities. On the other hand, the "old immigration," which is more closely related racially and culturally to the native population, is largely located in the small towns and in the open country. Furthermore, intermarriage in the case of the old immigration is more likely to take place between aliens and natives of the same ethnic stocks, German immigrants, for example, marrying German-Americans; Irish, Irish-Americans. Under these circumstances,

No effort has been made, so far as I know, to determine the precise condition under which hybridization actually takes place. Some of these conditions are of a rather subtle psychological nature, and not easily accessible to observation and description. However, the inter-breeding of races is ordinarily one of the incidents of cultural contact, and amalgamation is, as a matter of fact, one of the indices, perhaps the ultimate index, of the extent to which cultural fusion in any given case has actually taken place.

The common market place has always been the natural meeting place of peoples of different races and cultures. Men come together first of all to effect an exchange of goods and services. As it is because men are useful to one another that they come together at all, so it is because they are different from one another that they are useful.

When peoples of divergent racial stocks come together to main-tain a permanent, common life, a *modus vivendi* is established, in the first instance, on the basis of economic necessity. Under these circum-stances people of divergent racial stocks ordinarily live, as do the gypsies in our modern world, in relations that are symbiotic rather than social. In that case they treat one another as utilities rather than as persons. It is possible for races to live indefinitely in such a condition of symbiosis, contiguous in space, but culturally isolated; each group in its own world, and neither enjoying or seeking status in the other. This seems to be the situation in which all pariah people live; but it is true, to some degree, of every people that maintains or seeks to maintain an independent cultural life and tradition, while occupying the territory and participating in the economic life of another and different cultural group. This was, and to some extent is today, the case of the Jew, when, in the very center, at the very core of a national and cultural life not quite his own, he continued to live in his ghetto more or less an alien and a stranger to the community about him.[2]

It is evident that man's biological and his cultural interests are not always in harmony, and that social and political organizations are

---

intermarriage between native- and foreign-born peoples is not an accurate index of the blending of divergent racial stocks. Of the older immigration the Irish have the lowest rate of intermarriage, 299.5 for every 1,000 marriages. The Ger-mans, with a ratio of 704.7 exogamous unions for every 1,000 marriages, have the highest. In every case, however, the rate of intermarriage is higher among the older than the new immigration (*Census Monograph 7: Immigrants and Their Children* [1927]).

[2] Louis Wirth, *The Ghetto* (Chicago, 1928), chap. xiv, "The Social Signifi-cance of the Ghetto." See also Ludwig Lewisohn, *Israel* (New York, 1925).

frequently either a compromise or, to speak in sociological terms, an accommodation in the attempt to reconcile them. Slavery, caste, and even social classes may be regarded, in one of their aspects, as devices for maintaining and enforcing this symbiotic relation, and at the same time of limiting more intimate and personal contacts.

Social distances are, however, difficult to maintain, and the measures intended to preserve them are invariably only partially successful. Furthermore, sexual interest, which is still one of the most powerful motives in human conduct, operates independently and often counter to the interests represented by the organization of society. Romantic love, which is proverbially interested in the exotic and unfamiliar, not infrequently crosses racial barriers, and is never completely inhibited by class and caste taboos.[3]

It follows from what has already been said that hybridization does not proceed everywhere and always with the same facility and at the same tempo. Statistics of intermarriage of immigrant and native stocks in the United States indicate that assimilation and amalgamation are taking place at different rates in different groups. In fact, the rate of intermarriage is different in every different nationality.

An investigation based upon 79,704 marriages in New York City, out of a total of 171,356 for the years 1908-12, inclusive showed that the intermarriage rates for the Jews and the Negroes are less than those of all other national or racial groups.[4]

The intermarriage ratio of the Negroes born in the United States was 1.17 for every 100 marriages. For Jews born in the United States, it was 4.26. The author's comment is that "just as differences of

---

religion explain the low proportion of intermarriages between Jews

[3] It is psychologically true that only the unfamiliar and not completely controlled is interesting. This is the secret of the interest of modern scientific pursuit and of games. States of high emotional tension are due to the presentation of the unfamiliar—i.e., the unanalyzed, the uncontrolled—to the attention. And although the intimate association and daily familiarity of family life produce affection, they are not favorable to the genesis of romantic love. Cognition is so complete that no place is left for emotional appreciation. Our common expressions "falling in love" and "love at sight" imply, in fact, unfamiliarity; and there can be no question that men and women would prefer at present to get mates away from home, even if there were no traditional prejudice against the marriage of near kin (W. I. Thomas, *Sex and Society* [Chicago, 1907], pp. 196-97). See also Morris T. Price, *Christian Missions and Oriental Civilization: A Study in Cultural Contact*, pp. 286 f.

[4] M. A. Drachsler, *Intermarriage in New York City: A Statistical Study of the Amalgamation of European Peoples* (New York, 1921), pp. 21-22.

and non-Jews, so differences in color account for the small proportion of fusion between the Negro and the white." [5]

Not only does interbreeding take place at different rates for different racial stocks, but the incidental consequences of interbreeding need to be sharply distinguished. For example, when Jews intermarry with Christians, their children become, nominally at least, either Jews or Christians. Under ordinary circumstances the large proportion become Christians. [6]

On the other hand, when Negroes interbreed with other races, the offspring of such unions do not have the same freedom of choice. The mixed bloods are either, as in the case of the mulattoes of the United States, incontinently classed as Negroes, irrespective of the degree of the racial mixture, or they occupy, as half-castes and mixed bloods, a position somewhere between the two. In any case, the mulatto, conscious of his mixed origin, unwilling to accept the inferior status of his Negro ancestors, invariably constitutes, even in the United States, a distinct racial category and a separate social class. The consequence is that the mulatto is never completely identified with, or assimilated to, either one race or the other.

Fouillèe says: "In discussions of the race problem there is one factor of supreme importance which has been so far disregarded—to wit, the opinion or *idea* which a race has of itself and the influence exerted by this idea." [7]

Physical and racial marks, when they become the basis of class or caste consciousness, acquire a unique significance because they cannot be eradicated. A man may change his costume or his speech, but he cannot change his color.

It is a notorious fact that class and caste distinction have been very largely based upon racial differences. Visibility, to use the vocabulary

[5] It is evident that relative numbers and the sex ratio are factors that need to be considered here. In Copenhagen, where 89 per cent of the Jews of Denmark live, there are 68 mixed marriages to every 100 Jews. But in this instance the proportion of Jews in the total population is very small. A. F. Stone (*Studies in the American Race Problem*), quoting the censuses of 1860, 1870, 1880, and 1890, where separate enumeration of the mulattoes was made, says, "The results disclose the fact that where the proportion of negroes to the whites is lowest, the proportion of the mulattoes to the total negroes was highest."

[6] Prussian statistics of *The Religion of Children of Mixed Marriages Living with Their Parents* show that, according to the census of 1905, of 7,016 children of mixed marriages, 1,591, or 22.67 per cent, elected to be Jews, but 5,229, or 74.53 per cent, were classed as Christians. See Ruppin, *op. cit.*, pp. 175 f.

[7] Alfred Fouillèe, "Race from the Sociological Standpoint," *Papers on Inter-Racial Problems*, ed. G. Spiller (London, 1911).

of the navy bulletins, seems to determine not merely the existence of caste and class distinctions, but the vigor with which the discriminations which correspond to them will be enforced. When the physical differences between races are so pronounced that the hybrids constitute a distinguishable physical type, they almost invariably occupy a separate social category and are recognized as a distinct class or caste.

The mulatto, the name given without distinction to all Negro-white hybrids of the United States, is not, to be sure, in all cases distinguishable either from the black man, on the one hand, or the white man, on the other. He is, however, everywhere recognized as a distinct class, even though his position and his status are different in every country in which mixed bloods are sufficiently numerous to play an independent rôle.

It is, in fact, the rôle which the mulatto plays, and the position that he occupies in relation to the black man and the white, that determines in every case the character of the existing race relations and the local race problem.

In the United States the mulattoes are on the whole, with some important exceptions, the cultural advanced guard and the leaders of the Negro people. The two most eminent figures among Negroes in the United States, Booker T. Washington, and W. E. B. du Bois, were both mixed bloods. In recent years the Negroes have developed a literature dealing exclusively with Negro life. Most of the contributors to this literature are mulattoes, but the first writer to gain general recognition, Paul Lawrence Dunbar, was a full-blooded Negro.

In the West Indies, and particularly in those islands where the Negroes are in the majority, the mixed bloods are classed as "colored," and enjoy a more or less independent status. They are largely represented in business, in the professions, and in the so-called "white collar" jobs, and they constitute a respectable middle class between the dominant white officials and the black peasantry. In South America and particularly in Brazil, where Negroes and mixed bloods constitute more than 60 per cent of the population, there is, strictly speaking, no color line. Nevertheless, here, as elsewhere, the white man is invariably at the top, and the black man and the native Indian are at the bottom. Lighter-colored mixed bloods occupy the middle positions, and a successful black man generally insures his own status and that of his children by marrying a lighter-colored woman. As Lacerda puts it: "The mulatto himself endeavors, by marriage, to bring back his descendants to the pure white types," and "The marriages between

metis and whites are no longer disdained as they formerly were."
The mixed blood rises by a process of social and sexual selection,
"which removes from the descendants of the *metis* all the characteristic features of the black race." [8]

In South Africa, where racial antagonism is more intense than it is
even in the United States, the situation is a little confused. The distinction between the hybrid people and the native blacks is everywhere maintained, but the "colored people," as the mixed bloods are
called, occupy a higher status in Cape Colony than they do in the
other provinces. In general, the situation in Cape Colony approaches
that in Jamaica and other West Indian Islands under English domination. In Natal, however, and particularly in the Boer States, the Transvaal, and the Orange Free State, race relations conform more nearly
to conditions in the United States. [9]

II. THE MENTALITY OF THE MULATTO

I have discussed in some detail the conditions under which hybridization ordinarily takes place and the rôle which the mixed bloods
ordinarily play in the community in which they find themselves, because I am convinced, as will appear a little later, that what I have
called the mentality of the racial hybrid—that is to say, his peculiar
mental bias, the character of the intelligence which he displays, and
the general level of the intellectual life he has achieved—is very largely
due to the social situation in which his mixed origin inevitably puts
him. He is biologically the product of divergent racial stocks, but
just because of that fact he is, at the same time, the cultural product
of two distinct traditions. He is, so to speak, a cultural as well as a
racial hybrid.

There have been numerous attempts in recent years to determine
with some precision, on the basis of intelligence tests, the native
ability of the Negro as compared with other racial stocks. These investigations, in spite of the industry and ingenuity with which they
have been carried on, remain inconclusive, largely because of the
difficulties in distinguishing between the factors of nature and nurture,

---

[8] Dr. Jean Baptiste de Lacerda, "The *Metis*, or Half-Breeds, of Brazil," *ibid.*
[9] Maurice S. Evans, *Black and White in South East Africa: A Study in Sociology* (New York, 1911), chap. x, "The Asiatic and Coloured Sub-Problem,"
p. 283-309. See also Raymond Leslie Buell, *The Native Problem in Africa* (New
York, 1928), Vol. I: *South Africa*, pp. 58-155.

of innate ability and cultural opportunity. For this and other reasons, the results obtained have turned out to be capable of several different and inconsistent interpretations.

In general, however, the intelligence tests have shown that at the present moment the intellectual *niveau* of the Negro is consistently below that of the white man. On the other hand, the same tests have shown the intelligence quotient of the urban population to be higher than that of the rural, that of the native white to be superior to that of a foreigner, and the mental grade of both native-white and Negro populations to be higher in the northern than in the southern states.[10]

When attempts have been made to distinguish between the intellectual capacities of pure and mixed bloods, the results obtained have generally shown that the mulattoes were superior to the Negroes. In all cases, however, the literate members of both races made a better showing than the illiterates, and the literate Negroes ranked higher than the illiterate whites. The whole question of the intelligence tests, so far as they bear upon the comparative innate mental capacities of the black man and the white, have been carefully and critically reviewed by Edward Byron Reuter in his volume, *The American Race Problem: A Study of the Negro*.[11]

Summing up the results of the United States Army tests upon Negroes and whites made during the mobilization of the Army in 1917, Dr. Reuter says:

Certain .... facts of interest and significance appear as the data of the examinations are studied. In all cases the literate members of every race made a better showing than the illiterates. Irrespective of the section of the country, the literate Negroes ranked higher than the illiterate whites. The Northern Negroes very greatly surpassed the Italians in America. In the Alpha tests the New York Negroes made approximately the same ranking as the Alabama whites, while in the Beta tests the New York Negroes

---

[10] Carl C. Brigham, *Study of American Intelligence* (Princeton, 1923). See also G. O. Ferguson, "White and Colored Schools of Virginia as Measured by the Ayers Index," *School and Society*, XII (1920), 171-74; "The Psychology of the Negro, an Experimental Study," *Archives of Psychology* (New York, April, 1916), No. 36. See also M. J. Mayo, "The Mental Capacity of the American Negro," *ibid.*, IV, No. 28 (1913). See also Barbara Stoddard Burke, "A Summary of Literature on the Determination of the Intelligence Quotient and the Educational Quotient," *Twenty-seventh Year Book of the National Society for the Study of Education* (1928).

[11] *Op. cit.* (New York, 1927), pp. 91-92. See also Margaret Mead, "The Methodology of Racial Testing: Its Significance for Sociology," *American Journal of Sociology*, XXXI, No. 5 (March, 1926), 657-67.

ranked approximately nine points superior to the Alabama whites. That is, the New York Negroes, on the basis of the tests, and in whatever the tests measure, are equal to or slightly superior to the whites of Alabama. Very clearly the accident of a Southern birth is a determining element in intelligence, as measured by the Army tests.

This means that the tests made to determine innate racial capacity may be, and possibly should be, interpreted as demonstrating that intelligence, so far as it is at present possible to measure it, is due to "increased education, greater freedom in social contact, greater incentives, higher economic status," rather than to innate and unalterable traits, as other interpreters of the results have contended.

If attempts to measure the native intelligence of Negroes have failed to show the differences that were expected, there is, nevertheless, no question at all in regard to the actual superiority of the mulatto in comparison to the Negro, provided superiority is measured by present achievements and by the relative status of each in the existing social order. Everywhere the mixed blood has, with certain outstanding exceptions, outclassed the Negro. Whatever estimate future investigators may put upon the native ability of either racial group, and without reference to what the future may show, the mixed blood as a class has shown himself more enterprising, and his progress, accordingly, has been more rapid. Not only in the learned professions and in politics, but particularly in literature and the expressive arts, the mulatto has outdistanced the Negro. This is perhaps less true in South Africa and the West Indies than it is in South America and the United States. Speaking of the *metis* of South America, Lacerda says:

No one, however, can dispute that they are keenly intelligent and have a disposition for letters and science, and a fairly political capacity. The *metis* of Brazil have given birth down to our own time to poets of no mean inspiration, painters, sculptors, distinguished musicians, magistrates, lawyers, eloquent orators, remarkable writers, medical men, and engineers, who have been unrivalled in their technical skill and professional ability. As politicians they are clever, insinuating, and very acute in profiting by any favourable opportunity to secure a position; they are usually energetic and courageous in the struggle, in which they use every weapon with equal zest.

Even in Haiti, where the black man first gained his personal freedom and his national independence, a relatively small number of mixed bloods, constituting less than 10 per cent of the whole population, hold most of the public offices and carry on most of the professions.[12]

Here, as elsewhere, however, the mixed bloods have had no monopoly of the superior positions. The black man who succeeds in demonstrating superior ability is almost certain to be adopted into the mulatto aristocracy. If he then marries, as he usually does, a mulatto wife, his children will inherit, by that fact, the superior status of the mixed blood.

The disposition of the black man who has achieved distinction to marry into the mulatto class, referred to by Lacerda in his "Observations on the *Metis* of Brazil," is so characteristic of the Negro in the United States that it has been maintained that the superiority of the mulatto is due in large part, at least, to social and sexual selection.[13]

This would seem to indicate that Negro aristocracy, like that of the English, is maintained in what is probably the only way any aristocracy can in the long run be maintained, namely, by systematically recruiting its members from the ranks of the inferior classes. However the mulatto may have achieved his present superiority, there seems to be no question that it exists and can be measured as soon as a satisfactory criterion of superiority can be found. In the study of the mulatto to which reference has already been made, Dr. E. B. Reuter undertook this task. He collected from all available sources a list of persons who were recognized by Negroes themselves as in some way exceptional. The lists he obtained in this way constitute a kind of Negro *Who's Who*.[14]

The inquiry as finally made took into consideration the relative

---

[12] Lothrop Stoddard, *The French Revolution in San Domingo* (New York, 1914). See also *The Magic Isle* (New York, 1928).

[13] "The mulatto group continually is being improved by the addition to it of the best blood of the Negro race. The black man of ability, in almost every case, marries into the mulatto caste; and his children, with whatever of their father's superior mentality they inherit, are mulattoes. So far as his superiority is inherited, it becomes an asset to the mulatto group. The black man of greatest ability, perhaps, of any black man in the race is married to a light-colored mulatto woman. The most widely known black man of the race has a wife who is near white. The black man who approached nearer to genius than any other man the race has produced, married a light mulatto. The rule is almost without an exception that the black man of consequence marries into the mulatto caste. The mulatto group thus, on the assumption of the transmission of superior mental capacity, tends to become not only a culturally but a biologically superior group" (Edward Byron Reuter, *The Mulatto in the United States* [Boston, 1918], pp. 396-97).

[14] *Ibid.*, p. 186.

status of 4,267 persons, of whom 614 were men and 3,650 were women, all of them persons rated by Negroes themselves as in some sense exceptional. Of this number it was found that 447 were full bloods, and 3,820 were mulattoes. This means that while the ratio of full bloods to mixed bloods in the Negro population at the time this study was made was about 4 to 1, the ratio of mulattoes to Negroes of full blood among the 4,000 leaders of the races was 8½ to 1. The thing may be stated more emphatically: On the basis accepted for the purposes of this study, the chances of a mulatto child of developing into a leader of his race are thirty-four times as great as the chances of a black child. Twenty per cent of mixed bloods among the American Negroes have produced 85 per cent of the race's superior men.

III. THE MULATTO AS A PERSONALITY TYPE

It is often said of the mulattoes, as of mixed bloods generally, that they inherit the vices of both parent-races and the virtues of neither.[15] It is, however, notoriously difficult to assess moral qualities, particularly since traits which under certain circumstances may be regarded as vices are under other circumstances reckoned as virtues.

It is, in any case, interesting that there are, or seem to be, characteristics which, whether they are the results of one kind of crossing or another, are attributed to mixed bloods as such. It suggests, what has indeed been asserted, that the mixed blood, without respect to his racial origin and merely because of the rôle he is called upon to play, constitutes a distinct personality type. Mulattoes, as a class, exhibit certain personality traits which distinguish them from Negroes, with whom they are identified in the United States and South Africa, as well as from the whites, with whom they are disposed to identify

---

[15] "There is a widely accepted theory that the result of a union between white and black, or indeed between white and any coloured and backward people, is a breed which seems to combine all the weaknesses and vices of both parent stocks and none of the virtues of either. This does not seem to me to apply in the case of these Eur-Africans. Physically they are a fine people, in some cases with a colour and complexion distinctly attractive, not the sickly yellow of many other half-breeds, but a light brown with a tinge of red; both men and women often large, robust, well set up, with a tendency to corpulence, and with good features. They do not often display the energy and will power of their fathers, but to some extent this is due to lack of opportunity; their undefined status and anomalous position, and the deadening influence of their narrow and restricted environment. In any case they do not substantiate the somewhat cynical generalization I have quoted, for their general conduct is good, and they do not seem to have any specially vicious tendencies" (Evans, *op. cit.*, p. 300).

themselves elsewhere.[16] They are, as I have said, more enterprising than the Negroes, more restless, aggressive, and ambitious. The Negro, by contrast, is described by one who has known them on the plantations in the South as "docile, tractable and unambitious," and invariably contented and happy "when free from the influence of the mulatto and the white man." The author is describing a character of the Negro peasant with whom the black man is ordinarily identified.[17]

The mulatto and the mixed blood are often sensitive and self-conscious to an extraordinary degree. They do not have, on the other hand, the *insouciance* and *naïveté* which makes the Negro invariably so ingratiating and agreeable a companion. Mulattoes, also, are keenly aware of the defects of the Negro, but because their status is so intimately bound up with his, they are not able to view these defects with the same objectivity and tolerance as the white man does.[18]

One of the consequences of his more intense self-consciousness is that the mulatto lives at a higher tension than the Negro. He is more intelligent because, for one thing, he is more stimulated, and, for another, takes himself more seriously.[19]

We are bound to recognize the fact that intelligence, like consciousness, is an incident of action, and the intellectual attainment of an individual or a race is a function of their activities. Restlessness, while not identified with thought, and not in any sense a substitute for it, is nevertheless the first and most elementary response to a problematical situation that requires reflection. The restlessness, aggressiveness, and what may perhaps be described as the general egocentric behavior of the mulatto as compared to the Negro may, and probably does, have a temperamental basis. They are usually attributed, some-

---

[16] E. B. Reuter, "The Personality of the Mixed Blood," *Publication of the American Sociological Society*, XXII, 52-59.

[17] Alfred H. Stone, "The Mulatto Factor in the Race Problem," *Atlantic Monthly*, XCI, 658-62. See also Stone, *Studies in the American Race Problem.*

[18] See W. H. Thomas, *The American Negro: What He Was, What He Is, and What He May Become*, for a frank and candid expression of the attitude of the mulatto toward the Negro at the date this volume was published (1901). It must be remembered, however, that attitudes change and, with the gradual rise of the Negro, the traditional attitude of the mulatto toward him has been greatly modified.

[19] See a paper by W. E. B. Du Bois, "The Talented Tenth," in the volume, *The Negro Problem*, by Booker T. Washington and others. This is a plea for the higher education of the Negro. It is based on the general conception that the Negro masses can only hope to improve their status as a result of the advances made by the so-called "talented tenth." This talented tenth, however, was composed then, as it is now, very largely of mixed bloods.

times by the mulattoes themselves, to the infusion of the blood of the dominant race. These lines are from a poem entitled "The Mulatto to His Critics," which at once reflects temper and explains, in terms of popular psychology, the temperament of the mulatto.

> Ashamed of my race?
> And of what race am I?
> I am many in one.
> Through my veins there flows the blood
> Of Red Man, Black Man, Briton, Celt and Scot,
> In warring clash and tumultuous riot.[20]

Temperament in the case of the mulatto has, however, been reinforced by tradition—tradition that goes back to the days of slavery and life on the plantation. The mulatto slaves claimed and were granted privileges on account of their color. Frances Kemble, in her reminiscences of life on a Georgia plantation, relates that she was accosted one day by a mulatto woman who wanted to be put in some other form of work than field labor. She stated that hoeing in the fields was particularly hard on her "on account of her color," and then explained that "being a mulatto she considered field labor a degradation." [21]

Anyone at all familiar with the records of plantation life will recall numerous incidents which clearly, though quite unconsciously, reveal the fact that the mulatto was, so to speak, the favored child, the "white-haired boy" of the plantation.

The mulatto made a better appearance than the Negro and was chosen for that reason, as well as for others, to be the house servant. In the homes of well-to-do planters he acquired the manners of the superiors with whom he was associated. The mulatto slaves, partly because they were so largely house servants, and sometimes the children of their master, were the first to be emancipated. Of the Negroes in the southern states in 1860, but 10 per cent were free. On the other hand, of the mulattoes, 40 per cent were free.[22]

Mulattoes, partly because they were the first to gain their freedom, were very largely concentrated in cities, in both the South

---

[20] Joseph S. Cotter, Jr., in *Negro Poets and Their Poems* (Washington, D.C., 1923), by Robert T. Curlin.

[21] Frances A. Kemble, *Residence on a Georgia Plantation*, p. 194.

[22] See Reuter, *The Mulatto*, p. 113, where the census figures for 1850 are recorded.

and the North.[23] Some of them, particularly in the port cities of the southern states—Charleston, Savannah, Mobile, New Orleans—were sufficiently well to do to be themselves owners of slaves and thus able to give their children the advantages of a relatively superior education, either abroad or in the northern states. In Charleston and in New Orleans there was and is a colored aristocracy composed of these mixed bloods and their descendants. In spite of, or just because of, the fact that they were so generally the favored class among the slaves, the mulattoes, in proportion to their numbers, seem to have furnished a larger quota of fugitive slaves. It was from these fugitive slaves that the ranks of the antislavery societies in the North were recruited. Among these fugitive slaves the most conspicuous was Frederick Douglass, himself a mulatto, a distinguished orator, and the first man of Negro blood to achieve a national reputation.

The mulatto and the mixed blood are, for the reasons I have described, the product of a double inheritance, biological and cultural, that is different from that of the black man. If the mulatto displays intellectual characteristics and personality traits superior to and different from those of the black man, it is not because of his biological inheritance merely, but rather more, I am inclined to believe, because of his more intimate association with the superior cultural group.

Furthermore, the mixed blood, with the indubitable evidence in his features and in the color of his skin of his kinship with the dominant white race, was bound to reflect that whatever justification there was for holding the black man in a position of permanent insubordination, it did not apply to the same extent to the brown. The black man might dream of a return to Africa, to the land of his fathers, in order to set up there an independent state where he might work out his own salvation and that of his race. But such future could not appeal with the same force to the mixed blood, particularly since his father was in most instances a white man, while his mother was frequently an Indian. As a matter of fact, the amount of Indian blood in a mulatto is considerable, much larger than is generally recognized, and the brown man has, very naturally, clung to the traditions of his white and Indian ancestor. All this has contributed to make him a very dif-

[23] In Savannah, Georgia, in 1860, 18.1 per cent of the Negro population were mulattoes; in the rest of the state the proportion of the mixed to pure bloods was 8.2. In Charleston, S.C., the proportion of mixed to pure bloods was 28.2; the rest of the state was 5.5. In New Orleans 48.9 per cent of the Negro population was mulatto, and in the rest of the state the proportion of the mixed to pure bloods was 11.0. See *ibid.*, p. 115.

ferent man physically and culturally from the Negro and, above all, to give him a very different conception of himself. This is, in part at least, the basis of that restlessness and instability to which reference is so frequently made in writings on the subject of mixed races.

So far as the existing and intellectual superiority of the mixed bloods requires an explanation other than that of heredity, I am disposed to find it in the stimulating influences of his unique environment.[24] The mulatto shares more or less completely the life-experiences of two unassimilated races. He is not able, for that reason, to identify himself completely with either. The situation is at once anomalous and untenable, and it imposes upon the mulatto, foremostly and before all others, the task of finding a solution. This task, which is, for the mixed blood, so intimate and personal a matter, is at the same time difficult enough to call into action all his energies. The race has, in fact, become, in the United States at least, the center and focus of the intellectual life of the whole Negro race. It has so completely absorbed the interest and attention of a certain number of the intellectuals of the race as to become to them an obsession.

It is inevitable that an interest so dominating and actual should have a profound influence, not only upon the intelligence, but upon the personality of the mixed blood, who is, by his very origin, more directly concerned than anyone else. It is certainly true of the mixed bloods of the United States, who have achieved real distinction, that they have often displayed a degree of intelligence of which their parents were apparently quite incapable. This is eminently true in the case of Frederick Douglass and Booker T. Washington, who in their day and time were the two most eminent leaders of their race. Both were born in slavery and had, for that reason, very little oppor-

---

[24] Lacerda is convinced that mixed bloods frequently achieve an intellectual superiority which cannot be explained by heredity. He said: "Galton's deductions in regard to hybridity in animals cannot be wholly applied to human half-breeds. In the case of man there is an inheritance of moral and intellectual qualities that follows no fixed and absolute rules. Under the influence of agencies of which we do not know the nature, the intellectual qualities often reach, in the mixed progeny of the white and black, a degree of superiority which cannot be explained in terms of heredity, either remote or proximate. Some unknown force gives rise in them to an intelligence that is capable of developing to a pitch that neither of the parents could reach. It is, in fact, common to find, as the offspring of a white of very mediocre intelligence, mated with a negress of the lowest grade of culture, an individual of considerable intellectual power; just as if one of the effects of crossing in the case of man was precisely to improve the intelligence, or the moral and reflective qualities which distinguish individuals of the two races crossed" (p. 380).

tunity for an education of a formal sort. Both were, no doubt, men of superior native intelligence, but it was the conjuncture of events and the rôles which each in his time was called upon to play that enabled them to achieve the distinction and exercise the influence upon national affairs which they actually did. It was in their tasks, and in the association and activities which these tasks imposed, that these men gained their education.[25]

It has been the disposition of the mixed bloods, wherever they have been denied the status of the dominant race, to compensate themselves by withdrawing from association with the Negro and establishing a separate caste. Where they have succeeded in completely segregating themselves, as they have in some instances in South Africa and the United States, they have either deteriorated, physically and culturally, or they have at best remained stationary and not shared in the general economic and cultural progress of the race as a whole. This is true of the little mulatto aristocracies that established themselves in Charleston and New Orleans before the Civil War. It is particularly true of those little isolated communities of mixed Indian, Negro, and white populations—peoples that established themselves in the foothills of the Blue Ridge Mountains of Virginia, North Carolina, South Carolina, and Tennessee, or in other settlements on the outskirts of civilization in other parts of the southern states. These communities of free Negro and Indian origin withdrew themselves during slavery days from intimate association, not only with the black man, but with the white, in order to maintain their freedom and to escape identification with the despised free-Negro class. They now frequently claim to be white but are not accepted as such.

In these isolated settlements the mixed bloods succeeded in achieving their independence and securing for themselves rcognition as distinct from neither the Negroes or the mulattoes. They were given, for one thing, separate schools, separate from both Negro and white, but they did not escape in this way the inevitable deterioration which isolation from participation in the cultural life of the larger community invariably brings.[26]

The same thing seems to have taken place in the case of the

[25] See Booker T. Washington, *My Larger Education,* and Frederick Douglass, *My Life and Times.*

[26] See Arthur Esterbrook and Ivan V. McDougall, *Mongrel Virginians: The Win Tribe.* This study is devoted particularly to one of these hybrid racial groups but contains references to eleven others in that general region of the Blue Ridge.

Griquas, a mixed-blood people in South Africa, as has taken place in these isolated mixed-blood communities in the southern states. Maurice Evans, speaking of the Griquas, says: "The Griquas are a degenerate, demoralized, dissolute people, weak, lazy and thriftless." [27]

Even the so-called "cape colored" of Cape Colony, South Africa, who long enjoyed in that colony a freedom and a status which was not accorded them elsewhere in South Africa, are, according to recent reports, declining in numbers relative to other elements in the population. "Apparently," says Leslie Buell, "this group [cape colored] which contains some of the leading non-Europeans in South Africa is beginning to degenerate." [28]

While it is true that the mulatto in the United States, as is the case of the mixed blood generally, has been disposed to escape from the racial coil in which his origin and his history have involved him by separating himself from the masses of the Negro race, the vigor with which the racial line has been drawn against him has compelled him to take another course.

More and more in the course of his struggle for position and status in the white's man world the brown man has chosen to throw in his fortunes with the black and make the Negro's cause his own. He has made himself not merely the leader but the teacher, the interpreter, and in some sense the emancipator of the race. In this struggle the black man, as education has been more widely diffused, has begun to play a more important rôle. However, the mulatto, in spite of his smaller numbers, still largely represents the intellectual class of the race.

This struggle, gathering in breadth and intensity, which Lothrop Stoddard has described as "the rising tide of color," has been at once an inspiration and a discipline to the mulatto. What is more, it has given him a cause and a career, the influence of which upon his intellectual life can hardly be overestimated, for intelligence and intellectual life, as I have said before, are incidents of action, and it is only the sense of participation in the great action that gives individuals or races the courage and the *élan* that is necessary to rise from a lower to that higher cultural level of intellectual life which is standard in the modern world.

---

[27] Quoted in *Black and White in the Southern States*, pp. 25-26.
[28] *Op. cit.*, I, 11.

INDEX OF NAMES

UBJECT INDEX

FREE PRESS PAPERBACKS

A Series of Paperbound Books in the Social and Natural Sciences, Philosophy, and the Humanities

These books, chosen for their intellectual importance and editorial excellence, are printed on good quality book paper, from the large and readable type of the clothbound edition, and are Smyth-sewn for enduring use. Free Press Paperbacks conform in every significant way to the high editorial and production standards maintained in the higher-priced, case-bound books published by The Free Press of Glencoe.

Many of these books are available in their original cloth bindings.
A complete catalogue of all Free Press titles will be sent on request